BUSINESS ECONOMICS IN A RAPIDLY-CHANGING WORLD

INTERNATIONAL (CORPORATE) GOVERNANCE: A ONE-DOT THEORY INTERPRETATION

Business Economics in a Rapidly-Changing World

Additional books in this series can be found on Nova's website under the Series tab.

Additional E-books in this series can be found on Nova's website under the E-books tab.

Business Issues, Competition and Entrepreneurship

Additional books in this series can be found on Nova's website under the Series tab.

Additional E-books in this series can be found on Nova's website under the E-books tab.

BUSINESS ECONOMICS IN A RAPIDLY-CHANGING WORLD

INTERNATIONAL (CORPORATE) GOVERNANCE: A ONE-DOT THEORY INTERPRETATION

PETER KIEN-HONG YU
EDITOR

Nova Business and Management Publications, Inc.
New York

For permission to use material from this book please contact us:
Telephone 631-231-7269; Fax 631-231-8175
Web Site: http://www.novapublishers.com

LIBRARY OF CONGRESS CATALOGING-IN-PUBLICATION DATA

International (corporate) governance : a one-dot theory interpretation /
editor, Peter Kien-hong Yu.
p. cm.
Includes bibliographical references and index.
ISBN 978-1-61122-645-4 (hardcover : alk. paper)
1. Corporate governance. 2. Industrial management. I. Yu, Peter
Kien-hong, 1953-
HD2741I5883 2010
338.6--dc22
2010041369

Published by Nova Business and Management Publications, Inc. † New York

DEDICATION

To my father, who went to Taiwan Province from Guangdong Province in August 1949 working on board the last ship of China Merchants Steam Navigation Company (CMSNC) (the May 1949 ship transported gold from Shanghai Port to Jilong Port) and who had been permanently settled down in the United States since December 1972.

CONTENTS

PREFACE

In July 2010, I drafted a short article. Its title is "Issues in the Study of Social Science."

In the article, I said will discuss some important issues related to social science, including the study of business and management.

At the outset, it should be pointed out that scholarship means to me the following criteria in the order of importance: logic, contribution, consistency, preciseness, closeness to reality, etc. In July 2010, I realized that I should have included the term, consistency. In spring 2008, when I first drafted the chart, as shown in the first chapter, I only mentioned logic, contribution, preciseness, closeness to reality, etc.

Academics must put logic in the first place. One should convince oneself first before persuading others to accept your description, explanation, and inference of certain phenomena. Logic may have to do with inductive method, deductive method, a hybrid of inductive and deductive methods, etc. In April 2010, one of my colleagues said, in the study of business, we should rely on logics (as opposed to logic). I have been in the trade for many years, and what I heard was an eye-opener.

However, after pondering for a few weeks, I realized that my one-dot theory, which is accompanied by my crab and frog motion model, has logics. My response accordingly is as follows: We have to be consistent in whatever we do. Logics could be the following: taking the inductive method at time/space sequence (1); a hybrid of both inductive and deductive methods at time/space sequence (5); and the inductive method at time/space sequence (1,000) again. What the researcher had non-dialectically done is tantamount to do the following from Kuching to Singapore in summer 2010. In the non-dialectical first leg, he or she swam to the shore of the city-state. In the second leg, the person walked for a few miles. In the final phase, the same person hitchhiked to the flooded Orchard Road. In short, applying logics implies that one must be dialectical. Non-dialectically, it cannot be done, because it emphasizes cause and effect or portrayed in terms of deduction or a linear thinking.

Contribution means one has to come up with something that nobody has done before. The two co-authors of the best-seller, *Blue Ocean Strategy*, succeeded in doing that, almost. However, by taking both the classical and applied ways, they failed to properly acknowledge that they did not do a good job in taking the classical way, which is a representation of certain phenomena (as opposed making or generating something for a company, for instance, in applied way),[1] and, more importantly, a version of the *Yin* and *Yang* diagram.

---

[1] Conversation with D. P. Dash, dated April 13, 2010, in his office.

When an academic applies a model or theory to describe, explain, and infer or predict certain phenomena, he or she should use it consistently. One cannot apply a different model or theory for a different paragraph, section, or chapter.

Preciseness, as opposed to accuracy, is called for when we conduct research and writing. The choice of words is particularly important. If we are precise, we can be closer to reality.

What should we do to further enable us to be closer to reality? One of the basic things to do is to choose your unit of analysis. In the study of political science or international relations/affairs, it is usually the country. However, when we study business, we usually have to rely on the unit of analysis of company. It is better for us to adopt both units of analysis. This is because sometimes a company is at the mercy of a central government. In that context, we have to first understand the latest policy of the government. For example, business style would certainly be affected, when in the late 1970s, mainland China gradually changed its economic structure from the central planning to that of market economy with Chinese characteristics.

There are other issues that we can discuss. First, if one does not apply a model or theory in their study, one can be easily labeled as a pseudo-scientist. However, if one does do that, a researcher (as opposed to a practitioner) can be easily tautological.

Fairness is another problem. We can only choose a classical way to make a critique of a publication, whose author(s) had chosen the same classical way. It is not fair, if one selected the classical way to make a critique of the applied way and vice versa.

Third, many academics are trying to challenge others, to the extreme of decimating the same. I can give one example. After World War II, many American political scientists began to quantify political science or the study of politics. Before that, we were told that politics is an art. The major, influential academic journal was firmly in the hands of those political scientists who subscribe to the quantitative method. If you do not apply mathematical formulas, your paper will be immediately rejected by the editor(s) in the first round of review. Only in recent years, did we see qualitative papers being published in that journal. Why is that so?

Well, those academics who think that only quantification of politics can be scientific finally realized that it is not possible for them to beat a qualitative study of politics. For a long period of time, this kind of struggle has also taken place between traditional Chinese herbal medicine, which is holistic, and Western medicine, which is applied. A May 2010 news report carried this headline: Traditional medicines making a comeback.[2] In other words, traditional or complementary medicines are fast regaining their popularity among Ibans, because, for certain sicknesses, taking certain herbs and roots are more effective and do not give any side effects. What I am saying is that compromise must be made between different camps. They should learn to cooperate and coordinate in their research and writing. This means adopting both the classical way and the applied way, so as to be closer to reality in generating their findings.

In sum, before entering the world of social science, one must ask oneself the following tough question: Do you want to spend your time, energy, etc. on doing something that will never enable you to find a law, as the law in natural science? Don't forget: 1) Everything in social science can be falsified, and, if you choose the applied way, you will realize that a

[2] *Borneo Post* (hereinafter BP)(Sarawak, Malaysia), May 21, 2010, p.D2. The headline of another edition carried "Chinese Traditional Medicine Gaining Acceptance." See *ibid.*, July 13, 2010, p.14.

model or theory discovered by you cannot last for a long period of time; and 2) politicians and business people do not put logic in the first place. Can we come up with a law in social science, when we the researchers have already distorted reality, unless one has already found a suitable model or theory to rationalize everything? Here, we can insert the term, Occam's razor ("the simplest explanation is usually the correct one").

To digress, I would like to mention a few other things. First, in February 2010, my school head in an email to me and others said the term, international (corporate) governance [i(c)g], is "VERY SIGNIFICANT [sic]." That phrase has emboldened me to choose i(c)g as the book title. To the best of my knowledge, nobody has ever coined the term, which is integrated from three other terms, international governance, international corporate governance, and corporate governance. One has to learn to rationalize the seemingly contradictory terms. This can be done only dialectically.

Second, the chapter, entitled International Regimes and Non-regimes in Confucian (Corporate) Governance: A Critique of Blue Ocean Strategy's Metaphor and Methodology, was an invited talk for the international conference, Accelerating Economic Revival through Innovation and Reform, at Women's Christian College, University of Madras, Chennai, India, February 5-6, 2010. I would like to especially thank the following academics, namely, Anita Rajendran and Margaret Ratha Rani, who permitted me to reprint the research paper on Confucian (Corporate) Governance and Blue Ocean Strategy (BOS). I also would like to thank the Cengage Learning Australia for using the diagrams, which were originally published in the third Asia Pacific, 2009 edition of Danny A. Samson and Richard L. Daft's Fundamentals of Management,[3] plus the editor of *International Journal of Business and Management* (IJBM) (Canada) for the permission to reprint the slightly updated paper on the high speed rail in Taiwan Province, Republic of China (ROC) and the publisher of Oxford Academic Publishing (U.K.) for the permission to reprint the paper on *The Study of Politics and Non-Politics Should Begin with One Dot.* To follow the footstep of Yadong LUO in his *Global Dimensions of Corporate Governance* (2007), I would like to state the following: Every effort has been made to trace copyright holders and to obtain their permission for the use of copyright material. The lead author apologizes for any errors or omissions in the book and would be grateful if notified of any corrections that should be incorporated in future reprints or editions of this book. Last but not least, I wish to thank Lisa LeeHua NGUI for helping me to take out the term, Buddha, from that pure circle and to add that curve in the last page of this Preface, which can help a reader to better understand my writings or a researcher to structure his or her writing logically, systematically, and coherently at both the macro- and micro-levels. In passing, it should be noted that, in September 2010, I suddenly realized that the *Yin* and *Yang* diagram can be twisted or flipped standing up in the shape of the JOO/ZHU diagram, as readers will see later in the Preface.

Third, I wish to thank Director WANG Su Chen for copy-editing my article on the World Trade Organization (WTO).

[3] Specifically, "p.92; p.118; PowerPoint slide on Mechanistic versus Organic Organizations, which accompanies the textbook; p.217, p.260, p.450, p.454, p.483; p.576; and the cartoon from the PowerPoint slide, which accompanies the textbook." From SAMSON, D. *Fundamentals of Management,* 3E. © 2008 Cengage Learning Australia, a part of Cengage Learning, Inc. Reproduced by permission.

Fourth, in the last few years, Taipei-based books like Win Join Book Company, Ltd. and Ta Tong Book Company have partially supported my One-dot Center, which was first created in April 2007. I am grateful to them.

Fifth, I thought of including the chapter on levels of international (corporate) governance, which was presented at an international conference of Fudan University, Shanghai, in July 2010, but I did not do so. Therefore, readers are urged to read the paper which has a possibility to be published in Zhenglai DENG and Sujian GUO's *China's Searches for Good Governance: Inside and Outside China*. The edited book has a good chance to be published by Palgrave Macmillan (New York) in spring 2011. This writing attempts to offer a fuller picture of what governance is all about. It is very important that readers must have a whole picture first. In passing, this book is related to the one-dot theory. If readers want to read my paper, Redefining Company as an International Regimes and/or Non-International Regimes-related Artificial Person: A One-dot Theory Interpretation, and Making Sense of the Regime's Dimension of Investment, plus my other paper, Conceptualizing Taiwan, Xinjiang, Tibet, etc. as One Dot: Contrasting and Testing Three One-dot Theories, which was presented at Harvard University in November 2010, please contact me.

Sixth, to be honest, when I graduated from New York University (NYU), I was not well versed in methodology. After reading and writing over the last few decades, I think I am pretty confident about research methods, both dialectical and non-dialectical, because I made the following statement in late 2004 after applying my one-dot theory and the crab and frog motion model: A dialectical/crab and frog motion remark is just the opposite of a non-dialectical/crab and frog motion (usually deductive, linear, or cause and effect) remark, or, at best, they must meet half-way.

Seventh, each chapter is either related to the title of the book or the sub-title. If one challenges me, saying he or she does not see the application of the one-dot theory in a certain chapter, my reply is simple and straightforward: Look at the entire chapter, and you will see a dot. Come to think of it, each word or a section in a chapter is but a partial dot of a larger or fuller dot, whatever that is.

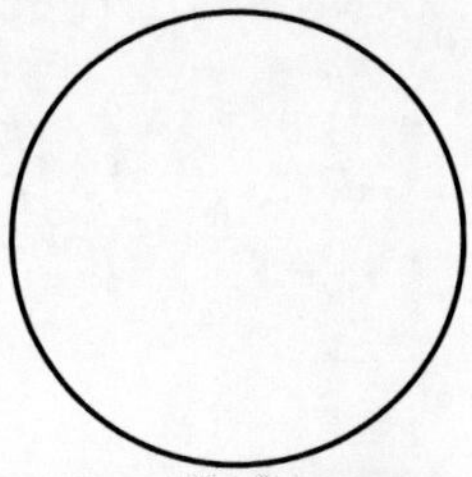

The *Yin* and *Yang* diagram

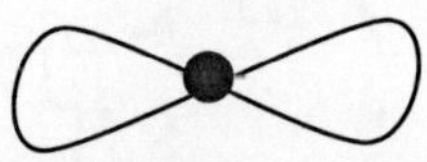

Source: 朱慧慈 /Judith JOO/ZHU
Huici *LaoShi*'s
WuJiZhenYuan

1 2 3 4 5 A B C D E

time/space sequence (1)
time/space sequence (2)
…………………………..
time/space sequence (n)

Source: 俞劍鴻/Peter Kien-Hong
YU's crab and frog motion
model, September 1994

Peter K. H. YU, Swinburne University of Technology, Austrlia, Sarawak Campus
December, 2010

In: International (Corporate) Governance
Editor: Peter Kien-Hong Yu

ISBN: 978-1-61122-645-4

Chapter 1

ONE-DOT THEORY AND THE CRAB AND FROG MOTION MODEL

Peter Kien-hong Yu and Chunli Zhang

ABSTRACT

This paper is an in-depth study of one dot by using different approaches and methods in social science. Because one dot can be a theory, it must be accompanied by a model, and the name of the model is called the crab and frog motion.

Arguably, everything can be simplified or compressed in terms of a dot. It is suggested that we should apply the Yin and Yang diagram to describe and explain, if not infer or predict, the one dot.

For the first time since September 1994, the second co-author has in August 2010 tried to apply mathematical formulas to shore up the verbal model.

Keywords: one dot, theory, model, dialectics, methodology

INTRODUCTION

In spring 2008, the lead co-author of this chapter, to his best ability, developed the following methodology framework to study social science, which can be applied to philosophy, science, paradigms, schools of thought, theories, and models. Because the term, ontology, has been mentioned, we may have to include discussion on religion (divinity) or the information, data, and analysis related to supernatural forces/power, such as God, Buddha, and Allah, if and when necessary.

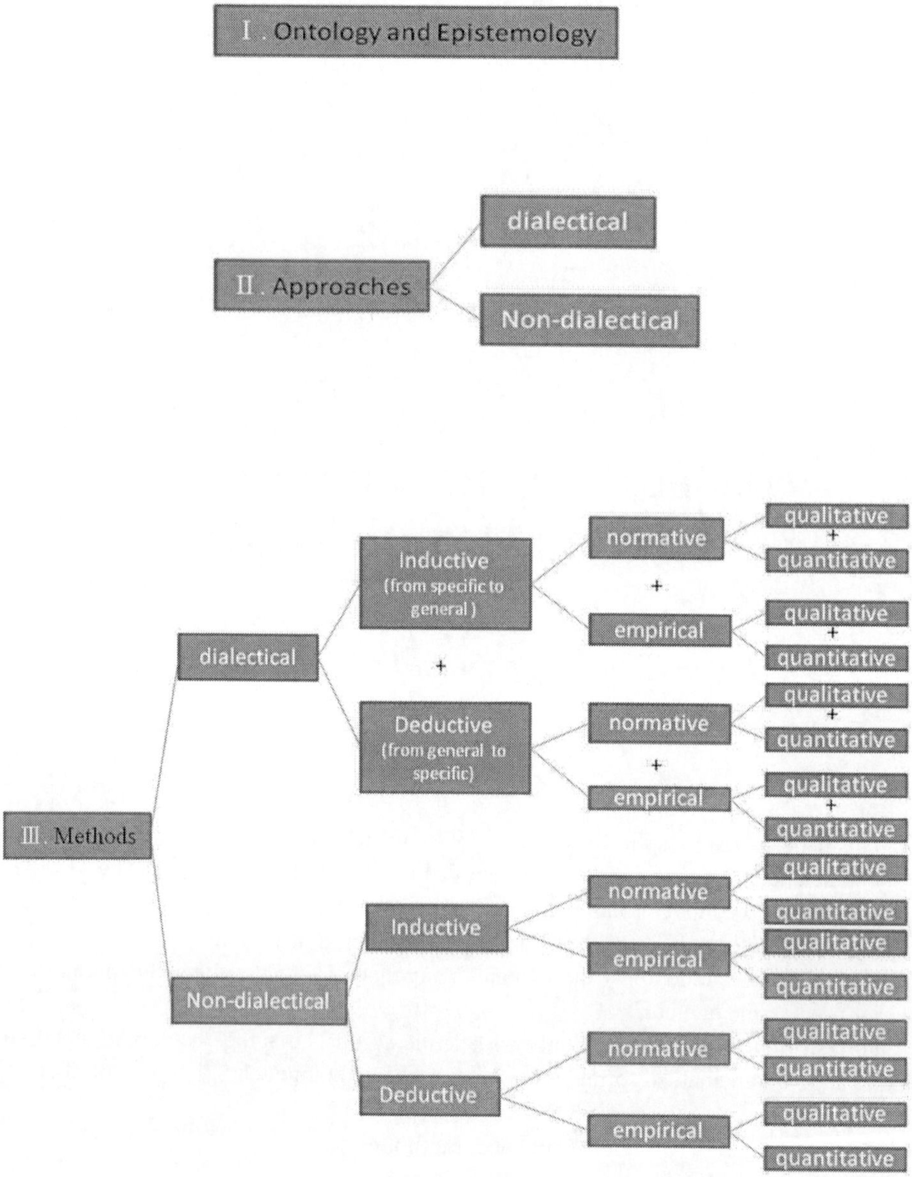

In this study, the whole framework will be applied to describe, explain, and infer one dot as a theory from both dialectical and non-dialectical perspectives.[4] Because a theory must be accompanied by a model but not vice versa, the lead co-author will also describe and explain my crab and frog motion model as time comes. Other synonyms for the term, crab and frog motion, are dialectical and scientific from the Chinese Communist perspective.

[4] See Peter Kien-hong YU, *God is, by Inference, One Dot: Paradigm Shift* (Boca Raton, Florida: Universal-Publishers, 2010), Chapter 1. In April 2010, this author was told that there are two ways of conducting research and writing, classical way and applied way.

THE ONTOLOGY AND EPISTEMOLOGY OF ONE DOT

What is ontology? Simply put, it is a metaphysical study of Being. Being is something that exists somewhere in the abstract or non-abstract world that we know. Human beings live in a three-dimensional world. However, an 11-dimensional theory exists, which unites all string theories (and supersedes them).[5] Thus, we can always ask: Does one dot exist? If it does not, we do not have to continue our study. However, if it does exist, we have to touch upon epistemology, which is related to validity and limits of looking at everything from the one dot perspective.

The lead co-author can immediately come up with five examples, whereby academics and experts had expressed the things that they want to show or conceptualize in terms of one dot or within a circle, which is but a dot:

- Power or power capacity by Gene Sharp;[6]
- The global business environment model by John J. Wild, *et. al.*[7]
- Three tiers of noncustomers depicted in terms of three overlapping circles;[8]
- The little red dot, referring to the Republic of Singaporc (ROS);[9] and
- Integration and Universality of Knowledge from the Islamic Perspective, especially in the 21st century.[10]

Concentric circles/*TongXinYuan* are another good example. In short, many academics and experts are fond of applying a dot or a circle, because *everything* can be easily described and explained, if not inferred or predicted, as a dot or within a circle. It is, therefore, a valid way of conducting research and writing. However, the way those authors had drawn or conceptualize the dot or the circle cannot be more persuasive and even powerful than applying the Chinese *Yin* and *Yang* diagram Plus the Five Elements:

---

[5] http://en.wikipedia.org/wiki/M-theory, accessed on June 29, 2010. According to a British scientist, it is not possible for human beings to understand the complex and complicated universe. See *ShiHua Daily News* (hereinafter SHDN)(Sarawak, Malaysia), June 14, 2010, p.13.

[6] Gene Sharp, *The Politics of Nonviolent Action* (Boston: Porter Sargent Publishers, 2006).

[7] John J. Wild, *et. al. International Business: The Challenges of Globalization*, 4th ed. (Upper Saddle River, Pearson and Prentice Hall, 2008), p.xv and pp.29-31.

[8] W. Chan Kim and Renee Mauborgne, *Blue Ocean Strategy* (Boston, MASS.: Harvard Business School Press, 2005), p.104.

[9] Tommy Koh and Chang Li Lin, eds., *The Little Red Dot: Reflections by Singapore's Diplomats* (Singapore: World Scientific, 2005). See also ZHENG WenHui, *Singapore: The Little Red Dot* (Singapore: LanDianTuShuSiRenYouXianGongSi, 2009). In August 1998, the then president of the Republic of Indonesia (RI) referred to the city-state as a red dot.

[10] *Education and Social Development* (Bangi, Selangor: Faculty of Education, Universiti Kebangsaan Malaysia, 1998), p.64, as cited in Nazaruddin Hj. Mohd Jali, *et. al.*, *Malaysian Studies* (Harlow, England: Pearson and Hall Prentice, 2007), pp.277-278. A "Balanced and Harmonious Human Being" model has also been shown.

It looks simple yet it is profound. we will elaborate on the diagram immediately after the next paragraph.

Conceptually, we can think of a longhouse, high-rise, or a train as a dot. If we look at each one of from a distance, it is definitely a dot. However, can a dot be a line, house, air, water, and even God? It is possible to regard a dot as a line, assuming that a small insect is looking at a human being, for example. However, the same creature is not a line for sure, if we look at it at a close range, unless we are talking about an even smaller insect looking at it.

A dot could be the diagram as depicted above. However, it is not a pure dot, because there are something in the dot. A pure dot is like talking about the term, universe, whereas a non-pure dot is cosmos, which refer to order plus chaos at the same time. We see, for example, one small, black dot in the white portion of the whole dot and another small, white dot in the black portion of the whole dot. In other words, if a dot is to be pure, it must be presented in terms of a circle, with nothing inside. It should be a blank, white circle, assuming that white is pure. Otherwise, we will be confused, when we talk about, for example, Singapore as a little red dot. Several questions can be asked. Is red pure? In *Blue Ocean Strategy*, red means bloody or competition. Are we talking about the whole dot in red? Obviously, we are not, because the whole dot is consisted of two-half dots, with at least two colors. Or are we talking about the little (red) dot in the white portion of the whole dot or the little (red) dot in the black portion of the whole dot? Obviously, we are not, because only Singapore is mentioned. However, if we say Singapore in the context of the Association of Southeast Asian Nations (ASEAN) or in the context of the relationship between Singapore and its giant neighbor, the Republic of Indonesia (RI) or the Federation of Malaysia (FOM), then we are closer to reality or the diagram itself. Furthermore, what does the curved line, shaping like a snake, in the diagram refer to? Obviously, it is not the red dot. It actually reflects the middle way or what Confucius had said about the *ZhongyongZiDao/middle way*? We can, if we use the following drawing, which in the Chinese Daoist parlance is called *WuJiZhenYuan* and which is but a version or, to be more precise, a simplification of the *Yin* and *Yang*:

That is to say, the middle way is that dot in the middle, which could be or could not be red, depending on the context.

In sum, the *Yin* and *Yang* diagram can rationalize the five examples. Can each example rationalize the other four examples plus the *Yin* and *Yang* diagram? It is very doubtful.

Indeed, everything can be regarded as a dot, including God, by inference. We ought to ask the next epistemological question: What are its limitations, if any? A human being exists. It is a dot. This is a fact. In the context of God, the human being is a partial dot, because we are part of Him and because most Catholics and Christians believe that God is everywhere. He is omnipresent. If there is a partial dot, by inference, the fuller dot must be something else, if not God. The only question is that no one has met God. That is the only and sole limitation. If a person is a Buddhist, he or she can accept the fact that Buddha is a dot, when looking at the Buddha statute. A statute is a dot. In this connection, he or she may say that it was Buddha who first created everything. If so, this means that God is a late comer. However, how did Buddha create God? Has Buddha ever met or shook hands with God? When facing an issue, who has the final say? Nobody has the answers or can answer those tough questions. To an atheist, both God and Buddha do not exist. If so, there is no limitation at all him or her to regard everything as a dot. The limitation simply does not exist.

Since we are studying the dot at the social science level, we just need to be logical, not religious, metaphysical, etc. As such, we can proceed to the approaches and methods.

THE APPROACHES

To simplify everything at the outset, we can say that there are two approaches: dialectical and non-dialectical. So, a researcher must decide on either one of them, because we want to be closer to reality when we conduct research and writing. If he or she decides to conduct a comparative study, then the researcher can use both approaches. For example, in chapter two, he or she applies the dialectical approach and, in chapter three, the other approach. And, in the fourth chapter, he or she would compare and contrast the findings, reminding the readers that the study has been relying on the same source materials, which is very important.

Indeed, there is a striking difference between the two approaches. After testing more than 60 cases on China and other topics, this is what the lead co-author would say and have been repeatedly saying it: A dialectical/crab and frog motion remark is just the opposite of a non-dialectical/crab and frog motion (usually deductive, linear, or cause and effect) remark, or, at best, they must meet half-way. One can easily rationalize non-dialectical things by applying the dialectical approach, whereas it is more difficult the other way around.

To elaborate, on the one hand, what is a dialectical approach? Basically, it can be traced back to the Chinese *Yin* and *Yang* Plus the Five Elements. Although many, if not most, non-Chinese find it hard to understand, Karl H. Marx applied dialectics. Hence, we see terms like thesis, anti-thesis, and synthesis. Things constantly change. As a result of having a dialogue or clash between thesis and anti-thesis, a synthesis eventually emerges. After that, the synthesis, if it still exists, could break down into thesis and anti-thesis again. A pattern would be flowing that way, until the synthesis becomes extinct one day, and the process ends.

Marx must have been heavily influenced by the Chinese philosophy of *Yin* and *Yang*, so were MAO Zedong, ZHOU Enlai, DENG Xiaoping, CHIANG Kai-shek, after retreating to the Taiwan area, CHIANG Ching-kuo, LEE Teng-hui, etc. To some extent, Dr. SUN Yat-sen, the founder of the Republic of China (ROC), sometimes also applied dialectics. This is unavoidable and inevitable, because many, if not most, Chinese idioms are structured in terms of *Yin* and *Yang*. It is easier for a group on the same side to speak the same language, so as to communicate well. We must not forget that Chinese scholars, including Confucius, since ancient times tried to correlate almost everything in terms of *Yin* and *Yang*. The Nobel Prize winner, YANG Zhengning, vehemently opposes that way of conducting scientific research and writing. Yet, when he said there is no clash between science and religion eventually, even if there is now, he had been dialectical, because he is talking about two things at the same time.

On the other hand, what is a non-dialectical approach? We may say that it is just the opposite or 50% of dialectical approach or anything that is not related to dialectics. However, in the real world, it is difficult to find a writing, however short and brief, which does not apply at least what one academic called inner dialectics. In other words, the non-dialectical approach at the macro-level is not dialectical. Yet, to organize one's writing, he or she must be dialectical sometimes within the writing at the micro-level. For example, we often hear people say "on the one hand" and "on the other hand" within an essay. By doing that, the author has already been dialectical, because the author is talking about two or more things at the same time, which may be different. If so, the two things may engage in a dialogue or even clash, resulting something else after a period of time.

Take game theory as another example. The theory itself can be non-dialectical. However, when we proceed to look at the matrix, we see plenty of inner dialectics at work: There are at least two players; there are two numbers in each box; one box may be chosen to against another box, etc.

Before the lead co-author prove that a dialectical remark is just the opposite of a non-dialectical remark, or, at best, they must meet half-way, let me describe and explain his crab and frog motion model, each number, letter, word, or term of which is part of his one-dot theory.

The following model, which, if looked at from far away, could be two half-dots (1 2 3 4 5 as the first half-dot and A B C D E as the second half-dot) or simply one dot if we look at its entirety[11]:

1 2 3 4 5 A B C D E

time/space sequence (1)
time/space sequence (2)
....
time/space sequence (n)

1 means 100% of a concept or whatever;
3 means 50% of a concept or whatever;
5 means 1% of a concept or whatever.

E means 100% of a concept or whatever;
C means 50% of the concept or whatever;
A means 1% of the concept or whatever.

---

[11] *Zheng, fan, shun,ni, zhen,* and *wei.* There are many dots in the world. For example, each of a Polka dot means "each of a number of round dots evenly spaced to form a pattern on fabric." See *Oxford Student's Dictionary*, p.792.

The 1 2 3 4 5 spectrum is equivalent to what the lead co-author call the safe zone, and the A B C D E spectrum, the danger zone. 5 is the middle way/golden mean/road/path/line/track in the safe zone and A, the middle way/golden mean/road/path/line/track in the danger zone.

When one makes a move at any time/space sequence, he or she is thinking of only one most important Number or Letter, and, therefore, there will be no contradiction whatsoever. In the course of making moves, the dialectician is performing a crab or side-ways motion. For example, he or she began at 5. In the next time/space sequence, he or she may go to A. At the third time/space sequence, the same dialectician may move back to the safe zone and stay at 1. In this connection, the phenomena of the negation of negation, the affirmation of negation, the affirmation of affirmation, and the negation of affirmation will appear before time/space sequence (n) is reached. This process is known as the sub-dialectical game. It should be pointed out that there are three basic stages [or (nodal) points] of development: nascent, ascendant, and mature for the Numbers and mature, descendant, and moribund for the Letters. In other words, 5 is nascent; 3, ascendant; and 1, mature. On the other hand, E is mature: C, descendant; and A, moribund. Last but not least, a series of other, relevant dialectical, theoretical models must be applied, in order to amply describe, explain, and infer (or predict) more phenomena. When a dialectician no longer applies the first crab and frog motion model constructed by him or her, he or she is said to have leaped or jumped from the first crab and frog motion model to second or another crab and frog motion model.

At this juncture, a caveat should be added, that is, whenever we use the word, versus, it means that dialectics is involved and that the concept or whatever on the left extreme, say Yes or 1 will eventually defeat, co-opt, absorb, etc. the concept or whatever on the right extreme, say No or E at time/space sequence (n). However, in the process, the following arrangement may be necessary, such as flexibly positioning Yes at 1 and No at 5. In other words, a contradictory or even adversary relationship between Yes and No at the beginning has been transformed into a non-contradictory, non-adversarial relationship later on, meaning that whoever chose Yes or whoever opted No should learn to tolerate the existence of each other, because they are both in the safe zone spectrum.

In sum, a crab and frog motion player performs two roles when playing games, that of a crab by moving side-ways[12] and a frog by leaping or jumping from one model to another model as he or she sees fit. Such is the magic beauty of dialectics.

To demonstrate that it is easier to rationalize everything by applying the dialectical approach, the following five examples are basically taken from Chapter 1 of the lead co-author's earlier publication, *God is, by Inference, One Dot: Paradigm Shift.*[13]

---

[12] Crabs can also have *xiaoshuibu* (quick short steps). In other words, they can move straight forward. See *United Daily News* (UDN)(Taipei), February 12, 2007, p.A10. In Yilang County, Taiwan Province, Republic of China (ROC), there is a crab museum. Not all crabs can be eaten, because some of them are poisonous. Poison could be dangerous. See Formosa Television (Taiwan, ROC), dated February 7, 2008.

[13] See Peter Kien-hong YU, *God is, by Inference, One Dot: Paradigm Shift* (Boca Raton, Florida: Universal-Publishers, 2010), pp.25-29.

Example 1

Non-dialectical, linear thinking, with no inner dialectics: A yes is a yes is a yes. A no is a no is a no. In other words, the two like water and fire cannot mix. For example, when a father in the morning tells his children that in the afternoon they will go to watch a movie directed by LEE Ang, which immortally shake the souls of movie-fans, he encounters a contradiction when he decides not to go to the same theater to watch the same movie. This is because in his mind he is non-dialectically thinking (at least) two contradictory concepts at the same time, even if an earthquake struck in the afternoon, which can enable the father to make up an excuse or to have a justification, pointing at the collapsed theater, not to go: both yes and no. However, there would be no contradictions when he, applying the lead co-author's crab and frog motion model, is thinking of "yes" at a particular time/space sequence, to be followed by another "yes" or "no" at the next time/space sequence, to be followed by another "no" at the third time/space sequence. By the same token, he would face a contradiction, by not applying the lead co-author's crab and frog motion model, when he said "no" in the morning and "yes" in the afternoon regarding watching the same movie. In a word, non-dialectically, the father simply cannot dissolve the contradiction, when even a five-year old child may sense something is wrong, if not illogical.

However, dialectically, the father can dissolve the "yes" and "no" contradiction, if he applies any one of the following models: Yes at 1 and No at E; No at 1 and Yes at E; Yes at 1 and No at 5; No at 1 and Yes at 5; etc. The crucial, key point is that whenever making a move, the dialectician would think of only one concept, be it Yes, No, or its mixture (such as 3, if Yes is 1 and No is 5) at any time/space sequence. As such, there would be no contradiction whatsoever.

Example 2

Many, if not most, Chinese idioms should be understood in terms of dialectics, as mentioned earlier. This is because one's understanding of the idiom could be more precise and closer to what the dialectician who originally coined the idiom had in mind or, simply, reality.

At this juncture, the lead co-author proposes to dialectically and non-dialectically analyze the Chinese term, *Sheng* (birth), *Lao* (age/getting older), *Bing* (illness), and *Si* (death). This idiom is a good example of both a dialectical and non-linear thinking as well as a non-dialectical and linear thinking. Indeed, we are born, even if it means by the cloning technology. Then, on the next split second or half-a-second, we become older at time/space sequence (2). As we become older, we can sometimes get sick. Death comes when our heartbeats stop. However, a question ought to be asked: Is this linear pattern precise or closer to reality? The answer is no, unless we construct a dialectical model, because not all human beings follow that pattern due to the fact that each one of our experience could be different. In other words, the linear thinking can be easily faulted or the taken-for-granted pattern theory falsified.

Birth can be positioned at 5 and age, 4. Illness can be put at 2 and death, 1. 3 could be regarded as a mixture of both 1 and 2 as well as both 4 and 5. At time/space sequence (1), a baby is born. He or she is at 5 in the safe zone, to begin with. If everything does not flow smoothly, he or she may die. In other words, the baby does not have to go through the extensive age and illness phases or process. Needless to say, it would be best, if public opinion polls were conducted--and dialecticians like MAO would certainly welcome that--to find out how many people followed the taken-for-granted pattern as mentioned in the Chinese idiom and how many did not normatively move from 5 to 4 to 3 to 2 and, finally, to 1. In life, it is a fact that many of us move back and forth, like a crab, between 4 and 2.

Some babies could die in mothers' bodies. For those babies, they would be placed in the Non-Birth, Age, Illness, and Death spectrum or the danger zone. This makes sense, because they are not related to the birth, age, illness, and death spectrum, each one of which can be observed outside of their mothers' bodies.

Example 3

When the People's Republic of China (PRC) was created, there were roughly 550 million people. In June 1953, the Chinese mainland (*NeiDi*)/China proper completed its first census. A little over 600 million people were registered. In July 1979, the then PRC Vice-Premier endorsed the one-child policy, which was first adumbrated by DENG earlier in the same year. Beijing began to implement its one-child policy initially at some provinces and later to the whole country. To circumvent the rather-inhumane policy, a couple gave the same Chinese name to their five children. The following model perhaps was in their mind: One Name (at 1) versus Many Names (at E). Another way of saying the same thing is: Each Number in the spectrum refers to each child. The eldest child would be positioned at 1, whereas the youngest child at 5, each having the same name. This has been logically presented, because the eldest child was born first at time/space sequence (1), to be followed by the second child at time/space sequence (2), etc. At least the couple had dissolved the contradiction, and this is certainly acceptable to the Chinese mind.

Example 4

The summer 2008 Olympic torch relay and related remarks can be analyzed. First, let me provide some facts:

1. The International Olympic Committee (IOC), Lausanne, Switzerland; Chinese Taipei Olympic Committee (CTOC); and Beijing Organizing Committee for the XXIX Olympiad (BOCOG) are involved.
2. In February 2007, both Taipei and Beijing reached a consensus in writing on the relay route.
3. In April 2007, Beijing announced the route, mentioning that the torch would arrive in Chinese Taipei from the Socialist Republic of Vietnam (SRV) on April 30, 2008 and that Taipei, Hongkong Special Administrative Region (SAR), and Macao SAR are designated "as in its domestic leg relay." Beijing demanded an extra condition, saying the CTOC "is responsible for coordinating all relevant parties to not use any flag, emblem, or anthem other than those [described by the IOC] during the torch relay."

4. Right after, Taipei, fearful that the contiguity of Taiwan and Hong Kong could make the island a part of the PRC's territory, rejected the planned 24 kilometers (km) route on the grounds that it downgraded the ROC's status as a sovereign, independent state. In other words, the relay should not enter or exit Taiwan via the Chinese mainland, Hongkong, or Macao. What it prefers is to reverse the order, for example, from Taipei to Hanoi.
5. Beijing, worried about the fact that supporters of the Taiwan independence movement could have displayed separatist flags, slogans, or symbols, responded by saying Taipei reneged on an agreement to host a stop on the summer 2008 Beijing Olympic torch relay.
6. In August 2007, a consensus was reached in which Chinese Taipei would be defined as *JingWaiLuxian* ("an overseas city," "overseas route," "a city of an outside territory," or "part of China's domestic route rather than in the international circuit"). (In passing, it should be pointed out that, as an extension of the "One China, Respective Interpretation," Beijing made a remark regarding the location of the Taiwan Pavilion in the Expo2010 Shanghai China site from May 1 to October 31, 2010: "The location of the Taiwan Pavilion is a dot in Zone A, which hosts the China Pavilion and national pavilions for Asian countries except Southeast Asian ones. The China Pavilion is also a dot in Zone A.")
7. September 20, 2007 was the cut-off date for negotiations on the relay. A few days earlier, Beijing suddenly renewed a condition, saying the CTOC "is responsible for coordinating all relevant parties to not use any flag, emblem, or anthem other than those [described by the IOC] during the torch relay." The IOC has clear rules regarding the national flags. To be sure, the term, all relevant parties, is too broad, to Chinese Taipei, because the CTOC said it can only regulate the personnel involved in the relay and no one else. On September 21, the IOC announced that "[t]he route will now have to go ahead without a stop in Chinese Taipei." Taipei, on September 21, decided to let the torch to bypass Chinese Taipei.
8. The ROC is the first country to decline or reject the relay in the IOC history.
9. In January 2008, the PRC's Ministry of Foreign Affairs (MOFA) said it strongly opposes anyone using the Olympic Games to hype political issues, such as Darfur region in the Republic of Sudan (RS), which violates the Olympic spirit and principle. In August 2008, its president made a similar remark.
10. As of August 8, 2008, the opening day of the Olympic Games, the ROC still maintains diplomatic ties with 23 countries in the world. In the same month, the ROC MOFA said it is not political if those countries' dignitaries and officials were invited by Beijing leaders to attend the Olympic Games.

Non-dialectically and linearly, it is difficult to describe and explain the following route, because contradictions obviously exist: The torch will go to Japan from Australia; then, it will go to the Republic of Korea (ROK), to be followed by the Democratic People's Republic of Korea (DPRK); from DPRK, the next leg is to go to the SRV; after that, it is Chinese Taipei; from there, Hongkong will be next, to be followed by Macao and, finally, the destination, Beijing. In other words, we just need to pose the following questions: Can we regard the Olympic games as purely sports? Can we regard the Olympic games as purely politics? Can we regard the Olympic games as a mixture of politics and sports? Can we regard the Olympic games as a mixture of (pure) sports and (pure) politics? Last but not least, can we separate politics from sports?

Obviously, there are a lot of contradictions, because, non-dialectically, sports are sports and politics is politics. However, if at each time/space sequence, one only thinks one Number or Letter in the lead co-author's crab and frog motion model, there is no contradiction whatsoever. So, from Australia to Japan, it is sports; from Japan to ROK, it could be 3 or a mixture of politics and sports, because the DPRK, out of national pride, may want the torch to go to its capital first; from the ROK to DPRK, it is a mixture of politics and sports, unless friction has already been resolved beforehand; from the DPRK to the SRV, it is sports; from the Southeast Asian country to Chinese Taipei, it is sports; from Chinese Taipei to Hongkong, it is politics, because, due to national pride, the former, regarding itself as least as a political entity superior to Hongkong and Macao, prefers the torch goes to another country, not Hongkong; from Hongkong to Macao, it is sports; and, the final leg is still sports, because Macao is part of the PRC. In any case, if there are arguments, a public opinion poll should be conducted, so as to clarify how many people are at 1, 2, 3, 4, or 5 respectively at each time/space sequence.

Example 5

The following question was posed in a Fall 2007 class: What do you see: (solid) ________? A graduate student from the United States, Michael L. Miller, said it is a line. The author replied saying your thinking is linear, because, to this graduate student, a line is a line is a line. However, dialectically, the following drawings could also be interpreted or seen as a line: , if we look at it from a distance or flip it by only looking at the cross-section of the two-oval shaped drawing; x-ray or laser light or even the cellular telephone line, which has been termed "the world's longest umbilical cord"[14]; …….., such as an ant's pheromone trail;[15] and imaginary line, such as axis in the outer space, which is "[a]n imaginary line that passes through the center of a planet or *star*, around which the object rotates"[16] or the middle line between the ROC and the PRC as a result of signing the December 1954 U.S.-ROC Mutual Defense Treaty, which was initiated by the United States. Dialectically, I will put ________ at 1; 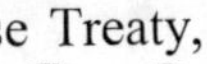 at 2; x-ray or laser light at 3; …….. at 4; and imaginary line at 5. Needless to say, there could be other types of lines, such as the chemical equator, which is a 50-kilometer wide boundary separating the Northern Hemisphere's dirty air from that of the less polluted Southern Hemisphere. Reporting in the *Journal of Geophysical Research—Atmospheres*, a group of climatologists found this world-wide weather "barrier" that can block air pollution from traveling southward.[17]

A word can be added. It is not possible for Miller to see the solid line since birth to time/space sequence (n). This is because when he was one year old he cannot recognize that kind of line as being solid. Someday, if he were to be in charge of handling the Taiwan Strait

---

14 Parents may use the telephone to find out where are their children. See *Taipei Times* (hereinafter TT), (Taipei), September 13, 2008, p.9.

15 An ant moves by dots. "Each dot represents two hundredths of a second." See *UDN*, December[illegible]p.6. Dots make up a line.

16 Heather Couper and Nigel Henbest, *Space Encyclopedia* (London: Darling Kindersley, 1999), p.290.

17 *China* Post (hereinafter CP)(Taipei), November 16, 2008, p.1.

crisis, he would most likely remind both sides of the Taiwan Strait that an imaginary line exists since the mid-1950s. In passing, it should be noted that Cardinal Paul SHAN Kuo-Hsi likened life to a tunnel.[18] Life is abstract, while tunnel can be regarded as a line, if not a dot. In other words, is life a line or a dot? If life has a history, it is a timeline. A timeline is a dot, too. In short, Miller has to change throughout his life by being dialectical. Otherwise, he cannot rationalize everything logically, systematically, and coherently.

The Methods

Again, methods can be either dialectical or non-dialectical. When conducting a comparative study, both methods are used. The first method can be applied in chapter two, for example, and the second one, chapter three. Dialectically, both methods must be used, so as to rationalize *all* the phenomena, minus one.[19] The lead co-author will first discuss the dialectical method.

The dialectical method can be further understood as both inductive and deductive. It has logics, as opposed to logic. On the one hand, inductive reasoning is from specific to general. It is normative. On the other hand, deductive reasoning is the opposite or general to specific. It is empirical.

The Chinese usually prefer the inductive way of reasoning, whereas many, if not most, social scientists in the West tend to dislike it, preferring the deductive way of reasoning. The former, after seeing, hearing, or conceptualizing something, would list down the findings in the order of importance: Point 1, Point 2, Point 3, and so on and so forth. However, the problem with this kind of reasoning is that what if the first or tenth point contradicted with Point 50 or 500? Because we are in academia, we have to express ourselves logically. Obviously, the inductive reasoning has this limitation, if a contradiction can be spotted.

To be sure, the Chinese are more concerned about having a whole picture first. The inductive reasoning can help them to decide on two most important concepts at the very beginning of each game. For example, we want to talk about the One China principle. This is one concept, which could be put at 1. Then, the Chinese would think of its opposite, that is, non-One-China principle or E. After that, the Chinese would play a role of a crab, going back and forth in between those two concepts or points. As mentioned earlier, the Chinese would use a series of dialectical models, so as to emerge as the winner at time/space sequence (n).

People in the West usually adopt a non-inductive reasoning, that is, they prefer deductive reasoning. In other words, having a whole picture is not their foremost concern.

People in the Middle East are similar to the Chinese. They want to have a whole picture first and then look at the details. However, their approach is not dialectical. In March 2010, one of my students who had lived in the Kingdom of Saudi Arabia (KSA) for some 20 years shared with us the logic in the Middle East. The first Saudi Arabian would say yes to, say, A. The second Saudi Arabian would also say yes to A. And, the third one would likewise say yes to A. However, all of them could still be saying no. Why? To each one of them, the whole picture is yes. Since A is a detail, A may be no to all of them. However, to a person who maintains a linear thinking, A is A is A. In other words, how can it be Non-A?

---

[18] *ZhongguoGuangboGongsi* (Taipei), November 16, 2008, at 4 pm.

[19] When all the human beings become extinct, the crab and frog motion model may no longer be able to be applied by anyone in the world.

Coming back to the application of the lead co-author's model, the Number and Letter spectrums in the crab and frog motion model can be regarded as a result of inductive reasoning. 1 carries the most weight in the safe zone or the order of importance, whereas E, also the most weight in the danger zone or the order of importance.

So, where do we put one dot? Normatively, it is placed at 1. "75% of one dot" + "25% of one dot" could be places at 2. "Two-equally-half dots" could be at 3. "25% of one dot + 75% of one dot" is positioned at 4. And, "1% of one dot + 99% of one dot" is located at 5. The Letter or A B C D E spectrum refers to "Non-One-Dot."

Can the one dot be deduced? By deduction, we are talking about cause and effect, and it has a linear reasoning. Because of this, we have that, and that will further lead to other related things. So, a dot is a dot is a dot, just as a rose is a rose is a rose. Or one can use a train as a good analogy. One coach is connected to another coach and finally the locomotive or vice versa. For example, "two-equally-half dots" is one dot or vice versa.

If one has fully understood the logic of dialectics, he or she would agree that, by applying or being able to apply both inductive and deductive reasonings, one can be much closer to reality. This implies that other writings are intellectual exercises. However, there is nothing wrong with this, so long as we present ourselves logically.

Non-dialectically, one can only be either inductive or deductive. Since most social scientists in the West prefer the latter reasoning, induction has become a marginal way of reasoning.

Normatively, if things do not change, indeed, one dot is one dot is one dot. It is what ought to be. However, empirically, is this really so? Let us look at the Earth, which is but a dot in another bigger dot, the Milky Way. Was our globe one piece? Did part of it become our Moon, when another asteroid, comet, or something else struck it? What about Mars? What we are trying to drive at is that our Earth could begin as one dot. Later, two or three dots emerged, namely, Earth and Moon or Earth, Moon, and Mars. We cannot rule out a possibility, that is, someday, the three entities, to wit, our Earth, Moon, and Mars could become one entity again, or even the Milky Way could become part of another galaxy, which could be even a bigger dot, after impact. Dialectically, this is what we see: Our Earth becoming two or three entities, only to become one again someday, which could be one million or billion years later. Using the crab and frog motion model, we can rationalize everything logically. However, non-dialectically, this phenomenon cannot be described and explained, unless accompanied by inner dialectics.

On the one hand, a dialectician will be both qualitative and quantitative. The former means using words to describe, explain, or infer or predict something, while the latter refers to using mathematical formulas to find out truth, if it is possible. MAO in early 1927 published his field trip in surveying the status of the peasants in his poor and backward Hunan Province. In September 1920, he even called for the deconstruction of one China or one dot into 27 pieces, including the creation of the *HunanGongheGuo* (Republic of Hunan). To him, it is no big deal, because, we have bear in mind that Chinese history is characterized by the dialectical phenomenon of *HeJiuBiFen* and *FenJiuBiHe* (empires wax and wane, kingdoms cleave asunder), and a Chinese usually does not dispute that saying.

On the other hand, a non-dialectician is not obliged to be both qualitative and quantitative. Moreover, he or she may not really understand the crucial term, *HeJiuBiFen* and *FenJiuBiHe*.

MATHEMATICALLY SHORING UP THE THEORY AND MODEL

The one-dot theory can help us to make a better decision also under irrationality and lack of adequate information. Thus, it is different from the game theory, which basically assumes that all human beings are rational. Application of the one-dot theory can offer long-term observation and interpretation of changes in human behavior and policy line/path. It follows that we can figure out the kind of factors involved, thereby helping us to infer/predict future development and enabling us to pragmatically make adjustments to as well as to control and command the strategy and tactics. Figure 1 is a description and explanation of the one-dot theory's dynamic operation in terms of the coordinates.[20]

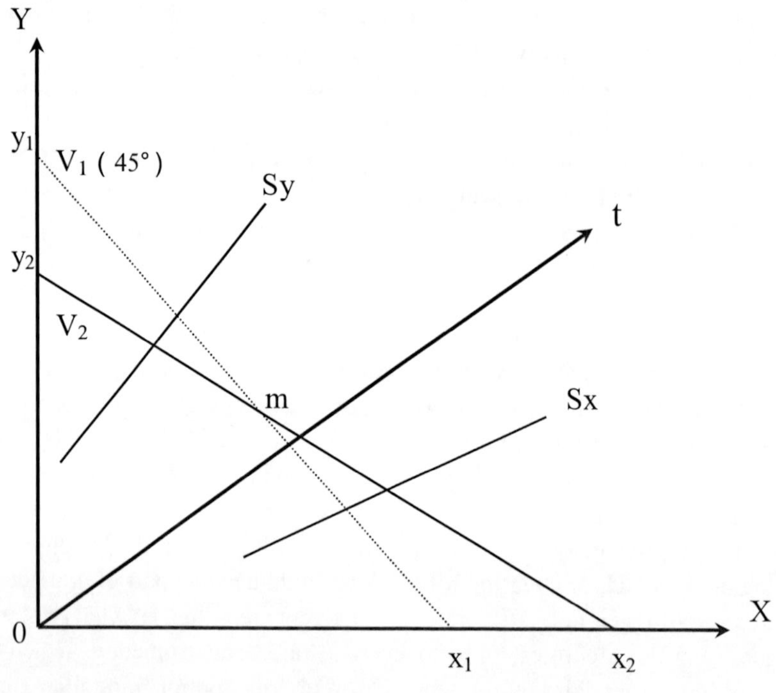

Figure 1. Decision-making under irrationality and lack of adequate information.

Axis X and Axis Y refer to the positive extreme/pole and the negative extreme/pole, respectively. Axis t reflects the changing process at different time and space dimensions. Axis V_1 is equivalent to the equilibrium of a decision's beneficial result, when there are no specific

---

20

基於「一點理論」可以在非理性與資訊不足的情境下，滿足最適當決策之選擇，故不同於只探讨理性的博奕理論（game theory）。運用「一點理論」將可長期觀察並解釋人類行為與政策路線之變化，據以瞭解變化因素與推論未來可能發展，進而提出務實性與整體性的調整与控制策略和战术。茲以座標圖說明其動態運作之方式。

ideology line/path nor policy line/path. Under $x_1 + y_1 = C$, C is a constant, resulting the following function:[21]

$$f(x,y) = |\Delta x / \Delta y| = 1$$

However, in the process of real decision-making, an ideology line/path, policy line/path, or experience-oriented policy will be involved. So, V_2 refers to the line of a decision's beneficial result, which is related to the policy line/path. V_2 intersects with V_1 at m. D, on the line of $x + ky = D, k > 1$, indicates a constant. Thus, in the Sx zone, we have:[22]

$$|\Delta x / \Delta y| > 1$$

While in the Sy zone, we have

$$|\Delta x / \Delta y| < 1$$

Similarly, $mx_2 > my_2$ can also be proven true in the basic triangular relationship between $\triangle x_1mx_2$ and $\triangle y_1my_2$.

$$\therefore Sx > Sy$$

Thus, when the situation is chaotic, thereby making us not able to make rational analysis, or when rationality has been constrained by an ideology line/path and policy line/path, decision-making must fall on Line Sx in the relevant $\triangle x_1mx_2$ zone, rather than on Line Sy in the $\triangle y_1my_2$ zone, so as to get the most beneficial result.

The value of the one-dot theory is that it can help us to make the most appropriate decision, when we face (mother) nature in a realistic situation. Under incomplete rationality and lack of adequate information, we will be subjectively affected by the latent influence of ideology line/policy and policy line/path, while integrating external resources, in an effort to (re-)formulate our specific ideology line/path and policy line/path. However, the one-dot

---

21 X與Y兩軸分別代表正反兩端，t軸則為不同時空的變化過程，V_1為無特定意識型態/政策路線的決策效益均衡線，在線上的$x_1+y_1=C$，C為常數，故可得其函數為$f(x,y)=|\Delta x / \Delta y|=1$。

22 然在實際決策過程中，必然具有意識型態與政策路線，或因政策累積之經驗取向，V_2表示具有政策路線的決策效益線，V_2交叉V_1之中點於m，在線上的$x+ky = D$，$k>1$，D為常數，故在Sx區域可得$|\Delta x / \Delta y|>1$，而在Sy區域則為$|\Delta x / \Delta y|<1$；同理，在$\triangle x_1mx_2$與$\triangle y_1my_2$的三角形基本性質中，亦可證明$mx_2>my_2$。$\therefore Sx>Sy$。因此，當處於渾沌不明之情境而無法使用理性分析時，
或因意識型態、政策路線而採有限理性之決策時，應使決策落於Sx線在$\triangle x_1mx_2$的相關區域，必然優於Sy區域在$\triangle y_1my_2$之決策選擇，將可獲致最大效益。

theory can make up the shortcomings by enabling us to expand qualitative and quantitative resources and to integrate positive and negative dimensions of phenomena.[23]

Conclusion

As can be seen, the common denominator of all things, tangible or intangible, in the past, present, and the future is a dot. A dot is a theory not a model, because, in each model, there should be at least two concepts related to each other. Dot and Non-dot constitute a framework. It can be called a model.

Some academics and experts may find the one-dot theory merely amusing, lacking academic or scholastic rigor. To some extent, we agree. However, if there is no other theory which can be common denominator of all things in the world, then we have to choose the one-dot theory for the time being. If criticism is still leveled at the one-dot theory, then, we have to ask what about the game theory? It is fun to play games. Yet, many economists and non-economists have received Nobel Prizes by applying the game theory. To be sure, serious business begins with the crab and frog motion model or the matrix in the game theory. It is by applying a model that we can rigorously test whether the model can, indeed, describe and explain as well as infer, if not predict, more phenomena than other models or theories. If a dialectical model has been rightfully constructed, it can help us to predict future. The lead co-author has proven that, for example, human beings cannot be globalized again, once some of us can live on the Moon, for example, on a permanent basis.[24] [If someone died in the International Space Station (ISS) or his or her remains were already in outer space, the globalization process can be immediately regarded as ended, because the remains are no longer part of our planet.] The only problem, as we see it, is, when researchers apply the lead co-author's theory and model, which is shored up by the second co-author's mathematical formulas for the first time in August 2010, to describe, explain and infer, if not predict, phenomena, whether skeptics or detractors can be more convinced.

---

[23]

一點理論的價值，在於呈現人類在自然世界中的真實情境，必然受到主觀習性的潛在影響，整合外界資源而為意識型態與政策路線，形成不完全理性與資訊不足的情境，如何選擇最適決策，我們應用一點理論，以獲致正面與反面的整合效應，擴大資源的質與量，滿足決策之最適選擇。

[24] To be sure, some human remains are already in outer space, because they do not want to be buried on Earth. In February 2010, Barack H. Obama, II proposed to the U.S. Congress to freeze the Federal Government budget to return to the Moon. Instead, he focussed on developing commercial space transport. Mainland China plans to land on the Moon before 2017.

In: International (Corporate) Governance
Editor: Peter Kien-Hong Yu

ISBN: 978-1-61122-645-4

Chapter 2

MANAGEMENT DIAGRAMS: CONSISTENTLY CONVERTING THEM IN TERMS OF A SERIES OF *YIN* AND *YANG* DIAGRAMS

Peter Kien-Hong Yu, Chui Ching Ling, and Bibiana Chiu Yiong Lim

ABSTRACT

In April 2010, the lead co-author, for the first time, heard from his colleague that there are the classical way and the applied way to conduct research and writing on business. Later in the same month, he was also told that logics (as opposed to logic) should be adopted.

There are many diagrams, charts, tables, etc. in a business or management book. Some of them were adapted from the other publications. However, unless the author(s) have, from the very beginning to the last word in the publication, applied ONE model and/or theory of their choice, contradictions, which can easily lead to confusion, would inevitably surface.

This paper attempts to logically, systematically, and coherently, conduct a critique of selected diagrams as shown in a best-selling textbook on management and the PowerPoint slides, which were prepared by the publisher and adapted by a lecturer.

The lead co-author will apply his one-dot theory and the crab and frog motion/*Yin* and *Yang* diagram/*TaiJiTu* model and consistently convert those 10 randomly selected diagrams on management in terms of the theory and a series of the model. By doing so, the co-authors have consistently adopted both the classical and applied ways.

Keywords: Management, research methods, dialectics, *Yin* and *Yang* diagram, one-dot theory

In June 2009, the lead co-author entered into the world of business and management study, with trepidation, although fully aware that it is but part of social science.[1] In April 2010, the lead co-author was reminded by his colleague that the unit of analysis for business and management is usually the company, whereas the unit of analysis for international relations/politics/affairs is usually the country.[2] At the same time, the lead co-author, for the first time, heard from the same colleague the term, applied[3] way (of conducting research and writing on business), which can enable us to create/bring forth/generate/make that which does not exist (as opposed to the classical way, which is a representation *of*--not *for*--something). Later in the same month, the lead co-author was again told by the same colleague, who is fond of transdisciplinarity (TD), which recognizes "the existence of different levels of reality governed by different types of logic,"[4] that we have to apply logics (as opposed to logic), when we conduct business and management studies.

It was not until early June 2010 that the lead co-author realized that the statement that we have to preferably adopt the applied way and to preferably apply logics, when we conduct research and writing on business and management, can be easily challenged, if we apply the lead co-author's one-dot theory and the crab and frog motion/*Yin* and *Yang* diagram/*TaiJiTu* model, which can be traced back to some 3,100 years and which is a version of dialectics.

In this paper, the lead co-author will first introduce the crab and frog motion model. In the second section, The co-authors will convert all the selected 10 management diagrams in terms of the lead co-author's one-dot theory and a series of crab and frog motion models. In other words, each non-dialectical diagram can be regarded as a dot, and the co-authors will construct a series of models, which are necessary, in order to comprehend the original diagram, which could be adapted from or be a version of other diagram(s). In the third section, we will point out some findings. And, in the last section, we will say something about academic study of business and management.

THE CRAB AND FROG MOTION MODEL

The model's structure is as follows:

1 2 3 4 5 A B C D E

time/space sequence (1)
time/space sequence (2)
....
time/space sequence (n)

To elaborate, 1 means 100% of a concept or whatever; 3 means 50% of a concept or whatever; 5 means 1% of a concept or whatever. E means 100% of a concept or whatever; C means 50% of the concept or whatever; A means 1% of the concept or whatever.

---

[1] It should be noted that international relations/international affairs overlap with international business at least 80%.

[2] One academic journal stated the following: "The journal addresses the burning questions of management at all levels, namely international organizations and communities, state, region and company," access on July 30, 2010.

[3] Or performative way. What is needed is a model for creating that which does not exist.

[4] See its November 1994 charter.

The 1 2 3 4 5 spectrum is equivalent to what I call the safe zone, and the A B C D E spectrum, the danger zone. 5 is the middle way/golden mean/road/path/line/track in the safe zone and A, the middle way/golden mean/road/path/line/track in the danger zone.

When one makes a move at any time/space sequence, he or she is thinking of only one most important Number or Letter, and, therefore, there will be no contradiction whatsoever. In the course of making moves, the dialectician is performing a crab or side-ways motion. For example, he or she began at 5. In the next time/space sequence, he or she may go to A. At the third time/space sequence, the same dialectician may move back to the safe zone and stay at 1. In this connection, the phenomena of the negation of negation, the affirmation of negation, the affirmation of affirmation, and the negation of affirmation will appear before time/space sequence (n) is reached. This process is known as the sub-dialectical game. It should be pointed out that there are three basic stages [or (nodal) points] of development: nascent, ascendant, and mature for the Numbers and mature, descendant, and moribund for the Letters. In other words, 5 is nascent; 3, ascendant; and 1, mature. On the other hand, E is mature: C, descendant; and A, moribund. Last but not least, a series of other, relevant dialectical, theoretical models must be applied, in order to amply describe, explain, and infer (or predict) more phenomena. When a dialectician no longer applies the first Crab and Frog Motion model constructed by him or her, he or she is said to have leaped or jumped from the first crab and frog motion model to second or another crab and frog motion model.

At this juncture, a caveat should be added, that is, whenever we use the word, versus, it means that dialectics is involved and that the concept or whatever on the left extreme, say, Yes or 1, will eventually defeat, co-opt, absorb, etc. the concept or whatever on the right extreme, say, No or E, at time/space sequence (n). However, in the process, the following arrangement may be necessary, such as flexibly positioning Yes at 1 and No at 5. In other words, a contradictory or even adversary relationship between Yes and No at the beginning has been transformed into a non-contradictory, non-adversarial relationship later on, meaning that whoever chose Yes or whoever opted No should learn to tolerate the existence of each other, because they are both in the safe zone spectrum.

In sum, a crab and frog motion player performs two roles when playing games, that of a crab by moving side-ways[5] and a frog by leaping or jumping from one model to another model as he or she sees fit. Such is the magic beauty of dialectics.

Indeed, if one looks at the model from a distance, it is but one dot. Besides, each component in the model is but part of the one-dot theory.

CONSISTENTLY CONVERTING THE MANAGEMENT DIAGRAMS

In this paper, it is appropriate to apply the *Yin* and *Yang* diagram, , which is related to the lead co-author's theory and model, to study the term, management, and other related diagrams. This is because, throughout the chosen book, *Fundamentals of Management*

[5] Crabs can also have *XiaoShuiBu* (quick short steps). In other words, they can move straight forward. See *United Daily News* (UDN)(Taipei), February 12, 2007, p.A10. In Yilang County, Taiwan Province, Republic of China (ROC), there is a crab museum. Not all crabs can be eaten, because some of them are poisonous. Poison could be dangerous. See Formosa Television (Taiwan, ROC), dated February 7, 2008.

(Samson and Daft 2009),[6] dialectical terms can be easily detected. Although Samson and Daft may not aware that what they have done by at least adopting inner dialectics, they are supposed to be consistent throughout their book from writing the first word to the last word. Examples are many, with a brief explanation.

1. One Dot[7]

This is a good example.[8] However, by just looking at the diagram, can one tell which dimension in the general environment carries more weight than other dimensions? It is difficult, because even the two co-authors said "the dimensions that influence the organization over time but often are not involved in day-to-day transactions with it."[9] Yet, we see in the book that the international dimension was discussed first and legal/political, last, implying that the former is more important than the latter. In the crab and frog motion model, we have scale mechanism, reminding readers that 1 is more important than 5, at least normatively.

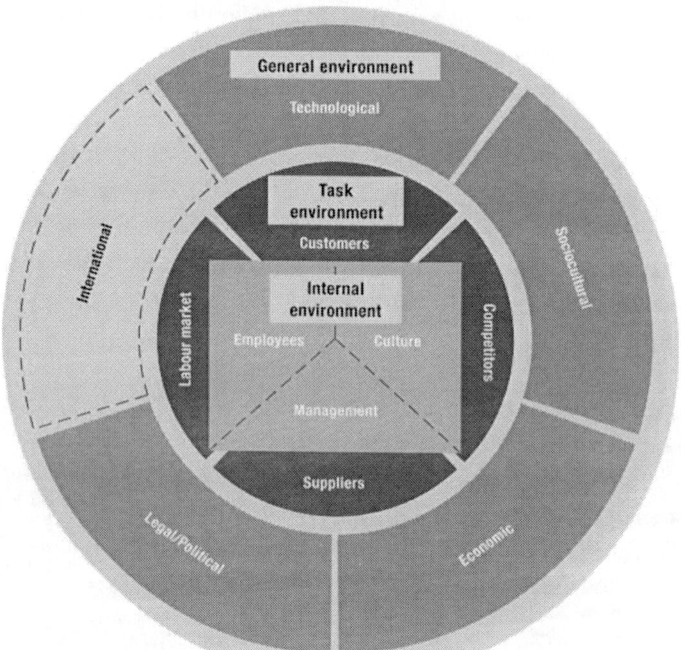

[6] Danny A. Samson and Richard L. Daft, *Fundamentals of Management*, third Asia Pacific ed. (Victoria, Australia: Cengage Learning Australia, 2009).

[7] *Ibid.*, p.92. The general environment is the outer layer of the environment. There are other dots. See, for example, *ibid.*, p.104, p.140, p.185, p.233, p.254, p.300, p.402, and p.571. However, the structures inside are all different. From SAMSON, D. *Fundamentals of Management,* 3E. © 2008 Cengage Learning Australia, a part of Cengage Learning, Inc. Reproduced by permission.

[8] John J. Wild, *et. al.* also presented their study of international business in terms of a dot. See their book, John J. Wild, Kenneth L. Wild, and Jerry C. Y. HAN, *International Business: The Challenges of Globalisation*, 5th ed. (New Jersey: Pearson and Prentice Hall, 2010).

[9] Samson and Daft, pp.92-98.

2. Mechanistic Versus Organic Organizations[10]

The word, versus, is dialectical. Many academics and experts, who have a linear-thinking or are used to the cause and effect study, failed to recognize this. In other words, by applying, at least, inner dialectics, they should not feel uncomfortable with dialectics, some of whom mistakenly think that dialectics is associated with Marxism. As a reminder, the *Yin* and *Yang* diagram appeared before Marxism.

3. 1 = Not well at all; 2 = Not very well; 3 = Moderately well; 4 = Very well; 5 = Extremely Well

This is similar to a five-point Likert scale (1 = lowest importance and 5, highest importance). "Not well at all" represents one extreme and "extremely well," another extreme. The spectrum can be expanded or reduced. For example, a manager may have ten roles to play in a company, that is, under the category of informational: monitor, disseminator, and spokesperson; under the category of interpersonal: figurehead, leader, and liaison; and under the category of decisional: entrepreneur, disturbance handler, resource allocator, and negotiator.[11] In this context, what one should do is to construct the 1 2 3 4 5 6 7 8 9 10 spectrum or the A B C D E F G H I J spectrum. For example, 1 refers to monitor; 5, leader; and 8, disturbance handler.

4. Making the Leap: Becoming a New Manager[12]

In the crab and frog motion model, one has to often leap or jump from one model to another model, though all the structures remain the same. This is necessary, because, sometimes, we cannot use the first model to describe and explain, if not to infer or predict, certain new phenomena. As a next step, we have to build a new model or a series of other crab and frog motion models.

5. Adversarial Orientation and Partnership Orientation[13]

A dialectical relationship has at least a (partial) adversary, due to the existence of the safe zone (or partnership orientation) and danger zone (or adversarial orientation) structure, if we look at the whole model. At time/space sequence (n), we will be able to see the end result of the game.

---

[10] *Ibid.*, p.357 and p.359 as well as the PowerPoint.
[11] *Ibid.*, p.31.
[12] *Ibid.*, p.26.
[13] *Ibid.*, p.108.

6. Paradox[14]

A dialectical/crab and frog motion remark is just the opposite of a non-dialectical/crab and frog motion (usually deductive, linear, or cause and effect) remark, or, at best, they must meet half-way.

Because some readers may still be confused, we will first apply the *Yin* and *Yang* diagram to describe and explain, if not infer or predict, the term, management, which is again but a dot. First, we must conceive management as a pure dot, with nothing inside. It comes in the shape of a circle, which means 360 degrees, embracing all types of management from A to Z, such as Theory Z or what I called JapanAm Theory (Japan + America), if we refer to the 1986 *Gung Ho* movie, which means a management perspective that incorporates techniques from both Japanese and Western management practices. However, it does not represent everything, because there are other things in the world, both tangible and intangible.

Here, the *Yin* and *Yang* diagram comes in. In other words, there is management and non-management. Management could be represented by the white portion in the diagram and non-management, the black portion. By the latter, it could refer to a company car, chief executive officer (ceo), etc., that is, tangible and intangible things related to management. Couched in terms of the crab and frog motion model, management is 1 2 3 4 5 and non-management, A B C D E. Another way of saying the same thing is management versus non-management.

In real life, we may well sometimes have to position management at 1 and non-management, 5. In that context, what does A B C D E stand for in terms of the whole model? It is non-"management-and-non-management," or something totally not related to management and the company, such as asteroid, universe, etc. Here, we must insert another model, that is, management and non-management related to the company versus (as opposed to and) non-management not related to the company. We must also have the following structure in mind: One *Yin* and *Yang* diagram on the left versus the other *Yin* and *Yang* diagram on the right. Another way of saying the same thing is the left *Yin* and *Yang* diagram versus the right *Yin* and *Yang* diagram. The right *Yin* and *Yang* diagram in this context could be asteroid versus non-asteroid (which could be, for example, universe).

What does the small black dot in the white portion and, for that matter, the small white dot in the black portion, represent? To be sure, the small black dot in the white portion could refer to something in the black portion, and vice versa. In other words, they co-exist. In passing, it should be noted that, just as the small black dot or the small white dot, respectively, can be expanded, it can be reduced, too, respectively.

What about the crooked line in the middle of the diagram, which looks like a snake? It represents the middle road/path/line or both 1 in the safe zone or A in the danger zone, depending on the time/space sequence. To be sure, both 1 and A can constitute another dialectical model.

At this juncture, we will select 10 diagrams from the Samson and Daft book. Readers can compare and contrast them, only to find that the two co-authors neglected or had failed to integrate all the diagrams in the book into one grand diagram at the very beginning of the book. What they did had confused readers, young and old alike. To be sure, books like *Blue Ocean Strategy* and *International Business: The Challenges of Globalisation* have the same

[14] *Ibid.*, p.317.

shortcomings. However, we will show how they can be converted in terms of a series of the crab and frog motion model.

I. [15]

Mechanistic versus Organic organisations

Mechanistic ***(In Stable Environments)***	**Organic** ***(In Dynamic Environments)***
• Rigid hierarchical relationships	• Collaboration (both vertical and horizontal)
• Fixed duties	• Adaptable duties
• High formalisation	• Low formalisation
• Formalised communication channels	• Informal communication
• Centralised decision authority	• Decentralised decision authority

At least five, major crab and frog motion models with the same structure are needed: 1) Mechanistic Organizations versus Organic Organizations; 2) Organic Organizations versus Mechanistic Organizations; 3) In Stable Environments versus In Dynamic Environments; 4) In Dynamic Environments versus In Stable Environments; and 5) Rigid hierarchical relationships at 1; Fixed duties at 2; High formalization at 3; Formalized communication channels at 4; and Centralized decision authority at 5; which is another way of representing Mechanistic Organizations, as well as Collaboration (both vertical and horizontal) at E, Adaptable duties at D; Low formalization at C; Informal communication at B; and Decentralized decision authority at A, which is another way of representing Organic Organizations.

If we want to be in-depth, we can construct a series of other models, for example, Rigid hierarchical relationships versus non-Rigid hierarchical relationships. By the latter, it can be Fixed duties, High formalization, etc.

II.

In chapter 9 on page 359, we see the following rating/grading: Disagree Strongly, represented by 1 2 3 4 5. Agree Strongly represented by 1 2 3 4 5. In Chapter 10 on page 392, we see the following rating: 1 = not well at all; 2 = not very well; 3 = moderately well; 4 = very well; 5 = extremely well. In Chapter 13 on page 508, we see the following rating: very important ← 1 2 3 4 5 6 7 → very unimportant.

The above-mentioned ratings are very confusing. How do we convert different ratings logically, systematically, and coherently? First, we must first identify three major models, namely, Disagree Strongly versus Agree Strongly; “not well at all” versus “extremely well;” and “very important” versus “very unimportant.” Second, Disagree Strongly should be 1 2 3 4 5, and Agree Strongly, A B C D E. The same logic applies to the second rating, namely, the

[15] From SAMSON, D. *Fundamentals of Management,* 3E. © 2008 Cengage Learning Australia, a part of Cengage Learning, Inc. Reproduced by permission.

"not well at all" spectrum is 1 2 3 4 5 and the "extremely well"'s, A B C D E. As to the last example, the model should be restructured as follows: "very important" is equivalent to 1 2 3 4 5 and "very unimportant," A B C D E.

III.[16]

Environment and culture

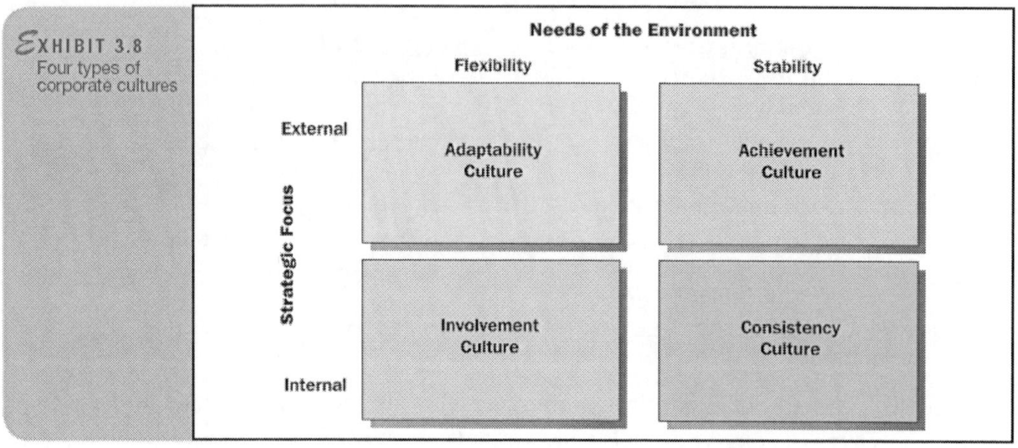

Source: Based on Denison, D.R. and Mishra, A.K. (March-April 1995). Toward a Theory of Organizational Culture and Effectiveness. *Organization Science,* 6, no. 2: 204-23; Hooijberg, R. and Petrock, F. (1993). On Cultural Change: Using the Competing Values Framework to Help Leaders Execute a Transfromational Strategy. *Human Resource Management* 32, no. 1: 29-50; and Quinn, R.E. (1988). Beyond Rational Management: Mastering the Paradoxes and Competeing Demands of High Performance. San Francisco: Jossey-Bass.

A series of models are needed to describe and explain the diagram. If presented well, the models can help us to infer or predict future, even to time/space sequence (n). We can name some of them: Needs of the Environment versus Non-"Needs of the Environment;" Strategic Focus versus non-"Strategic Focus;" Achievement Culture at 1, Consistency Culture at 2, Involvement Culture at 4, and Adaptability Culture at 5; External at 1 and Internal at 5; and Flexibility at 1 and Stability at 5. Since this diagram is derived from several sources, we also need to have the following model: All the authors to be put in the safe zone spectrum. In other words, we have to tolerate all of their contributions, however contradictory they are. The crab and frog motion player has to decide where to place the first author, second author, and so on and so forth, accordingly in 1 2 3 4 5.

[16] From SAMSON, D. *Fundamentals of Management,* 3E. © 2008 Cengage Learning Australia, a part of Cengage Learning, Inc. Reproduced by permission.

IV.[17]

Goals, Plans and performance

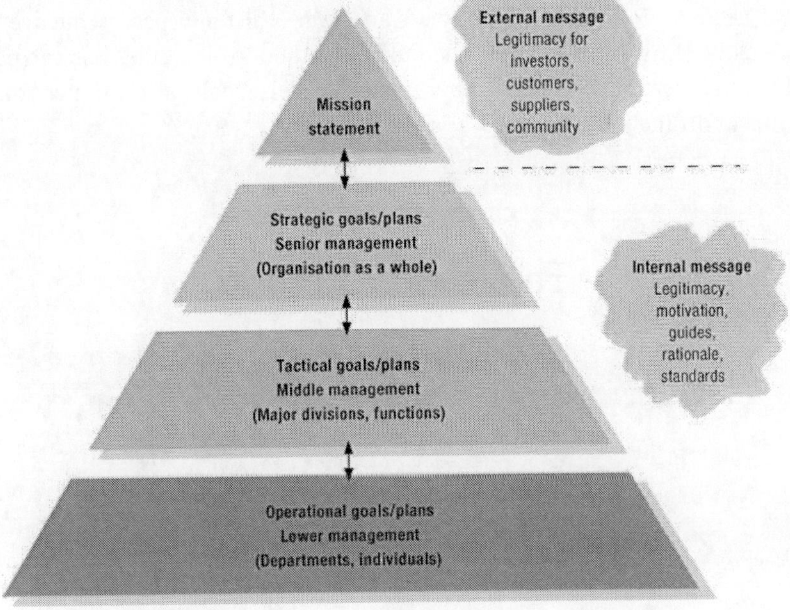

This is a pyramid-shaped diagram. As such, it simply means that "Mission statement" should be positioned at 1, because 1 carries the most weight. "Strategic goals/plans..." should be placed at 2. "Tactical goals/plans..." should be put at 4. And, the last level should be 5. "External Message" and "Internal Message" should also be constructed and be put at 1 and 5, respectively.

V.[18]

Maslow's hierarchy of needs

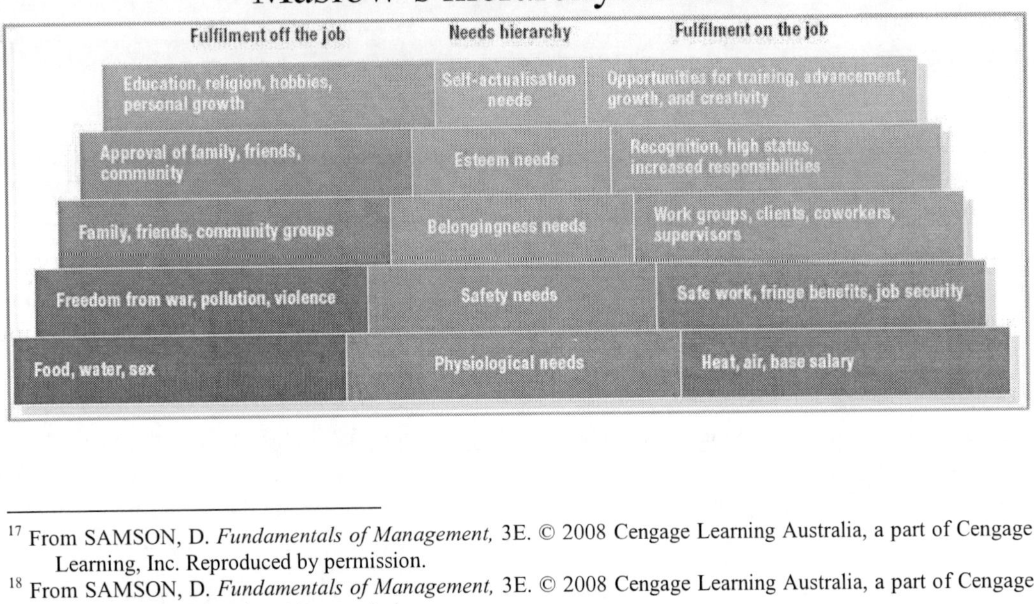

---

[17] From SAMSON, D. *Fundamentals of Management,* 3E. © 2008 Cengage Learning Australia, a part of Cengage Learning, Inc. Reproduced by permission.

[18] From SAMSON, D. *Fundamentals of Management,* 3E. © 2008 Cengage Learning Australia, a part of Cengage Learning, Inc. Reproduced by permission.

Abraham H. Maslow's hierarchy or theory of human needs was originally presented in a pyramid-shaped diagram. Another model saying the same thing is as follows: Self-actualization needs at 1; Esteem needs at 2; Belongingness needs at 3; Safety needs at 4; and Physiological needs at 5. In this model, we start from 5 at time/space sequence (1). Like a crab, we gradually move from 5 to 1. Since the co-authors of the 2009 book expanded upon the original pyramid, we have to build other related models, such as "Fulfilment on the job" at 1 and "Fulfilment off the job" at 5.

VI.[19]

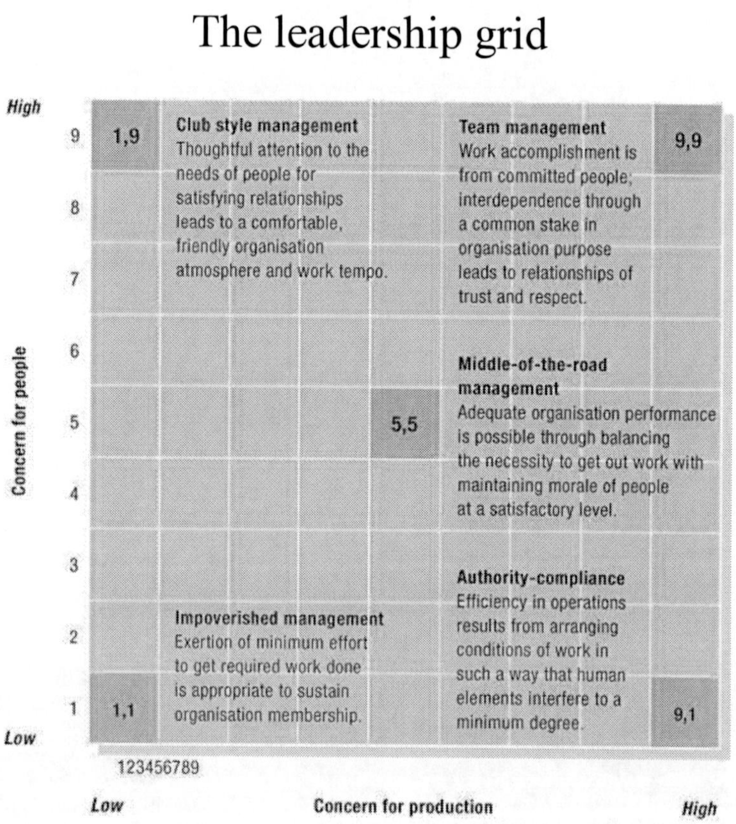

This is a complex and complicated diagram. Depending on each leader of the company, any arrangement is possible. For example, we can put "Club style management" at 1, while "Team management" could be placed at 3. To simplify everything, we can use Foxconn Technology Group (FTG), as an example. It is a multinational business group anchored by the Hon Hai Precision Industry Co., Ltd. in Taiwan, Republic of China (ROC), which makes products for Apple, Nokia, Dell, Sony, and Panasonic, and which employs an estimated 420,000 people in the Chinese mainland (*neidi*), including 300,000 in Shenzhen, a city of sub-provincial administrative status in Guangdong Province. From January to June 2010, 10 out of its 12 Shenzhen plant employees leapt to their deaths from their apartments, to be

[19] From SAMSON, D. *Fundamentals of Management,* 3E. © 2008 Cengage Learning Australia, a part of Cengage Learning, Inc. Reproduced by permission.

followed by other incidents in July 2010. Some protesters say that the company was making money by exploiting workers. In other words, the founder of Foxconn, Terry T. Gou, was more concerned about production than people. In June 2010, Gou, under pressure, shifted to "middle-of-the-road" style from "Authority-compliance" style by rising 30% of his employees' wages, if one qualifies after assessment, which could spell a historic end to cheap labor in the mainland.[20] Needless to say, the crab and motion player has to decide by himself or herself where to position, for example, middle-of-the-road management style.

VII.[21]

Hersey & Blanchard's situational theory

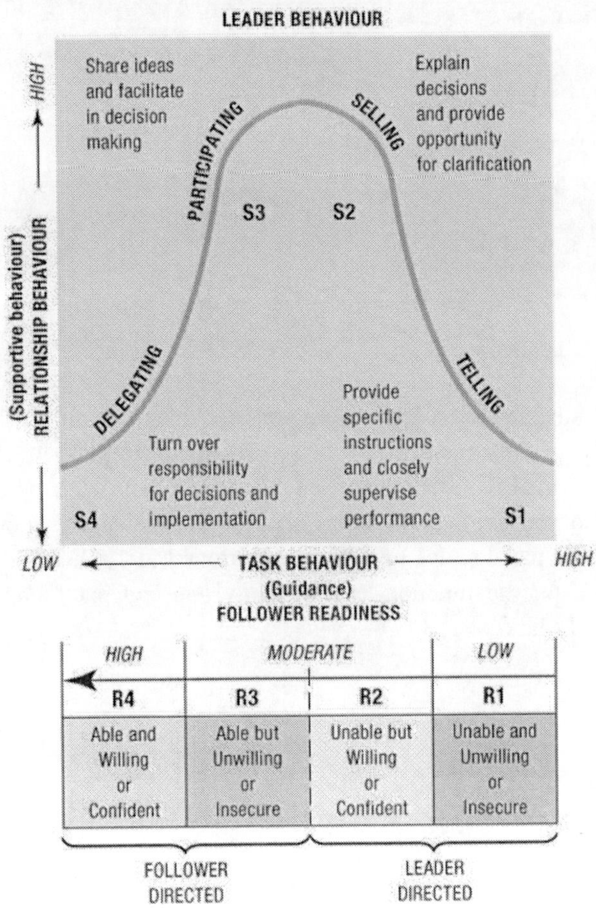

Paul Hersey and K. H. Blanchard's situational leadership model "is a contingency approach to leadership that links the leader's behavioural style with the task readiness of employees."[22] Their point is simple and straightforward: People low in task readiness, due to little ability, training, or insecurity, need a different leadership style from those who are high

[20] *Borneo Post* (hereinafter BP), June 10, 2010, p.B10.

[21] From SAMSON, D. *Fundamentals of Management,* 3E. © 2008 Cengage Learning Australia, a part of Cengage Learning, Inc. Reproduced by permission.

[22] Samson and Daft, p.454.

in readiness to lead them.[23] So, for leader behavior, we can position relationship behavior at 1 and task behavior, 5. In another model, "telling" could be at 1; "selling," 2; "practicing," 4; and "delegating," 5. What does 3 stands for? It stands for a mixture of 1 and 2 as well as 4 and 5. As for follower readiness, we need at least two models: high at 1; moderate at 3; and low at 5, plus putting R4 at 1; R3 and R2 are equivalent to 3; as well as R1 equal to 5. Needless to say, what we have written down only shows a partial picture. We need more crab and frog motion models, if we want to see a fuller picture.

VIII.[24]

Levels of strategy

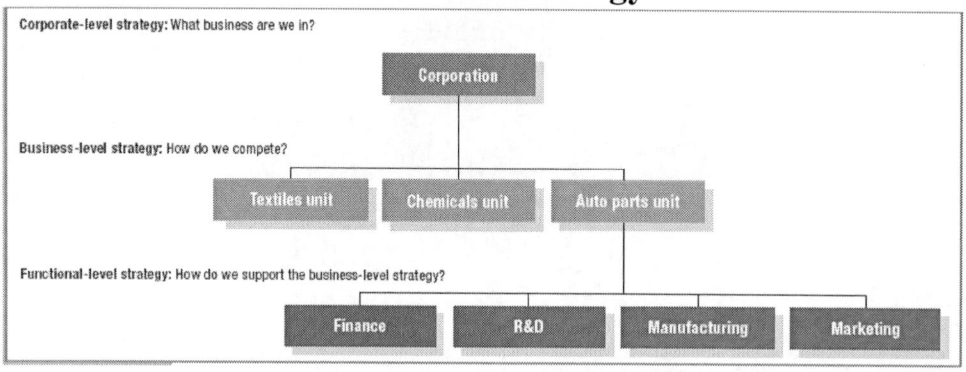

It is not difficult to construct a series of models for this diagram. Corporate-level strategy should be placed at 1; business-level strategy, 3; and functional-level strategy, 5. Since corporation does not equal to textiles unit, chemical unit, and auto parts unit, we need the following model: Corporation versus non-Corporation. However, another way of saying corporation is, for example: textiles unit, to be positioned at 1; chemical unit or 3; and auto parts unit or 5. And, for the function-level strategy, we can put Finance at 1; R & D, 2; Manufacturing, 3; and Marketing, 5.

[23] *Ibid.*

[24] From SAMSON, D. *Fundamentals of Management,* 3E. © 2008 Cengage Learning Australia, a part of Cengage Learning, Inc. Reproduced by permission.

IX.[25]

Managing team conflict

Styles to handle conflict

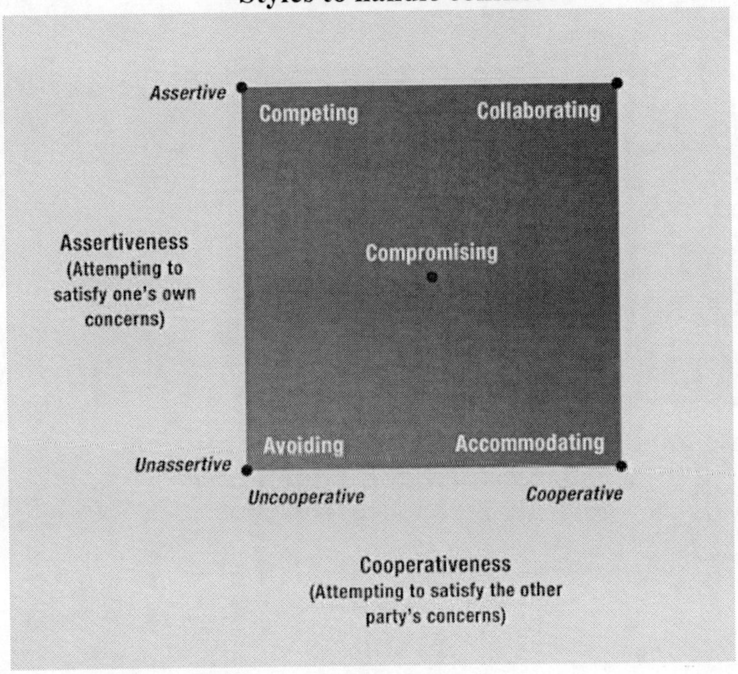

The diagram is obviously non-dialectically built. However, inner dialectics exists, such as assertive versus unassertive as well as cooperative versus uncooperative. Managing team conflict can be done dialectically, that is, by applying the crab and frog motion model. Depending on the manager, the assertiveness style could be 1 and the cooperativeness style, E. A manager may also have to accommodate both styles, by positioning the first style at 5 and the second style, 1. In other words, 3 would be a mixture of both 1 and 5. At certain time/space sequence, both 1 and 5 are needed, certainly.

In the diagram, we also see the term, compromising, in the middle of the square or box. This is like 5 in the safe zone of the crab and frog motion model and A in the danger zone.

X.[26]

A few models are needed in the seemingly contradictory paragraph. "To be a Failure" should be put at 1, because, normatively speaking, at time/space sequence (n), the man wants to reach there. The second model is: "To Reach My Goal" (or 1) versus "Not to Reach My Goal" (or 5). Before reaching the goal, the man has to rely on the third model: Success (or 1) versus Failure (or 5). Since the man mentioned success twice in the second sentence in the cartoon, he was at 1, standing for success, twice or at time/space sequence (1) and time/space sequence (2). In sum, a seemingly contradictory paragraph can be and has been dissolved.

---

[25] From SAMSON, D. *Fundamentals of Management,* 3E. © 2008 Cengage Learning Australia, a part of Cengage Learning, Inc. Reproduced by permission.

[26] From SAMSON, D. *Fundamentals of Management,* 3E. © 2008 Cengage Learning Australia, a part of Cengage Learning, Inc. Reproduced by permission.

"My goal is to be a failure. If I reach my goal, I'll feel successful and if I don't reach my goal, I'll feel successful too!"

FINDINGS

Many findings are in order. First, all the chosen (or non-chosen) diagrams in the 2009 book are in a mess. They come in different internal structures, shapes, sizes, etc. There is no logic, system, or coherence, if we lump and look at them together. Intuitively, had we chosen other diagrams, the result is the same--confusion begets confusion. There could be logic, if we look at each one of them, respectively. However, this may not be 100% true, because some diagrams were adapted, and, therefore, the two co-authors of the book may have distorted the research method(s) of those original diagrams. In short, an undergraduate student can be easily confused, to say the least.

Second, in this intellectual exercise, we have consistently tried to convert all the non-dialectical diagrams into the dialectical ones. By doing so, the lead co-author had, for the first time in July 2010, revised the order of what scholarship means to him in the following original order of importance: logic, contribution, preciseness, closeness to reality, etc. He would put the term, consistency, in the third place, to read: logic, contribution, consistency, preciseness, closeness to reality, etc.

Third, the lead co-author's one-dot theory and the crab and frog motion model or the crab and frog motion model and/or theory can be applied when a researcher or practitioner is facing a question of what way to choose: classical way and/or applied way. This is because everything can be interpreted as a dot. Needless to say, a dot could be a partial dot of a larger dot. As a step further, the 1 2 3 4 5 A B C D E framework can be applied to describe, explain, and infer, if not predict, certain phenomena.

Fourth, to apply logics, one must be dialectical. Yet, by applying the lead co-author's model, one should realize that it can embrace all the logics in the world by virtue of the safe zone spectrum, which can be expanded. Thus, the inductive method could be placed at 5; deductive, at 1; and a mixture of them, at 3. Please read the first and last chapters in this book.

In passing, it should be pointed out that logics cannot be non-dialectical. For example, at point 1 in time, one applied the inductive method; at point 2 in time, one switched to the deductive method; at point 10 in time, one adopted the inductive method again. This is like saying one wants to travel from Kuching, Sarawak, Malaysia to Shanghai, mainland China. In the first leg of the trip, one tried to swim from Kuching to Xiamen City, Fujian Province. In the second leg, one rode on a bicycle. In the third leg, one spent 10 hours walking along the provincial road. And, in the last leg, one drove a car to reach the direct-controlled municipality. In short, although the traveller reached the destiny, he or she did not choose a consistent way.

Fifth, we do need to apply logics to study management and, for that matter, business. As shown, we have throughout the sections applied at least two types of logic to describe and explain all the 10 selected diagrams. However, there is consistency. Can the same model and theory be applied to study other diagrams in the same book or other books? The answer is clear: Yes, it can be easily done.

Sixth, because the lead co-author's theory and model can accommodate both classical and applied ways, the end result of our study or analysis should be closer to reality. The only problem is that we have to rely on a series of crab and frog motion models to represent each diagram, which is cumbersome to many, if not most, academics and experts. However, since each model's structure is the same, there should not be too much of headache for readers to comprehend or grasp everything in a short period of time. Meetings can be shortened, if the participants use and share the same logics.

Seventh, what needs to be done, as the second co-author suggested, is to integrate all the small and big crab and frog motion models into one biggest model and to present them at the outset. The third co-author also concurred, adding the biggest model should be applicable to all situations and phenomena.

Eighth, by applying the lead co-author's theory and model, the study can be considered philosophical. “My philosophy is....” This sentence was uttered by the wife of the lead co-author's brother, when he was staying at their house in late 2001. The philosophy of the father of scientific management, Frederick W. Taylor (1856-1915), is: "In the past the man has been first. In the future, the system must be first."[27] Non-dialectically, whoever made that kind of statement--my philosophy is....--should not change a bit throughout his or her life. Is this possible? The answer is clear: No. Thus, Taylor switched the word from man to system. Man is not equal to system. To be sure, we cannot rule out the possibility that man can be put in the first place again in the future. It is always possible that, after another asteroid striking our planet, we the human beings have to go back to the stone age.

Nonetheless, dialectically, one can, depending on each time/space sequence, because one can comply with 1%, 50%, or even 100% of his or her philosophy in the philosophy versus non-philosophy framework. Thus, "man must be first" can be placed at 5, while "system must be first" can be positioned at 1, whereas 3 can be a hybrid of both 1 and 5, due to the fact that some criticisms of the scientific management have been levelled at Taylor, such as "did not appreciate the social context of work and higher needs of workers; did not acknowledge

---

[27] *Ibid.*, p.62.

variance among individuals; [and] tended to regard workers as uninformed, and ignored their ideas and suggestions."[28]

Ninth, the early study of management, as we know it today, emerged during the 19th and early 20th centuries or what some academics called the classical perspective.[29] At that time, not many academics and experts would think of first using the term, governance. Joan E. Spero and Jeffrey A. Hart, in their 7th edition book, *The Politics of International Economic Relations*, have urged us to move from the perspective of management to (international) governance. Morten Ougaard and Anna Leander, in their 2009 book, pointed out that, over the past two decades, the role of business in global governance has become increasingly topical. Our sincere plea is to venture into the study of international (corporate) governance, which is an integrated term of international governance, international corporate governance, and corporate governance.

If we were to add another term, business, the whole picture, non-dialectically, and half-picture, dialectically, would be more complex and complicated, as we often mention both business and management together.

The ultimate question is: Can you put the three terms together in our model or in any one of the non-dialectical diagrams mentioned above? Yes, it can be easily done, if one applied the crab and frog motion model. We can put governance at 1; business, 3; and management, 5. At time/space sequence (1), people concerned with business were at 3. Since the 19th century, people began to attach great importance on management. And, in recent decades, the emphasis has been first shifted to governance and then management, because the latter is but a part of the former.

Tenth, when the Dutch East Indies Company (DEIC) (or Vereenigde Oostindische Compagnie in Dutch), as a first artificial person in the world of business, was created in March 1602,[30] there was no technology. Can we, apply the following model: Man at 1, Science at 3, and Technology at 5? The answer is: Yes. Human beings existed first at time/space sequence (1). Science followed, say at time/space sequence (1,000). Then, we have technology. In other words, when we have all three, we simply look at man, science, and technology together at the specific time/space sequence, when technology emerged. What this means is that the crab and frog motion model covers the past, present, and the future. In other words, building a right model can enable us to predict future. Non-dialectically, it cannot be done, because man is man is man, unless inner dialectics has been applied later on, using such phrases as "on the one hand" and "on the other hand."

11th, often we hear both experts and laymen, saying that their attempt in conducting research and writing is to bridge the gap between research and practice or to put theory into practice. Once having understood the lead co-author's theory and model, one should realize that reality can easily be slotted into the one-dot theory and the crab and frog motion model.

12th, if one does not apply a model or theory, he or she can be easily labelled as a pseudo-scientist. However, when one does apply a model or theory, he or she may be criticized as being tautological. However, to a practitioner, such may not be the case, because he or she is making initiatives, and such a criticism cannot be levelled against him or her.

13th, if scholarship means the following in the order of importance, we have fulfilled at least the first four criteria: logic, contribution, consistency, preciseness, closeness to reality,

[28] *Ibid.*, p.63.
[29] *Ibid.*, p.61.
[30] It became defunct or bankrupted in March 1798.

etc. There is logic in the paper. The term, logics, is also applicable. We have made contribution to at least tell the two co-authors that they should be consistent in using or showing management diagrams. Indeed, there is consistency. The lead co-author's model and theory are precise, by virtue of the spectrums and time/space sequence components, because, for example, each time/space sequence may refer to a half-a-split second. And, because the dialectical model is both normative and empirical, the study should be closer to reality.

14th, many subscribers to linear thinking or cause-effect are not aware that they have to adopt inner dialectics, in order to continue their description, explanation, and inference. A dual-track approach/strategy is one finest example. In June 2010, the United Nations (UN) slapped the fourth comprehensive package of (tighter, crippling, or paralyzing) sanctions on the Islamic Republic of Iran (RIOI). The first round was made in December 2006. Before making the punishments, dialogue and negotiations as well as the threat of sanctions took place. In a word, the dual-track approach is precisely dialectical.

CONCLUSION

Since ancient China, the Chinese scholars tried to correlate everything in terms of *Yin* and *Yang*. We are carrying on the baton in the relay, so to speak, so as to enable us to rationalize *everything* logically, systematically, and coherently. The lead co-author emphasizes the word, everything, because it can be easily done.

We were told that there are seven (deadly) sins in corporate mismanagement or mis-governance, to wit, gluttony, lechery or the bet, the loafer, the cheat, avarice, envy, as well as pride and ambition or the sun king (Singh 2009). Arguably, the problem or what the lead co-author called the 8th sin with social science is that, often, when we study a topic, we did not put logic in the first place. This applies to business and management, politics, etc. What the non-dialecticians have done is actually distorting reality, even if one attempts to apply the grounded theory, trying not to have preconceived ideas.[31] To be sure, managers or, for that matter, ceos, cannot put logic in the first place. They must put profit in the first place. Without profit, their company cannot survive. If their company cannot survive, logic does not mean a thing, unless logic can generate profit or revenue. However, a well established company may have to be concerned with logic, for example, when they place an advertisement in the mass media, trying to convince prospective buyers. Even so, some advertisement statements may not be logical, because they do not fit into all consumers' needs.[32] Thus, the following model is needed: Profit at 1 and logic, 5.

It remains to be seen whether or not other academics and experts who apply game theory, system theory,[33] rational (choice) theory, etc. can be equally successful in converting information, data, and analysis into their choice of model and/or theory. Intuitively, it is doubtful, because both game theory and rational (choice) theory, which does not accompany with at least one model, presume that all the human beings are rational at all times, which is not so. Besides, the structure of their models could, most likely, differ. In this connection, the

---

[31] If a person is not religious, he or she should go back to the split second just before the Big Bang. If the person is religious, he or she should go back to the moment before the existence of God, Buddha, etc., because God is a Being, something which can influence our mind and heart.

[32] Conversation with Vie Ming TAN, dated June 10, 2010.

[33] Samson and Daft, pp.72-73.

shortcoming of the system theory is precisely that black-box or what Samson and Daft called Transformation process (or management/production technology), in which we do not know what is 100% really going on.

In sum, it is not difficult to convert information, data, and analysis into the lead co-author's model and theory, which can, needless to say, still be falsified, when all the human beings become extinct, meaning that nobody can apply the crab and frog motion model and the one-dot theory and, therefore, what the lead co-author have done since September 1994 by constructing the dialectical model would be in vain.

APPENDIX I. CONVERTING THE CHINESE PEOPLE'S LIBERATION ARMY PYRAMID AND DOCTRINAL DISCOURSE IN THREE-DIMENSIONS

The diagrams below can also be applied to the study of business and management. They were drawn by an expert on Chinese Communist military affairs, which are definitely dialectical, but whose logic is not dialectical.[34]

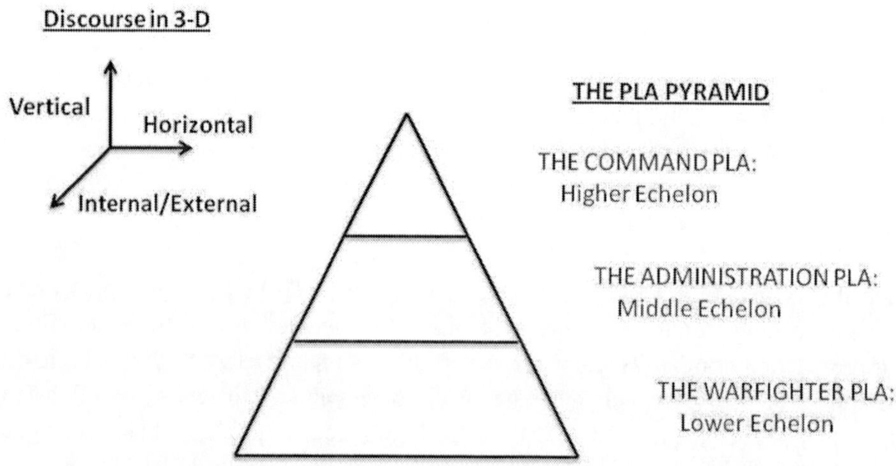

It is not difficult to convert them dialectically. Again, a series of crab and frog motion models are needed: Horizontal at 1 and Vertical at 5; Vertical at 1 and Horizontal at 5; Internal at 1 and External 5; Internal at 1 versus External at E; and so on and so forth. As to the pyramid, the dominant model is: Higher Echelon at 1; Middle Echelon at 3; and Lower Echelon at 5. Is it possible to position Higher Echelon at 1, while Middles Echelon is placed at E and Lower Echelon at C? This possibility cannot be ruled out, because there could always be struggles over budget, for example, between military officials who belong to or side with different echelons. In short, the main point is that everything has been structured consistently.

---

[34] Andrew Scobell, "Discourse in 3-D: The PLA's Evolving Doctrine, Circa 2009" in Roy Kamphausen, David Lai, and Andrew Scobell, eds., *The PLA at Home and Abroad: Assessing the Operational Capabilities of China's Military* (Carlisle, PA.: Strategic Studies Institute, U.S. Army War College, June 2010), p.102.

REFERENCES

Kamphausen, Roy, David Lai, and Andrew Scobell, eds. (2010), *The PLA at Home and Abroad: Assessing the Operational Capabilities of China's Military* (Carlisle, PA.: Strategic Studies Institute, U.S. Army War College).

Samson, Danny A. and Richard L. Daft (2009), *Fundamentals of Management*, third Asia Pacific Ed. (Victoria, Australia: Cengage Learning Australia).

Singh, Udai Vir (2009), *7 Deadly Sins of Corporate Mismanagement : What They Don't Teach in Business Schools* (New Delhi: Pentagon Press).

Wild, John J., Kenneth L. Wild, and Jerry C. Y. HAN (2010), *International Business: The Challenges of Globalisation*, 5th ed. (New Jersey: Pearson and Prentice Hall).

In: International (Corporate) Governance
Editor: Peter Kien-Hong Yu
ISBN: 978-1-61122-645-4

Chapter 3

Redefining Global Business as International Regimes-Related Trade and Commerce: Navigating through an Ocean without Confusion by Applying the One-dot Theory

Peter Kien-Hong Yu and George Kwang Sing Ngui

Abstract

Many academics take for granted the real meaning of the term, global business. In this paper, the co-authors attempt to offer a new interpretation by associating it with international regimes, which is a positive concept, benefiting all the countries, political and/or economic entities, and individuals like you and me.

To rationalize all the information, data, and analysis, the lead co-author of this chapter applies his one-dot theory, which is accompanied by his crab and frog motion model, throughout the study.

If a businessman or a transnational corporation is looking for a niche in the market, thinking of others first by tip toeing the line of forming, maintaining, and sustaining international regimes can enable a businessman or a transnational company to make profits, without competition for a longer period of time. Such should be strategy, as opposed to implement the Blue Ocean Strategy (BOS), which is not truly global nor being able to be sustained for a longer period of time.

Keywords: (international) governance, international regimes, business (without competition), one-dot theory, *Yin* and *Yang* Diagram

There are five keywords for this research paper, namely, (international) governance, international regimes, business (without competition), one-dot theory, *Yin* and *Yang* Diagram. Actually, the keyword, (international) governance refers to two terms, governance and international governance. What is applied at the governance level should also be applied to the international governance level. By the same token, business (without competition), refers to two terms. One is business with competition and the other, business without competition. If one has fully grasped the term, international regimes, he or she should realize that it must be mentioned when we study governance at almost all the levels. Likewise, as can be seen later on, the *Yin* and *Yang* Diagram is but part of the one-dot theory.

The keywords have been on purpose arranged in that order. The reasons are two-fold. First, they by themselves could be non-dialectically confusing. For example, some academics would simply use the term, governance, when the issues that they have touched upon actually are related to the world.[1] Others would add adjectives like international and global. Still others would narrow down their study of governance to merely contemporary Germany or the Asia-Pacific region.[2] The same thing speaks for the term, business. Thus, we have international business,[3] global business,[4] and world business.[5] There is one unique book, which mentions international business in the title and global business in the subtitle, and the publisher happens to have adopted the term, world trade, as part of the name for the company.[6] Oddly enough, *Glossary of International Trade* does not even carry entries for global business, international business, or world business,[7] as if readers can distinguish them without any problems or the terms can be used interchangeably, which is not really true. As can be seen later on, depending on the context, they can have different connotations. Second, they could be non-dialectically contradictory. For example, depending on the context, *Yin* and *Yang* could be contradictory or at odds.

In this paper, the co-authors will first introduce the lead co-author's crab and frog motion model. Because a model does not have to have a theory but a theory must have a model, the one-dot theory must be accompanied by a one-dot model. In the second section, the co-authors will try to slot in the information, data, and analysis into the model, thereby enabling us to figure out whether it is possible to rationalize everything. In the third section, we will point out some major findings. In the section that follows, we will briefly sketch what kind of global business can be conducted in relation to international regimes, without competition for a longer period of time.

---

[1] See, for example, William M. Lafferty, ed., *Governance for Sustainable Development: The Challenge of Adapting Form to Function* (Chelteham, U.K.: Edward Elgar, 2004).

[2] See, for example, Simon Green and William E. Paterson, eds., *Governance in Contemporary Germany: The Semisovereign State Revisited* (Cambridge, U.K.: Cambridge University Press, 2005) and Richard Maidment, David Goldblatt, and Jeremy Mitchell, eds., *Governance in the Asia-Pacific* (London: Routledge, 1998).

[3] John D. Daniels, Lee H. Radebaugh, and Daniel P. Sullivan, *International Business: Environments and Operations*, 10th ed. (Upper Saddle River, N.J.: Pearson/Prentice Hall, 2004).

[4] See, for example, Charles W. L. Hill, *Global Business Today*, 6th ed. (Boston: McGraw-Hill/Irwin, 2009).

[5] See, for example, John S. Hill, *World Business: Globalization, Analysis and Strategy* (Mason, Ohio: Thomson and South-Western, 2005).

[6] See Charles Mitchell, *A Short Course in International Business Ethics: Combining Ethics and Profits in Global Business* ((Petaluma, CA.: World Trade Press, 2009).

[7] *Glossary of International Trade* (Petaluma, CA.: World Trade Press, 2009).

The Crab and Frog Motion model

The following model, which, if looked from a distance, could be two half-dots (1 2 3 4 5 as the first half-dot and A B C D E as the second half-dot) or simply one dot if we look at its entirety[8]:

1 2 3 4 5 A B C D E

time/space sequence (1)
time/space sequence (2)
…………………………..
time/space sequence (n)

1 means 100% of a concept or whatever;
3 means 50% of a concept or whatever;
5 means 1% of a concept or whatever.

E means 100% of a concept or whatever;
C means 50% of the concept or whatever;
A means 1% of the concept or whatever.

The 1 2 3 4 5 spectrum is equivalent to what I call the safe zone, and the A B C D E spectrum, the danger zone. 5 is the middle way/golden mean/road/path/line/track in the safe zone and A, the middle way/golden mean/road/path/line/track in the danger zone.

When one makes a move at any time/space sequence, he or she is thinking of only one most important Number or Letter, and, therefore, there will be no contradiction whatsoever. In the course of making moves, the dialectician is performing a crab or side-ways motion. For example, he or she began at 5. In the next time/space sequence, he or she may go to A. At the third time/space sequence, the same dialectician may move back to the safe zone and stay at 1. In this connection, the phenomena of the negation of negation, the affirmation of negation, the affirmation of affirmation, and the negation of affirmation will appear before time/space sequence (n) is reached. This process is known as the sub-dialectical game. It should be pointed out that there are three basic stages [or (nodal) points] of development: nascent, ascendant, and mature for the Numbers and mature, descendant, and moribund for the Letters. In other words, 5 is nascent; 3, ascendant; and 1, mature. On the other hand, E is mature: C, descendant; and A, moribund. Last but not least, a series of other, relevant dialectical, theoretical models must be applied, in order to amply describe, explain, and infer (or predict) more phenomena. When a dialectician no longer applies the first crab and frog motion model constructed by him or her, he or she is said to have leaped or jumped from the first crab and frog motion model to second or another crab and frog motion model.

At this juncture, a caveat should be added, that is, whenever we use the word, versus, it means that dialectics is involved and that the concept or whatever on the left extreme, say Yes or 1 will eventually defeat, co-opt, absorb, etc. the concept or whatever on the right extreme,

[8] *Zheng, fan, shun,ni, zhen,* and *wei.* There are many dots in the world. For example, each of a Polka dot means "each of a number of round dots evenly spaced to form a pattern on fabric." See *Oxford Student's Dictionary*, p.792.

say No or E at time/space sequence (n). However, in the process, the following arrangement may be necessary, such as flexibly positioning Yes at 1 and No at 5. In other words, a contradictory or even adversary relationship between Yes and No at the beginning has been transformed into a non-contradictory, non-adversarial relationship later on, meaning that whoever chose Yes or whoever opted No should learn to tolerate the existence of each other, because they are both in the safe zone spectrum.

In sum, a crab and frog motion player performs two roles when playing games, that of a crab by moving side-ways[9] and a frog by leaping or jumping from one model to another model as he or she sees fit. Such is the magic beauty of dialectics.

CONCEPTUALIZING FROM GOVERNANCE TO BUSINESS

In this section, we will first tackle the term, governance. It comes in many dimensions. Once determined, we can proceed to discuss the private sector, which usually refers to business. This is because there are, indeed, an increasing number of academics who are tying business with (global) governance, as interdependence among states intensifies. We will also try to show that there are at least three levels of governance, that is, global, international, or world, and how we would arrange them dialectically. After having done that, we will discuss the international regimes dimension of business, because, when we discuss governance at almost every level, we have to deal with the intertwined international regimes. In a word, governance at almost all levels has to involve international regimes and, in turn, touches upon business, especially at the global level.

"Which should come first" has been a perennial, philosophical question, until recently. The causality dilemma between the chicken and egg can be said as being settled in July 2010 by a group of British scientists, who scientifically proved the vital role of a protein, which was found only in a chicken's ovaries, used to kick-start the egg's formation.[10] What about the other dilemma, namely, internationalization and globalization?

According to John S. Hill, they are often used interchangeably in the general business press. However, in his *World Business: Globalization, Strategy and Analysis* book,[11] "*internationalization* occurs when firms extend products and services in overseas markets, usually from their home country" while "[g]lobalization is the process by which businesses create value by leveraging their resources and capabilities across borders; it includes the coordination of cross-border manufacturing and marketing strategies." As a result, internationalization is the first stage in the globalization process." By the same token, later on, we will also spell out the reason why it is necessary to mention global business first.

Business is tied to governance. Indeed, the co-editors of *Business and Global Governance* pointed out that their book will be of interest to students and scholars of Business Studies, International Relations, International Politics, and International Political Economy as

---

[9] Crabs can also have *xiaoshuibu* (quick short steps). In other words, they can move straight forward. See *United Daily News* (UDN)(Taipei), February 12, 2007, p.A10. In Yilang County, Taiwan Province, Republic of China (ROC), there is a crab museum. Not all crabs can be eaten, because some of them are poisonous. Poison could be dangerous. See Formosa Television (Taiwan, ROC), dated February 7, 2008.

[10] http://www.msnbc.msn.com/id/38238685/ns/technology_and_science-science/ and http://news.cnet.com/8301-11386_3-20010563-76.html, accessed on July 23, 2010.

[11] John S. Hill, p.303.

well as for practitioners, who are in the public and private sector.[12] In passing, it should be noted that some academics would add the third sector, with non-governmental organizations (NGOs) at the supranational level, national non-profit organizations at the national level, and local groups at he sub-national level as the finest example, which is quite different from transnational corporations at the supranational level, national corporations at the national level, and local businesses at the sub-national level, which belong to the private sector.[13]

How do we conceptualize governance, which involve both the public and private sectors? We can treat the two sectors as being one dot or a pure circle with nothing inside. Then, we ought to ask the next question, that is, is it possible to have 100% governance, at almost all levels, embracing both sectors? The answer is: No. So, we have to construct a new model, governance versus non-governance. The former is equivalent to the safe zone spectrum and the latter, the danger zone spectrum, which could refer to a zillion things, such as sand, storm, air, a baby, etc. We can conceptualize the framework as one pure dot versus non-"one pure dot."

Because we are studying governance, not non-governance, we need only focus on the one pure dot, which, to repeat, refers to both public and private sectors, each constituting a half-dot. Sometimes, the priority could be reversed. Instead of mentioning the public sector first, we mention the private sector first. This possibility cannot be ruled out. For example, a central government may be in heavy national debt. Foreign transnational corporations may donate some money to help the poor people in that country. As another example, in July 2010, the Economic and Social Council of the United Nations (ECOSOC) awarded "Special Consultative Status" to the Taipei-based Buddhist Tzu Chi Foundation (TCF), an acknowledgement of its outstanding charity and medical work in more than 70 countries around the world.

Since international regimes, which can be defined as a set (or sets) of at least 15 criteria/core elements/features (including those four as mentioned by Steven D. Krasner) in the contexts of (fragmented) issue-area, (fragmented) issue-areas, and issue-regimes, transcends national boundaries or both public and private sectors, we should bear in mind that they can exist in both sectors. The only problem is that can we identify the proper or appropriate ones at a point in time, so as to solve or resolve the issue in an area. For example, we often see the term, exchange-rate regimes, in books related to business and management, or the term, disclosure regimes in books related to corporate governance.[14]

However, many community-centered arrangements at the end of 2001, for example, do not bear that unique word, regime, such as exchange arrangements with no separate legal tender, involving 40 countries; currency board arrangements, involving eight countries; other conventional fixed peg arrangements, involving 41 countries; pegged exchange rated within horizontal bands, involving five countries; crawling pegs, involving four countries, exchange rates within crawling bands, involving six countries, managed floating with no pronounced

[12] See Morten Ougaard and Anna Leander, eds., *Business and Global Governance* (London: Routledge, 2010) and Kevin Farnsworth, "Governance, Business and Social Policy: International and national dimensions" in Patricia Kennett, ed., *Governance, Globalization and Public Poicy* (Cheltehham, U.K. Edward Elgar, 2008), pp.35-55.

[13] Robert O. Keohane and Joseph S. Nye, Jr., "Introduction" in Joseph S. Nye, Jr. and John D. Donahue, eds., *Governance in a Globalizing World* (Washington, D.C.: Brookings Institution Press, 2000), p.13. See also William C. Clark's, which was adapted from Keohane and Nye, on p.99.

[14] See, for example, Yadong LUO, *Global Dimensions of Corporate Governance* (Malden, MA.: Blackwell Publishing, 2007), p.2.

path for exchange rate, involving 42 countries, and independently floating, involving 186 countries.[15]

After having narrowed down our focus from governance to business, we still have to distinguish what global business, international business, and world business are? Are they similar or different? While terms like global learning, global web, and global economy, global marketplace, and global terrorism have been mentioned, the author of *Global Business Today* did not bother to define what is global, as opposed to international.[16] On page 35, he said "[a]n international business is any firm that engages in international trade or investment." Ironically, Michael R. Czinkota, Ilkka A. Ronkainen, and Michael H. Moffett in their *Fundamentals of International Business*, without defining what international business is, defined global business as: "Global business consists of transactions that are devised and carried out across national borders to satisfy the objectives of individuals, companies, and organizations. These transactions take on various forms, which are often interrelated. Primary types of international business are import-export trade and foreign direct investment (FDI). The latter is carried out in varied forms, including wholly owned subsidiaries and joint ventures. Additional types of international business are licensing, franchising, and management contracts."[17]

On the one hand, Oded Shenkar and Yadong LUO, while silent on global business, defined international business as "business activities that involve the transfer of resources, goods, services, knowledge, skills or information involving two or more countries."[18] In passing, it should be noted that, in the preface, they reminded readers that "[t]his book offers a fresh and unique perspective on international business: First, it takes a truly *global* rather than a U.S. perspective, providing balanced coverage… [italics ours]."[19] On the other hand, John D. Daniels, Lee H. Radebaugh, and Daniel P. Sullivan include transactions involving governments of two or more countries as international business,[20] and this is unique as contrasted to other definitions. What is confirmed here is that business can be government-related or government-owned. In the Chinese mainland (*neidi*), we do see many state-owned enterprises (SOEs).

To John S. Hill, world business "refers to commercial activities performed to promote the transfer of technologies, goods, services across national boundaries."[21] The problem with this usage is whether we can apply it to talk about intercelestial business, global business, or supranational business. To be sure, the noun, world, may also refer to oneself, as Hill wrote: world business can contribute to the well-being of countries, companies, and individuals.[22] An individual is a person. Inside oneself, there could be many things going on, including exchange of intangible things. For example, Robert B. Oxnam, who is a well-known expert on Asia, in his September 2005 book, *A Fractured Mind: My Life with Multiple Personality Disorder*, said that, once in his life, he has had 11 personalities, including old man, young

---

[15] Daniels, Radebaugh, and Sullivan, p.294.
[16] He on page xiv said "[c]onsistent with this goal, over the last six editions, I have…."
[17] See their book, *Fundamentals of International Business* (Mason, OH.: South-Western Educational Publishing, 2003).
[18] See their book, *International Business*, 2nd ed. (Thousand Oaks, CA.: Sage Publications, 2008), p.556.
[19] *Ibid.*, xiii.
[20] Daniels, Radebaugh, and Sullivan, p.674.
[21] John S. Hill, p.4.
[22] *Ibid.*, p.2.

man, males, and females.[23] That being so, certain types of exchanges must have been carried on. If so, the same word, world, can refer to a particular nation, country, or state.

Dialectically, in this study, we would put global business, which is defined as international regimes-related trade and commerce at 1; international business at 3; and world business positioned at 5 in the lead co-author's crab and frog motion model. The reason is simple and straightforward, that is, we should be consistent, because, when we discuss international regimes, we should realize that each regime applies to all the countries, political and/or economic entities, and individuals like you and me here and there, at least in our globe or Earth.

Findings Related to Information, Data, and Analysis

Many major findings can be discussed. First, when business people conduct trade and commerce, do they put logic in the first place? The answer is not really, at least subconsciously. However, we did find one book on business practices, mentioning Western and non-Western logic: "Form of logic, on the one hand, are formal, syllogistic deductive arguments used in Western countries such as France or Great Britain in which it is critical to have sound premises, or inductive arguments such as those used in the United States, in which objective evidence and representative examples are critical. On the other end of the continuum, alternative forms of heuristics are legitimate, such as circular logic or arguments based on honor or relationship."[24] A few comments can be made. First, it is a surprise to see that even the Americans prefer the inductive way. We tend to doubt it. Arguably, they are like the French and the British, who prefer the deductive method, characterized by linear thinking and cause-and-effect. Second, in this study, the crab and frog motion model actually adopts both the inductive and deductive methods. The spectrums are structured inductively, and the time/space sequence component, deductively. Needless to say, the people in the Middle East have their own unique and interesting way of thinking and reasoning, that is, circular or looping,[25] which is quite close to the Chinese way of thinking and reasoning.[26] They would first try to figure out the boundary and then look at the details. So, they may say yes to the whole picture, whatever that is, and no to a specific detail, without contradicting themselves.

Second, the sub-title of *Chindia* is *How China and India Are Revolutionizing Global Business*. The editor of the 2007 book urged us to reshape our world and our business, if you have one, because we have to engage with China and India, due to their stunning rise in the new global market.[27] The book was edited at a time when the study of international governance and international regimes began to be topical or timely, at least in the Chinese mainland. Yet, the editor or none of the other authors have mentioned the term, international regimes, at least after a search of the index. The closest terms are intellectual property and panda, because they are certainly related to international regimes. The former is associated with the copyright regime and the latter, the panda-protection regime. In this connection, on

---

[23] See his book, *A Fractured Mind: My Life with Multiple Personality Disorder* (New York: Hyperion, 2005).

[24] Camille P. Schuster and Michael J. Copeland, *Global Business Practices: Adapting for Success* (Mason, OH.: Thomson Higher Education, 2006), p.34.

[25] *Ibid.*, pp.184-186. For the Japanese and Korean logic, see pp.162-163. For the African logic, see pp.202-203.

[26] *Ibid.*, pp.136-140.

[27] See Pete Engardio, ed., *Chindia: How China and India are Revolutionizing Global Business* (New York: McGraw-Hill, 2007).

page 109, the term, international norm, was mentioned. This term is also related to international regimes, because, to James C. Hsiung, two synonyms for the term, (pre-set or customary) norms, are regimes and institutions [such as the United Nations (UN) Security Council or international tribunals], and an example of a key norm is sovereignty, adding "[a] regime consists of norms, but includes principles, rules, procedures and, hence, a structure of convergent expectations of decision makers. A set of norms may also be called regime, for short."[28]

However, international regimes-related trade and commerce *qua* business is different from business related to China and India. The former is *truly* global, as opposed to what Shenkar and LUO said,[29] and it constitutes the brand new "megamarkets," whereas the latter could still be cut-throat, because, when the lead co-author of this chapter was attending an international conference in the fourth largest city in the Republic of India (ROI), Chennai, in February 2010, what he heard from the Indian participants is that India should overtake China. In August 2010, it is confirmed that the People's Republic of China (PRC) is the second largest economy in the world. What this suggests is that there will still be competition, trade war, etc. That is to say, even if they form an alliance by becoming the biggest force, which can reshape the world economy, what they do may not benefit the rest of the world, due to competition between Chindia and Non-Chindia. In short, both China and India cannot 100% revolutionize global business but international regimes-related trade and commerce can.

Third, from the year 1500 to the year 2000, we saw various grand theories related to international business: mercantilism (which is the first or pre-classical theory of international trade), absolute advantage, comparative advantage, factor proportions theory, international product life-cycle theory, new trade theory, and national competitive advantage. In February 2005, we saw the emergency of the Blue Ocean Strategy (BOS) theory, which was put forward by W. Chan KIM and his female student, Renee Mauborgne, and which tells us how to seek a niche[30] by creating uncontested market space and making the competition irrelevant.[31]

To challenge the two BOS co-authors, we need only to ask ourselves one question: Can watching the Canadian Cirque du Soleil to Curves (Circus of the Sun) benefits us all? The answer is a resounding no. Poor people, with an income of one or two American dollars per day, can become poorer, if they spend money on watching the circus. Therefore, the BOS itself is not a regime. As such, human beings do not really need circus, for the sake of survival or in order to survive.

Fourth, a company can only trade with another country's company. This is already international. Yet, if the former is selling products related to international regimes, the company can be said as being conducting a truly global business, given the nature of each regime, which calls for each individual on Earth under the shadow of future to be involved in the past, present, and the future. The only problem is that each regime is fragile.

---

[28] James C. Hsiung, "Norms, Power, the Power of Norms, and Community: Essentials of International Governance" in Peter K. H. Yu, *et. al.*, eds., *International Governance, Regimes, and Globalization: Case Studies from Beijing and Taipei* (Lanham, MD.: Lexington Books, 2010), p.10, p.12, p.16, p.20, and p.22.

[29] Shenkar and LUO, p.xiii.

[30] Niche was mentioned in Engardio's book. See pp.347-349.

[31] W. Chan KIM and Renee Mauborgne, *Blue Ocean Strategy: How to Create Uncontested Market Space and Make the Competition Irrelevant* (Boston, MA.: Harvard Business School Press, 2005).

Fifth, a book on governance should cover some issues related to international regimes. Joseph S. Nye, Jr. and John D. Donahue are fully aware of this linkage.[32] Yet, many do not. They only discuss mechanisms, instruments, and international norms.[33] For example, William M. Lafferty had one section on a holistic, interdependent and contingent program, he did not mention the term, international regimes, which is an indispensable tool of governance, in his introduction.[34] Jorgen Wettestad also did not structure his writings in terms of international regimes, mechanisms, and measures, although the latter two words were mentioned in his book.[35] The major reason for mentioning this is because we can conduct global business related to mechanisms and measures, as we will elaborate in a later section.

Sixth, business can have many dimensions, such as the political dimension, economic dimension, social dimension, cultural dimension,[36] etc. We can also mention the international regimes dimension of business. Although international regimes also come with different dimensions, such as political and scientific,[37] the point of departure differs diametrically from that of other dimensions of business. The latter must think of the others and the former, the self in general or the company in particular, even if a businessman attaches first importance on ethics as opposed to profits.[38]

Seventh, KIM and Mauborgne gave an incomplete picture of a market without competition. They only mentioned the term, market universe. They should have also mentioned the existence of market cosmos in the book. The former implies a market without competition, because, the term, universe, connotes order, whereas the latter embraces both order and chaos. Their blue ocean can be correlated as market universe or what we called one-dot or one pure circle in the lead co-author's jargon. However, in real life, we should treat market universe, which is the safe zone spectrum in the crab and frog motion model, in co-existence with market cosmos, which is equivalent to the danger zone spectrum. This is because the two BOS co-authors mentioned the term, red ocean, which is bloody, fraught with cut-throat competitions. Needless to say, we also have to take the following into consideration: market universe *and* market cosmos versus non-"market universe *and* market cosmos." Only by making this clear, can we have a fuller or whole picture of business, to wit, international-regimes related trade and commerce and non-"international-regimes related trade and commerce."

Eighth, some regimes may not directly enable some business people to do business, such as implementation of the preferential tariff regime but their mechanisms and measures can. An example of it has to do with the banana trade war: "In April of 1999, the World Trade

---

[32] Robert O. Keohane and Nye, "Introduction" in Joseph S. Nye, Jr. and John D. Donahue, eds., *Governance in a Globalizing World* (Washington, D.C.: Brookings Institution Press, 2000), pp.19-22. See also Volker Rittberger, ed., *Global Governance and the United Nations System* (Tokyo: United Nations University Press, 2001) and John N. Clarke and Geoffrey R. Edwards, eds., *Global Governance in the Twenty-first Century* (Hampshire, U.K.: Palgrave Macmillan, 2004),

[33] See, for example, William M. Lafferty, "Introduction" in *id.*, ed., *Governance for Sustainable Development: The Challenge of Adapting Form to Function* (Cheltenham, U.K.: Edward Elgar, 2004), p.5 of chapter 1 and Helge Jorgens, "Governance by Diffusion" in *ibid.*, pp.247-248 of chapter 9.

[34] See p.20.

[35] See Jorgen Wettestad, *Designing Effective Environmental Regimes; The Key Conditions* (Cheltenham, U.K.: Edward Elgar, 1999).

[36] See, for example, Garry P. Ferraro, *The Cultural Dimension of International Business*, 5th ed. (Upper Saddle River, N. J.: Pearson/Prentice Hall, 2006).

[37] Wettestad, pp.30-32.

[38] See, for example, Charles Mitchell, *A Short Course in International Business Ethics: Combining Ethics and Profits in Global Business* ((Petaluma, CA.: World Trade Press, 2009).

Organization (WTO) ruled that the European Union (EU) violated international trade law by establishing quotas and tariffs on bananas from Latin America imported by U.S.-based Chiquita Brands International, Dole Foods, and Fresh Del Monte Produce. At the same time, the EU allowed licensed access for bananas from former colonies in Africa, Asia, and the Caribbean. According to the WTO ruling, the arrangement cost the United States $ 191 million in trade opportunities. The banana business is hardly lucrative. Retail prices and sales of bananas have been falling for years, margins, and narrow, the crop is susceptible to disease and transportation is tricky. At 800 to 900 euros per ton, European banana prices are double those in the United States, but the growers barely benefit. The Center for International Economics in Canberra, Australia, estimates that only $150 million of the $2 billion this arrangement costs European consumers finds its way to the banana growers. The main beneficiaries are the firms that hold the banana import licenses. Still, bananas represent a major export for many developing nations…, proving a crucial source of employment. The Latin American nations whose banana exports have been restricted in Europe have been hopeful that the WTO ruling will eventually bear fruit. In 2001, during an all-night session during which a stunned WTO official kept murmuring 'they are talking about bananas, they are talking about bananas,' the United States and Ecuador reached an agreement [effective May 2001] with the EU to replace the quote structure with a preferential tariff regime by 2006, thus ending nine years of the Banana War."[39]

Needless to say, some people may ask the following question: Is it correct to say that the preferential tariff regime cannot benefit all the individuals, including each businessman? The answer lies in the following word, area. We can always carve out the area, such as the headquarters of Dole Foods, where the business people cannot or did not make profit. By doing so, there would be no logic problem.

Ninth, would all the business people be able to engage in trade and commerce, which are related to international regimes? The reason for posing this question is that are all the human beings good-natured? If some of them are bad, those people would not conduct or even try to engage in non-international regimes-related business, because they cannot embrace others first in community-centered arrangements. Is that the reason why we seldom see the term, international regimes, appearing in books related to business and management? This calls for concern, because governance must be understood as international regimes and non-regimes and because it is said that trade between nations can be traced back to as far as 2000 B.C., not just the last several hundred years, when tribes in Africa took dates and clothing to the Middles East's Babylonia and Assyria and exchanged them for spices and olive oil.[40] At that time, certain types of regimes must have existed, such as making arrangements to cope with the onslaught of typhoons.

Tenth, doing business is not easy. A senior lecturer, who specializes in strategic management, observed that 8 or 9 out of 10 businesses usually fail. The same thing speaks for maintaining a regime. Each regime is fragile, admittedly. Thus, the WTO dares not to equate the principle of "More Competitive" as a component of a trade regime, while four other principles are clearly related to the trade regime (as opposed to the world trade regime), to

[39] Shenkar and LUO, pp.19-20.

[40] Ricky W. Griffin and Michael W. Pustay, *International Business: A Managerial Perspective*, 5th ed. (Upper Saddle River, NJ: Pearson and Prentice Hall, 2007), p.8.

wit, Without Discrimination, Freer, Predictable, and Beneficial for Less Developed Countries.[41]

Global Business Related to Environmental Regimes

Environment affects us all in a globalizing or partially globalized world. A European travelling in an African desert is equally at risk as a native African. The issue involved is human security. The same thing speaks for those scientists who are working in the North Pole, exposing to similar danger.

Wettestad studied environmental regimes, and he was trying to design them effectively. In this section, we can suggest some global businesses without competition that we can do.

Regimes by themselves usually cannot generate business. For example, Wettestad mentioned the acid and ozone regimes, the global climate regimes, atmospheric regimes, etc. However, if we look at the financial, verification, compliance (strengthening), or institutional mechanisms (as opposed to the fundamental mechanisms of rationalism and norms, which cannot)[42] and measures, such as in June 1990 setting up a Multilateral Fund (MF) in Paris to cope with the ozone issue, businesses can be generated here and there in the world, even in outer space.

Institutions need to be set up to monitor, for example, the Oslo Convention (OSCON) on Marine Dumping or Convention on Long-range Transboundary Air Pollution (LRTAP). Center for Naval Analyses (CAN) and the Institute for Public Research (IPR) also can play roles. Experts need to be employed to, for example, report on emission stabilizations or reductions. They certainly need devices, equipments to carry out their mission and fulfil their tasks. Engineers are involved in designing those things and business people have to promote and sell them. To clear up chemically polluted rivers and seas, inflicting damage on fish, for example, workers must be hired. To reduce cost, foreign workers may be needed. This also means business. In short, many people can be involved in the pan-global business loop, even analysts at the CNA have to be fully committed to small businesses.[43]

Conclusion

We will draw upon several points. First, there are two ways, when we deal with social science, to wit, taking the classical way and/or the applied way. The latter, though more practical, is simply too narrow in scope and the theory and/or model generated can be easily falsified, while the former can be more rigid in theoretical validity after repeated tests. The sincere plea is that both camps should closely cooperate and coordinate with each other, so as to bring about a research end-product or write up closer to reality. To repeat, a model or theory discovered by taking the applied way may easily be falsified by a meta-model or meta-theory. As such, academics who adopt the grounded theory should realize that what they have spent in figuring out a theory for a company or a group of companies may be wasted.

---

[41] "About the WTO," www.wto.org, accessed on July 23, 2010.
[42] Wettestad, p.14.
[43] http://www.cna.org/about/contracts/small-business, accessed on July 28, 2010.

Second, many transnational corporations claim to be global. The Coca-Cola Company (CC) is such an example, and Shenkar and LUO concur. Yale University has been endeavoured to be global, when it faces close to 10,000 universities and colleges in the world. However, the former must think about its profit first, recalling that its rival, Pepsi-Cola Company (PepsiCo), bankrupted twice in the last century. It is also not possible for the prestigious university in Connecticut to spend its limited tangible and intangible resources in interacting with some 1,500 known degree/diploma mills, which only sell that piece of paper, without requiring students to fulfill all the normal requirements. As can be seen, there are limits as to what they can do. Therefore, they cannot be truly global.

Last but not least, when human beings can live in outer space's bases, the definition for the term, global business, may have to be again modified, to read intercelestial, international regimes-related trade and commerce. This possibility cannot be ruled out, because it has been reported that extra-terrestrial creatures do exist and they have been trying to send messages to us human beings.[44]

[44] *See Hua Daily News* (hereinafter SHDN)(Sarawak, Malaysia), July 24, 2010, p.13.

In: International (Corporate) Governance
Editor: Peter Kien-Hong Yu

ISBN: 978-1-61122-645-4

Chapter 4

THREE THEORIES RELATED TO THE WORLD TRADE ORGANIZATION (WTO): A ONE-DOT THEORY CONCEPTUALIZATION

Peter Kien-Hong Yu

ABSTRACT

There are at least three theories related to the World Trade Organization (WTO) since January 1995: 1) It is an international regime; 2) it can become a regime; and 3) it can be used to form, maintain, or sustain the World Trade Regime (WTR).

Because human beings cannot remember everything after reading a journal article or a book, this author attempts to apply his one-dot theory to conceptualize each above-mentioned theory.

In this study, the WTR, under the scenarios, situations, or circumstances of urgency, insecurity, perception, and convergent expectation (or a convergence of expectations) will be regarded as the original, whole dot, composing, comprising, or encompassing a set (or sets) of at least 15 criteria/core elements/features, involving both the public sector authorities such as a national government agency and the private sector authorities such as scientific, professional and/or epistemic, or donor communities. Hence, the first theory is equivalent to a dot facing another dot; the second, a partial dot, together with a non-partial dot, becoming an original, whole dot; and the last one, one dot or the lower-level-of-analysis dot to be more precise, which is at the second level or equivalent to mechanism in the context of three levels, namely, international regimes, mechanisms, and measures, supporting or shoring up the original, whole dot (or regime), which is at the highest level of analysis.

In the concluding section, I will argue that we the human beings cannot succeed in fully converting the WTO into a WTR [as opposed to (multilateral) (free) trading regime], unless something happens, such as the dwindling of human population.

Keywords: World Trade Organization, World Trade Regime, (free) trade regime, International Regimes, one-dot theory

Everything, tangible or intangible, can be simplified or compressed into a dot. By inference, the term "everything," can include the supernatural force, God, which is the ultimate dot.[1]

This paper applies my one-dot theory, which can be defined as a whole, composing, comprising, or encompassing (an infinite number of) partial dots. When we talk about the partial dots, we are actually talking about the model (as opposed to the theory, which is at a higher level), and each partial dot in the model is but a part of the original, whole dot, which is at the highest level. Each partial dot could, again, be made up of (an infinite number of) other partial dots.

To put it another way, depending on the context, a dot can be parsed into at least two half-dots.[2] One is called original, whole dot, which is at the highest level, and the other, partial dot, which could be at a lower level. A partial dot or partial dots can support or shore up the original, whole dot.

Despite its prominence, the World Trade Organization (WTO) or Economic United Nations (EUN) is still poorly understood, as some academics lament in October 2002. One professor of economics even said that "... in a world with increasing globalization the global institutions [such as the WTO] appear to be increasingly irrelevant."[3] As the world becomes more complex and complicated, it is doubtful that the WTO can be fully understood even by its employees.

There are at least three theories related to the WTO. First, some academics do regard or refer to the WTO as a regime.[4] Some of them even said that, when formally organized, many of the international regimes can be considered intergovernmental organizations.[5] Second, the WTO can one day become a World Trade Regime (WTR), as opposed to the multilateral trading regime. Last but not least, the WTO can be used to form, maintain, or sustain the WTR.

What constitutes a WTR or what does a WTR embody? Steven D. Krasner asks: "How can regimes be defined?" or as Robert O. Keohane said "[a]rguments about definitions are often tedious."[6] I will first cite several definitions on international regimes, and readers have to bear in mind that definitional issues and a lack of conceptual clarity have not yet been resolved.[7] Most academics and experts like to quote Krasner's definition in the early 1980s, which has gained almost universal acceptance:[8] "implicit or explicit principles, norms, rules

---

[1] See my manuscript, God is One Dot: Paradigm Shift or the short article, Is the God Particle Part of a Larger Dot, God? The One-dot Working Papers Series, Vol.1 (December 2008) (No. 4), 14 pages and God, by Inference,,is One-dot: Paradigm Shift (Boca Raton, Florida: Universal-Publishers, 2010). On August 11, 2010, the author came across the following book by Hugh Ross, The Fingerprint of God, which was first published in 1989. A fingerprint is a dot.

[2] We can say it takes two half-Chinas to make a whole China. "Two-half Chinas" or liangbandezhongguo has no meaning. Email from James C. Hsiung, dated December 14, 2006. In other words, one can love both the Republic of China (ROC) on Taiwan and mainland China at the same time, since patriotism is a form of love.

[3] Graham Bird, "On Solving the World's Economic Problems by Doing Something Unfashionable," World Economics, Vol.8, No.2 (April-June 2007), pp.119-131 at p.131.

[4] http://en.wikipedia.org/wiki/International_regime, accessed on November 17, 2008 and .

[5] Ibid. Some academics use international regimes and international institutions interchangeably.

[6] Robert O. Keohane, "The Demand for International Regimes," International Organization, Vol.36, No.2 (Spring 1982), pp.141-171 at 157-158.

[7] http://www.beyondintractability.org/essay/international_regimes/.

[8] See his edited book, International Regimes (Ithaca, N.Y.: Cornell University Press, 1983), Mitsuo Matsushita, Thomas J. Schoenbaum, and Petros C. Mavroidis, The World Trade Organization: Law, Practice, and Policy (Oxford: Oxford University Press, 2003), p.584.

and decision-making procedures around which actors' expectations converge in a given area of international relations." Some academics attempted to elaborate on them by giving some concrete examples. Here, we see the four criteria/core elements/[9]features: principles, norms, rules, and decision-making procedures. Mark J. Valencia and Yoshihisa Amae in the early 21st century still subscribe to Krasner's. To them, regime means "sets of implicit or explicit principles (beliefs of fact, causation, and rectitude), norms (standards of behavior defined in terms of rights and obligations), rules (specific prescriptions or proscriptions for action), and decision-making procedures (prevailing practices for making and implementing collective choice around which actor expectations converge)."[10] Keohane and Joseph S. Nye, Jr. in the early 1970s define regimes as "an interstate agreement regulating a particular area of world affairs, usually monitored or managed by an interstate organization."[11] In the late 1970s, they have defined regimes as "sets of governing arrangements."[12] Still other academics simply say that "regimes are by definition, instances of international cooperation."[13]

Arguably, none of their definitions are adequate.[14] Mine can offer a fuller picture or a more complete picture of what should be qualified to be called international regimes, involving both the public sector authorities such as the 192-member United Nations (UN) as of August 2010, World Bank (WB), and a national government agency; the (purely) private sector authorities such as non-governmental organizations (NGOs), transnational corporations, as well as scientific, professional and/or epistemic communities; or public-private combinations, such as the Bank of International Settlements (BIS): They have to do with a set (or sets) of at least 15 criteria in the contexts of (fragmented) issue-area, (fragmented) issue-areas, and issue-regimes. It goes without saying the issue is called (free) trade, covering, *inter alia*, agriculture, services, trade rules, industrial tariffs, and intellectual property. However, there are many terms related to this issue: (regional) trade agreement[15]; trade barriers; trade deficits; trade discrimination; trade issues; trade negotiation(s); trade obstacles, such as tariffs as well as customs regulations and practices; trade policy; trade policy instruments such as tariffs, quotas, non-tariff barriers, anti-dumping and safeguard measures, safeguard clauses, grey areas, rules of origin, and administrative measures; trade policy interactions; (free) trade rationale; (multilateral) trade reform; unfair trade; trading arrangements; trading countries; trading institution; trading nations; trading partners; trading rules; trading system; etc. That is to say, we must include at least the following criteria, so that beginners would find international regimes less abstract a term to deal with and to grasp: 1) It must be remembered that the word "regime" at the international level, based on experience, is always non-dialectically positive or dialectically 100% positive, beneficial to all the countries, political and/or economic entities, and individuals like you and me, whereas the same word at the national or domestic level is usually negative; 2) principles; 3) norms; 4)

---

9 http://www.beyondintractability.org/essay/international_regimes/.

10 See their article, "Regime Building in the East China Sea," Ocean Development and International Law (hereinafter ODIL), Vol.34, No.2 (2003), p.189.

11 See Robert O. Keohane and Joseph S. Nye, Jr., eds., Transnational Relations and World Politics (Cambridge, MA.: Harvard University Press, 1972).

12 Ibid., Power and International Interdependence (Boston: Little, Brown), p.19.

13 http://en.wikipedia.org/wiki/Regime_theory, accessed on November 17, 2008.

14 James C. Hsiung wrote the following words: "In addition to being adequate, a definition must be parsimonious (and elegant, to boot)." His email dated December 14, 2008.

15 When the World Trade Organization was established, all but three (to wit, Japan, the Republic of Korea (ROK), and Hongkong) of its original 120 members were parties to at least one of the 62 regional trade agreements then in force.

rules; 5) decision-making procedures; 6) pan; 7) we are all on the same side; 8) one for all, all for one (in the Daoist sense?),[16] as opposed to collective security's one for all and all for one;[17] 9) community-centered arrangement(s); 10) cooperation; 11) coordination; 12) avoidance of mutually damaging outcomes;[18] 13) no power struggle; 14) transparency; and 15) each regime can mitigate anarchy, tension, (scientific) uncertainty, and mistrust.

A brief critique is in order. First, from Krasner to academics who define regimes as instance of international cooperation, none of them can show us students of international regimes that the term is positive both dialectically and non-dialectically to begin with. There is cooperation among, for example, members of the North Atlantic Treaty Organization (NATO) or institution like the collective security. However, there could be tension, conflict, and so on and so forth between the NATO members and the non-members such as the Warsaw Pact or between the members who subscribe to the same collective security arrangement and those who do not. Sometimes, we also see tension, conflict, etc. even among the NATO members and the collective security members. Second, it is said that the international regimes studies have been on-going since the 1970s, beginning with the issue of the protection and preservation of the environment.[19] In the 1980s, emphasis shifted from environment to international security and other issues. Nowadays, students of international regimes are looking into the role of private sector authorities, that is, leaders in different industries and transnational corporation. Most students would be lost, unless we help them to discern the positive nature of a regime at the international level. For example, we can talk about the Danube River regime, as opposed to the Danube River system. Otto Popper in November 1943 applied the term to study the Danube River regime. In this example, even adversaries during World War I, World War II, and the Cold War must cooperate with each other, or they will suffer together, because each country, each international political or economic entity, or each individual can, for example, dump toxic chemicals or wastes into the river in the middle of night. Third, Keohane and Nye should add the word "community-centered," because we have to talk about supranational forces, such as the European Union (EU) in action. Fourth, Valencia and the Japanese maritime expert have expanded on Krasner's definition. However, especially under urgency, we do not have to talk about, for example, rectitude, if it is defined as "the quality or state of being straight" or "moral integrity."[20] And, in the context of my 15 criteria, Krasner's definition reflects only a partial picture and failed to demonstrate that, especially under urgency, it does not matter which school of thought, be it (neo-)Realist, (neo-)Marxist, etc., each one of them will have the urge to form, maintain, or sustain a certain regime or regimes, so as to resolve a related issue. In other words, international regimes do not have to be always treated as an intervening variable.

In sum, this author will apply his own definition to study the WTO and the WTR.

---

[16] Beijing has been promoting harmonious society for some time. A theoretician in the mainland said it is fundamentally Daoist. When you think of wuwo (無我), there will be no comparison and contrast as well as competition, all of which would lead to struggle. See http://www.chinareviewnews.com, search dated March 10, 2007.

[17] 大馬的民主行動黨 (Democratic Action Party) 創黨元老張守江說"爭取民主 [fighting for democracy] 是一項人人為我,我為人人的大眾事業."參閱詩華日報(馬來西亞),2007年2月12日,第A11版.

[18] John Vogler, The Global Commons: A Regime Analysis (New York: John Wiley & Sons, 1995), p.18.

[19] Ming Chuan Weekly (hereinafter MCW)(Taipei), December 26, 2005, p.2.

[20] http://www.merriam-webster.com/dictionary/rectitude.

A Critique of the Three Theories

In this section, I will apply my one-dot theory to describe and explain each theory and to argue that the third theory makes more sense. We cannot rule out the second theory, if the population of human beings has drastically dwindled.

A Critique of the First Theory

This theory simply ontologically treats the WTO as a dot and the WTR as another dot. This implies that, if they are equivalent to each other, we did not have to create the WTO in January 1995. When we see most international relations academics describing the General Agreement on Tariffs and Trade (GATT) and the WTO as being "virtually coterminous" with the global trade regime, because they focus on the regime's principles, norms, and rules, and largely disregard decision-making procedures,[21] the WTO is certainly not yet a dot. Similarly, when we read the annual World Trade Report, saying that "[a]mong the greatest challenges… is how to integrate developing economies into the system in a manner that contributes to their growth and development aspirations,"[22] we can interpret it to mean that the system is not yet a regime, because there exists the possibility of having negative things happen within a system. There are also some academics of law, who stated that the WTO is "one of the most important intergovernmental organizations in the world."[23] Later in the same publication, they referred to the WTO as an international organization, with a legal personality, legal capacity, and sufficient privileges and immunities.[24] Another professor of economics regarded the WTO as a global agency or institution.[25] Indeed, the WTO and the WTR are not the same, because "WTO law is not a self-contained system, conflicts may arise between the covered agreements and non-WTO customary or conventional law."[26] We just have to look at the following facts.

The WTO glossary or dictionary and terminology database do contain terms related to the three levels. The first level is international regimes, the second one, mechanisms, and the third, measures. Here are the findings.

At least in the WTO glossary, which has 186 entries, we do not find terms related to the first one.[27] As to mechanism, we do see the term, "transitional safeguard mechanism," which means "[i]n textiles and clothing, allows members to impose restrictions against individual exporting countries if the importing country can show that both overall imports of a product and imports from the individual countries are entering the country in such increased quantities as to cause--or threaten--serious damage to the relevant domestic industry."[28] As to the third level, we do see five entries. First, countervailing measures: "Action taken by the importing country, usually in the form of increased duties to offset subsidies given to producers or

---

[21] Theodore H. Cohn, Governing Global Trade (Hampshire, U.K.: Ashgate, 2002), p.1 and p.25.
[22] http://english.people.com.cn/90001/90778/90858/6315309.html, dated December 5, 2007 at 10:30.
[23] See Matsushita, Schoenbaum, and Mavroidis, inside jacket of the book.
[24] Ibid., p.14.
[25] Bird, p.131.
[26] See Matsushita, Schoenbaum, and Mavroidis, p.74.
[27] Accessed on September 27-28, 2008 and May 4, 2010.
[28] http://www.wto.org/english/thewto_e/glossary_e/transitional_safeguard_mechanism_e.htm.

exporters in the exporting country."[29] Second, the following is mentioned, "export-performance measure: Requirement that a certain quantity of production must be exported." Third, local-content measure or "[r]equirement that the investor purchases a certain amount of local materials for incorporation in the investor's product" has been mentioned. Fourth, we see safeguard measures: "Action taken to protect a specific industry from an unexpected build-up of imports--generally governed by Article 19 of GATT. The Agriculture Agreement and Textiles and Clothing Agreement have different specific types of safeguards: 'special safeguards' in agriculture, and 'transitional safeguards' in textiles and clothing."[30] And, fifth, the glossary has the following term, trade-balancing measure: "Requirement that the investor use earnings from exports to pay for imports."[31]

However, the WTO website also contains the WTO terminology database. To be sure, most of them do not have definitions. Some of them do have sources or notes, such as relating to a certain document. They are: adjustment measures; Agreement Establishing the Trade Policy Review Mechanism; Agreement on Trade-Related Investment Measures; agri-monetary measures; amber box measures; anti-dumping measure; anti-inflationary measures; anti-surge mechanism; border adjustment measures; border measures; China's Administrative Measures on Imported Sprits in the Domestic Market; China's Transitional Review Mechanism; circumvention of anti-dumping duty measures; Committee on Trade-Related Investment Measures; compensatory measure; contingency measure; corrective measures; cost efficiency of measures; countervailing duty measure; countervailing duty measures (CVD measure); Decision on Measures Concerning the Possible Negative Effects of the Reform Programme on Least-Developed Countries and Net-Food Importing Developing Countries; Decision on Measures in Favour of Least Developed Countries; Declaration on Dispute Settlement Pursuant to the Agreement on Implementation of Article VI of the [GATT] 1994 or Part V of the Agreement on Subsidies and Countervailing Measures; differential measures; discriminatory measures; dispute settlement mechanism (DSM); easy money measures; emergency safeguard measure; emergency safeguard mechanism; exchange rate mechanism; export competition measures; final anti-dumping measure; final countervailing measure; final measures; governmental measures; grey area measure; Group on Quantitative Restrictions and Other Non-Tariff Measures; Implementation Review Mechanism; import licensing measures; import relief measure; Inventory of Non-Tariff Measures; item-related non-tariff measures; market-making measures; market regulating measures; measures exempt from reduction; measures in effect, measures in force; measures necessary to protect human, animal or plant life or health; measures taken for balance-of-payments purposes; monitoring mechanism; Negotiating Group on Non-Tariff Measures; Negotiating Group on Rule Making and Trade Related Investment Measures; Negotiating Group on Subsidies and Countervailing Measures; Negotiating Group on Trade-Related Investment Measures; non-market mechanisms; non-recurring measure; notification of emergency measures; Notification of laws, regulations and administrative procedures relating to safeguard measures; Notification of pre-existing Article XIX measures; Notification under Article 12.1 (a) of the Agreement on Safeguards on initiation of an investigation (extension of existing measure) and the reasons for it; Notification under article 12.4 of the Agreement on Safeguards before taking a provisional measure referred to in Article 6; Notification under

[29] http://www.wto.org/english/thewto_e/glossary_e/countervailing_measures_e.htm.
[30] http://www.wto.org/english/thewto_e/glossary_e/safeguard_measures_e.htm.
[31] http://www.wto.org/english/thewto_e/glossary_e/glossary_e.htm.

article 12.7 of measures subject to the prohibition and elimination of certain measures under Article 11.1 of the Agreement on Safeguards; Notification under Article 5.1 [Articles 5.1 and 5.5] of the Agreement on Trade-Related Investment Measures; one-time measures; outline measures; outstanding measures; protective measures; provisional measure; provisional safeguard measure; prudential measures; pump-priming measures; quantitative restrictions and other non-tariff measures; reallocation measures; recognition of autonomous liberalization measures; recognition of autonomous liberalization measures; rehabilitation measures; relief measures; remedial measures; restrictive import measures taken for balance-of-payments purposes; review mechanism; revocation of measures; special safeguard mechanism; specific measure; trade-based measures; transitional review mechanism; transitional review mechanism under Article 18 of the Protocol of Accession of China; transitional safeguard mechanism; Transparency Mechanism for Regional Trade Agreements; undertakings repealed with imposition of provisional measures; undertakings repealed without imposition of provisional measures; withdraw measures of liberalization (to);

We do see terms related to regimes, which can be classified into *imperium* group of international regimes and *dominium* group of international regimes, the former of which is related to terms like sovereign rights and state-organized and the latter group is related to terms like property rights and institution-organized:[32] bonded transport regime; bonded transport regime and guarantees; contractual trade regimes; flat tariff regime; important licensing regime; import licensing regimes; memorandum on foreign trade regime; Questions and replies to the Memorandum on the foreign trade regime; tariff-only regime. However, there were no definitions, unlike the glossary.

It should be noted that in the list there is no mention of such terms as (certain) dispute settlement regimes; anti-dumping regimes, as mentioned by some academics;[33] "a series of regimes (e.g. 'diary products regime,' 'sheep-meat regime," which offer farmers a guaranteed price (intervention price), independent of global market conditions;[34] import-substituting regimes as a means of stimulating industrialization;[35] investment regime, which was codified in the Foreign Investment Law (FIL), which came into force in December 1993, and which was one of a series of measures designed to liberalize trade and capital markets prior to entry into North America Free Trade Area (NAFTA) from January 1994;[36] special regimes, which are applicable only to certain market sectors, such as agriculture, textiles and clothing, as well as information technology, one example of which is the MultiFibre Arrangement (MFA) under the GATT or the WTO Agreement on Textiles and Clothing (ATC), allowing states to impose high quotas on imported clothing and textiles;[37] the GATT subsidy regime;[38] market-oriented trading regime (as opposed to fair and market-oriented trading system)[39] that is as free as possible from restrictions and distortions;[40] establishing different import regimes and

---

[32] From James C. Hsiung's classification. Donald Puchala's are formal and informal.

[33] Julie Soloway and Andrey Anishchenko, "Agenda Setting for a Millennial Round: Challenges and Opportunities" in Rugman and Boyd, Ch.3 on p.55 and p.57. See also David Palmeter, The WTO as a Legal System: Essays on International Trade Law and Policy (London: Cameron May, 2003), p.91.

The WTO does have the term, anti-dumping measure.

[34] Robin H. Pedler, "The EU in the WTO" in Rugman and Boyd, Ch.7 on pp.181-182.

[35] Nigel Pain, "Opennedd, Growth and Development" in Rugman and Boyd, Ch.9 on p.217.

[36] Ibid., p.239.

[37] Matsushita, Schoenbaum, and Mavroidis, p.135 and p.141.

[38] Ibid., p.135.

[39] Ibid., p.140.

[40] Ibid., p.135.

maintaining equality within each regime;[41] European Community (EC)'s discriminatory import regime for bananas that favored the African-Caribbean-Pacific countries;[42] a tariff-only regime for bananas that meets the interests of all parties involved; regimes of trade protection,[43] interim regime,[44] liberal trading regime,[45] contingency protection regime, which is applied to transatlantic trade and rooted in the WTO,[46] confrontational and corrosive regime,[47] own-country trade regimes/own-country import or export regimes or other country trade regimes/other country import or export regimes,[48] *sui generic* regimes for the protection of plant varieties that suit their agricultural systems,[49] the over-strict Intellectual Property protection regime,[50] the (weak) patent regime,[51] commodity support regimes,[52] the EU sugar regime,[53] (domestic) risk regulation regime,[54] the WTO-inconsistent import policy regime,[55] the counterfactual regime(s),[56] or the WTO regime of countermeasures and enforcement.[57]

It is also interesting to note that the GATT does not have the DSM. Yet, law professors mentioned the GATT dispute settlement regime,[58] which, according to this author, is at the highest level of analysis, to be followed by mechanisms and measures.

From the above-mentioned regimes, mechanisms, and measures, we can say that they reflect partial reality, because, if the WTO is equivalent to the WTR, then, we would not see any negative things, even though we do see many individual regimes at work within the WTO. For example, in August 2008, the Republic of China (Taiwan) in the name of "Separate Customs Territories of Taiwan, Penghu, Kinmen and Matsu (Chinese Taipei)" for the first time, joined by the United States and Japan, claiming that under the WTO Information Technology Agreement (ITA), which is signed by virtually all the world's countries and that the EU had pledged duty-free treatment for the three products, asked the WTO to settle a case in its favor against the EU by ordering the latter to eliminate its import

---

[41] Ibid., p.148.

[42] The European Community (EC)'s scheme was found to be inconsistent with Article I of the General Agreement on Tariffs and Trade (GATT) as well as several other World Trade Organization (WTO) agreements. See ibid., p.366 and p.384.

[43] Pain, p.243.

[44] Tim Josling, "Bananas and the WTO: Testing the New Disoute Settlement Process" in Timothy E. Josling and Timothy G. Taylor, eds., Banana Wars: The Anatomy of a Trade Dispute (Oxon, U.K.: CABI Publishing 2003), pp.169-194 at p.191.

[45] Palmeter, p.7.

[46] Ibid., p.59.

[47] Ibid., p.99.

[48] John Hillary, "Trade Liberalization, Poverty and the WTO" in Homi Katrak and Roger Strange, eds., The WTO and Developing Countries (New York: Palgrave Macmillan, 2004), Ch. 3 on pp.40-56.

[49] Dwijen Rangnekar, "Implementing the Sui Generis Option in the TRIPs Agreement" in ibid., Ch. 5 on p.88.

[50] Ruth Mayne, "The TRIPs Agreement and Access to Medicines: An NGO Perspective" in ibid., Ch.7 on p.162.

[51] Homi Katrak, "The Indian Pharmaceutical Industry and Consumer Welfare: Prospects under the TRIPs Regime" in ibid., Ch.8 on p.165 and p.167.

[52] Tim Rice, "Farmgate: The Developmental Impact of Agricultural Subsidies" in ibid., Ch.12 on p.260 and p.261.

[53] Ibid., p.278. The regime "guarantees all producers the same level of support that they received under their previous national sugar policies. The regime is now a very complex mixture of 'market support' instruments, from minimum support prices and intervention buying, to import duties, export refunds and production quotas." ActionAid believes that the regime needs fundamental reform. See p.285.

[54] Michael Trebilcock and Julie Soloway, "International Trade Policy and Domestic Food Safety Regulation" in Petros C. Mavroidis and Alan O. Sykes, eds., The WTO and International Trade Law/Dispute Settlement (Cheltenham, U.K.: Edward Elgar, 2005), Ch.8 on p.203.

[55] Kym Anderson, "Peculiarities of Retaliation in WTO Dispute Settlement" in ibid., Ch.9 on p.242.

[56] Ibid.

[57] Joost Pauwelyn, "Enforcement and Countermeasures in the WTO: Rules are Rules—toward a More Collective Approach" in ibid., Ch.17 on p.425.

[58] Matsushita, Schoenbaum, and Mavroidis, p.135.

duties on certain high-technology products, such as liquid crystal displays (LCDs), of which the ROC is one of the world's biggest producers.[59] In the following month, DBS established panels to deal with the matter. In other words, we first see the WTO system, and, inside this system, we see regimes, mechanisms, and measures at work, beneficial to all the member governments, at least in theory. If they do not, then we say the regimes, mechanisms, and measures have failed, or have been derailed, or violated.

In short, the WTO is not equivalent to the WTR.

CAVEATS

First, if the WTO cannot be regarded as a regime, we should regard it as two half-dots. That is to say, it takes two half-WTOs to make a whole WTO. In other words, one half of the WTO is related to regimes and the other half, non-regimes, which could refer to many negative things, such as disputes.

Second, if the WTO cannot be regarded as a regime, can we at least regard it as a multilateral trading regime? Quite possibly so, if qualification will be made. This is because the scope of enquiry for a multilateral trading regime is narrower than a WTR. In other words, the term "multilateral trading regime" may only apply to some members. Besides, the term "multilateral trading system," implies that it has many negative phenomena in the other part of the same system. For example, the WTO stated in December 2007 that the system has contributed significantly to post-war prosperity but it has not delivered all it could and still confronted by formidable challenges, both short-term and longer-term.[60]

Third, if the WTO can be regarded as a regime, can it also be regarded as an institution? One academic said the WTO is an example of institution in general[61] or a contract (as opposed to a charter) organization.[62] This author cannot accept it as such, because institutions could be either good or bad. Indeed, the WTO still has many internal problems, such as the need to improve the dispute settlement system, the necessity of strengthening rules on service trade, the urge of managing the relationship between environment challenges and trade, energy and trade, and so on and so forth.[63]

Fourth, we often see the term, the "WTO regime" or its predecessor, the "GATT regime," which had governed world trade from April 1947 to the end of 1994. It should be noted that they are not the same. If they are, there is no need to form the WTO regime. Thus, only the latter has, for instance, the centralized dispute settlement mechanism(s) (DSMs) or "the new institutional structure of the WTO provides greater legal coherence among its wide-ranging rights and obligations."[64] The principal mechanism for dealing with problems which arose

---

[59] China Post (hereinafter CP)(Taipei), August 1, 2008, p.1 and http://www.taipeitimes.com/News/biz/archives/2008/08/20/2003420845, dated August 20, 2008.

[60] http://english.people.com.cn/90001/90778/90858/6315309.html, dated December 5, 2007.

[61] See James C. Hsiung, keynote speech, "International Governance & Regimes: Mitigation of Anarchy," presented at an international conference held at the Graduate School of International Affairs, Ming Chuan University (Taoyuan, Taiwan, ROC), December 15, 2003, p.12.

[62] Gilbert Winham and Anna Lanoszka, "Institutional Development of the WTO," in Alan M. Rugman, "The World Trade Organization and the International Political Economy," in Rugman and Gavin Boyd, eds., The World Trade Organization in the New Global Economy (Cheltenham, U.K.: Edward Elgar, 2001), Ch.2 on p.23.

[63] http://english.people.com.cn/90001/90778/90858/6315309.html, dated December 5, 2007.

[64] Jeffrey J. Schott, WTO 2000: Setting the Course for World Trade (Washington, D.C.: Institute for International Economics, 1996), p.1 and p.3.

due to future actions or non-actions of one or more GATT contracting parties concerning matters covered in the GATT is diplomatic consultation.[65] However, it should be noted that both the anti-dumping and countervailing duty actions are consistent with the GATT and the WTO's Uruguay Round Agreement of April 1994, which commenced in September 1986.

Fifth, when we use the term, the WTO regime, we should also think about the principle substantive obligations of a free trade regime, such as tariffs, quotas, and barriers to trade; most-favoured-nation (MFN)[66] and national treatment; safeguards; export controls; and services.[67]

Sixth, there are many regimes within the WTO or, for that matter, the GATT. Some regimes may disappear, as in the case of the Bretton Woods Trade regime, which, by the mid-1980s, was no longer adequate to deal with a highly integrated world economy characterized by oligopolistic competition, scale economies, ad dynamic comparative advantage.[68]

Seventh, the WTO did not mention the investment regime. Other academics and experts have mentioned it in their writings. It is interesting to note that many experts on economics believe that an investment regime is not necessary, because markets can play a role to discipline errant states and firms. Robert Gilpin pointed out that "[t]here is evidence to the contrary… . [A]n international agreement could 'lock in' the trend toward liberalization and national policies affecting [foreign direct investment], eliminate distortions caused by governmental 'beggar-thy-neighbor' policies, and reduce conflicts among states and multinational firms."[69]

Eighth, Jeffrey J. Schott said in the mid-1990s that "[o]verall, the WTO is working well"[70] or, according to Alan M. Rugman in the early 21st century, the WTO "is in a crisis."[71] These remarks alone strongly evidence that the WTO does not equal to the WTR, because the former is yet to benefit all the member governments and non-member governments and due to the existence of the key "triad" members, namely, the United States, EU, and Japan or the Quad, adding Canada, which, sometimes would only seek to benefit themselves first. To be sure, sometimes, the United States and EU push for unilateralism, in view of the fact that their domestic economies are vast and that effective regional groups in the rest of the world are lacking, which can challenge them.[72] We also see triad-based trade disputes, illustrating that the WTO is in trouble for three reasons. First, "it is a technical body, lacking in political power and even political understanding." Second, "… its acute lack of political skill led it to make the dreadful mistake of giving standing to non-governmental organizations at the abortive Seattle Millennium Round of December 1999." Third, "the catalyst for the ultimate failure of the WTO may, somewhat paradoxically, be a technical decision. The United States has lost a chance to the EU involving export subsidies paid for many years by the US Domestic International Sales Corporation (DISC). The potential scale of retaliation by the EU against the United States runs into several billions of U.S. dollars. In contrast, the 'wins' by

---

65 Matsushita, Schoenbaum, and Mavroidis, p.19.

66 The most-favoured-nation principle implies especially favourable treatment. It is a principle of non-discrimination, which is quite the opposite of special treatment. See ibid., p.143.

67 See Matsushita, Schoenbaum, and Mavroidis, p.cii.

68 Robert Gilpin, Global Political Economy: Understanding the International Economic Order (Princeton, N.J.: Princeton University Press,, 2001), p.221.

69 Ibid., p.301.

70 Schott, p.48.

71 Alan M. Rugman, "The World Trade Organization and the International Political Economy," in Rugman and Boyd, Ch.1 on p.1.

72 Ibid.

the United States against the EU on the bananas and beef hormones cases were both under US$200 million."[73]

Ninth, there is a debate about governance and the "democratic legitimacy" of the WTO.[74] Another academic of WTO alerted readers in his article title: Better Rules for a New Millennium: A Warning Against Undemocratic Developments in the WTO.[75] To be sure, if the WTO were the same as the WTR, the former does not have to discuss the issue of democracy, because all the members and each individual are on the same side.

Tenth, books like *Tariff Negotiations and Renegotiations under the GATT and the WTO: Procedures and Practices*[76] and *Interpreting WTO Agreements*[77] may confuse those students of international regimes who have just begun the study. If the WTO were not a regime, we will see many negotiations and bargainings. However, once becoming a WTR, there is no need to have negotiations and bargainings. People involved need only to make sure the said regime can be maintained and sustained. In short, there is no need for interpretation as to whether negotiations and bargainings are needed.

A Critique of the Second Theory

This theory is telling us that a partial dot can become the original, whole dot, given time. However, before the emergence of the latter, there would be many other dots in the WTO, as mentioned in the last section related to the nine regimes, such as bonded transport regime. Needless to say, some dots are not related to regimes. For this reason, even if the WTO becomes a regime, the non-WTO members must also be a regime, in order to be a genuine WTR. There are two ways to conceptualize what I said.

First, we look at the biggest dot. This dot is the WTR. Inside this dot, we see the WTO as a dot and the non-WTO as another dot. In other words, both of them make up the biggest dot. However, if the WTO becomes a regime, it is still a partial dot of the biggest dot, namely, WTR. That is to say, the non-WTO dot must also become a regime, in order for us to see the realization of the biggest dot. Second, we can regard the WTO as an eclipsed moon. If it becomes a regime, it must be a fuller moon. However, this fuller moon must be understood in terms of a concentric circle, which is a full moon. When the WTO becomes a WTR, the former disappears. However, this may take a long period of time, say, 10,000 years, because if all of the members agree to comply, we still have to monitor a million transnational corporations, trading companies, etc. to comply with the WTR.

Writing in the mid-1990s, Schott pointed out that "[b]y 2000, world trade in merchandise goods and commercial services will likely exceed $8 trillion, or $2 trillion more than was transacted in 1995. By that date, the [WTO] will likely have more than 130 member countries, which account for about 95 percent of world trade…."[78]

---

[73] Ibid., pp.19-20.

[74] Matsushita, Schoenbaum, and Mavroidis, p.608.

[75] See Marco C.E.J. Bronckers's in Mavroidis and Sykes, Ch.23 on pp.621-640.

[76] Anwarul Hoda, Tariff Negotiations and Renegotiations under the GATT and the WTO: Procedures and Practices (Cambridge: Cambridge University Press, 2001).

[77] Asif H. Qureshi, Interpreting WTO Agreements: Problems and Perspectives (Cambridge: Cambridge University Press, 2006).

[78] Schott, p.23.

We often see the term, trade regime[79] (as opposed to domestic trade regime)[80] or multilateral trading regime.[81] Immediately, one should realize that we are talking about the issue of free trade and where it has been conducted. After pin pointing the regime-related issue, we should figure out the area, synonyms of which include sphere, electron, region, place, etc. Three related terms are often used: (fragmented) issue-area, (fragmented) issue-areas (to wit, one issue affecting two areas), and issue-regimes (one issue affecting at least two regimes). After having done that, we should then find out which scenario, situation, or circumstance: Urgency, convergent expectation (or a convergent of expectations), insecurity, and perception. The scenario, urgency, always comes first. Regimes can work well under this urgent scenario, situation, or circumstance. More importantly, as a next step, we should consider the above-mentioned 15 major criteria in order to call a regime a regime at the international level. Needless to say, we can add other criteria, if and when necessary. The criteria can also be used to compare and contrast regimes and international law, other international organizations, international institutions, NGOs, transnational corporations, and mass media. Only by fulfilling the 15 criteria, can we say that the WTO has evolved into a WTR.

This author will try to find out whether each criterion can be found in the WTO. I will first find evidence to support the thesis that a particular criterion does exist. Then, I will try to find evidence to the contrary.

1) Positive Nature

It must be remembered that the word "regimes" at the international level, based on experience, is always positive to begin with, beneficial to all, whereas the same word at the national or domestic level is usually negative. By all, it particularly refers to investors, foreign companies, truckers, governments, and so on. Consumers can also be benefited, due to more choices and lower prices.[82]

However, there were exceptions to the contrary. In December 2008, the ROC succeeded in accession into the Agreement on Government Procurement (AGP) under the WTO, meaning that it can bring in an additional US$7-8 billion worth of investments per year. The AGP can also ensure non-discriminatory treatment amongst domestic and foreign goods, services and suppliers, and to enhance the transparency of the public procurement system. However, what about those WTO members, which are yet to access into the AGP? Up to signing up to the WTO rules on government procurement, only 40 countries and regions that have done so, including the United States, Europe, Japan, the Republic of Korea (ROK), and the Republic of Singapore (ROS), but excluding mainland China.[83]

---

[79] See, for example, John H. Barton, The Evolution of the Trade Regime (Princeton, N.J.: Princeton University Press, 2006).

[80] Winham and Lanoszka, Ch.2 on p.31.

[81] At Lima, Republic of Peru (ROP) in November 2008, HU Jintao of mainland China mentioned the term, multilateral trading regime. However, the Chinese translation was duobianmaoyitixi for the same term, which is a mistake. See http://www.chinareviewnews.com/doc/1008/0/8/3/100808378.html?coluid=1&kindid=0&docid=100808378&mdate=1123084607, dated November 23, 2008.

[82] http://www.wto.org/english/thewto_e/whatis_e/tif_e/fact2_e.htm.

[83] http://news.morningstar.com/newsnet/ViewNews.aspx?article=/DJ/200811280302DOWJONESDJONLINE000393_univ.xml, dated 11-28-08 3:02 AM EST and *CP*, November 30, 2008, p.1.

2) Principles

There are a number of simple, fundamental principles run throughout all of the WTO documents or agreements, such as trade without discrimination [MFN: treating other people equally and National treatment: Treating foreigners and locals equally]; freer trade: gradually, through negotiation; predictability: through binding and transparency; promoting fair competition; encouraging development and economic reform.[84] In organizing their assessment of the implications of mainland China's accession, some authors pin pointed the GATT and the WTO's five basic principles: nondiscrimination; market opening; transparency and predictability; undistorted trade; and preferential treatment for developing countries.[85]

Under DSM, there is a principle of compulsory adjudication, permitting retaliatory measures against the violating country.[86]

However, there were exceptions to the contrary. In the short term, less developed countries seem to suffer, because they usually do not have the capital, management expertise and skills, etc. to carry out efficient, profitable trade. However, the WTO believes that, in the long run, they are giving more time to adjust, greater flexibility, and special privileges, such as access to the developed countries' markets.[87] How to go about carrying this out? There are four important exceptions to the key GATT principle of non-discrimination:[88]

1. Developed countries can give tariff preference to developing countries.
2. Countries entering into regional free trade agreements do not need to extend the preferences negotiated in this context on an MFN basis.
3. A country can invoke temporary "safeguard" protection to one of its industries suffering serious injury due to a surge of imports.
4. Temporary quantitative restrictions can be invoked by a country with serious balance of payment problems.

3) Norms

There are many agreements, contracts, etc. [as opposed to charter in the UN] in the WTO. When it comes to the question of compliance, they become norms.

However, there were exceptions to the contrary. For example, norms may apply only the non-Triad members.

4) Rules

The WTO emphasizes the rule of liberalizing trade. However, it is not just about this rule, and, in some circumstances, its rules support maintaining trade barriers--for example to

---

[84] http://www.wto.org/english/thewto_e/whatis_e/tif_e/fact2_e.htm.

[85] Deepak Bhattasali, Shangtong Li, and Will Martin, China and the WTO: Accession, Policy Reform, and Poverty Reduction Strategies (Washington, D.C.: World Bank and Oxford University Press, 2004), p.2.

[86] Winham and Lanoszka, Ch.2 on p.31.

[87] http://www.wto.org/english/thewto_e/whatis_e/tif_e/fact2_e.htm.

[88] Rugman and Boyd, p.4.

protect consumers, prevent the spread of disease, or protect the environment.[89] Other rules can also be mentioned: trade in services, trade-related investment measures, and intellectual property rights.[90]

Regulations are related to rules. The former usually refers to details, whereas the latter, general things. We do see Regulation on Anti-dumping and Anti-subsidy of the People's Republic of China (PRC) and Regulations of the PRC governing Customs Protection of Intellectual Property Rights in the WTO website.

However, there were exceptions to the contrary. WTO members, before becoming a regime, can easily circumvent obligations.

5) Decision-making Procedures

The procedures and customary practices under the old GATT are generally retained in the WTO's decision-making processes, which are quite unusual.[91] There are several types of WTO decisions: general decision-making; interpretations; waivers; and amendments.[92] Specifically, dispute resolution panels and the WTO Appellate Body are involved.

However, there were exceptions to the contrary. Many trade diplomats, environmentalists, and academics are concerned about the small tribunals, which lack democratic legitimacy but which can determine profound issues, such as the relationship between trade and environmental values or trade and labor values.[93]

6) Pan

Pan is related to an issue which could be here and there, because each regime has to do with an issue in a given area. We can also mention issue-area or issue-areas. An issue can also involve a few regimes. First, there do not seem have many regimes within the WTO. Does it mean that the WTO cannot become a WTR? The crucial test is on the word, area, which could refer to a place such as a supermarket, a big place such as the Earth itself, or even electron. In August 2010, Stephen Hawking even warned that, to avoid extinction, Earthlings must colonize space within the next two centuries.[94] In other words, a trade regime may be easily in existence, whereas a world trade regime could not easily come about. Even if it does, it will take a long period of time for it to be successful, say 1,000 years.

Second, area could be, as mentioned in the glossary or terminology database: foreign trade zone, pest free area; provisional area; scheduled territories; special economic area; special economic zone; sterling area; submissions posted on the provisional area; territorial nature of industrial property rights; territorial product; territories entitled to receive preferential treatment; trading area; and unified economic area.

---

[89] http://www.wto.org/english/thewto_e/whatis_e/tif_e/fact2_e.htm.
[90] Schott, p.1.
[91] Matsushita, Schoenbaum, and Mavroidis, pp.12-14.
[92] Ibid.
[93] Joel P. Trachtman, "The Domain of WTO Dispute Resolution" in Mavroidis and Sykes, Ch.4 on pp.78-79.
[94] http://www.thestar.com/news/world/article/845893--stephen-hawking-says-we-must-flee-earth, accessed on August 11, 2011.

The term, area, could also be abstract. One of the examples is the (multilateral) trading system. Within a particular trading system, we could see the following: agriculture, textiles and clothing, banking, telecommunications, government purchases, industrial standards and product safety, food sanitation regulations, intellectual property, and much more, plus WTO agreements and a wide range of activities. In another trading system, we could see lesser activities, because some countries may not have to buy and sell telecommunications all the time.

Third, the WTO chose the word "world," as opposed to the word or adjective, "global." To be sure, "world" is more flexible. It could mean "oneself," the inner world. It could refer to the nation-state system. It could be global or near-global. It could also be intercelestial. The ashes of human beings could be on the Moon in late 2009 or early 2010.[95] In other words, there could be trade and commerce conducted between the Earthlings and Mooners after 2014, when the Americans can be staffed on a permanent basis on the Moon, if the American president changes his mind.

Yet, we see the following statement: "Simply put: the [WTO] deals with the rules of trade between nations at a *global* or *near-global* level. But there is more to it than that (emphases mine)." In other words, the WTO is restricting the trading rules to our Earth.

However, there were exceptions to the contrary. If we say the WTO regime, we are saying that it applies to all members. Each member is a country or at least an entity. This means that we are talking about area in general or territory in particular. However, within the WTO, many individual regimes exist. Here, we are saying that some regimes do not apply to some members sometimes. This would make a difference between the WTO regime and individual regime.

7) We Are all on the Same Side

In order for the WTO to become a WTR, all the member governments must be on the same side. As a next step, all the non-WTO member governments must join as well. Otherwise, the WTO cannot become a one-dot, by being a WTR.

As mentioned earlier, there are rules which make all the member governments to be on the same side, and they are related to the benefiting of all trade barriers, such as protecting consumers or preventing the spread of disease.[96]

However, there were exceptions to the contrary. First, one way of looking at the WTO is as a forum for member governments to negotiate trade agreements. "The first step is to talk. The WTO was born out of negotiations, and everything the WTO does is the result of negotiations. The bulk of the WTO's current work comes from the 1986-94 negotiations called the Uruguay Round and earlier negotiations under the GATT. The WTO is currently the host to new negotiations, under the 'Doha Development Agenda' launched in [November] 2001." In short, so long as there are disputes as well as negotiations and evening bargains, all the WTO member governments cannot be on the same side.

[95] CP, March 29, 2008, p.8.
[96] http://www.wto.org/english/thewto_e/whatis_e/tif_e/fact1_e.htm

Second, the United States uses the multi-track strategy of bilateral, regional, and multilateral trade negotiations simultaneously. To redress this balance, a Transatlantic Free Trade Agreement (TFTA) had been advocated.[97]

Third, one academic pointed out that Articles VI and XIX of the GATT 1994, and the WTO Agreements on Anti-Dumping, Subsidies and Countervailing Duties, and Safeguards, together with the WTO Dispute Settlement Understanding *qua* contingency protection regime appears to be decided one-sided, hence manifesting shortcomings.[98] To elaborate, in the months from July 1999 through July 2001, the United States imposed definitive anti-dumping duties on EC exporters on six occasions, and the latter imposed none on U.S. exporters. During the same period, the United States imposed definitive countervailing duty orders against EC exporters five times, while the EC imposed none against the former. The story is similar with safeguard measures, which are generally imposed on a MFN basis, and not against the trade of specific countries.

8) One for all, all for One (in the Daoist Sense?),[99] as Opposed to Collective Security's One for all and all for One

First, Pascal Lamy is the fifth incumbent Director-General of the WTO. His appointment took effect in September 2005 for a four-year term. In April 2009, WTO members reappointed him for a second four-year term, starting on September 1, 2009. The title of his message to the visitors of his WTO website is: "A world trade system for the benefit of all."[100] This implies that Lamy is thinking of others. The WTO also has the principle of national treatment, that is, giving others the same treatment as one's own nationals.[101] In this connection, he once served as advisor to Poul Nyrup Rasmussen, who was the prime minister of Denmark from January 1993 to November 2001 and who was the President of the Party of European Socialists (PES) since April 2004. Again, this implies that he has a group of people in mind, unlike a capitalist, who would usually only think of his or her profits first.

Second, when the WTO becomes a WTR, it is still not fully one for all and all for one. In other words, the non-WTO members must also play a role to materialize this criterion.

However, there were exceptions to the contrary. First, there is no entry on the term, international regimes, in the WTO glossary or the terminology database. This calls for serious concern. This is because we cannot take for granted that each delegation from each country does understand the jargon, which is difficult to grasp, especially by the Chinese, Japanese, and Koreans for example. Many delegates may not be aware that mechanisms are measures are under international regimes or at lower levels of analysis. Besides, some terms are hard to be understood by a layman, such as "pump-priming measures." To be sure, there is no definition for this term in the WTO glossary and terminology database. In addition, some

[97] Rugman and Boyd, p.7.

[98] Palmeter, pp.59-60.

[99] Beijing has been promoting harmonious society for some time. A theoretician in the mainland said it is fundamentally Daoist. When you think of wuwo (無我), there will be no comparison and contrast as well as competition, all of which would lead to struggle. See http://www.chinareviewnews.com, dated March 10, 2007.

[100] http://www.wto.org/english/thewto_e/dg_e/dg_e.htm

[101] http://www.wto.org/english/thewto_e/whatis_e/tif_e/fact2_e.htm

regimes, mechanisms, and measures as mentioned in all the publications, conferences, meetings, etc., were neglected to be included in the glossary and the terminology database.

9) Community-centered Arrangement(s)

Terms like cartel arrangements, credit arrangements, delayed delivery arrangements, exchange arrangements, institutional arrangements, orderly marketing arrangement, and swap arrangement do appear in the WTO terminology database, with 5,656 entries. They are different from the term, "community-centered arrangements," in international regimes.

However, there were exceptions to the contrary. For instance, starting haze may not be community-centered.

10) Cooperation

Cooperation can be easily understood. As of August 2010, there are 153 members in the WTO. The WTO oversees about 60 different agreements, which have the status of international legal texts. Member countries must sign and ratify all WTO agreements on accession. Compromises must be made or we see trade negotiations doomed to failure.[102] In the 1980s, we do see many developing countries, which began to unilaterally liberalizing their trade regimes and undertaking much more substantial reform of their domestic policies than developed countries.[103]

At this juncture, perhaps we can mention the GATT's Article XIX, which is an escape clause or "safeguard" that allows a government to temporarily suspend a concession agreed upon in a previous negotiation if its import-competing industry is injured as a consequence of a temporary surge in import volume. It is a safeguard that promotes greater cooperation and prevents a breakdown in cooperation that would otherwise occur were imports to surge.[104]

However, there were exceptions to the contrary. This is understandable, because 14 states and 2 territories so far have no official interaction with the WTO.[105] In other words, they do not have to comply with those agreements, such as Agreement on Agriculture (AoA), General Agreement on Trade in Services (GATS), Agreement on Trade-Related Aspects of Intellectual Property Rights (TRIPs), Sanitary and Phyto-Sanitary (SPS) Agreement, and Agreement on Technical Barriers to Trade (TBT).

11) Coordination

Once becoming a WTO member, many changes have to be done. For example, to separate the regulatory and operational function of the Ministry of Posts and Telecommunications (MPT), as well as to respond to changes in technology and administrative reforms, the PRC Government created the Ministry of Information Industry

[102] Soloway and Anishchenko in Rugman and Boyd, Ch.3 on p.48.
[103] Ibid., pp.49-50.
[104] Kyle Bagwell and Robert W. Staiger, "Enforcement" in Mavroidis and Sykes, Ch.1 on pp.12-13.
[105] http://en.wikipedia.org/wiki/World_Trade_Organization, dated October 19, 2008.

(MII) in March 1998. Months later, the MII split China Telecom, which was the sole basic telecommunications services provider in the mainland up to 1994, into three state-owned companies and reinvigorating China United Telecommunications Corporation (Unicom).[106]

However, there were exceptions to the contrary. For example, a country can elicit the escape clause, choosing not to coordinate with another WTO member.

12) Avoidance of Mutually Damaging Outcomes[107]

The WTO strives for harmony. So, we see the following statement: "The most harmonious way to settle these differences is through some *neutral* procedure based on an agreed legal foundation (italics mine)."[108]

First, it is mistake for Lamy to say that the WTO is "[a] world trade system for the benefit of all."[109] In the WTO glossary and terminology database, we see the following terms, bearing the word, system: The world trade system[110] fair trading system; the GATT system; general accounting system; import licensing system; international and regional systems; international monetary system; mailbox system; market-oriented agricultural trading system; multilateral system of notification and registration of geographical indications for wines and spirits; multilateral trading system; multiple rate system; tariff system; and UN system.

Unless a system has become a regime at the international level, there are bound to have negative things in it. In his website message, Lamy mentioned trade barrier, poverty, imbalances, losers, fragile economies, etc. Lamy further points out that the WTO is a modern system to solve trade disputes. Even so, negative things still exist. So, to avoid mutually damaging outcomes, each WTO member has to cooperate and coordinate by not dumping, for instance.

However, there were exceptions to the contrary. For instance, only after several years, do we see direct shipping link between the ROC and PRC in December 2008, when both parties know for sure that it can save them money for maritime transport, if ships do not have to go to a third port.

As another example,[111] which has to do with the EU banana regime versus the WTO's increasingly liberalizing trade regime, the EU only amended its banana regime seven times, and it did not fully comply with the WTO's two compliance panel findings. In November 2008, the WTO judges again for the 8th time upheld a ruling against the EU in the long-running "banana war," pitting Brussels against the United States and Latin American producers.[112] U.S. Trade Representative, Susan C. Schwab, stated that "[i]t is time for the EU to do the right thing and implement a tariff-only regime for bananas that meets the interests of all parties involved."[113] In short, time is needed for EU to dismantle its discriminatory banana

[106] Mari Pangetsu and Debbie Mrongowius, "Telecommunications Services in China: Facing the Challenges of WTO Accession" in Bhattasali, Li, and Martin, Ch.10, pp.157-158.
[107] John Vogler, The Global Commons: A Regime Analysis (New York: John Wiley & Sons, 1995), p.18.
[108] http://www.wto.org/english/thewto_e/whatis_e/tif_e/fact1_e.htm.
[109] http://www.wto.org/english/thewto_e/dg_e/dg_e.htm.
[110] Trade Policy Reviews 2008: A multilateral assessment of the effects of policies on the world trading system (Geneva: World Trade Organization, 2008).
[111] See Gordon Myers, Banana Wars: The Price of Free Trade A Caribbean Perspective (London: Zed Books, 2004) as well as Josling and Taylor.
[112] http://www.javno.com/en/economy/clanak.php?id=208045, dated November 26, 2008 , at 17:10 pm.
[113] Ibid.

regime, the implication of which is to form a global banana regime, benefiting all the producers and consumers here and there.

13) No Power Struggle

The WTO operates on a *one country, one vote* system. When it comes to voting, there are bound to be factional politics. However, it should be noted that actual votes have never been taken.[114] This is because decision-making is generally by consensus or consensus governance model, and relative market size is the primary source of bargaining power.

However, there were exceptions to the contrary. First, the advantage of forging a consensus is that it encourages efforts to find the most widely acceptable decision. The main disadvantage is that we will see many rounds of negotiations to arrive at a consensus, plus the tendency for final agreements to use ambiguous language on contentious points that makes future interpretation of treaties difficult.[115]

Second, there is no need to have negotiations and/or bargaining when it comes to governing the members of the WTO. Yet, we see a lot of them going on since the inception of the WTO. The WTO admits it: "Trade relations often involve conflicting interests" and agreements often need interpretation.[116] Or the WTO states that it is not a superman, just in case anyone thought it could solve--or cause--all the world's problems![117] Gilbert Winham and Anna Lanoszka wrote: "The WTO is moving toward a regime of 'permanent negotiations', in which the organization begins to look more like a typical national legislature and less like the occasional diplomatic encounters of international relations."[118] If one is puzzled, he or she could be easily misled or confused. Why do we see negotiations and/or bargaining? This is because governance at any level has failed, derailed, or being violated. In short, the WTO is not working well.

Third, the WTO states that "[m]any WTO agreements require governments to disclose their policies and practices publicly within the country or by notifying the WTO."[119] However, not all of the WTO agreements were complied with by all the members. Therefore, we can constantly see power struggles in the foreseeable future.

Fourth, by just looking at the term "dispute settlement," we know that some fellow-members are violating trade rules, and other members will use the multilateral system of settling disputes, involving the Dispute Settlement Body (DSB) panels, the Appellate Body, the WTO Secretariat, arbitrators, independent experts and several specialized institutions, instead of taking action unilaterally.[120]

Fifth, the United States is armed with section 301 of the Trade Act of 1974 and variants known as "Super 301," requiring the President to implement retaliatory measures against countries that are identified as restricting American trade and which fail to reform their market opening laws rapidly when a notice has been given, Super 301, and other laws.[121]

---

[114] http://en.wikipedia.org/wiki/World_Trade_Organization, dated October 19, 2008.
[115] Ibid.
[116] http://www.wto.org/english/thewto_e/whatis_e/tif_e/fact1_e.htm.
[117] Ibid.
[118] Winham and Lanoszka in Rugman and Boyd, Ch.2 on p.30.
[119] http://www.wto.org/english/thewto_e/whatis_e/tif_e/fact1_e.htm.
[120] http://en.wikipedia.org/wiki/World_Trade_Organization, dated October 19, 2008.
[121] Matsushita, Schoenbaum, and Mavroidis,, p.46.

Sixth, China became politically divided in December 1949. There was certainly a power struggle between both sides of the Taiwan Strait. As it turned out, Beijing became the 143rd WTO member in November 2001. The ROC's accession to the WTO was approved 24 hours after that of the PRC. In January 2002, Taipei became a member.

14) Transparency

The WTO states that the trade rules "have to be 'transparent' and predictable."[122] Therefore, transparency is an obligation. Under the General Agreement on Trade in Services (GATS), transparency operates on three levels, such as WTO members must promptly publish all relevant measures of general application "which pertain to or affect the operation of this Agreement."[123] The WTO's dispute settlement activities can significantly enhance transparency.[124] The AGP is one good example. It is certainly called for, so that "unfair" practices, such as export subsidies, dumping products at below cost to gain market share, and quotas to set limits on quantities of imports would not hurt the trading system.[125]

However, there were exceptions to the contrary. The Third World Network (TWN) has called the WTO "the most non-transparent of international organisations," because "the vast majority of developing countries have very little real say in the WTO system."[126]

15) Each Regime Can Mitigate Anarchy, Tension, (Scientific) Uncertainty, and Mistrust

First, before becoming a member of the WTO, a WTO's working party will examine issues of discrepancy between the WTO rules and the applicant's international and domestic trade policies and laws. When the General Council (GC), which is the WTO's highest-level decision-making body in Geneva and which meets regularly to run the WTO, or Ministerial Conference (MC), which is the top-most decision-making body of the WTO, which can make decisions on all matters under any of the multilateral trade agreements, and which tends to meet every two years, approves of the terms of accession, the applicant's parliament must ratify the Protocol of Accession (PA) before it can become a member. In a word, once becoming a WTO member government, there is an increased order in the world trade system.

However, there were exceptions to the contrary, notably about the TRIPs Agreement.[127] This interesting agreement cannot resolve many issues resulting from different intellectual property regimes in different countries. For example, the United States employs a first-to-invent criterion for priority in patent applications, while the rest of the world uses a first-to-file system. Although this discrepancy has not been harmonized under the TRIPs Agreement, the former should make a compromise. If so, there will be only one regime on intellectual property.

---

[122] http://www.wto.org/english/thewto_e/whatis_e/tif_e/fact1_e.htm.
[123] Matsushita, Schoenbaum, and Mavroidis, pp.242-243.
[124] Rugman and Boyd, p.4.
[125] http://www.wto.org/english/thewto_e/whatis_e/tif_e/fact2_e.htm.
[126] http://en.wikipedia.org/wiki/World_Trade_Organization, dated October 19, 2008.
[127] See Matsushita, Schoenbaum, and Mavroidis, p.398.

One of the other most serious charges leveled against the WTO is that it endangers food, safety and environmental standards, as well as public health.[128] To reverse this anti-globalist charge, some law professors point out that WTO norms have made real impact, making sure that national governments and authorities would learn to satisfy international norms and international constituencies.[129]

Can the WTO become a WTR one day and how long would that take? This is like looking at the title of the following book: *Governing the Internet: The Emergence of an International Regime*.[130] In other words, just as the Internet could become a regime someday, the WTO can become a regime, too, provided that there is a reduction of population on Earth for it to work like a regime.

A thorough check of the WTO website tells us that, indeed, there are many regimes, mechanisms, and measures in that world economic body, as the last section has shown. If the WTO is filled with nothing but regimes, it can be qualified to be called a WTR.

However, 32 of the 50 *countries* named by the *UN* as "least-*developed countries*" (LDCs or Fourth World countries) are *WTO* members. The Cambodian Government, the UN Industrial Development Organization and the WTO held a conference on trade in November 2008 in the Siem Reap Province.

CAVEATS

First, how long would it take the WTO to become a WTR? Nobody really knows. Many factors are involved. For example, it must fulfill the 15 criteria. As another example, if the sanctions mechanism can work well, then the possibility increases. And, if the issue of trade is related to human rights, then the whole picture would be more complex and complicated.

Second, a regime outside of the WTO may also be a concern of the WTO, because it sparked transatlantic trade wars, dating back to World War II. The case in point is the EU banana regime, as mentioned earlier.[131] Almost every country in Europe is a WTO member. Washington is also a member, which was lobbied by the American companies, namely, Chiquita Brands (CB), Del Monte, and Dole Food Company (DFC), to the courts of the WTO. In other words, in the context of EU and its ex-colonies or African, Caribbean, and Pacific (ACP) countries, which belong to the Lome Convention (previously called the Yaounde Convention), and to EU producers, a regime exists in general and a Banana Protocol in particular, for the benefit of all. However, in the context of the United States and the aforementioned entities, the banana regime did not work well, because cheaper bananas produced by United States companies, which can be up to 60%, originating from the Caribbean, could not sell well in EU, because EU's banana regime gives preferential treatment to its ex-colonies producers, such as the United Kingdom (UK) siding with the Commonwealth Caribbean, and places tariffs, quotas, and distribution barriers to U.S.

---

[128] Ibid., p.486.

[129] Ibid., p.519.

[130] Marcus Franda, Governing the Internet: The Emergence of an International Regime (Boulder, CO.: Lynne Rienner, 2001).

[131] Rugman and Boyd, pp.8-10 and Pedler in Rugman and Boyd, Ch.7 on pp.172-176. For a list of reports related to the European Communities's regime for the importation, sale and distribution of bananas, see Giorgio Sacerdoti, Alan Yanovich, and Jan Bohanes, eds., The WTO at Ten: The Contribution of the Dispute Settlement System (Cambridge: Cambridge University Press, 2006), p.xxx.

companies in Europe. For the record, the GATT has ruled against the EU two times, but the latter has been reluctant to comply fully, choosing instead to modify its restrictive regime[132] or regulations thereby producing a new regime in June 1998[133] and to let the former to reexamine the court case. In short, since the dispute began in February 1996, unless the gap between the ex-colonies producers and U.S. banana farmers has been drastically reduced, the banana regime, involving 40 member countries, such as the Windward Islands (Dominica, St. Lucia and St. Vincent, and the Grenadines), which get between 50% and 70% of their export earnings, can only be regarded as working but not well here and there, unless the inconsistency between the EU banana regime and the WTO trade rules obligation has been resolved.

A CRITIQUE OF THE THIRD THEORY

This theory is asking us to look at the WTO as a lower-level dot of analysis supporting or shoring up another dot, WTR, which is at the highest level of analysis and very abstract.

As can be seen, in the WTO, there are international regimes (accompanied by mechanisms and measures) and non-regimes, which are not related to international regimes, mechanisms, and measures. Thus, when we say the WTO as an institution, a traffic cop,[134] or an umbrella organization governing the international trading system,[135] we are saying using the international regimes in the WTO to support or shore up the WTR. In other words, we are not saying that we should use the non-regimes to support or shore up the WTR. Any such attempt would only bring about negative effects, consequences, etc., because some institutions are bad, such as the human trafficking institution or the International Monetary Fund (IMF) which cannot alone solve or stabilize the world-wide financial crisis, which, according to a financial analyst/trader, Jeffrey S. L. Yu, began with the troubling housing market or the sub-prime lending crisis in the United States in spring 2006 or so, and which burst in July 2008, with a nose dive two months later.[136] In December 2008, George W. Bush, for the first time, admitted that the United States is in recession, after the release of official data showing the worst monthly job losses since 1974.[137] In January 2009, a majority of top economists thought the recession would officially end in the third quarter of 2009, which would make this the longest downturn since World War II.[138] In July 2009, the American president said he sees "the beginning of the end of the recession."[139] In November 2009, the EU's recession began to inch out.[140] In July 2010, the U.S. Treasury Secretary dismissed fears

---

[132] Pedler in Rugman and Boyd, Ch.7 on p.174.

[133] Ibid., p.175.

[134] Rugman and Boyd, p.2.

[135] Ibid.

[136] Email from him, dated November 18, 2008. According to the findings of National Bureau of Economic Research, the U.S. economy began to decline in December 2007. See China Times (hereinafter CT)(Taipei), December 3, 2008, p.A2.

[137] http://www.thewest.com.au/aapstory.aspx?StoryName=535544, dated December 6, 2008.

[138] The Malaysian Reserve (Kuala Lumpur), January 12, 2009, p.11.

[139] Borneo Post (hereinafter BP)(Sarawak, Malaysia), July 31, 2009, p.B4 and October 31, 2009, p.B4. Paul Krugman in August 2009 said "Great Depression 2.0" was avoided but recovery slow. See ibid., August 11, 2009, p.B12.

[140] Ibid., November 23, 2009, p.B3.

of a double dip recession but warned of a slow U.S. recovery with the economy only gradually gaining strength.[141]

CAVEATS

In the eyes of Marco C. E. J. Bronckers, the WTO remains an international organization like many others.[142] He also wrote the following sentences: "…, these attractions of the WTO (package deals and enforcement) must not be exaggerated. They do not turn the WTO into a 'world government'."[143] The reason for citing this passage is to remind readers that it is not possible for the WTO to become a global government. Therefore, there is no need to discuss constitutional democracy in the WTO.[144]

CONCLUDING REMARKS

Terms like trade regime and multilateral trading regime already exist. However, they only apply to certain areas. Unless there is a dwindling of human population, arguably, the WTR cannot surface. Even if did, it cannot last long, because we only need to have one minor dispute and the WTR can be regarded as not being able to work 100%.

However, we need to form, maintain, and formulate the WTR. This is because if there is order in the global market, more people can be benefited. A sanctions regime must be formed, so that it can punish those countries, political entity, economic entity, and each individual who does not comply with international law, etc. A watchdog may also need to be set up, so as to check and balance those sanctions regime workers. Needless to say, school children should be taught about international regimes and, more importantly, to appreciate and put them into practice.

This paper attempts to reconceptualize the structure, which is as follows: The WTR, as an entity, should be shored up by the WTO, international law, other international organizations, international institutions, NGOs, transnational corporations, mass media, etc.

Needless to say, depending on the context, the WTO itself can be regarded as a dot. If so, it can be called the WTO dot. However, this WTO dot is still part of the WTR dot, the latter of which applies to both the WTO (members) and the non-WTO (member governments). The WTO dot also has to maintain and sustain the WTR dot. In other words, in general, the scope of enquiry for the WTR is larger than that for the WTO; and, in particular, the WTO is a half-dot or a partial dot, and the non-WTO, another half-dot or a partial dot.

---

[141] Ibid., July 27, 2010, p.B11.

[142] Bronckers in Mavroidis and Sykes, p.625.

[143] Ibid., p.624.

[144] Ernst-Ulrich Petersmann, "Constitutionalism and WTO law: From a State-centered Approach towards a Human Rights Approach in International Economic Law" in ibid., Ch.24 on p.652.

FINDINGS

There are several important findings. First, it is easier to simplify or compress everything, tangible or intangible, as a dot.[145] A dot is the common denominator of everything that one can think of, conceive of, imagine, etc. So, the WTO is a dot. In the context of WTO and non-WTO, WTO is only a partial dot. It follows that a concentric study[146] may have to be conducted. To dissolve all the contradictions, one may have to take the dialectical approach and the related methods.

Second, the World Bank in 1989 began to use the term, governance, in one of its reports.[147] Others followed, for example, in 1990, Robert Wade's book title is *Governing the Market*.[148]

Third, once the WTR has emerged, there will be a different set-up or a different way of playing the ball-game, so to speak. When the WTR is in existence, the WTO will shore up the WTR, along with international law, other international organizations, international institutions, etc., in addition to having a sanctions regime. Otherwise, the WTR can easily fail, be derailed, or violated.

Fourth, trade regime can easily surface,[149] because it can be applied here and there and therefore, it is certainly different from the term, WTR, which refers to a bigger area, usually the whole world. Because the area for the latter is bigger, it is, ironically, more difficult to form, maintain, or sustain.

Fifth, to qualify as a regime, only four criteria are needed, according to Krasner. However, the test should be more rigid, when we examine the 15 criteria. By doing so, many students of regimes would be easily disappointed, seeing that a regime can easily fail or they would erroneously think that regimes should be studied under idealism.

Sixth, dialectically speaking, the emergence of a WTR cannot be ruled out. This is because we should always think about a scenario whereby the total population of human beings can be reduced. During the Cold War of the last century, there was the desolate scenario of the nuclear winter. As one example, the Free World led by the United States was often thinking of using nuclear weapons to attack the Communist camp, led by the former Soviet Union. As another example, we still remember the 13-day Cuban Missile Crisis in October 1962. Even after the Cold War, nuclear winter cannot be ruled out. In August 2007, a nuclear-armed B-52 bomber flew from Minot Air Force Base, which is near the Canadian border to Barksdale Air Force base, which is in Louisiana and near the Gulf of Mexico.[150] The airmen did not follow the rules on handling such munitions, because they were unaware of such lethal cruise missiles. In other words, the warheads are supposed to be removed before the flight. After the end of the Cold War, there is a shortage of military people with the

---

145 The only thing left to examine is whether God is a dot. See my forthcoming study, God is One Dot: Paradigm Shift.

146 There is an academic journal called Concentric: Studies in Linguistics/同心圓: 語言學研究(Taipei).

147 World Bank, Subsaharan Africa: From Crisis to Sustainable Growth (Washington, D.C.: World Bank, 1989).

148 See his book, Governing the Market: Economic Theory and the Role of Government in East Asian Industrialization (Princeton, N.J.: Princeton University Press, 1990).

149 See John H. Barton, Judith L. Goldstein, Timothy E. Josling, and Richard H. Steinberg, The Evolution of the Trade Regime: Politics, Law, and Economics of the GATT and the WTO (Princeton, N.J.: Princeton University Press, 2006). The authors begin by examining the institutions' rules, principles, practices, and norms from their genesis in the early postwar period to the present.

150 CP, October 21, 2007, p.3.

right skills, training, and mentality followed. The U.S. Air Force later punished 70 airmen involved in the incident. Last but not least, the University of Cambridge professor, Martin Rees, predicted that the 21st century is our last one.[151]

Seventh, if the WTO were a hegemon, when it comes to trade, the WTR can be easily be maintained and sustained.[152]

Eighth, it is possible for the WTO to become history. This is because the WTO can become a WTR, at least theoretically.

Ninth, can we the human beings be able to be globalized again, as a result of economic globalization? The word, "globalization," became an entry in an English dictionary in 1961 for the first time. This means that human beings began to be conscious of the globalization process, the end result could be the emergence of a global village. However, if globalization is related to our globe, the Earth, then, as early as the late 1990s, we should already realize that we the human beings cannot be globalized as one family again. We can first assume that Adam and Eve were the first human beings. They were globalized once by living together. When their children or grandchildren began to disperse or migrate to other places, human beings can be said as being localized. It should be noted that, in April 1997, Celestis, Inc., a unit of Houston-based Space Services Incorporated (SSI), began its service of sending the ashes of hundreds of people from 14 nations into space. In early March 2008, it was reported that Robotic lunar landers in late 2009 or early 2010 would carry capsules containing a portion of cremated remains of persons in a payload to the lunar surface for the first time.[153] Since the late 1990s, we can say that we are living in a globalizing world. The momentum has been picked up by the creation of the WTO in January 1995. However, we the Earthlings cannot ever be considered as being one family again, especially, when at least one person who will want to be the first to die on the Moon, and not on Earth, so as to remain in history. In short, the history of the Earth has already been incomplete since April 1997. The date could be earlier, if we consider the crew of seven members who lost their lives in January 1986 in the space shuttle Challenger, which broke apart 73 seconds into its flight.

Tenth, we can use the term, issue-regimes. Are there regimes in the WTO, which has that kind of characteristic? The issue of trade can be easily tied to the health regime and the environmental regime. Needless to say, shipment of tainted or contaminated milk powder can affect health and the environment. In the WTO, we do see a committee on trade and environment in the GC.

11th, the word, "world," is flexible. It could mean oneself. It could refer to the nation-state system. It could also be intercelestial. When human beings can be staffed on a permanent basis on the Moon, there could be trade and commerce conducted between the Earthlings and Mooners.

---

[151] Martin Rees, Our Final Century: The 50/50 Threat to Humanity's Survival (Oxford: Heinemann, 2003).

[152] See Gilpin, pp.82-93.

[153] CP, March 29, 2008, p.8.

In: International (Corporate) Governance
Editor: Peter Kien-Hong Yu
ISBN: 978-1-61122-645-4

Chapter 5

INTERNATIONAL REGIMES AND NON-REGIMES IN CONFUCIAN (CORPORATE) GOVERNANCE: A CRITIQUE OF *BLUE OCEAN STRATEGY*'S METAPHOR AND METHODOLOGY

Peter Kien-Hong Yu, Kiat Sing Heng, Lisa Hua Ngui Lee and Mung Ling Voon

ABSTRACT

This paper applies the lead author's Crab and Frog Motion model or the one-dot theory to describe and explain, if not to infer or predict, Confucian governance, which can also be applied to the study of, for example, international (corporate) governance.

Because Confucianism advocates, *inter alia*, harmony, international regimes, which is familiar to the people in the West and yet foreign to most people in the East and which can be defined as a set (or sets) of at least 15 criteria/core elements/features in the contexts of (fragmented) issue-area, (fragmented) issue-areas, and issue-regimes, can be discussed as a tool for fostering harmony.

Later, the lead author applied the same model or theory to conduct a critique of the metaphor and methodology of the 2005 international bestseller, *Blue Ocean Strategy* (*BOS*). It is found that the co-authors, W. Chan KIM and Renee Mauborgne, of that Harvard Business School Press (HBSP) book did not use the metaphor well, and they should have said that they, while choosing both the classical and applied ways, were subconsciously adopting *Yin* and *Yang* plus the Five Elements[1] or the lead author of this chapter's crab and frog motion model (or further simplified as and/or compressed into one-dot theory) without realizing it and did not do a good job in their application of dialectics in general or the lead co-author of this chapter's methodology in particular.

To be sure, one of the biggest findings is that it is better to set sail to the strategy of manufacturing goods and services related to international regimes (as opposed to non-regimes) than applying the *BOS*, so as to really maximize or even guarantee a

[1] Dialecticians use the elements to reconcile the *Yin* and *Yang*.

company/corporation's profit, paraphrasing the two co-authors, in a truly uncontested market place, thereby making the competition not relevant, at least for a longer period of time, because many business people have not yet realized that regimes have become increasingly indispensable in a partially globalized or globalizing world, which is increasingly characterized by national sovereignty at bay.

Keywords: international (corporate) governance, international regimes, Confucianism, methodology, dialectics

INTRODUCTORY REMARKS

In February 2005, *Blue Ocean Strategy* (*BOS*) became an instant, co-authored bestseller, coming out in 41 languages.[2] The lead co-author of this book travels a lot and recently attended a *BOS* Conference, which was held in October 2009 in Kota Kinabalu, capital of the Malaysian state, Sabah.[3] A "Sibu in the Blue Ocean" public forum was also held in November 2009 in the Sarawak, Malaysian town.[4] Before that, he was in Kuala Lumpur, promoting the *BOS*.

There are many keywords in a publication, be it a newspaper opinion piece, an academic paper, or a thick book. In this paper, the co-authors will mention some relevant keywords in this Harvard Business School Press (HBSP) book. The purposes are two-fold: 1) to demonstrate that W. Chan KIM and Renee Mauborgne's use of the metaphor [5] did not give a fuller or full picture; and 2) to point out that their writing should be dialectical or that they did not realize that they were applying the lead co-author of this chapter's crab and frog motion model (or further simplified as and/or compressed into one-dot theory), because the lead co-author of this chapter can easily apply his dialectical model to conduct a critique of their problematic metaphor and methodology, due to the fact that KIM and his female student applied both classical and applied ways of conducting their research and writing. The classical way applied a model and/or theory from the very beginning and the latter applied way, figuring out a model and/or theory from collected information and data, with no preconceived ideas, if possible.[6]

---

[2] I have heard of this book a few years ago and included their recent publications in my proposed unit of study. However, I only began reading their book in November 2009. See W. Chan KIM and Renée Mauborgne, "Blue Ocean Strategy" *Harvard Business Review*, October 2004, pp.76-85; *id.*, *Blue Ocean Strategy: How to Create Uncontested Market Space and Make the Competition Irrelevant* (Boston, MA.: Harvard Business School Press, 2005) and *id.* (September 2009), "How Strategy Shapes Structure," *Harvard Business Review*, 13 pages. On November 11, 2009, I emailed the two authors that their strategy is but a version of *Yin* and *Yang* plus Five Elements.

[3] *Borneo Post* (hereinafter BP), October 23, 2009, p.17.

[4] *Ibid.*, October 29, 2009, p.21.

[5] http://en.wikipedia.org/wiki/Blue_Ocean_Strategy, accessed on November 11, 2009.

[6] This is similar to the grounded theory method.

My Crab and Frog Motion Model[7] and One-dot Theory[8]

The lead co-author of this chapter is a political scientist by training. In August 2009, he began to teach business courses, namely, Foundations of International Business (FIB), Asia Business Context (ABC), Organization and Management (OM), as well as Comparative Regional Businesses (CRB) with trepidation.[9] At the beginning, he thought he had ventured into a field which is vastly different from Political Science or International Relations (IR)/Politics (IP)/or Affairs (IA). After reading the compulsory textbooks, such as *Business in Asia and Pacific*, he told one Australian convenor that 80% of the contents are similar to IR, and she agreed.[10] After all, we are all social scientists in a world of interdisciplinary studies, trying to apply a dialectical or non-dialectical approach and method(s) to describe, explain, and infer or predict business phenomena, so as to be logical, [11]systematic,[12] and coherent[13].

The lead co-author of this chapter's model is called crab and frog motion, which is, as he realized in October 2007, merely a version of *Yin* and *Yang* plus the Five Elements, which can be dated back to more than 3,000 years. Most people have seen it, and a 19th century physicist Niels Bohr in the West had applied it in his attempt to describe and explain the complimentarity of science/scientific attitude and religion/religious attitude:[14]

The diagram is a simplification of complex and complicated reality. Other synonyms for the lead author of this chapter's crab and frog motion model are dialectical and scientific.

"Seeing is believing" had been mentioned by KIM and his co-author,[15] and throughout their book, the lead co-author of this chapter detected many crab and frog motion, dialectical, or scientific terms: a market universe composed of two sorts of oceans: (bloody) red and blue (p.4); red ocean(s)/red waters (p.5 and p.23) and blue ocean(s)/blue waters (p.5 and p.23); explicit or implicit strategy (p.42); customers and noncustomers (p.102); hot spots and cold spots (p.157 and p.158); industries never stand still and continuously evolve;[16] the market universe never been constant;[17] carrots and sticks;[18] balance the scales;[19] etc.

---

[7] This word can be found in, for example, KIM and Mauborgne (2005), p.209.

[8] This word can be found in, for example, *ibid,* p. 177, p.209, and p.210.

[9] This word can be found in, for example, *ibid.*, p.171. They wrote: "Trepidation builds as people are required to step out of their comfort zone and change how they have worked in the past."

[10] Email from her, dated July 31, 2009.

[11] This word can be found in, for example, *ibid.*, p.28, p.29, and p.40.

[12] This word can be found in, for example, *ibid.*, p.19 and p.30.

[13] This word can be found in, for example, *ibid.*, p.43. The word, incoherent, can be found in *ibid.*, page 42.

[14] See Frederick Grinnell, *Everyday Practice of Science* (New York: Oxford University Press, 2009), p.181.

[15] The quotation can be found in p.152.

[16] The words can be found in, for example, *ibid.*, p.6.

[17] *Ibid.*

[18] The words can be found in, for example, *ibid.*, p.184.

[19] The words can be found in, for example, *ibid.*, p.190.

It is also very interesting to see that the two *BOS* co-authors used the term, leap-frog[20] (which is "a game in which one player bends down and is vaulted over by another player"[21]) on page 31. Their thinking again resembles the crab and frog motion model. In this model, one can normatively leap-frog from E to D, to C, to B, to A, to 5, to 4, to 3, to 2, and to 1, and vice-versa. One can also leap or jump from one dialectical framework to another crab and frog motion model. In short, the two co-authors, like dialecticians, were, while employing dialectical words, concepts, etc., constantly engaged in dialogues.[22]

The crab and frog motion model can be further simplified as and/or compressed into what the lead co-author of this chapter called a one-dot theory, which is at a higher level but interrelated and, yet, not oversimplified.[23] KIM and Mauborgne's market universe[24] (as opposed to market cosmos, which is a combination of order and chaos) is actually equivalent to one pure dot, with nothing chaotic inside, that is to say, changes and shifts in the market universe (and later on, perhaps cosmos) can be described, explained, and inferred or predicted by the one-dot theory. People who adopt the crab and frog motion model have to first think of two extremes, and they would navigate in between those extremes like a crab by making normatively leap-frog moves or empirically side-ways moves. When you have two extremes, you have already set up a framework and have a fuller picture. One uses this framework to describe, explain and infer or predict certain phenomena. If one cannot apply it, one would or should leap[25] or jump[26] to another framework. If not, one cannot continue to describe, explain, or infer or predict unrelated phenomena.

Once decided upon a model or theory, one can rely on its internal logic to rationalize, hopefully, everything, so as to be closer to reality. The dialectical model is simply the following:

1 2 3 4 5 A B C D E

time/space sequence (1)
time/space sequence (2)
....
time/space sequence (n)

1 2 3 4 5 is a spectrum or what the lead co-author of this chapter called the safe zone, while A B C D E is another spectrum or what he refer to as the danger zone. Each spectrum can be expanded or contracted. For example, 1 2 3 4 5 can be expanded to become 1 2 3 4 5 6 7 8 or 1 to 1,000; or contracted to be only 5 A. Scale[27] is involved. 1 means 100%; 3, 50%; and 5, 1%, while E means 100%; C, 50%; and A, 1%. As can be seen, there is a scale, that is, from E to A, there is a downward trend of movement, whereas from 5 to 1, there is an upward trend. Anyway, 1 weighs the most and 5 the least. Also, E weighs the most and A, the least. Whenever confronted with a dilemma, one would go to the middle road or 5 of the safe zone

[20] This word can be found in, for example, *ibid.*, p.31.
[21] http://www.merriam-webster.com/dictionary/leap-frog, accessed on November 10, 2009.
[22] The word can be found in, for example, *ibid.*, p.139.
[23] This word can be found in, for example, *ibid.*, p.191. They wrote: "At the risk of oversimplification...."
[24] There is a distinction between the words, cosmos and universe.
[25] This word can be found in, for example, *ibid.*, p.17.
[26] This word can be found in, for example, *ibid.*, p.34 and p.161.
[27] This word can be found in, for example, *ibid.*, p.13.

or A of the danger zone in 1 2 3 4 5 A B C D E. There could also be a middle road between 5 and A. Due to its flexibility, such is the beauty of dialectics.

An Interpretation of Confucian Governance

Someone may ask how the 2005 book is related to Confucianism. The answer is simple and straightforward: to have a fuller picture is important, because the thesis of that book is related to Confucianism and, as such, we cannot do without the discussion of international regimes, which is a set (or sets) of at least 15 criteria/core elements/features in the contexts of (fragmented) issue-area, (fragmented) issue-areas, and issue-regimes and which "will become more important for two reasons--the proliferation of collective goods issues and the erosion of state capacity that makes it impossible for individual states or groups of them to cope with challenges to their well-being and prosperity."[28]

At the outset, it must be pointed out that governance comes in terms of many dimensions, such as international, global, corporate, administrative, shared, etc. Supernatural forces/power at the religion level, could also be taken into consideration, sometimes. This is because, ontologically, a business tycoon may go to a church, for example, and thank God, saying, because of God, he or she has made a high profit or avoided a big loss. At the social science level, partnership between the public and private sectors is taken for granted, especially due to the rapid rise of civil society, whereby people can have a bigger voice without having to fear about the political repercussions. Arguably, Confucian governance offers a fuller picture than the 2005 book[29] or a largest, holistic picture since time immemorial, because it has juxtaposed (mother) nature and man in one framework.

Confucius is an ancient Chinese sage and philosopher. It is not possible for anyone to remember every word of what he said or wrote, even Confucius himself will forget what he wrote or said when he became older. So, what we should do is to simplify or compress his words and deeds in terms of the following 12 Chinese characters, starting with *TianRenHeYi* [that man is an integral part of (mother) nature], to be followed by *WaiShengNeiWang* (variously translated as Confucian doctrine of exercising perfect self-cultivation and benevolent governance; internal king/emperor and external holy/sage; domestic sage; being an inner sage so as to rule the outside world; the principle of saint inside and king appearance; inside the king and outside the saint; the outer sageliness and inner kingliness) and *HeErBuYi* (*Hexie*/harmony without uniformity; harmony comes in terms of different degrees at this place or that).

The first four Chinese characters, *TianRenHeYi*, is the largest, holistic picture. [There could be another concept related to *TianRenHeYi qua* the roof or eaves on top of the first four characters, called *TianXia* (literally translated as All-under-Heaven), which could be likened to a pure dot, with nothing inside.] Applying the crab and frog motion model, which is 1 2 3 4 5 A B C D E, *Tian* is 1, *Ren*, 5. *Tian* could be Heaven, (mother) nature, or environment. If we were talking about 10,000 years ago, we the human beings were still at the mercy of Heaven or (mother) nature. Now, we are in a better position, because, sometimes, we can use scientific instruments and devices to cope with (mother) nature. Of course, there is a long way

[28] Email from Richard W. Mansbach, dated March 18, 2009.

[29] See back flap of the book.

to go to overcome, for example, global warming or to find renewable energy resources, in view of the rapid depletion of petroleum. *TianRenHeYi* is 3 or the mixture/hybrid of 1 and 5. At 3, we see balance in the safe zone spectrum, which could bring about harmony, because we the human beings know that it is not possible for us to be greater than Heaven or conquer (mother) nature. If *Tian* is at 1 and *Ren* at E, then human beings will be defeated by *Tian* at time/space sequence (n). Where to place *TianRenHeYi*? 5 perhaps is the place in this *Tian* versus *Ren* model. However, in so doing, we are still at the mercy of *Tian*, because we cannot forget the last move by *Tian* at time/space sequence (n), which strongly suggests the end of humankind (as early as 2012, according to one recent movie?). Or you can put *Ren* at 1 and *Tian* at E. Then, one is saying that *Ren* will defeat *Tian* at time/space sequence (n). However, intuitively, this is more difficult, if not impossible at time/space sequence (n). We can only occasionally say that or apply the model. Needless to say, there is no difficulty in linking the three different kinds of frameworks. We just have to create other frameworks between, for example, the first framework and the third framework, when we make a jump.

After introducing the largest, holistic picture of Confucian governance, it is necessary to create a second crab and frog motion model, by focusing only on *Ren*. This means that you have to jump or leap from the largest, holistic picture to another smaller picture or model. Then, you have a Man versus Non-Man model. At 1, Man is 100%, whereas at 5, Man could be only 1%, and the latter is not impossible, because there could also be (mad) scientists who try to mix human being with Non-Man, an example of which is a beast. Mermaid is one example.

When you focus on *Ren*, you are actually referring to *Sheng* (sage; wise person) and *Wang* (king or boss of a company). Here, again, another model must be created: *WaiShengNeiWang* (at 1) versus Non-*WaiShengNeiWang* (at E), which could be anything other than *Sheng* and *Wang*. To be sure, whenever the word, versus, is used, it means that there is definitely struggle, conflict, friction, etc. When the word, and, is used, it means that one concept is at 1 and the other concept, 5. For example, *Sheng* at 1 and *Wang*, 5. Here, it implies that *Sheng* and *Wang* must learn to tolerate each other's existence, which can bring about 100%, 50%, or 1% of harmony. Other people including employees should perceive a boss as *Sheng*, who has the wisdom, while the boss must also behave like a king.[30] By being a king, the boss has to know how to reward and punish his counterparts, employees, etc., according to the rules and regulations. Otherwise, chaos could follow.

The king, needless to say, has to keep in mind of the other two phrases, which can be seen in Confucius' *Analects*: *JiSuoBuYu, WuShiYuRen* (if one does not want to have, do not impose on other people) and *JiLiLiRen*, *JiDaDaRen* (live and let live; conduct themselves in society do their own self-cultivation, but also conduct themselves in society so that others can do the self-cultivation; themselves to seek accessible, but also let others seek accessible; or literally "Just as you would like to establish yourself in the world, so allow others to establish themselves. Just as you seek to understand things, so allow others the same opportunity").[31]

When one engages in business, maintaining and sustaining harmony should be constantly in a boss' mind. Chaos is not good to the business people in the long run, because profit cannot be guaranteed, when there is a lack of peace and tranquility. So, another smaller

[30] James MacGregor Burns's marvelous first political biography on the then U.S. President, Franklin D. Roosevelt, *Roosevelt: The Lion and the Fox*, does not really fit here, because a sage should not be foxy.

[31] http://en.wiktionary.org/wiki/%E5%B7%B1%E7%AB%8B%E7%AB%8B%E4%BA%BA%EF%BC%8C%E5%B7%B1%E9%81%94%E9%81%94%E4%BA%BA, accessed on November 8, 2009.

picture or model will have to be created, namely, *HeErBuYi* versus Non-*HeErBuYi*. *HeErBuYi* is at 1 and Non-*HeErBuYi* at E. After having jumped or leaped to this model, one would again navigate in between those two extremes, like a crab.

A series of models are needed to present everything logically, systematically, and coherently as well as to rationalize everything. Another picture or model is needed, so as to remind people that they co-exist and must learn to tolerate their existence: Put the first four Chinese characters or *TianRenHeYi* at 1, the second idiom or four characters, namely, *WaiShengNeiWang* at 3, and *HeErBuYi* at 5. Why *HeErBuYi*? It is because Confucius recognizes that each one of us (be it a boss, an employee, or each company) is different (and unique). However, the boss of a company must promote harmony among the different employees (with different characteristics and propensities) and foster a harmonious relationship with those companies which cooperate or even compete with his or her company.

To maintain or sustain harmony, using international regimes as a tool is a desideratum, because each regime can benefit all the countries, political/economic entities, and individuals like you and me, as we shall see the more the better later on.

A Critique of KIM and Mauborgne's Book

On page 19, KIM and his student mentioned their methodology or practical methodologies,[32] which incorporates approaches and methods, to support their thesis. Because they have mentioned the term, market universe, we can say that they have used both classical and applied ways. The latter is similar to grounded theory method. In their website, the *BOS* "presents a theory, tools, and frameworks to allow your company to break away from the competition and create a blue ocean of new market space":[33]

Basic tools of BOS

- The strategy canvas
- The Four Actions framework
- Eliminate-Reduce-Raise-Create Grid

The initial litmus test for *BOS*: focus, divergence, and compelling tagline

Frameworks/methodologies Applicable to Strategy Execution

- Tipping Point Leadership approach
- Four Organizational Hurdles framework
- Kingpins approach, Fishbowl management, atomization
- Hot spots, cold spots and consigliere approach

[32] This word can be found in, for example, *ibid.*, p.24.
[33] http://www.blueoceanstrategy.com/abo/test.html, accessed on November 11, 2009.

- 3 E principles of Fair Process

Additional Tools/methodologies/Frameworks for Strategy Formulation

- The six paths framework
- The sequence of *BOS*
- Buyer Utility map
- Buyer experience cycle
- The profit model of *BOS*
- Price corridor of the mass model
- Four Step Visualizing Strategy Process
- Pioneer-Migrator Settler Map
- Three tiers of noncustomers framework
- Six Thinking Hats

We will first find loopholes in their metaphor, to be followed by a critique of their methodology.

They mentioned the metaphor of market universe, which is made up of the blue ocean and the red ocean. This is definitely a problem. The two co-authors were actually referring to *Yin* and *Yang*, respectively, and they should have used the term, market cosmos, which has both order and chaos. To them, the red one is bloody, fraught with competition, while the other one is just the opposite. In real life, is it possible to distinctively separate them? The answer is a resounding no. This is because, even if we refer to the red ocean as bloody, we can still see international regimes at work, such as the trade regime, foreign exchange regime, corporate governance regime, business policy regime, etc., which can, if working at least 1%, benefit all the parties.[34] Thus, to thoroughly apply the crab and frog motion model, they should have said that the red ocean is old (as opposed to bloody), while the blue one is new, with no competition. In other words, in the former, we see new, and, in the latter, we see old. This kind of arrangement is precisely *Yin* and *Yang*.

To put it another way, the *Yin* and *Yang* diagram is not equivalent to the blue ocean. A pure circle or dot with nothing chaotic inside should represent the blue ocean. This is equivalent to market universe, with no competition. If we say the white portion in the diagram is equivalent to the blue ocean or uncontested market and the black portion, red ocean, it is still misleading, because there is a dot in the white portion/blue ocean and there is another dot in the black portion/red ocean. So, what should be properly presented is that the blue ocean is new and the red ocean is old. In other words, within the black portion/red ocean, you see white portion/blue ocean, which can represent new ideas, for example, for the circus industry; and within the white portion/blue ocean, you can see old ideas in the same circus industry. If we do not equate the blue ocean as new and the red ocean as old, then it does not make sense when we see the red ocean in terms of a dot within the blue ocean or white portion, because

---

[34] The *Yin* and *Yang* does encourage innovation. So, if the red ocean is old, the dot in the red ocean would be blue or new. New implies innovation. Discussion with Mung Ling VOON, dated August 18, 2010.

the blue ocean is suppose to have no competition. Needless to say, the dot in each portion can be enlarged, reduced, or remain the same. If so, the portion, either white or black, will change accordingly.

In a word, the lead-co-author of this chapter did not notice their negligence or failure to give a proper, fuller picture, when he was reading their book in late October 2009 for the first time, until on November 13, 2009, when he watched a video clip, where KIM, in an interview, said the following phrase: blue ocean created in the middle of the red ocean.[35] This phrase is equivalent to the black portion/red ocean with a dot which represents the blue ocean. That is to say, no where can we find the same phrase in the book, not even the cover page.

We can have two categories for approach: dialectical and non-dialectical. The question which ought to be asked at this juncture is: Had the two *BOS* co-authors done a good job in presenting and applying their methodology? If not, their book can be called into serious question.

Many people, after reading their 2005 book, can certainly retain the following sentence--How to create uncontested market space and make the competition irrelevant--and, of course, the successful example, Cirque du Soleil (Circus of the Sun), which has been represented in terms of a strategy canvas, which is "an analytic framework that is central to value innovation and the creation of blue oceans" on page 40.[36]

However, methodologically speaking, KIM and Mauborgne have failed to do a good job. They did not clearly spell out their approach and method(s) in either the first or second chapter. I do not think that they have fully grasped approaches and methods. For example, they are vague regarding whether they are using the inductive method, deductive method, or both. One contributor to *Wikipedia* said "a deductive process was not followed."[37] Only dialectically, can one employ both inductive and deductive methods in a publication. That is to say, non-dialectically, it is either induction or deduction. Indeed, it is very easy to challenge the two *BOS* co-authors, as to why they applied the inductive method in this paragraph and deductive in another paragraph or section, or chapter.

Many authors on business books like to mention models. One example is the most well known and most basic business model, which is called the shopkeeper model, involving "setting up a store in a location where potential customers are likely to be and displaying a product or service;" the ACER's fast-food business model,[38] or global business environment model.[39] The two *BOS* co-authors' Chapter 4 focuses on the big picture. Methodologically, the big picture should be the model. Yet, we did not even see a verbal model, let alone a drawing in that chapter for us to see clearly how everything has been integrated. Many things, such as the four actions framework, the profit model of *BOS*, etc. had been scattered here and there, incoherently. In a word, we do not have a full picture, let alone a conceptual or mental map.

On page 42, they mentioned the term, an incoherent strategy, with a question mark at the end. This section was followed by another section called Strategic Contradictions. They wrote the following words on the same page: "When a company's value curve looks like a bowl of

---

[35] http://www.youtube.com/watch?v=wv_RsRATivo&feature=related, accessed on November 13, 2009.

[36] KIM and Mauborgne (2005), p.25.

[37] http://en.wikipedia.org/wiki/Blue_Ocean_Strategy, accessed on November 16, 2009.

[38] See, for example, Sonia El Kahal, *Business in Asia Pacific* (Oxford: Oxford University Press, 2001), p.211.

[39] John J. Wild, Kenneth L. Wild, and Jerry C. Y. Han, *International Business: The Challenges of Globalisation*, 4th ed. (Frenchs Forest, New South Wales: Pearson, 2008), Preface and p.31.

spaghetti--a zigzag with no rhyme or reason, where the offering can be described as 'low-high-low-low-high-low-high' – it signals that the company doesn't have a coherent strategy. Its strategy is likely based on independent substrategies. These may individually make sense and keep the business running and everyone busy, but collectively they do little to distinguish the company from the best competitor or to provide a clear strategic vision." The two *BOS* co-authors suffer from the same problem. Obviously, "low-high-low-low-high-low-high" does not match the non-dialectical inductive or deductive reasoning. One's logic can easily get stuck, not being able to flow smoothly. There is a lack of a train of thought. However, "low-high-low-low-high-low-high" can be dialectically expressed by applying the crab and frog motion model, as shown below, although we need a series of them, which could be, to some people, cumbersome:

First possible model: Put high at 1 and low at 5;
Second possible model: Put low at 1 and high at 5;
Third possible model: Put high at 1 and low at E;
Fourth possible model: Put low at 1 and high at E;
etc.

In short, at each time/space sequence, one looks at only a number or a letter, and there will be no contradictions strategically or tactically, unlike what the HBSP authors said, and this dialectical movement is certainly closer to reality, because can a company be successful all the time? To be sure, a dialectical/scientific/crab and frog motion remark is just the opposite of a non-dialectical/crab and frog motion (usually deductive, linear, or cause and effect) remark, or, at best, they must meet half-way. Such is the paradox,[40] to a non-dialectician. However, to a dialectician, it is magic, because the crab and frog motion model enables himself or herself to rationalize everything, from A to Z. To be sure, non-dialectically, either inductive or deductive, one cannot swim[41] from red waters to blue waters, because they are at odds. To be sure, blue waters could be in the red waters or co-exist with red waters. However, one can do such a thing, dialectically.

It is also a mistake to treat red oceans as representing all the industries in existence today, where as blue oceans denote all the industries not in existence today or the unknown market.[42] On page 119, the authors also said: "... blue ocean strategists represent a significant departure from red oceans...." In other words, unless applying the crab and frog motion model, it is not possible to see this phenomenon, because red oceans could be placed at 5 and blue oceans, 1, while a mixture of blue and red oceans is 3, which, in life, does exist, and le Cirque is the finest example.

To mention it again, what should be properly said? Blue ocean should be new and red, old. In the new ocean, we do see some old things, and vice versa. This again corresponds to what the *BOS* co-authors said about the Canadian circus. Dialectically, blue ocean(s) can coexist[43] with red ocean(s). In the latter, we do see aspects of blue ocean(s), for example, in

[40] This word can be found in, for example, KIM and Mauborgne (2005), p.64.

[41] The translator of the Republic of China (ROC) version of the 2005 book used the Chinese character of *you*/swim. See http://happycwhite.googlepages.com/itcs.b5, accessed on November 6, 2009. KIM and his student also used the word, swim.

[42] KIM and Mauborgne (2005), p.4.

[43] This word can be found in, for example, *ibid.*, p.190.

existence initially as an idea, and vice versa, when business people rush to copying those who implement the *BOS*. So, conceptually, it is a mistake to treat the two types of oceans as if they are not related to each other or to say or imply red oceans cannot exist in blue oceans,[44] even KIM and Mauborgne mentioned that le Cirque retained acrobats and other thrilling performances, while adding artistic flair and intellectual wonder to the acts.[45] In other words, the new circus contains old things, and vice versa.

We should not forget that KIM and his student did not put a question mark after the following two words for the section: strategic contradictions. However, they did pose the following question: Are there strategic contradictions? In other words, to them, there are non-dialectically contradictions. To be sure, dialectically, there is no contradiction from time/space sequence (1) to time/space sequence (n), because when making a move only one number or letter is thought about. If there are still contradictions, it is only 50%.

On page 177 in the 2005 book, the co-authors wrote: "The theory was good. In practice, however, things took an unpredicted turn." Because they failed to present a logical, systematic, and coherent theoretical framework in the second chapter or even the first, which has to do with analytical tools and frameworks, it is very difficult for theoreticians to relate to what they said in the first chapter to all the figures (e.g., p.40), maps (e.g., p.96 and p.121), index (e.g., p.140), etc., or the strategic canvas. On page 136, they displayed "The Profit Model of *BOS*." By looking at this model alone, one can tell that the co-authors do not really understand what a model or theory is. The following arguments justify this: 1) They must tell us in writing or present us with a linkage of this profit model with the framework as presented in the second chapter or even the first. In other words, they have not integrated all of the models and theories as mentioned in the book into one larger logical, systematic, and coherent model, preferably shown in a drawing.

We must not forget that a model or theory could clash with another model or theory in the same publication. They even mentioned on page 17, whole-system approach and on page 30, complex business models. As an academic, we are supposed to dissolve the possible or potential contradictions when we see two or more models or theories in a publication. It is well known that, if we were studying the same issue, one author may come up with a conclusion which is just the opposite of another book writer's conclusion. In fact, sometimes, the same author may contradict himself or herself, if you carefully read *all* of their publications; and 2) since they applied the Profit Model of *BOS* in Chapter 6, a legitimate question can be posed: Why cannot they apply another (better) model or theory for the same chapter?

Sometimes, the way they draw their diagram is similar to the crab and frog motion model, as shown in Figure 2-6 on page 38. The following terms were mentioned, when the *BOS* co-authors depicted the strategy canvas of Southwest Airlines: Price; Meals; Lounges; Seating class choices; Hub connectivity; Friendly service; Speed; and Frequent point-to-point departures. In the same canvas, two words are used: high and low. This kind of arrangement resembles the crab and frog motion model. However, one who applies the crab and frog motion model needs two models to express the same thing. First, it is: Price (or 1); Meals (or 2); Lounges (or 3); Seating class choices (or 4); Hub connectivity (or 5); Friendly service (or 6); Speed (or 7); Frequent point-to-point departures (or 8) spectrum versus the Non-Price;

[44] *Ibid.*, p.5.
[45] *Ibid.*, p.15.

Meals; Lounges; Seating class choices; Hub connectivity; Friendly service; Speed; Frequent point-to-point departures (or E) spectrum. The second crab and frog motion model is High versus Low, which again can be expressed in terms of several possible models, as mentioned earlier.

KIM and his co-author wrote on page 96: "[t]hese are businesses whose strategies fall on the margin between red oceans and blue oceans." Inductively, this phenomenon is possible. However, deductively, this phenomenon cannot be expressed in terms of a linear thinking or a train of thought, simply because the three types of strategies cannot be connected with or linked to each other. In the crab and frog motion model, margin could be either 5 or A.

The *BOS* co-authors mentioned a number of theories in their book, such as the theory of endogenous growth (pp.209-210), the new growth theory (p.210), etc. They also mention the game theory, that is, on page 211, mentioning the term, non-zero-sum game or on pages 137 and 143, win-win game. They should not have done that, unless they tell us where each of them can be shown in their frameworks, such as the Four Actions framework on page 29 or the biggest model. Otherwise, confusion begets confusion. Indeed, *BOS* as a theory[46] may clash with the game theory. For example, in the latter, player A may fight against player B. In other words, there would be no harmony and no more competition free.

FORMING, MAINTAINING, OR SUSTAINING[47] REGIMES VERSUS FORMULATING OR IMPLEMENTING THE *BOS*

Both international/global governance and international regimes can be regarded as the theory. However, if international/global governance is the theory, then international regimes are the tool[48] or we can treat regimes as a sub-theory, unless we conduct a comparative study, which may yield different, heuristic findings. There are at least 15 core elements of a particular regime: 1) positive nature; 2) principles; 3) norms; 4) rules; 5) decision-making procedures/practices; 6) pan; 7) we are all on the same side; 8) one for all, all for one (in the Daoist sense?),[49] as opposed to collective security's one for all and all for one; 9) community-centered arrangement(s); 10) cooperation; 11) coordination; 12) avoidance of mutually damaging outcomes;[50] 13) no power struggle; 14) transparency; and 15) mitigation of anarchy, tension, (scientific) uncertainty, and mistrust.

There are many examples of regimes. *Imperium* group of international regimes, which is related to sovereign rights and they are state-organized: the diplomatic regime;[51] the national

[46] See note 33.
[47] This word can be found in, for example, *ibid,* p.5.
[48] This word can be found in, for example, *ibid,* p.35.
[49] Beijing has been promoting harmonious society for some time. A theoretician in the mainland said it is fundamentally Daoist. When you think of *wuwo*, there will be no comparison and contrast as well as competition, all of which would lead to struggle. See http://www.chinareviewnews.com, search dated March 10, 2007.
[50] John Vogler, *The Global Commons: A Regime Analysis* (New York: John Wiley & Sons, 1995), p.18.
[51] According to LEE Seng Giap, "[s]ince as of now there seems to be no Chinese translation capable of doing what the English original term can do, you may, at least for the time being until there is such a Chinese coinage, consider the "dichotomy" approach of separating the "software aspect" from the "hardware aspect" in terms of Chinese translation. For example, in the case of "外交國際(泛)領域**暨議題**," in the "software aspect." you can call it "外交國際泛制"or "外交國際範制" or "外交國際規制" or whatever suitable term you can think of. In the "hardware aspect." you may call it "外交國際組織/機構/聯盟/中心" or some other suitable

security regime; the (human) security regime; the anti-war regime;[52]the arms control, disarmament, and non-proliferation regime; the anti-terrorism/counter-terrorism regime; the human rights regime; the international protection regime;[53] the foreign aid regime; the global refugee regime; the environmental regime, etc.

Dominium group of international regimes, which is related to property rights and they are institution-organized: the global ocean regime; the deep seabed regime; the outer space regime; the counter-piracy regime; the international business policy regime; the barrier-reduction trade and commerce regime; free and fair international trade of carbon storage services regime; the foreign investment regime; the foreign exchange/flexible exchange rate regime; the anti-money launderers regime; the intellectual property regime; the international telecommunications regime; the whaling regime, the panda protection regime, etc.

If one has fully understood what an international regime is, one would agree with us, saying harmony, though (very) fragile, does exist.[54] If a certain regime can be maintained or sustained, there is certainly harmony, even if it means Confucian-style or 1%.

In this connection, we do not need to ask the following question as posed by the two *BOS* co-authors on page 101 in Chapter 5: "How do you maximize the size of the blue ocean you are creating?" This is because there are so many regimes and they are becoming more important than ever. Besides, each regime [as opposed to international law, international organizations, international institutions, non-governmental organizations (NGOs), and mass media], can benefit all the countries, political/economic entities, and individuals like you and me. Reportedly, by 2011, there could be 7 billion people on earth and by 2050, 9 billion people.

On the one hand, there are many similarities between having blue oceans and maintaining and/or sustaining regimes. In the preface, the *BOS* co-authors said their *BOS* can enable them to build "a future where customers, employees, shareholders, and society win" plus maximizing opportunities and minimizing risk, so can the strategy of maintaining and sustaining the manufacturing of products of regime-related goods and services. (Please read the chapter on redefining global business.) On page 23, the two *BOS* co-authors wrote the following words: Effective *BOS* should be about risk minimization and not risk taking. Indeed, if business is related to regimes, then it is definitely about risk minimization and not risk taking.

On the other hand, differences can be noted. First, the two *BOS* co-authors use strategic move (as opposed to the typical way of using company or industry[55]) as the unit of analysis for their research.[56] Each move can deliver products and services that opened and captured new market place, with a significant leap in demand.[57] However, depending on the issue for

---

nomenclature. In this instance, the Chinese language seems to be more "specific," less "embracing" and less "liquid" than the English. The "dichotomy" approach may hopefully show you the way out of this "Chinese linguistic rigidity or bind." Email from him, dated December 14, 2006.

[52] This regime has been developed since the signing of the August 1927 Kellog-Briand Pact in Paris, providing for the renunciation of war as an instrument of national policy. However, it failed.

[53] Multilateral institutions designed to protect clearly defined classes of people such as religious minorities, ethnic minorities, and refugees within sovereign states. The common good is a value that represents the fundamental goals of a collectivity and its in many ways at the core of its *raison d'etre.* See Bruce Cronin, *Institutions for the Common Good: International Protection Regimes in International Society* (Cambridge: Cambridge University Press, 2003), p.12.

[54] This word can be found in, for example, *ibid,* p.15.

[55] http://en.wikipedia.org/wiki/Blue_Ocean_Strategy, accessed on November 11, 2009.

[56] KIM and Mauborgne (2005), p.10.

[57] *Ibid.*, p.11.

each regime, the unit of analysis could be the country, political/economic entity, or each individual. Thus, we have to study various dimensions of business, such as political, economic, cultural, etc. Second, the swarm theory can be related to the regime study, while it conceivably cannot do so when we discuss blue ocean, unless we talk about oceans.

CONCLUSION

Several findings can be noted. First, Peter LIAO Sheung Kwan of the Hongkong-based Asian Knowledge Management Association (AKMA) attempted to decode the *BOS*.[58] He did not really succeed, because he failed to strongly suspect that KIM has been influenced by *Yin* and *Yang* plus the Five Elements, especially when we look at the sentence, which was written by him, as mentioned earlier: a market universe composed of red oceans and blue oceans.[59] So, a chief executive should not have commented that "KIM and Mauborgne's strategies are not only *original* but practical [italics ours]."[60] However, because it is very difficult for many, if not most, people to accept or even appreciate dialectics or the crab and frog motion model, on purpose or unintentionally distorting it as Marxist, KIM and Mauborgne must have on purpose chosen other words to express the same dynamics of *Yin* and *Yang* plus the Five Elements. As for the lead co-author of this chapter, after many years of frustration since September 1994, he, for the very first time, in this paper began to use the term, crab and frog motion, so as to keep a distance from the Marxist distortion and to, more importantly, attract the attention of more readers. Ironically, like the lead co-author of this chapter, KIM and his female student did not escape from the tunnel vision[61] of *Yin* and *Yang* plus the Five Elements. Needless to say, a tunnel could be very wide or narrow.

Second, by applying a model or theory, it means that we have to accept a tunnel vision, because we are locked into a series of models and/or theories. However, the Confucian model of *TianRenHeYi*, to be followed by *WaiShengNeiWang* and *HeErBuYi* certainly is not narrow, because *Tian* is mentioned, which could refer to the environment, universe, or even multiple universe.

Third, regimes and blue ocean(s) are similar. If goods and services are provided in terms of regimes, the market will be vast, since everyone knows that he or she will be benefited and, therefore, will buy or get that particular goods and services. Because of vast demand, this means lower (operation) cost and more profit. Arguably, the strategy for manufacturing goods and services in terms of regimes is better than the *BOS*, because trade and commerce involving international regimes is truly global business. Ask yourself: Does everyone need circus? Can everyone be benefited from watching the circus? Since few business people are aware of the regimes, regime-oriented manufacturing constitutes open waters, with no sharks.[62] To repeat, each regime does not have bad things inside. It only contains old things,

---

[58] http://www.akma.com.hk/image/c/publications/articles/f7.PDF, accessed on November 6, 2009.

[59] KIM and Mauborgne (2005), p.4.

[60] http://www.blueoceanstrategy.com/boo/executive_reviews.html, accessed on November 11, 2009.

[61] This phrase can be found in, for example, *ibid,* p.56.

[62] Red oceans are suppose to filled with sharks. See the two authors' website: http://www.blueoceanstrategy.com/abo/test.html, accessed on November 11, 2009. Many people were misled by Hollywood movies, thinking that sharks are fierce and man-eaters or they are not gentle and graceful sea creatures. Sharks do not attack humans and they are curious by the presence of divers in the water, according to an expert. See *BP*, September 30, 2009, p.4.

which must be also good. It is high time to set sail for it,[63] because the untapped market space for regime-oriented goods and services is not saturated at all. Regimes are global. Therefore, we can redefine global business as international regimes-related trade and commerce.

Fourth, the two co-authors said le Cirque, for example, has created a blue ocean of new, uncontested market space that as of yet has no agreed-on industry name.[64] We can propose to call it the reconciled (*TiaoHe*) industry consisted of new good things and old good things, which are but a hybrid.

Fifth, many people in the world do not really understand Chinese logic and they would criticize, distort, etc. what Chinese (Communist) leaders do and say, as if they are the real experts.[65] In September 2009, HU Jintao, the People's Republic of China (PRC) President, again addressed the United Nations (UN) in a four-point proposal for making the world a more lovely and harmonious place to live, calling for the international community to work together to bring about peace and prosperity that encompassed the following: security, free trade, climate change, and tolerance. On the final point,[66] HU advocated that the international community should acknowledge differences in cultural tradition, social values and systems, and respect the right of all countries to independently choose their "development paths." To be sure, first, this is precisely Confucian. HU in a sense has also re-embraced ancient Chinese philosophy. Second, security is a regime; trade is another regime, and climate change has to do with the environmental regime. Yet, citing some examples at the micro-level, critics say HU's proposals are rife with hypocrisy,[67] which is, dialectically not true or merely 50% true. This is because the Chinese (Communists) have succumbed to Confucianism by putting ethics (also known as moral philosophy or moral science) above politics and economic affairs, if they can. In other words, at the macro-level, the Chinese (Communists) have every intention to maintain harmony; however, at the micro-level, they can easily be criticized.

In sum, KIM and Mauborgne had not properly presented their metaphor. The metaphor is incoherent and confusing. Besides, the two co-authors actually need more explanation for the phrase, uncontested market space. A good conceptual metaphor should have a lot of implications that really will enrich the reader thinking and highlight the pattern of key characteristics in the domain.[68] And, there is a striking similarity between their logic and that of *Yin* and *Yang* plus the Five Elements. If so, they should have advocated regime-oriented goods and services, which is related to Confucian (corporate) governance but not really directly related to blue ocean(s). As a final word, the two *BOS* co-authors criticized Michael E. Porter's idea that successful businesses are either low-cost providers or niche-players.[69] Would they accept our humble criticism?

---

[63] Paraphrased from the blurb by *Publishers Weekly*, United States and *Business Week*, United States.

[64] KIM and Mauborgne (2005), p.18.

[65] One good example is a critique of ZHAO Tianyang's book, *TianXia TiXi* (A Philosophy for the World Institution) (Nanjing, China: Jiangsu Jiaoyu Chubanshe, 2005) by William A. Callahan. See his article, "Chinese Visions of World Order; Tianxia, Empire and the World," paper presented to International Studies Association Annual Convention, Chicago, February-March 2007.

[66] In November 2009, Assistant Minister of Infrastructure Development and Communication Datuk LEE Kim Shin said Malaysians of all races and religious beliefs must continue to uphold the spirit of tolerance. See *BP*, November 6, 2009, p.9.

[67] http://www.david-kilgour.com/2009/Sep_24_2009_04.php, accessed on November 8, 2009.

[68] http://www.ribbonfarm.com/2007/08/06/book-review-blue-ocean-strategy/, accessed on August 17, 2010.

[69] http://en.wikipedia.org/wiki/Blue_Ocean_Strategy, accessed on November 11, 2009.

In: International (Corporate) Governance
Editor: Peter Kien-Hong Yu
ISBN: 978-1-61122-645-4

Chapter 6

MARKETING X AS A UNIVERSITY OF GOVERNANCE: A ONE-DOT THEORY AND MODIFIED SWOT MODEL APPLICATION

Peter Kien-Hong Yu and Shawn S. F. Kao

ABSTRACT

This is a study of University X and plus, for the sake of comparison and contrast, a proposed carbon trading company at three different levels: international (good) governance, international (good) corporate governance, and (good) corporate governance. There could be a difference in the interpretation of the same thing at each level. The attempt is to find out whether the two corporate bodies can perform the same at all three levels. If not, what are some of the differences?

Keywords: international governance, international corporate governance, corporate governance, international regimes, corporations

The term, international (corporate) governance [i(c)g], was coined by me in summer 2009, when the lead co-author joined a new institution of higher education in June 2009, while trying to propose a new business minor. We can add an adjective, namely, good, to the same term, implying that we are not discussing bad governance. In March 2010, the lead co-author came across one book by Joan E. Spero and Jeffrey A. Hart, who urged us to move from the perspective of management, which does not really totally emphasize rules, norms, procedures, institutions, etc.[1] for the sake of benefiting all, to the perspective of governance, when we study international economic relations, for a good reason,[2] because management's scope of enquiry is narrower, whereas governance can incorporate the study of, for example,

---

[1] When we study international regimes, we can come up with at least 15 core elements, not just rules, norms, procedures, and institutions.

[2] Joan E. Spero and Jeffrey A. Hart, *The Politics of International Political Economy*, 7th ed. (Singapore: Cengageasia, 2010), Ch.1.

international (economic) regimes, implying the necessity of having community-centered arrangements, cooperation, etc. By all, we are referring to all the countries, political/economic organizations, and individuals like you and us.

Until February 2010, did our school head "recognise [i(c)g] as a VERY SIGNIFICANT [sic] curriculum development initiative within the Swinburne framework of business education."[3] Before that, our head said he was confused by that term.[4] However, the lead co-author told him that we can parse the term into at least three phrases or in three ways: international (good) governance, international (good) corporate governance, and (good) corporate governance. In other words, each term could mean differently from the other two but they should be understood together or holistically, so as to have a fuller or whole picture, because we are living in a globalizing world or partially globalized world, whereby international regimes have become more important than ever.[5]

For example, (good) corporate governance could be understood in terms of two levels, namely, firm/company-level or country-level. The firm-level implies local or within a national boundary, whereas the country-level is referring to international (good) corporate governance. And, once we see international (good) corporate governance at work, each transnational/multinational corporation may well have to be willingly surrender itself to become a tool or instrument of those people in the world who want to govern or are governing the international society, community, or even arena, especially when they try to form, maintain, or sustain international regimes under the following scenarios, namely, urgency, insecurity, convergent expectation, and perception, so as to solve or resolve issues, which concern us all under the shadow of future.

This paper attempts to apply the lead co-author's one-dot theory and its related series of frameworks to describe and explain, if not infer or predict University X's words and deeds, since its original intake of a number of students many years ago, at the firm-level and country-level, bearing in mind the implication that this institution of higher education may well willingly become a tool of those people who want to govern or are governing the world, especially under urgency. Whether it can be a tool will be compared and contrasted with a proposed offshore company, which conducts the business of carbon trading.

Using University X as a case study is appropriate, because it is a public land-grant technically private institution of higher education in the Asia-Pacific region. It is an international university, as one of its important documents stated the following term: one university spanning two countries. It is also a regional university, as its vision statement so state, attracting faculty members and students from several dozen countries as of today, thereby affording itself to willingly serve as a tool for those people who want to govern or are governing the world. To be sure, regional (or even global) is still international, because, depending on the administrative definition, a selected region can only include two countries or political/economic entities. If University X wants to be a global institution of higher education, it must first put forward a strategy plan of transforming it as an institution of higher education spanning all 190-plus countries.

[3] Email from Debiprasad Dash, dated February 26, 2010.

[4] On February 8 and 9, 2010, I presented international (corporate) governance to a foreign government official at the Swinburne University of Technology, Sarawak Campus, and our head was present.

[5] Pepsi and rival Coca-Cola adopted the May 2006 School Beverage Guidelines to stop selling sugared beverages in United States schools. Coca-Cola has said it won't sell sugared drinks in primary schools worldwide unless asked. In March 2010, Pepsi has started pulling its sugared soft drinks out of all the Republic of India (ROI) schools and globally by 2012.

A CRAB AND FROG MOTION CONVERSION OF THE MODIFIED SWOT MODEL

SWOT, evolved from the SOFT planning method, came about in the 1960s. The technique was devised by Albert S. Humphrey, and it can help us to identify the strategic factors of strengths, weaknesses, opportunities, and threats of a person or company. The usefulness of SWOT analysis is not limited to profit-seeking individuals or organizations. SWOT analysis may be used in any decision-making situation when a desired end-state (objective) has been defined or identified.[6]

Efforts to refine it have been made. For example, the Six Forces Model (SFM), namely, competition, new entrants, end users/buyers, suppliers, substitutes, complimentary products/the government/the public, is a market opportunities analysis model, as an extension to Michael E. Porter's Five Forces Model (FFM), which is a framework for the industry analysis and business strategy development and which has been challenged by some academics. Arguably, the SFM is more robust than a standard SWOT analysis model.[7]

In this paper, we will further modify the SWOT model by using the lead co-author's one-dot theory and its related series of frameworks to study the words and deeds of University X, the main reason being that we find SWOT analysis model too superficial.

It should be noted that, when we have a theory, we have to have a model to accompany it but not vice versa. That is the main distinction, and, therefore, we need to have two terms. It is not difficult to advance or find a (new) theory, when we apply the SWOT analysis model. It is what the lead co-author called the one-dot theory, when we look at the model in its entirety or from a distance. To be sure, each strategic factor, be it strengths, weaknesses, opportunities, or threats, is but part of the one-dot theory. The factors or words constitute a system, because, sometimes, we can lump the first two words together or we must discuss the first factor and the last factor at the same time, under certain scenarios, circumstances, or situations, which could be rapidly-changing.

The SWOT analysis model as presented by Humphrey is not in-depth. Before converting it, so as to be closer to reality, if it is approachable or reachable, it is necessary to introduce the crab and frog motion model. The following model, which, if looked at from far away, could be two half-dots (1 2 3 4 5 as the first half-dot and A B C D E as the second half-dot) or simply one dot if we look at its entirety from a distance[8]:

1 2 3 4 5 A B C D E

time/space sequence (1)
time/space sequence (2)
....
time/space sequence (n)

---

[6] http://en.wikipedia.org/wiki/SWOT_analysis, accessed on March 16, 2010.

[7] http://en.wikipedia.org/wiki/Six_Forces_Model, accessed on March 16, 2010 and http://en.wikipedia.org/wiki/Porter_5_forces_analysis, accessed on March 16, 2010.

[8] *Zheng, fan, shun, ni, zhen,* and *wei.* There are many dots in the world. For example, each of a Polka dot means "each of a number of round dots evenly spaced to form a pattern on fabric." See *Oxford Student's Dictionary*, p.792.

1 means 100% of a concept or whatever;
3 means 50% of a concept or whatever;
5 means 1% of a concept or whatever.

E means 100% of a concept or whatever;
C means 50% of the concept or whatever;
A means 1% of the concept or whatever.

The 1 2 3 4 5 spectrum is equivalent to what I call the safe zone, and the A B C D E spectrum, the danger zone. 5 is the middle way/golden mean/road/path/line/track in the safe zone and A, the middle way/golden mean/road/path/line/track in the danger zone.

When one makes a move at any time/space sequence, he or she is thinking of only one most important Number or Letter, and, therefore, there will be no contradiction whatsoever. In the course of making moves, the dialectician is performing a crab or side-ways motion. For example, he or she began at 5. In the next time/space sequence, he or she may go to A. At the third time/space sequence, the same dialectician may move back to the safe zone and stay at 1. In this connection, the phenomena of the negation of negation, the affirmation of negation, the affirmation of affirmation, and the negation of affirmation will appear before time/space sequence (n) is reached. This process is known as the sub-dialectical game. It should be pointed out that there are three basic stages [or (nodal) points] of development: nascent, ascendant, and mature for the Numbers and mature, descendant, and moribund for the Letters. In other words, 5 is nascent; 3, ascendant; and 1, mature. On the other hand, E is mature: C, descendant; and A, moribund. Last but not least, a series of other, relevant dialectical, theoretical models must be applied, in order to amply describe, explain, and infer (or predict) more phenomena. When a dialectician no longer applies the first crab and frog motion model constructed by him or her, he or she is said to have leaped or jumped from the first crab and frog motion model to second or another crab and frog motion model.

At this juncture, a caveat should be added, that is, whenever we use the word, versus, it means that dialectics is involved and that the concept or whatever on the left extreme, say Yes or 1 will eventually defeat, co-opt, absorb, etc. the concept or whatever on the right extreme, say No or E at time/space sequence (n). However, in the process, the following arrangement may be necessary, such as flexibly positioning Yes at 1 and No at 5. In other words, a contradictory or even adversary relationship between Yes and No at the beginning has been transformed into a non-contradictory, non-adversarial relationship later on, meaning that whoever chose Yes or whoever opted No should learn to tolerate the existence of each other, because they are both in the safe zone spectrum.

In sum, a crab and frog motion player performs two roles when playing games, that of a crab by moving side-ways[9] and a frog by leaping or jumping from one model to another model as he or she sees fit. Such is the magic beauty of dialectics.

Having said that, we can show a series of arrangements, with regarding to the four strategic factors of the SWOT analysis. As can be seen, they can be or are closer to reality. We will list a number of important possibilities.

[9] Crabs can also have *XiaoShuiBu* (quick short steps). In other words, they can move straight forward. See *United Daily News* (UDN)(Taipei), February 12, 2007, p.A10. In Yilang County, Taiwan Province, Republic of China (ROC), there is a crab museum. Not all crabs can be eaten, because some of them are poisonous. Poison could be dangerous. See Formosa Television (Taiwan, ROC), dated February 7, 2008.

Strengths

Strengths at 1 and Non-Strengths at E; Non-strengths at 1 and Strengths at E; Strengths at 1 and Weaknesses at E; Strengths at 1 and Weaknesses at 5; Weaknesses at 1 and Strengths at 5; Strengths at 1 and Opportunities at E; Strengths at 1 and Opportunities at 5; Opportunities at 1 and Strengths at 5; Strengths at 1 and Threats at E; Strengths at 1 and Threats at 5; Threats at 1 and Strengths at 5; Strengths at 1, Opportunities at 2, Weaknesses at 5 and Threats at 4; etc.

Following the above-mentioned footsteps, one can also spell out the models for the other three strategic factors, namely, Opportunities, Weaknesses, and Threats. One can certainly apply them flexibly. One also needs to construct a series of other models in order to connect one model as shown above with another model as shown in the last paragraph, if and when necessary. For example, how does one leap from the crab and frog motion model of Strengths at 1 and Non-Strengths at E to Strengths at 1 and Opportunities at 5? At time/space sequence (1), one may be positioned at 1. Next, because of his or her strengths, he or she created new opportunities for himself or herself. Because the first model did not mention the term, opportunities, he or she has to leap from the first model to the second model, which is Strengths at 1 and Opportunities at 5. Here, a new model must be constructed, to wit, Tying Opportunities with Strengths, which is put at 1 and Non-Tying Opportunities with Strengths, which is placed at E. Needless to say, we can coin other wordings, if one finds this model not precise enough. Having done that, one can still see a linear thinking at work, which can enable us to trace back to the origin, implying the following framework, which is also at work: Linear Thinking at 1, Non-Linear Thinking at 5, and a mixture of both thinking at 3.

In order not to confuse readers, we can simply parse the following sentence into a series of crab and frog motion models: University X is one of the top institutions in the world of higher education. The main models are as follows: University X at 1 and Non-University at E; Top Institution in the world at 1 and Non-Top Institution in the world at E; World of Higher Education at 1 and Non-World of Higher Education at E; Is at 1 and Non-Is at E; etc.

Needless to say, there are other minor models that we need to construct, such as Of at 1 and Non-Of at E. However, it is not necessary for us to show all of them, so long as we can convert the main ones to become our Table of Contents in a book or the structure in our research paper or monograph, which should be logically, systematically, and coherently presented.

CITING RELEVANT INFORMATION, DATA, AND ANALYSIS ABOUT UNIVERSITY X USING THE MODELS

Strengths at 1 and Non-Strengths at E. There is one country in the Asia-Pacific region, which has public universities, private ones, and several foreign universities having offshore[10] or foreign branch campuses. It can also attract many international students. In February 2010, for example, that country has 71,000 such students from abroad. By 2015, it plans to have an international student population of 120,000. And, by 2020, it hopes to have 200,000 of

[10] *Borneo Post* (hereinafter BP)(Sarawak, Malaysia), August 25, 2010, p.12.

them.[11] University X can recruit several hundred of them.[12] It perceives that more students can come to the offshore campus.

University X is located at a place, which is not far away from one of the developed countries in the Asia-Pacific region. The tuition plus room and board in the latter are usually more expensive than University X.[13] Besides, if one pursues his or her master degree or doctoral degree, University X does not usually charge anything, meaning no additional revenue.

University X emphasizes teaching and learning, so as to be more ahead of many others. Periodically, it would conduct workshops to help academics to be aware some of the teaching and learning skills.

The university has become stricter, in view of the fact that it has to pass three types of quality assurance tests, one given by the host country and the other two, main campus and the home country's quality assurance agency. For example, each academic staff has to declare what does he or she plan to achieve in the coming year. As another example, each academic staff has to come to office everyday, working close to 40 hours per week. As a third example, in the foreseeable future, each academic staff has to have publications of one kind or another in each year, following the home campus's standard. A list of acceptable academic journals has been distributed to the academic staff.

University X does care about the environment. So, on campus, one sees many signs, saying no-smoking. On some of them, a certain amount of money as penalty is mentioned, if a smoker does not comply with this rule, for example, by being close to the door entrance or a window. As another example, in November 2009 in the morning, suddenly a fire alarm broke out. As it turned out, it was a fire drill, and we see the university president on the scene. The university is serious about this drill, because it maintains an Emergency Response Team name-list, which includes the Building Warden, Floor Warden, and First Aider as well as it held a post mortem meeting in February 2010, which was attended by personnel from Fire & Rescue Department.

On the Non-strengths spectrum, we do see that many, if not most, citizens of the country, prefer to attend purely public universities, because they are cheaper, even though one of its ranking officials urged their students to discard the mentality that private higher learning institutions are not on par with the public ones, because the former are always closely monitored by the government.[14]

Opportunities at 1 and Non-Opportunities at E. We can mention a few. First, in two years' time, if University X can have 5,000 or more students, it could have a second campus in another location.[15] Second, some University X students, after completing their diploma studies, could be transferred to the main campus, so as to finish their bachelor degree. This can be regarded as an incentive.

However, speaking of the Non-Opportunities spectrum, in another publication, one important figure said "[i]n the next three years, we expect to have 5,000 students on campus" and another person mentioned in the same brochure "in the next five years."[16] Certainly, some

[11] *GuoJiShiBao* (hereinafter GJSB)(Sarawak, Malaysia), p.B1.

[12] It has close to 500 international students as of March 2010.

[13] *GJSB*, March 20, 2010, p.A17.

[14] *BP*, September 30, 2009, p.3.

[15] *BP*, September 30, 2009, p.3.

[16] *Graduation and Award Presentation Ceremony*, dated September 29, 2009, p.4 and p.6.

parents and prospective students will be confused. In this connection, what if the number of students dropped, given the intense competition?

Weaknesses at 1 and Non-Weaknesses at E. There are close to 10,000 universities and colleges in the world. University X ranks top-500, according to two different surveys, one conducted in London and the other, Shanghai. Due to the fact that University X must have a minimum of 5,000 students in order to begin to make a profit, it has to take almost every applicant. The following question ought to be asked: Can the university attract many brighter and more serious students? In this connection, how to teach students when the quality of students differ?

As to the Non-Weaknesses spectrum, the University X administration work hard to make sure that only qualified students, meeting minimum requirements, can continue their study. So, for example, at least 15 final examination scripts, which are randomly selected, have to be cross-marked by a convenor, who teaches at the main campus. In this connection, there could not be too many students who can receive high final grades. Explanations must be given if over 30% of the students in a unit of study failed to get a passing final grade of 50%.

Threats at 1 and Non-Threats at E. In August 2010, University X has about 3,500 students. However, in the same state, it has to face stiff competition from another foreign university, which comes from the same country, which is located at quite a remote place as compared to the location of University X, and which, according to a news report, has 2,800 students from throughout the country and over 40 other countries.[17] There is another pressure. That is to say, a local public university wants to have more students and it has vowed to become a research institution of higher education in 2015, based on its Research & Development (R & D) ongoing project, although it at the same time admitted that the grant provided by the federal government was not enough to cover the project but the public university would try to secure from state and international funding.[18]

University X has many local Chinese students (as opposed to those from mainland China and Taiwan). There are two new developments, which can put pressure on University X. First, in March 2010, a private, vocational college announced that it aims to double student population within the next five years and it will attract more students whose career is in wholesale and retailing, theme restaurants, operation management, etc., where University X is located.[19] Second, mainland China plans to set up one offshore campus in Malaysia, while facing student shortage in the next ten years, due to lack of new born babies. To barely survive, a private college or university in the Chinese mainland must have at least 6,000 students.[20] Otherwise, that institution of higher education would not be able to make a profit. When it has more than 11,000 students, one can see a smoother operation.[21]

University X also has to participate in International Education Fair (IEF), for the sake of attracting more prospective students. For example, in March 2010, one fair has held in Kuching, Sarawak, Malaysia. The competition is keen, because just by looking at computing, information technology, and science technology, we see 20 different colleges and universities having booths at the Permata Exhibition Hall.[22] As mentioned earlier, University X has many

[17] *BP*, October 26, 2009, p.8.

[18] *Ibid.*, March 16, 2010, p.2.

[19] *Ibid.*, March 23, 2010, p.D4.

[20] http://www.chinareviewnews.com, dated 2010-03-24 at 14:39:02 and accessed on March 25, 2010.

[21] *Ibid.*

[22] *BP*, March 19, 2010, p.20.

local Chinese students. Yet, Fuijan Province, mainland China-based *Huaqiao* University, which is subordinate to Overseas Chinese Affairs Office (OCAO) of the People's Republic of China (PRC)'s State Council (SC) also has a booth. Some of the prospective students may choose *Huaqiao* instead. A little over 9,000 university students from this country are studying in the Chinese mainland. In Semptember 2010, Guangdong Province-based, Jinan University contemplated the opportunity of having a foreign branch campus. And, in November 2010, National Taiwan University (NTU) has been thinking of having an offshore campus in Penang state.

After using the SWOT analysis model, can we relate the findings to good governance? There are some models regarding good governance, in addition to what the New York-based think tank, Ethisphere, is trying to do by conducting an evaluation of corporate ethics and companies with more than US$50 million in annual revenue, employing at least 100 workers. It evaluated more than 3,000 firms on seven factors, ranging from how seriously their top executives take corporate citizenship, to how they manage compliance, to the effect their ethical leadership has on industry rivals.[23]

According to the United Nations (UN), good governance has eight characteristics: consensus oriented, participatory, following the rule of law, effective and efficient, accountable, transparent, responsive, as well as equitable and inclusive. If University X practices them, would it be able to turn weakness into strength or threat into opportunity?

The answer is difficult to arrive at with hundred percent assurance. Yes, we can say that University X is consensus-oriented. This is because University X sometimes operates like a corporation, the university president usually has the final say but not 100%, because sometimes he or she must also adhere to the main campus and even the country's local government's policies and instructions.

Sometimes participation is compulsory, for example, each academic must show up at the graduation ceremony or certain workshops. At other times, some key administrators would hold meetings to resolve a pending issue.

Rule of law does play a major role at the university. There are several dozen policies. The problem is that one can easily detect contradictions and inconsistencies. For example, the workload model allows each academic to choose any two themes out of three, to wit, teaching, research, and service. Yet, the proposed research objectives require each academic to be involved in research and writing in one way or another.

To academics, they feel that there are effectiveness and efficiency. However, many students would complain that the service is usually slow.

Accountability is at work. One would be responsible for what he or she does or says, in the name of the university interest.

University X has become more transparent. For example, certain positions in some committees are being elected. As another example, the distribution of final grades would be known to colleagues in each academic unit. If one gives too high a grade, one may be asked to explain the reason(s).

In a corporate setting, responsive is demanded. Thus, one administrator said, if one has questions, he or she should not hesitate to ask. Needless to say, each academic is required to have office hours. Given the country's culture, academics have to actively help their students.

---

[23] *Ibid.*, March 23, 2010, p.B4.

Equitable and inclusive are in play. Samuel P. Huntington said, after the end of Cold War, seven or eight civilizations clash against each other. University X has all of those cultures. So far, each staff has learn to be objective in saying and doing things.

COMPARING AND CONTRASTING UNIVERSITY X AND A CARON TRADING COMPANY

In this section, we will first mention an offshore carbon trading company, for the sake of comparison and contrast, which so far is still on the paper but which will be soon or later launched by the Republic of China (ROC) on Taiwan.[24] An official at the Environmental Protection Administration (EPA) in Taipei said his country aims to engage in international carbon trading, despite its diplomatic isolation since the early 1970s, by helping its cash-strapped allies and friends in Africa and the Asia-Pacific region to develop clean energy projects, while at the same time it will try to reduce the emissions of greenhouse gases to ease the effects of global warming.[25] Investors would receive offsets in return, called Certified Emissions Reductions (CERs), which can be used toward emissions reduction goals or sold for profit. The December 2009 delivery CERs were trading around 11.30 euros (US$15.56) a ton in March 2010.[26]

What Taipei would do is to obtain carbon credits by promoting green technology, including solar energy plants or bio-fuel power plants, among nations in those 23 countries that have diplomatic relations with the ROC. This kind of arrangement is one of the key features of the December 1997 Kyoto Protocol on global warming, which is due to expire in 2012. To be sure, nations gathered in Copenhagen/Hopenhagen in December 2009 did not succeed in hammering out a successor treaty on climate change as expected.[27]

By engaging in carbon trade, Taipei perhaps can indirectly be part of the UN's Clean Development Mechanism (CDM), which allows rich nations to fulfil part of their greenhouse gas reduction commitments under the Kyoto pact by investing in projects that help reduce emissions in developing countries.[28]

In 2006, the International Energy Agency (IEA) ranked the ROC 22nd in the world for fuel-based carbon dioxide (CO_2) emissions at 270 million tons per year. It was No. 16 in terms of per-capita emissions, higher than Japan and the Republic of Korea (ROK).[29] The ROC's EPA said in March 2010 that the government would aim to cut emissions to 2005 levels by 2020 anyway, a reduction of at least 30 percent from projected levels. President MA Ying-jeou has said that he wants his nation's annual CO_2 emissions to fall to 214 million tons by 2025 and half that by 2050.[30]

Major CO_2 polluters in the Taiwan area include Taiwan Cement Corporation (TCC), Taiwan Power Company (TPC), and Formosa Plastics Corporation (FPC), according to the

---

[24] Emailed it and no confirmation from its Environmental Protection Administration (EPA) email, dated March 25, 2010.

[25] *BP*, March 19, 2010, p.A6.

[26] http://www.reuters.com/article/idUSTRE62G18Y20100317, accessed on March

[27] *BP*, March 19, 2010, p.A6.

[28] *Ibid.*

[29] http://www.reuters.com/article/idUSTRE62G18Y20100317, accessed on March 23, 2010.

[30] *Ibid.*

EPA.[31] It has not estimated how many credits the ROC on Taiwan would seek from Africa or how much it planned to invest in those countries.

University X is a corporate entity in the country. Although not a polluter, does it have the social responsibility of reducing CO_2? Or is it reducing CO_2, since using air conditioning is a must due to humid temperature almost every day? It does not really have academic staff, who are well-known experts on the environmental regimes. So, it cannot play a big role, even if it is called upon by the UN to give a lending hand.

The EPA's carbon trading company most likely is subsidized by the government, in whole or in part. It can play a role in the Taiwan area. Thus, we will see corporate governance at work. Since it is interested in helping its diplomatic allies, we will have to discuss international corporate governance. And, since the UN will appreciate what the ROC will be doing, the ROC in general and the carbon trading company in particular would willingly become a tool of the world body.

A word can be added regarding the UN model on good governance. Can it be applied to the carbon trading company? The answer is simple and straightforward: Until it is set up, we cannot really comment on it. Needless to say, before setting up the company, the officials in charge from the very beginning should recruit only those who really qualify, so as to avoid wasting limited tangible and intangible resources.

CONCLUSION

Several findings can be noted in this section. First, today, it is more than appropriate to first mention the term, governance and, then, management. If we were talking about the days immediately after World War II, we can first use the term, management, in view of the fact that, with the robust rise of civil society, most central governments in the world cannot have the final say regarding many issues. There must be closer cooperation and coordination between the public and private sectors, the latter of which could sometimes chip in some tangible and intangible resources. Community-centered arrangements should also be made, so as to solve or resolve regime-related issues. The term, governance, implies both state and non-state dimensions. After that, perhaps we can talk about management and other terms.

Second, the co-authors are confident that the study of i(c)g will become more important than ever. This is because the United States is concerned. On May 28, 2010, the American president in his 52-page *National Security Strategy*'s Preface and on page 21 mentioned the term, governance, the U.S. capacity to speak to other people's hopes, as well as American troops and diplomats, private sector, nongovernmental organizations (NGOs), and citizens, who all have a role to play. The term, international regimes, was also mentioned on page 13. On page 23, "a global nonproliferation regime" was mentioned. The term, international nonproliferation norms, was mentioned on page 24. The term, international norms, was mentioned on page 11, page 17, page 40, and page 50. On pages 12-13, he said international cooperation since World War II has been an architecture of institutions, organizations, regimes, and standards that establish certain rights and responsibilities of all sovereign nations. On page 19, he mentioned public-private partnerships. Last but not least, a section was devoted to (alternative) mechanisms of cooperation.

---

[31] *Ibid.*

Third, a handbook on corporate governance has a sub-title, and it prides itself as a *definite* guide.[32] However, this reference book did not touch upon international governance and, therefore, it cannot give us a fuller picture of what is going on at the same time regarding governance at various levels or at least beyond the firm-level and country-level. In other words, the Institute of Directors should revise and expand their handbook.

Fourth, picking a unit of analysis is very important, when we study international regimes. There could be two levels: country or political/economic organizations and individuals like you and me. This means that a regime would be harder to be successful, when we study the second level, because we need just one non-cooperating person to derail or ruin a particular regime. For example, we are not supposed to smoke on campus and yet someone is still doing in the toilet.

Fifth, SWOT analysis can be treated as a model. In this study, the co-authors have modified it. Applying a model does not mean that we have to mention a theory, which is at a higher level. However, mentioning it could help us to remember it or to impress upon others, because it is more difficult to be a theorist than a model-builder. Needless to say, we can treat many models, simply as a dot, such as the *Yin* and *Yang* diagram as well as game theory.

Sixth, can we promote University X as a university of governance, so as to be a pioneer in the world? Up to now, we see Oxford University (Oxon), Georgia Institute of Technology (GIT), Management and Science University (MSU),[33] and City University of Science and Technology (CUST). In August 2010, Curtin University of Technology changed its name by dropping the last two words, because it wants to be more than technology.[34]

Strictly speaking, if a higher institution of education emphasizes, for example, technology, it cannot teach courses that are not related to technology, unless we talk about the political dimension of technology, the economic dimension of technology, the social dimension of technology, the legal dimension of technology, etc. If University X fully understands the cutting-edge word, governance, it can teach courses related to natural science and social science. To repeat, when we use the word, governance, we must also talk about regimes. When we talk about regimes, we are actually talking about three levels: regimes, mechanisms, and measures. For mechanism, we can break it down into devices and institutions (which can be further divided into practices and organizations). Devices are related to science and technology, while institutions touch upon political science, economics, sociology, law, etc. In a word, governance is a comprehensive word, embracing virtually everything.[35] It is a niche to attract more students. Needless to say, well established institution like the oldest surviving one in the English-speaking world dating back to the 11th century, that is, Oxon, need not to be concerned about having good academics and students.

Last but not least, it is a mistake for the ROC to tie its attempt to set up a carbon trading company with that of its diplomacy or diplomatic isolation. This is because the former is supposed to be altruistic, while the latter is for the sake of national interest. What this means that much education is needed for high-ranking officials, including Barack H. Obama, II when he in the same May 28, 2010 publication, said international regimes involve only

---

[32] Institute of Directors, *The Handbook of International Corporate Governance: A Definitive Guide*, 2nd ed. (London: Kogan Page, 2009).

[33] *BP*, March 7, 2010, p.A2. The university is located in Selangor Darui Ehsan, Malaysia.

[34] *Ibid.*, August 25, 2010, 12.

[35] Martin Hewson and Timothy J. Sinclair, "The Emergence of Global Governance Theory" in *id.*, eds, *Approaches to Global Governance Theory* (New York: State University of New York Press, 1999), p.17.

countries. If they cannot grasp the term fully, can they really communicate with each other and expect the public to understand and even accept?

In: International (Corporate) Governance
Editor: Peter Kien-Hong Yu
ISBN: 978-1-61122-645-4

Chapter 7

CAN WE APPLY THE INTERNATIONAL (CORPORATE) GOVERNANCE THEORY TO STUDY THE COCA-COLA COMPANY?

Peter Kien-Hong Yu*

ABSTRACT

The new theory, international (corporate) governance i(c)g, actually can be broken down into three interrelated theories or sub-theories, depending on the context, namely, international governance, international corporate governance, and corporate governance.

When the Coca-Cola Company (CC) began to sell its first soda fountain drink or coke in May 1886, the theory, international governance, and, for that matter, the international regimes theory, was not conceived of. Because the international governance theory may well become a mainstream school of thought in a partially globalized or globalizing world in the foreseeable future, we can develop a new theory, i(c)g, to test whether or not we can use it or the new school of thought to describe, explain, and infer or predict the words and deeds of the Company.

The answer to the title is: Yes. However, by browsing the CC website, arguably, the Coca-Cola Company does subconciously form, maintain, and sustain corporate regimes and international corporate regimes. As to international governance regimes, it has not been practicing all of them or 100%, unless we look at the following international regimes, which can also be applied at the firm-level and country-level governance: environmental regime, human rights regime, human security regime, foreign exchange regime, as well as arms control, disarmament, and non-proliferation regime.

Last but not least, if the term, global business, can be redefined as international regimes-related trade and commerce, the CC can be said as having only conducted "global" business, so long as it belongs to the regular or even low-calorie carbonated drinks industry, which cannot benefit all people in the world.

* I would like to thank Silke Machold and A.A. Ligthelm for the helpful comments in the writing of this research paper. The normal caveat applies.

Keywords: Coca-Cola Company, corporate governance, international corporate governance, international governance, international regimes

The term, corporate governance, has been around for a long period of time, and many scholars have studied it in-depth.[1] M. C. Jensen and W. H. Meckling focused on the dominant agency theory. J. H. Davis, E. D. Schoorman, and L. Donaldson studied the stewardship theory. Jeffrey Pfeffer came up with the resource-dependency theory. And R. Edward Freeman developed the stakeholder theory. M. L. Mace argued for the managerial hegemony theory. Others like Morten Huse; C. M. Daily, D. R. Dalton, and A. A. Canella, as well as Yadong LUO either summarized (transnational) corporate governance theories or pointed out the global dimensions of corporate governance.

When the Dutch East Indies Company (DEIC) (or Vereenigde Oostindische Compagnie in Dutch), as a first artificial person in the world of business, was created in March 1602,[2] it began to attract discussions on some emerging issues, such as who are the players, namely, the shareholders, management, and board of directors; what does it mean to be the first multinational corporation in the world; and what are the implications of being the first public company to issue stocks.

Since day one, a company has to face both public and private dimensions. By public, we are usually talking about the government agencies, which can issue license and impose guidelines, and by private, the manufacturers, suppliers, customers, and consumers. In order to maintain and sustain profit, governance is necessary for a company. It refers to the authoritative activity of governing a company, so as to ensure profitability, if not expansion.

To many academics, corporate governance can be understood in terms of two levels, namely, firm-level and country-level. [3] A local company can exist without having to interact with, for example, foreign manufacturers suppliers, customers, or consumers. Therefore, our focus can be on a company's internal dynamics and its interactions with, for example, domestic consumers. Once a local company buys raw materials from abroad or sells its products to foreign customers and/or consumers, country-level corporate governance sets in. At this level, what we should be concerned is whether or not the firm-level and country-level

---

[1] See M. C. Jensen and W. H. Meckling, "Theory of the Firm," *Journal of Financial Economics*, Vol.3, No.4 (July 1976), pp.305-360; J. H. Davis, E. D. Schoorman, and L. Donaldson, "Toward a Stewardship Theory of Management," *Academy of Management Review*, Vol. 22, No.1 (January 1997), pp.20-47; Jeffrey Pfeffer, "Size and Composition of Corporate Boards of Directors: The Organization and its Environment," *Administrative Science Quarterly*, Vol.17, No.2 (June 1972), pp.218-228; R. Edward Freeman, *Strategic Management: A Stakeholder Approach* (Boston: Pitman, 1984); M. L. Mace, *Directors: Myth and Reality* (Cambridge, M.A.: Harvard University Press, 1971); Morten Huse, *Boards, Governance and Value Creation: The Human Side of Corporate Governance* (Cambridge: Cambridge University Press, 2007); C. M. Daily, D. R. Dalton, and A. A. Canella, "Corporate Governance: Decades of Dialogue and Data," *Academy of Management Review*, Vol.28, No.3 (July 2003), pp. 371-382; and Yadong LUO, "Corporate Governance and Accountability in Multinational Enterprises: Concepts and Agenda," *Journal of International Management*, Vol.11, No.1 (March 2005), pp.1-18 and *Global Dimensions of Corporate Governance* (Malden, MASS.: Blackwell Publishing, 2007). See also Andrei Shleifer and Robert W. Vishny, "A Survey of Corporate Governance," *The Journal of Finance*, Vol.LII, No.2 (June 1997), pp.737-783 and R. K. Yin, *Case Study Research, Design and Methods,* 3rd ed. (Newbury Park, CA.: Sage Publications, 2002).

[2] It became defunct or bankrupted in March 1798.

[3] See Institute of Directors, *The Handbook of International Corporate Governance: A Definitive Guide*, 2nd ed. (London: Kogan Page, 2009), 11-22, especially p.16 and p.17, which talks about country-level governance and firm governance.

governance can remain the same. If not, would governance need to be modified or even abandoned?

Strictly speaking, a local company can hardly exist in isolation, if it has to acquire raw materials from abroad. The picture becomes more complex and complicated, because the foreign exchange regime will be involved sooner or later.

Living in a rapidly shrinking world, I propose to integrate firm-level and country-level corporate governance with that of international governance, which will likely emerge as the next dominant, mainstream school of thought, supplanting, if not replacing, (neo-)Realism, which usually treats country or central government as the unit of analysis and which does not have to study the involvement of civil society. Due to this likelihood, it is necessary for us to coin a new term, international (corporate) governance [i(c)g]. This means that firm-level and country-level corporate governance must be understood in the context of the largest picture, international governance, respectively.

Thus, since summer 2009, I am actually talking about three terms at the same time: international governance, international corporate governance, and corporate governance. The third level or corporate governance cannot give us a whole picture. Whether or not a company practices good or even better governance can be easily challenged or falsified by the country-level governance. This is because a (transnational) company, at both the domestic and international levels, usually does not have enough power to control external political, economic, social, and technological factors. After World War II. many countries became revolutionary, socialist, or even Communist. Some remained feudalistic. Such a tide can drastically change a central government's policy of practicing capitalism. Thus, in autumn 1949, the Coca-Cola Company (CC) had no choice but to cease its sales of Coca-Cola[4] in the Republic of China (ROC) market, with an estimated 500-million consumers on the Chinese mainland (*neidi*) when the Chinese Communists forced CHIANG Kai-shek to retrograde to the Taiwan area.

A fuller picture would be to contrast firm-level corporate governance with that of country-level corporate governance or the second, international level, so as to see whether or not the former has affected the latter and vice versa. However, the whole picture should be the following: Would a company's corporate and international corporate governance be affected, respectively, by international governance in general and international regimes[5] in particular?

To be sure, when we discuss corporate governance or international corporate governance, we cannot neglect nor ignore regimes. Thus, we see terms like corporate regimes and international corporate regimes. By the same token, when we discuss international governance, we cannot neglect nor ignore international regimes, which are the best tool for good, if not better, governance, because those people who want to resolve a (fragmented) regime-related issue in a given area, broadly defined, do not have to waste a lot of energy, money, etc. Cooperation is always there, for example. A local company sometimes does not have to be international or global in order to become a tool of an international organization, such as the United Nations (UN), because it may have to be involved in an international regime, such as the environmental regime.

---

[4] The brand name had to be transliterated from English to Chinese, while the meaning of Delicious Happiness' was not lost in the process. See http://www.thecoca-colacompany.com/presscenter/presskit_olympicgames2008_delicious_happiness_background.pdf, accessed on May 23, 2010.

[5] See, for example, Peter K. H. Yu, *International Governance, Regimes, and Globalization: A Chinese (Communist) Perspective*, forthcoming.

In this paper, I will examine the CC's corporate governance or the firm-level, its performance record at the international corporate governance-level, and its record at the first, international governance level. The main purpose is to find out whether there are twists and turns, zigs and zags, and ups and downs in its holistic[6] governance and to see whether it is either a truly global or a "global" company.

A Brief Description of the Company[7]

In May 2010, the author for the first time began to browse the CC's website, so as to collect relevant information regarding this study.[8] Case studies have also been conducted on the Company.[9]

In May 1886, the best known ever sparkling (as opposed to still) beverage, coke, at five cents per glass that can quench thirst, was born by accident[10] in Atlanta City, the State of Georgia. During the first year, sales of the Coca-Cola soda fountain drink averaged a modest nine drinks per day. As of today, from special occasions to exceptional moments, the sparkling beverage servings total at a rate of 1.6 billion[11] each day, which are sold at 206 markets/nations/countries.

In mid-1890, a store owner began bottling the beverage to sell, using a common, portable, refillable glass bottle. In mid-1910, the CC began to use the distinctive, contour bottle, which became one of the most recognized icons in the world.

In December 1941, the United States began to fight in World War II. By that time, Coca-Cola was bottled in 44 countries, and 64 bottling plants were set up around the world to supply the American armed forces. In November 1942, General Dwight D. Eisenhower began to command the Allied forces in North Africa. In June 1943, he ordered three million bottles of coke to refresh the Allied troops over there.

In the 1950s, cans were also introduced, becoming generally available in the early 1960s. In May 1984, the CC Foundation (CF), a primary philanthropic arm and wholly funded by the CC, was incorporated under the laws of Georgia.[12] It was granted 501(c)(3) *tax-exempt status* by the *Internal Revenue Service (IRS).* On July 4, 1982, the sugar-free Diet Coke/Coca-Cola/Coca-Cola Light/Coke Light, as opposed to regular or no-calorie sparkling beverages, was introduced in the market. It is the very first, successful extension of the Coca-Cola

[6] The Coca-Cola Company (CC) chairman and chief executive officer (ceo), Muhtar A. Kent, mentioned this adjective in his November 2009 speech.

[7] See, for example, Frederick Allen, *Secret Formula: How Brilliant Marketing and Relentless Salesmanship Made Coca-Cola the Best-Known Product in the World* (New York: HarperBusiness, 1994); Mike Cheatham, *" Your Friendly Neighbor": The Story of Georgia's Coca-Cola Bottling Families* (Macon, Ga.: Mercer University Press, 1999); and Charles Elliott, *"Mr. Anonymous," Robert W. Woodruff of Coca-Cola* (Atlanta: Cherokee, 1982).

[8] Unless otherwise noted, all the information come from the Coca-Cola Company (CC)'s website, accessed on May 21, 2010.

[9] Danny A. Samson and Richard L. Daft, *Fundamentals of Management*, third Asia Pacific Ed. (Victoria, Australia: Cengage Learning Australia, 2009), p.168.

[10] Charles A. Rarick, *Cases and Exercises in International Business* (Upper Saddle River, NJ: Pretince Hall, 2003), p.2.

[11] There are 180 million people having diabetics. See *GuoJiShiBao* (Sarawak, Malaysia), May 27, 2010, p.Zeng2.

[12] Email from the Foundation, dated June 3, 2010.

trademark. In November 1984, both *Coca-Cola* and its successful rival imitator, Pepsi,[13] announced plans to stop using sugar in soft drinks, replacing it with high-fructose corn syrup.

However, in April 1985, the CC chairman of the Board of Directors made a biggest blunder ever on formula modification, by releasing a new taste for Coca-Cola, the first change in formulation in 99 years. In taste tests, people loved the reformulated beverage, commonly called "new Coke." In the real world, they had a deep emotional attachment to the original, begging in three months for a return of the original formula, which was later called the Coca-Cola classic. In April 2010, Coca-Cola China launched an eco-friendly, ultra-light weight bottle for its well-known drinking water brand, Ice Dew, thereby saving 16,400 tons in carbon dioxide (chemical formula CO_2) emissions, which is equivalent to 2,788 cars taken off the road or 101 acres of forest planted. In sum, the CC has turned a late 19th century invention into a successful, ubiquitous business.

Applying the Governance Theory

The CC must first think of its survival, even though it has a Secret Formula 4-Dimension Theater, trying to demystify our curiosity about everything it does. Because we are talking about business, trade secrets must be strictly maintained. [14] Thus, one of the key areas with the CC's Science Function does include Formula Governance. This may well mean that the title of an article must have constantly alerting each chairman and chief executive officer (ceo) of the CC: *First, Coca-Cola or Pepsi,*[15] unless the two companies choose to merge one day to reset a new refreshing world.[16]

In passing, it should be noted that, the Company has a term, the Coca-Cola System, and it is proud that it has 700,000 associates,[17] who can create "global reach with local focus" and operating through multiple local channels, although the Company candidly admitted that it does not own nor control most of its bottling partners, meaning that is has no ownership interest or a non-controlling equity interest.[18] This is certainly a potential weakness, implying that, if not governed well, the more than 300 bottling partners can collectively conduct a strike or make unreasonable demands on the Atlanta headquarters. Seeing the CC in crisis, Pepsi-Cola Company (PepsiCo), which also has a history of fun and refreshment since summer 1898, may grab the opportunity to gradually overtake the CC. This possibility cannot be ruled out, because PespiCo in the early 1920s and the early 1930s declared bankruptcy

---

[13] Regarding imitation, the Company wrote: "Imitation may be the sincerest form of flattery, but The Coca-Cola Company was none too pleased about the proliferation of copycat beverages taking advantage of its success."

[14] SIM Khoon Yong, a third generation vendor, tries to keep an old Sarawakian ice dessert favourite alive, by not revealing the recipe trade secrets or the "ang tao cang luk" ingredients. See *Borneo Post* (hereinafter BP)(Sarawak, Malaysia), May 24, 2010, p.B2.

[15] http://www.pepsi.li/?p=1401, accessed on May 23, 2010.

[16] Pepsi-Cola Company (PepsiCo) and rival Coca-Cola Company adopted the May 2006 School Beverage Guidelines to stop selling sugared beverages in United States schools. Coca-Cola has said it won't sell sugared drinks in primary schools worldwide unless asked. In March 2010, Pepsi has started pulling its sugared soft drinks out of all the Republic of India (ROI) schools and globally by 2012.

[17] According to another figure, it is 92,800 associates, more than 87% of them work outside of the United States. See http://www.coca-coalcompany.com/ourcompany/meet_out_people.html, accessed on May 21, 2010.

[18] In January 2006, the Company-owned bottling operations were brought together to form the Bottling Investments operating group.

twice,[19] so can the CC someday. And, in August 1977, a minister of industry in the Republic of India (ROI) said: "The manufacture of [CC] beverages should be Indianized."[20]

There are many models and theories for governance, as noted at the outset.[21] The Company has its own, which is quite different from, for example, the UN model, which has eight characteristics, in the order of importance: participation, rule of law, transparency, responsiveness, consensus oriented, equity and inclusiveness, effectively and efficiency, and accountability. In passing, it should be pointed out that, in December 2008, the UN Development Programme (UNDP), supported by Chinese Communist academics such as YU Keping, launched the China Governance Assessment Framework (CGAF) at the UN Representative Office in Beijing, covering the following 12 dimensions, including civic participation, human and civic rights, rule of law, legitimacy, social justice, social stability, openness of government affairs, administrative effectiveness, accountability, public service, and government cleanliness.

The Company does cooperate with international bodies. In March 2008, it joined the first, four-year, public-private partnership project, Water Resources Management and Drinking Water Safety in Rural Regions of China [namely, water-stressed provinces of Sichuan, Heilongjiang, Xinjiang, and Liaoning], among the UN Development Programme (UNDP),[22] the People's Republic of China (PRC)'s Ministry of Water Resources (MOWR), etc.

It is not difficult to find words, terms, etc. to match those eight UN characteristics. Let me cite some relevant passages.

Participation

The Coca-Cola Company launched several community water initiatives/programs in the Chinese mainland, so as to help raise awareness about the importance of water stewardship and inspire community actions. In its *2008 Corporate Contributions and Grants Paid*, we see that Beijing Environmental Protection Foundation (BEPF) received US$206,000 from the CF, the grant of which is to build and expand on the existing "Save a Barrel of Water" campaign to 10-20 elementary schools or approximately 150,000 students in 15 cities throughout the Chinese mainland.

Rule of Law

There are many corporate documents, such as Code of Business Conduct (CBC), which is available in 10 languages, in which each CC employee has to comply with. In addition, the

[19] http://www.coca-colaconversations.com/my_weblog/2008/07/when-coke-bottl.html, accessed on May 26, 2010.

[20] http://www.time.com/time/magazine/article/0,9171,915304,00.html, accessed on May 31, 2010.

[21] See, for example, http://www.garberconsulting.com/governance%20models%20what%27s%20right.htm; http://www.datagovernance.com/gbg_governance_models.html; http://www.google.com.my/images?client=firefox-a&rls=org.mozilla:en-US:official&channel=s&hl=en&q=governance,+models&um=1&ie=UTF-8&source=univ&ei=l3H_S7STJYa-rAefhcXWDg&sa=X&oi=image_result_group&ct=title&resnum=4&ved=0CC0QsAQwAw; and http://www.banffexeclead.com/Newsletter04/PDF/Leadership%20Acumen%2021%20V2%20Models%20of%20Corporate%20and%20Board%20Governance.pdf, accessed on May 28, 2010.

[22] It also has a Business Call to Action campaign. Water is a most pressing environmental issue. See *Borneo Post* (hereinafter BP)(Sarawak, Malaysia), June 21, 2010, p.12.

Company has expanded its compliance program around American trade sanctions, with supporting policies, training, and audits. And, it is committed to the anti-corruption laws of every country in which it operates, including avoiding corruption in any form, such as bribery. In December 2007, the Company became a signatory to the World Economic Forum Partnering Against Corruption Initiative (PACI).

Transparency

It is doing its best, even on the secret formula or the fragrant, caramel-colored syrup, containing an ingredient called 7X, that makes the coke, which has been kept safely in a Georgia bank vault during the Company's history and it is known to no more than 10 people in the world.[23] In Governance & Ethics, it was stated that "[w]e review our systems to ensure we achieve international best practices in terms of transparency and accountability." Regarding reporting and the CC's policies, the Coca-Cola Company will "strive to be transparent," including corporate political contributions.

Responsiveness

The Company focuses on four global priorities areas, to wit, Water Stewardship (conservation and sanitation), Fitness and Active Lifestyles (physical fitness and nutrition), Sustainable Packaging (recycling), and Education.

Consensus Oriented

The CC does seek advice from or invite respected experts to, for example, calculate the water benefits of projects which can replenish water it uses to make its products.

Equity and Inclusiveness

The Company is proud of its system(s), embracing different type of people.

Effectively and Efficiency

The Coca-Cola Company's water programs, embracing manufacturing processed, such as rinsing, cleaning, heating, and cooling, are designed to make efficient use of agriculture water, although it does not own any farms. In passing, it should be noted that, "[i]n 2008, on average [the CC] used 2.43 liters of water to produce a one liter beverage.... [It is] nearly half way to [its] 2012 goal of 2.17 liters per liter which will be a 20 percent improvement."

---

23 http://www.coca-colaconversations.com/my_weblog/history/page/2/, accessed on May 26, 2010 and http://www.time.com/time/magazine/article/0,9171,915304,00.html, accessed on May 31, 2010.

Accountability

It is making efforts to move our planet toward a lower carbon and greener future. Live Positively is a concept introduced by the Company. It is a way for the CC to think holistically and globally about all of its system's sustainability efforts. A Vice President is in charge of the Company's Global Procurement, Commercial Products Supply, Supply Chain Development, Quality, as well as Environment and Water functions. The Company through all marketing media, such as television, radio, print, the Internet, and mobile telephones, is also urging consumers to make sensible, balanced choices about their overall diet and getting enough physical activity. So, it is shifting portion of the responsibility to the consumer, because each consumer in general and each child in particular who are under 12 and who lack the presence of a parent or a caregiver has to decide whether or not to drink the sweetened carbonated soda water.

The CC has spelled out its Mission, (2020) Vision, and Values, when facing consumers; suppliers/supply chain partners; some 20 million customers including grocery/convenience stores; restaurants, such as having strategic/business alliance with McDonald's in over 31,000 locations or 118 countries; mass merchandisers, such as (street) vending partners/vendors, movie theatres, kiosks, and amusement parks; more than 300 bottling partners worldwide, ranging from small family-owned businesses to large international publicly traded companies; and, sometimes, its shareholders, not to mention its 92,400 employees, who have to engage in, for example, marketing, including brand strategy and identity, advertising, customer experience, promotions, sponsorships, direct marketing, internet marketing, consumer insight and measurement, regional marketing management and all acquisition, cross-sell, and retention activities.

Each Regime Applies to all Governance Levels

There are many levels of governance.[24] In this study, this author has introduced three interrelated levels of governance. A closer look suggests that we must not neglect nor ignore the study of international regimes, which can be defined as a set (or sets) of at least 15 criteria/core elements/features (including those four as mentioned by Steven D. Krasner) in the contexts of (fragmented) issue-area, (fragmented) issue-areas, and issue-regimes.[25] In this definition, which is developed by me, I have added 11 other criteria, such as one for all and all for one (in the Daoist sense?) as well as community-centered arrangements.

When we study regimes, it should be reminded that the term is 100% positive, benefiting all the countries, politico-economic entities, and individuals like you and me. It is not the same as a system, which could only first benefit the Coca-Cola Company.

It is possible that not all (international) corporate regimes can benefit other companies, local or otherwise. If so, we must say it clearly that the regime can only be applied to that particular company for a period of time. Needless to say, not all issues are regime-related.

---

[24] See my paper, "Do We Need to Discuss Legitimacy at All Levels?" paper presented at the International Conference on Legitimacy and Governance," Fudan Institute for Advanced Studies in Social Science, July 3-4, 2010, Fudan University, Shanghai, mainland China.

[25] See Peter Kien-hong Yu, *et. al. International Governance, Regimes, and Globalization: Case Studies from Beijing and Taipei* (Lanham, MD.: Lexington Books, 2010).

The Company's incumbent ceo and chairman, Muhtar A. Kent, since July 2008 and April 2009 respectively, in a December 2009 speech mentioned the term, (single) issue, adding, to the top 180 retail partners, which make up the Coca-Cola Research Council (CRC), the overwhelming issue or concern is sustainability. However, sustainability is not a regime in itself, because, so long as there are companies, trying to maintain and/or sustain themselves, there will be intense competition, unfair or even cut-throat practices, etc.

When we study each regime, we have to figure out the four major scenario(s), that is, urgency, insecurity,[26] convergent expectation, and perception. Kent, in his December 2009 speech at the December 2009 Copenhagen/Hopenhagen Climate Council (CCC), which tries to create awareness of the importance of the UN Framework Convention on Climate Change (UNFCCC or FCCC), which is an international environmental treaty produced at the UN Conference on Environment and Development (UNCED), informally known as the Earth Summit, mentioned the urgency of climate change and, for that matter, good governance. For the record, in March 2006, the Company became a signatory to the UN Global Compact,[27] affirming its commitment to the advancement of its 10 universal principles in selected areas, such as human rights, environment, and anti-corruption.

Some of the important regimes, which can be categorized into two groups, are as follows. *Imperium* group of international regimes: the diplomatic regime; the national security regime; the (human) security regime; the anti-war regime; the arms control, disarmament, and non-proliferation regime; the anti-terrorism/counter-terrorism regime; the human rights regime; the international protection regime; the foreign aid regime; the global refugee regime; and the environmental regime.

The Coco-Cola Company has been involved in activities related to the arms control, disarmament, and non-proliferation regime. This is because the Board of Directors has Sam Nunn, who is the ceo of the Nuclear Threat Initiative (NTI) since January 2001. From the *2008 Corporation Contributions and Grants Paid*, we noticed that US$100,000 was granted to Georgia Tech Foundation (GTF), Inc. to support the Sam Nunn School of International Affairs Coca-Cola Endowed Chair. The CC has also granted financial aid to meet the needs of refugee students and provided seed funds to the Colombia Foundation for Education and Opportunity (CFEO) helping those who have been affected by the armed conflict in that country, which can come under the human security regime.

We also see a number of international regimes related to the *dominium* group: the global ocean regime; the deep seabed regime; the outer space regime; the counter-piracy regime; the international business policy regime; the barrier-reduction trade and commerce regime; the import/export regime; free and fair international trade of carbon storage services regime; the foreign investment regime; the foreign exchange/flexible exchange rate regime; the anti-money launderers regime; the intellectual property regime; the international tele-communications regime; and the whaling/panda protection regime.

In the CC's Forward-looking Statements, we do see its concern about the fluctuations in foreign currency exchange rates.

Nonetheless, from the webpages that I have browsed, I do not find the term, international regimes, which can be understood in terms of three interrelated levels, to wit, regime,

[26] The term, food insecurity, was mentioned under "Replenish."

[27] http://www.unglobalcompact.org/, accessed on May 28, 2010.

mechanism, and measure, although I do see words like mechanism[28] and measure.[29] One reviewer of this paper said the CC used the term, system. In response, I told the reviewer that a regime is not the same as a system. Sometimes, what the Company subconsciously does are equivalent to one regime or another. For example, to help children with iron-deficiency anemia and malnutrition, it provided NutriJuice free of charge to approximately 36,000 elementary school students in the Philippines. This is precisely one for all. The problem is, of course, with limited budget, the Coca-Cola Company cannot afford to provide the drink to all needy school children in the world.

Regime is a very abstract term, whereas measure, the least, and mechanism is somewhere in between, because it could refer to device, such as the fountain dispenser or pump, or institution, such as the Board of Directors, which currently has 14 members, and 13 of whom are not employees of the CC, implying that the latter can offer the chairman and ceo to sometimes to think out of the box, the CF, and the CRC.

The Company certainly is aware or conscious of the environment and its related things such as global warming,[30] which was coined by Wallace Smith Broecker in an August 1975 research paper, and which is caused largely by human activity, resulting rising in rising sea levels, melting glaciers, and more heat waves[31], but not of environmental regime. The issues of water scarcity and poor quality certainly are part of the regime to be dealt with.

The Coca-cola Company is also concerned about human rights. At workplace, including its dealings with its suppliers, in which it has no control of, it would try to make improvements. It is required that all managers are expected to implement and enforce the Company policy of non-discrimination, equal employment opportunity, and affirmative action, as well as to prevent acts of harassment within their assigned area of responsibility.

The Company is certainly fully aware that drinking too much Coca-Cola may result in health problems, such as obesity and having a blackened stomach. Having too much caffeine intake is also not good. So, it would remind its consumers that "[w]hile there are many factors involved in obesity, the fundamental cause is an imbalance between calories consumed and calories expended," emphasizing that the company will play a leading role in identifying and implementing solutions to address issues of obesity, as they affect each drinker and its industry. Indeed, the Company has developed NutriJuice, an orange flavoured drink fortified with iron, zinc, lysine, and vitamins A and C. It also has other alternative still beverages, such as waters; ready-to-drink teas and coffees; sports and energy drinks; and milk-and-soy-based beverages.

Do Things Related to Regimes

Because the CC's networks, including its Coca-Cola Civic Action Network (Coca-Cola CAN), are quite strong, is it possible to educate consumers or advertise things related to international regimes on its bottles, cans, and other containers, thereby making it more

[28] This term was used in Responsible Marketing.

[29] See, for example, Carletta Ooton's webpage, who is the Chief Quality and Product Integrity Officer. The term, a key measure, can also be found in Our Stance on Child Labor.

[30] See, for example, James Hoggan and Richard Littlemore, *Climate Cover-up* (Vancouver, Canada: Greystone Books, 2009) and Katharine Hayhole and Andrew Farley, *A Climate for Change* (New York: Faith Words, 2009).

[31] *BP*, May 21, 2010, p.A4.

internationally appealing? The answer is none other than yes. However, political will is definitely called for. The president of the Bottling Investments Group (BIG) made the following remarks: "We feel *very good* about the progress we have made, and the quality of the investments we are making. Most of all, we feel *good* about the investments we are making in our people, which are paying off in a very rich way [italics mine]." In other words, when can we see "very good" in the second sentence, meaning that the CC should spend more money on improving people's health?

Needless to say, the Company can promote (the awareness of) international regimes in its bottles, cans, and containers. As part of its marketing strategy, Coca-Cola has been doing many things. It has devoted a significant amount for budget advertising expenses in mainland China. In order for the Chinese mainland consumers to relate to the brand, Coca-Cola has even integrated (ancient) Chinese elements ranging from zodiac animals to couplets in its advertisements.[32] In short, the CC is willing to adapt.

However, obstacles remain. Examples are many. First, as mentioned earlier, Kent, in his December 2009 speech mentioned the term, good governance, plus two other terms, smart policies and real leadership. In his September 2009 speech, he talked about corporate diplomacy, which is becoming as important as political diplomacy. However, no where in the CC website do we see the term, international regimes, not even in its introductory remark on Mission, Vision, and Values. The following words were written: "The world is changing all around us. To continue to thrive as a business over the next ten years and beyond, we must look ahead, understand the trends and forces that will shape our business in the future and move swiftly to prepare for what's to come." And, under values, we see the following words: Act with urgency.

Kent also gave talks at many prestigious universities. Likewise, we do not hear the term, international regimes, in his speeches. The closest terms are as follows: philanthropic; charitable; "Our activities touch almost everyone on the planet…;" the CF is "responsive to the citizenship needs of the communities where we live and work," "no one nation or business or individual has been immune from this global economic tsunami...," etc. If Kent and others[33] like Donald F. McHenry, who is a distinguished professor in the practice of diplomacy and international affairs and who is on the CC's Board of Directors since the early 1980s or even Clyde C. Tuggle, who is in charge of global public affairs and communications, who reports directly to Kent, and who is a member of the influential Council on Foreign Relations (CFR), do not conceptualize beneficial[34] things to all the human beings in terms of international regimes, others would not likely to be aware of international regimes.

Second, water will be a problem in the decades ahead. Some political observers even fear of seeing water wars.[35] The CC should not just care about water surrounding its suppliers, etc. There are many places which need to be taken care of. For example, we read news report, saying that water supply to small districts like Spaoh and Debak, as well as longhouses in the mid and upper Rimbas areas will be improved, once the upgrading of the Betong water

---

32 http://www.chinaknowledge.com/Marcom/Book-ChinaConsumer.aspx?subchap=2&content=8, accessed on May 23, 2010.

33 The CC headquarters has over 50 nationalities represented at the corporate center in Atlanta.

34 In his December 2009 speech, he also mentioned this word.

35 See, for example, Vadana Shiva, *Water Wars; Privatization, Pollution, and Profit* (New York: South End Press, 2002).

treatment plant, pipelines, and storage facilities are implemented under the 10th Malaysian Plan (10MP).[36]

The CC should continuously be aware of the surroundings, such as solid waste, which can contaminate water and do something about it. This is because "[g]lobally, the local authorities spend about 20 to 50 per cent of their revenue on solid waste." One Malaysian minister said, in 2002, Malaysians generated 17,000 tons of solid waste daily, 19,000 tons three years later, and this was estimated to increase to 30,000 tons by the year 2020, showing an unsustainable pattern.[37] What about in other countries? Fortunately, SAS & Coca-Cola Environmental Foundation (SAS & CEF) in recent years had funded projects related to waste management, recycling, and water resources.

In this connection, the Company certainly knows that top scientists have been calling upon the United States to move quickly to reduce greenhouse gas emissions and put a price on carbon, using emerging technologies, such as energy efficiency, renewables, nuclear, carbon capture and storage for coal plants and biofuels.[38] Does the CC plan to include them in its system? Again, fortunately, it is doing something about it, because, in December 2009, the Company began to collaborate with Greenpeace to commercialize a new refrigeration technology that will allow the carbonated industry to eliminate Hydrofluorocarbons (HFCs), which can contribute to anthropogenic radiative forcing emissions, in all of the Company's new vending machines and HFC-free coolers. As of now, the CC system owns approximately 10 million coolers, vending machines, as well as (automatic) fountain dispensers and related equipments. In addition, the CC has commercialized PlantBottle, which is the first plastic packing that is made from up to 30% plant-based material, thereby turning waste into environment-friendly resource.

Third, in 2007, approximately 79% of the Coca-Cola Company's unit case volume was produced and distributed by its bottling partners, and only "many of our bottling partners produce their own corporate responsibility reports…." Does this imply that some of them would not cooperate with the CC to collect and to consolidate economic, social, and environmental data or to implement some regimes, under scenarios of insecurity, convergent expectation, and perception, as opposed to urgency?

Fourth, the following statements can be found, if one wants to contact the CC: "Each year The Coca-Cola Company... receive a large volume of unsolicited communications from people outside the Company containing ideas or suggestions that the submitters believe may be of value to the Company. While the Company appreciates these suggestions, we must adhere to a long-standing policy. Our policy prevents us from considering ideas related to advertising, formula modifications to any of our existing products and recurrent concepts we have previously considered. If you believe your idea is not in one of these excluded areas, feel free to proceed to our submission form...."[39] In short, even if this author's suggestion of updating the package of or repack the Coca-Cola to its refreshing modernity is noble, it cannot directly reach the chairman and the ceo or even the CF chairperson.

Fifth, another brand printed the following 36 words on its can: "FUJI Apple--Flavoured Sparkling Drink: Enjoy a refreshing moment with Pokka Fuji Apply! With Vitamin C & Real Apple Juice, it is the perfect enjoyment for a cool fun time. Savour its delicious real taste

[36] *BP*, May 21, 2010, p.6.
[37] *Ibid.*
[38] *Ibid.*, May 21, 2010, p.A4.
[39] https://secure.thecoca-colacompany.com/ssldocs/contactus/cokesubmit/index.shtml, accessed on May 23, 2010.

today!" Why not use the same space to alert the importance of international regimes, since the CC does emphasize package variety?[40] This certainly can be done! Would it cost bottlers more money to print the message? The answer is obviously a resounding no.

CONCLUSION

Several findings are in order. First, in this study, this author has integrated three theories. By doing so, I have taken both the classical and applied way of conducting research and writing. In other words, the study should be closer to reality, by cross-fertilizing both ways.

Second, the Coca-Cola Company existed before the new term, i(c)g. After conducting the study, this author finds that it is possible to apply the i(c)g theory to describe and explain the Company, at least in recent decades.

Third, the CC has not yet realized that the term, regime, can conceptualize many of what it has been doing in the last several decades or reset (or even refresh) the world, a term used by Kent. This is like what Asa Griggs Candler did, when he sold his exclusive rights to bottle and sell the coke for the sum of only one U.S. dollar to and, in fact, never collected it from the two lawyers in July 1899.[41]

Fourth, can we treat the Company as a unit of study? Or must we sometimes treat it as a tool of the United States Department of Agriculture (USDA)[42] or any international organizations? The answer is both yes and no. In other words, we could be closer to reality, if we applied both ways, classical and applied. The classical way is a model of something, representing partial reality, whereas the applied way, having logics (as opposed to logic), can help a company to create/bring forth/generate/make that which does not exist profits.[43]

Fifth, participating in more regimes can reduce anti-Americanism[44] world-wide. It can offer a holistic[45] view of the human affairs.

Sixth, global business may be redefined as trade and commerce involving international regimes, because regimes are truly global and, needless to say, international. The CC is a "global company," not a 100% global company, because its products may not benefit all the people in the world.

Seventh, the Company will remain a tool of international bodies, if it chooses to be involved. This is because, unless it can use its CF budget to hold, for example, a series of global conference tackling the climate challenge, can it make the UN a tool.

Eighth, the UN model on governance can be applied to the most part to describe and explain the Company's corporate governance. Needless to say, this does not mean that the CC can 100% reveal its secret formula for making the most popular soft drink, coke.

---

[40] The Company has three principles, and one of them is Drink.

[41] He did not believe the idea of bottling would work, and he also did not have the start-up capital that would be required to set up bottling plants all over America. See http://www.jbwhitehead.org/resources_jbw.aspx, accessed on May 25, 2010 andhttp://www.coca-colaconversations.com/my_weblog/2008/07/when-coke-bottl.html accessed on May 26, 2010.

[42] The Company is engaged in the National Water Program of the United States Department of Agriculture (USDA).

[43] Conversation with D.P. Dash, dated April 12 and 20, 2010.

[44] The CC chairman and ceo is fully aware of this issue.

[45] The CC chairman and ceo mention this adjective in his November 2009 speech.

Ninth, not a single company can escape from not participating in a certain international regime. Would Kent be a second Candler, ignoring this author's bold idea, that is, start using the term, international regimes, and participate in more regimes, not just four?

Tenth, in the Chinese mainland, the Company launched a program, distributing 100,000 sets of playing cards with acquired immune deficiency syndrome (AIDS), tuberculosis, and malaria prevention information to migrant workers in areas where the incidence of disease is high. What about choose an alternative? The Coca-Cola Company's products in general and a bottle of coke itself are not related to regimes, because they cannot benefit all the people in the world, unless there is a regime-related message on each advertisement, bottle, can, or container. However, its contributions and grants to various international regimes, indeed, can benefit all the people in the world. As such, i(c)g can be used to theorize the CC's corporate performance.

Eleventh, the Company prides the fact that the popularity of Coca-Cola has made it truly universal. However, a distinction must be made, that is, not all international regimes are universal. For example, should pandas become extinct one day, human beings would not have to maintain or sustain the panda protection regime.

Last but not least, a word of suggestion can also be given here. The CC should mainly focus its contributions and grants on the Third World. Fundacion Privada Centre de Recerca Epidemiologia (FPCRE) received a grant of US$1,672,390 to conduct research on travel-related behaviors in Barcelona, Paris, Copenhagen, and Basel. This is a mistake, because those urban cities are well developed, if not rich. Besides, what does this kind of study have to do with behavioural changes from consumers and the business that supply them?[46] In this connection, in future, any applications from the Chinese mainland, except those from Xinjiang Uygur Autonomous Region (AR) and Xizang AR/Tibet should also be automatically declined, because the country has the highest foreign exchange reserves in the world, accumulating almost US$2.5 trillion for the first time in mid-2010. Needless to say, fewer financial contributions should be given to arts, because not all the people can be benefited by artistic works.

References

Allen, Frederick (1994), *Secret Formula: How Brilliant Marketing and Relentless Salesmanship Made Coca-Cola the Best-Known Product in the World,* New York: HarperBusiness.

Cheantham, Mike (1999), *"Your Friendly Neighbor": The Story of Georgia's Coca-Cola Bottling Families*, Macon, Ga.: Mercer University Press.

Daily, C. M., D. R. Dalton, and A. A. Canella, A.A. (July 2003) "Corporate Governance: Decades of Dialogue and Data," *Academy of Management Review*, Vol.28, No.3, pp. 371-382.

Davis, J. H., E. D. Schoorman, and L. Donaldson, L. (January 1997), "Toward a Stewardship Theory of Management," *Academy of Management Review*, Vol. 22, No. 1, pp.20-47.

Elliot, Charles (1982), *"Mr. Anonymous," Robert W. Woodruff of Coca-Cola*, Atlanta: Cherokee.

[46] This sentence is taken from Muhtar A. Kent's speech in December 2009.

Freeman, R. Edward (1984), *Strategic Management: A Stakeholder Approach* (Boston: Pitman).

Hayhole, Katharine and Andrew Farley, *A Climate for Change*, 2009, New York: Faith Words.

Hogan, James and Richard Littlemore (2009), *Climate Cover-up*, Vancouver, Canada: Greystone Books.

Huse, Morten (2007), *Boards, Governance and Value Creation: The Human Side of Corporate Governance* (Cambridge: Cambridge University Press).

Institute of Directors (2009), *The Handbook of International Corporate Governance: A Definitive Guide*, 2nd ed., London: Kogan Page.

Jensen, M. C. and W. H. Meckling (July 1976), "Theory of the Firm," *Journal of Financial Economics*, Vol.3, No.4, pp.305-360.

LUO, Yadong (March 2005), "Corporate Governance and Accountability in Multinational Enterprises: Concepts and Agenda," *Journal of International Management*, Vol.11, No.1, pp.1 - 18.

Mace, M. L. (1971), *Directors: Myth and Reality* (Cambridge, M.A.: Harvard University Press).

Pfeffer, Jeffrey (June 1972), "Size and Composition of Corporate Boards of Directors: The Organization and its Environment," *Administrative Science Quarterly*, Vol.17, No.2, pp.218-228.

Rarick, Charles A. Rarick (2003), *Cases and Exercises in International Business*, Upper Saddle River, NJ: Prentice Hall.

Samson, Danny A. and Richard L. Daft, *Fundamentals of Management*, third Asia Pacific Ed. (2009) (Victoria, Australia: Cengage Learning Australia).

Shiva, Vadana (2002), *Water Wars; Privatization, Pollution, and Profit*, New York: South End Press.

Shleifer, Andrei and Robert W. Vishny (June 1997), "A Survey of Corporate Governance," *The Journal of Finance*, Vol.LII, No.2, pp.737-783.

Yin, R.K., (2002), *Case Study Research, Design and Methods,* 3rd ed., Newbury Park, CA.: Sage Publications.

Yu, Peter K. H., "Do We Need to Discuss Legitimacy at All Levels?" paper presented at the International Conference on Legitimacy and Governance," Fudan Institute for Advanced Studies in Social Science, July 3-4, 2010, Fudan University, Shanghai, mainland China.

Id., forthcoming, *International Governance, Regimes, and Globalization: A Chinese (Communist) Perspective.*

Id., et. al., eds., (2010), *International Governance, Regimes, and Globalization: Case Studies from Beijing and Taipei,* Lanham, MD.: Lexington Books.

In: International (Corporate) Governance
Editor: Peter Kien-Hong Yu
ISBN: 978-1-61122-645-4

Chapter 8

NEAR-BANKRUPTCY OF THE TAIWAN HIGH SPEED RAIL CORPORATION: WHAT WENT WRONG?

Peter Kien-hong Yu and Jokull Johannesson

ABSTRACT

After a few delays, the Taiwan High Speed Rail (THSR), which is the largest current Build-Operate-Transfer (BOT) Railway Project in the world, with eight stations on the line connecting the metropolises of Taipei and Kaohsiung, began its passenger service in January 2007. However, by February 2009, it became very clear that the Taiwan area government must take over the THSR Corporation (THSRC) in one way or another, because the latter had already mired in enormous debts, loosing roughly two thirds of its capitalization. The THSR was only able to break even once in April 2008.

This paper spells out the major reasons behind the project's near-bankruptcy. Some questions will be posed: Who are involved? Who should be responsible for the failure? Should business entrepreneurs venture into High Speed Rail (HSR) projects in the future?

Keywords: Taiwan, BOT, turnkey, Taiwan High Speed Rail Corporation, business failure

1. INTRODUCTION

Build-Operate-Transfer (BOT)[1] refers to, depending on the context, approach, concept, formula, method, model, pattern, project, theme, etc. However, the concept has been in operation for centuries. BOT is a project financing and operating approach that has found an application primarily in the area of infrastructure privatization (Brown and Schmidt, 1999). [2]

---

[1] In Mandarin Chinese, it is *JianZhao, YingYung*, and *YiJiao*, respectively. For advantages and disadvantages, see John J. Wild, *et. al*, *International Business*, 4th ed. (Upper Saddle River, N.J.: Pearson and Prentice Hall, 2008), p.378.

[2] Brown, R. W., and Schmidt, P. (1999), BOT (Build, Operate and Transfer) an alternative to traditional data conversion and management, GISdevelopment.net ---> GITA 1999. Available from: http://www.gisdevelopment.net/proceedings/gita/1999/business/ba003pf.htm , accessed on May 8, 2010

For many countries, financial markets are shifting the way "debt capital is raised to fund the development of infrastructure. In the past, debt was raised directly from multilateral and export credit agencies or from sovereign governments themselves to provide turnkey financing. Recently, infrastructure developers have turned increasingly to portfolio-style credit in the form of capital pools, operating concessions and stand-alone utilities. This has changed the traditional contractor's role from being a service provider to being a business partner in the operation of the enterprise."[3] How does it work in the United States?

Most of the early turnpikes and canals in America are "operated on the principle that a grantor, usually but not always a government body, would offer an operating license to a concessionaire for a long term contract to develop and operate a transportation company with exclusive rights to a length of road or river. Over time, the concept was extended to include frontier postal services, local telephone services, electrical utilities and many municipal service functions such as land management. In this way, infrastructure upgrades were financed without public funding, and a method of long-term payback from operating revenues was established with a contract period deemed lengthy enough to make the operating concession a lucrative project."[4]

The expert continued by saying that "[in] the modern setting, a cash-strapped corporation, municipality, county or state will enter into a profit sharing agreement with a concessionaire. This profit sharing principle is the key aspect differentiating the BOT approach from the outsourcing arrangements commonly undertaken in the country. The concessionaire will operate as an independent business organization contractually accountable for a series of technical, operational and service related goals. The contract will often be setup such that the risk of revenue fluctuation is offset to the concessionaire by means of a fixed fee obligation to the owner. The upside to this arrangement, however, can be considerable if revenues are better than anticipated... ."[5]

A number of variations on the BOT theme has emerged from the experience of international infrastructure development, which differed mainly in the exact ownership and payment arrangement between the owner and the concessionaire on completion of the construction portion of the contract. The main approaches are summarized in Table 1:[6]

Due to rapid, changing trends, concepts like Build, Own, Operate, and Transfer (BOOT), Design, Build, Operate, and Transfer (DBOT), as well as Public-Private-Partnerships (PPP) (ZHAO and WANG)[7] have also been arisen in the outsourcing market. Needless to say, if things did not go smoothly, Build, Operate, Litigation (BOL) could surface.[8]

---

[3] *Ibid*

[4] http://www.gisdevelopment.net/proceedings/gita/1999/business/ba003pf.htm, accessed on May 8, 2010.

[5] *Ibid.*

[6] *Ibid.*

[7] See, for example, GuoFu ZHAO and ShouQing WANG, "Indicators of Social Impact Assessment for BOT/PPP Projects," http://management.kochi-tech.ac.jp/PDF/SOCIAL_MANAGEMENT_INFRA/SESSION_B4/smsri_29_Zhao.pdf, accessed on May 17, 2010.

[8] http://news.chinatimes.com/2007Cti/2007Cti-News/2007Cti-News-Content/0,4521,11051401+112009092600384,00,html, accessed on May 7, 2010. One example is that, filed in May 2005, the Taiwan High Speed Rail Corporation (THSRC)'s three-dimensional trademark failed to be accepted by the Taiwan area's Intellectual Property Office (TIPO) under the Ministry of Economic Affairs (MOEA), and, later, the Taipei High Administrative Court (THAC) in September 2007 endorsed TIPO's decision, because 700T lacks distinctiveness for registration purposes.

Table 1.

Build-Transfer-Operate	Build-Own-Operate	Build-Transfer-Operate	Build-Lease-Transfer
The contract will specify the upgrade and operation of the enterprise by the concessionaire for a fixed period of time followed by the transfer of all facilities and equipment back to the owner.	The concessionaire is essentially buying the basic facility in installments from the owner, with the facility and it's upgrades provided as security over the repayment period. On completion of the contract, ownership reverts to the concessionaire.	The concessionaire builds and transfers a facility to the owner but exclusively operates the facility on behalf of the owner by means of a management contract.	The concessionaire builds a facility, leases out the operating portion of the contract, and on completion of the contract, returns the facility to the owner.

Many of the Taiwan area government[9] officials are educated in the United States, such as MAO Chi-kuo, the incumbent Minister of Ministry of Transportation and Communications (MOTC) since May 2008 and the then second Director of the Preparatory/Preparation Office of the Bureau of High Speed Rail (BHSR) from September 1991 to March 1993.[10] Because of their past knowledge, training, and connections, one can assume that they would either encourage or propose to the government the novel, foreign BOT experience. To the people in the Taiwan area, it would mean that the private sector acquires permission to invest and set up the project. After a period of operation, the asset will be transferred to the government.[11]

1.1. Background of the High Speed Rail BOT in the Taiwan Area

The case study that we are discussing has to do with Taiwan Province's[12] BOT. An overall picture should be first given. It should be noted that Taiwan Island itself is well known for its rugged central mountainous terrain, which has restrained its migration and constrained the socio-economic growth mostly along the plains of the West coast areas or Western corridors, which has 94% of the island population.[13] The construction crosses 14 counties, 68 townships, and 32 urban planning districts. For years, in an effort to balance the development of northern Taiwan and southern Taiwan, which is about the same distance as New York City and Washington, D.C., demand for North-South intercity transportation and regional daily commuting and business trips began to be vocal. In response, the Taiwan High Speed Rail Corporation (THSRC) mapped out a strategy to form the THSR as the longitude,

[9] The official name of the Taiwan area is Republic of China (ROC).

[10] http://www.motc.gov.tw/mocwebGIP/wSite/ct?xItem=4266&ctNode=203&mp=2, accessed on May 20, 2010.

[11] http://www.hsr.gov.tw/homepage.nsf/beff9cd4905e8649482569210010e4a3/76ee4cc04fed6f13482570a100149a79!OpenDocument, accessed on May 10, 2010.

[12] Mainland China has a total of 6,552 kilometers high speed rail done for commercial operation (new lines plus upgraded old lines, ranking number one in the world, as of March 2010.

[13] http://www.skyscrapercity.com/showthread.php?t=367080, accessed on May 7, 2010.

and the district mass transit as the latitude, thereby becoming a public transit web and smaller trains and local buses will link the new stations to downtown.[14]

However, the construction engineers had to overcome many problems at several locations, for example, the Yunlin County section, where the elevated railway crosses Provincial Expressway No.78 in the county that has subsided by 55 centimeters over the past seven years.[15] As another example, at the southern section, the THSRC had to build 157-kilometer continuous viaduct, which is the longest elevated structure in the world.[16] Even before the operation, a series of commercial disputes "…has produced a remarkable hodgepodge: French and German train drivers who are allowed to speak only English with Taiwanese traffic controllers while operating Japanese bullet trains on tracks originally designed by British and French engineers."[17]

Informal planning began as early as the 1970s.[18] The first formal plan by the Ministry of Transportation and Communications' Preparatory Office of the BHSR for a 345-kilometer (207-mile) High Speed Rail (HSR) line, which has 48-kilometer tunnels along the way, linking the metropolises of Taipei and Kaohsiung began in July 1990. They were then approved by the Executive *Yuan* (equivalent to the cabinet) in June 1992 and the Legislative *Yuan* (branch) in July 1993. However, the latter scrapped the national budget for building the HSR line and stipulated the BOT method. In December 1994, the Encouragement/promotion of Private Participation in Transportation Infrastructure Projects Statute, stating the required rules and policies for the project including a clause saying the government can take over a BOT project, was passed by the Legislative *Yuan*. A tender invitation for Private Participation in Construction and Operation of Taiwan North-South HSR Project was thus made by the government in October 1996.[19]

Later, in a prolonged bidding process, the Taiwan HSR Consortium (THSRC) ran against the Chunghwa/Chinese HSR Consortium (CHSRC). The THSRC's bid was based on the hyper-modern technology platform of Eurotrain, a joint venture of General Electric Company (GEC)-Alsthom and Siemens AG, while CHSRC's bid was based on the *Shinkansen* [new main line (also known as the bullet train since October 1964)] technology of Japan. THSRC also promised to build the line entirely from private capital. In September 1996, the THSRC was selected the best applicant. The group, as the concessionaire, was renamed and formally incorporated with the same acronym, THSRC, in May 1998. Two months later, the literally BOT agreements were signed between the MOTC and the THSRC, which granted the latter a concession to finance, construct, and operate the HSR System for a period of 35 years and a concession for ultra-modern, attractive HSR station area development for a period of 50 years. In September 1999, there was a big earthquake in the Taiwan Island, which prompted the issuance of contracts of the civil infrastructure works, due to the concern of the design and construction methods. In March 2000, the first contract of the civil works was awarded and the construction of the HSR began. The Roll-out Ceremony for the sleek, bulbous-nosed THSR 700T trains took place in January 2004 at Kobe, Japan, marking the first time that the

[14] http://library.taiwanschoolnet.org/gsh2009/gsh5568/, accessed on May 7, 2010 andhttp://www.nytimes.com/2007/01/04/world/asia/04taipei.html, accessed on May 7, 2010.
[15] http://www.taipeitimes.com/News/taiwan/archives/2010/04/03/200346921, accessed on May 7, 2010.
[16] http://finderarticles.com/articles/ml_m0BQQ/is_11_46/ai_n26709598//, accessed on May 7, 2010.
[17] http://www.nytimes.com/2007/01/04/world/asia/04taipei.html, accessed on May 7, 2010.
[18] http://finderarticles.com/articles/ml_m0BQQ/is_11_46/ai_n26709598//, accessed on May 7, 2010 and http://en.wikipedia.org/wiki/Taiwan_High_Speed_Rail, accessed on May 8, 2010.
[19] http://www.skyscrapercity.com/showthread.php?t=367080, accessed on May 7, 2010.

Shinkasen exported its system to a foreign country. In January 2007, the futuristic train, run at maximum speeds of 300 kilometers (186 miles) per hour, began to welcome the first paying passengers for test rides. In the following month, normal operations officially began.

As it turned out, by February 2009, what was meant to be a source of pride, for example, holding the world record for having longest viaduct at 157.3 kilometers from Baguashan, a mountain park, in Zhanghua County to Zuoying District in Kaohsiung Municipal City,[20] had turned into a rich source of embarrassment, incurring enormous debts, which amounted to NT$70.2 billion (US$2.1 billion) in losses or roughly two thirds of its capitalization.[21] The corporation is supposed to start paying back the syndicate loan from 2009 to 2022. Yet, it is only able to pay back the interests.[22] Because the THSRC was unsuccessful, it is necessary for us to find out who should likely be accountable for the whole mess.

2. Who Should be Accountable?

There are several key players throughout the development. The first key player is the Taiwan area government. The second one is the original five shareholders of the THSRC, namely, Continental Engineering Corporation (CEC), Pacific Electric Wire and Cable Company (PEWC), Evergreen International Corporation (Evergreen), TECO Electric and Machinery Company (TECO Group), and Taipei Fubon Commercial Bank Company (TaipeiFubon). The third one can be regarded as the contractors, who can, in turn, *inter alia*, convince or endorse the multilateral and export credit agencies, bank creditor, or from sovereign governments themselves to provide turnkey financing. Last but not least, passengers and consumers (or consumer advocates) or even experts on BOT and tax-payers can be regarded as another key player.

2.1. The First Player's Fault: Government

It is not difficult to find fault with the government. First, some talk show guests in the Taiwan area accused the second player for setting up the *pianju* (hoax/fraud/swindle).[23] If so, did any central, provincial, and local officials or elected officials get personal gains or benefits or were they concerned with the integrity of HSR projections, including (commuter) ridership, costs, revenues, and associated public benefits? We can pose this question by simply citing the following three sentences: "California seems certain to leverage private funds for its $40 billion-plus high-speed rail project. But just how much can it demand from for-profit sources? And who will benefit?"[24] Another analogy has to do with the Union of Myanmar (UOM). In a March 2010 report, readers were told that even the military junta in the UOM, which imposed martial law and which seized state power in August 1988, has taken in the past six months steps to privatize the nation, trying to sell off about 250 petrol

[20] http://wapedia.cobi/en/Taiwan_High_Speed_Rail, accessed on May 7, 2010.

[21] *Borneo Post* (hereinafter BP)(Sarawak, Malaysia), September 28, 2010, p.B3. One writer say it could even be double of that. See *ShiHua Daily News* (hereinafter SHDN)(Sarawak, Malaysia), September 26, 2009, p.8.

[22] *SHDN*, September 25, 2009, p.11.

[23] *Ibid.*, September 26, 2009, p.8.

[24] http://www.thetransportpolitic.com/category/places/california-high-speed-rail/. accessed on May 7, 2010.

stations, four ports, and state-owned buildings including warehouses and cinemas. However, the following tough questions were raised: Does the military regime want to reform the economy or to take profits before the 2010 multi-party general elections, which was scheduled in November of the same year?[25] Perhaps one can make similar assertions about the government officials and politicians in the Taiwan area.

Second, early on, it was not clear how much it would cost to be able to operate the system and how serious construction cost overruns would be. The THSRC's website mentioned US$18 billion, making the project undoubtedly the largest privately managed and funded BOT project in the world at the time on initiation and perhaps even by June 2006.[26] Other sources, such as the January 4, 2007 report by the Associated Press (AP), mentioned US$15 billion.[27] The amount of money certainly included compensation for requisition of private land and resettlement for residents of demolished houses.

Third, in April 2009, if not earlier, the then THSRC chairwoman, Nita C. ING, began to sense that she might have to step down.[28] In September 2009, analysts were asking how would the government initiate a takeover, as it did two months later? Would it attempt to control the majority of the board of directors, given the fact that even the government is in financial difficulties plus the fact that, in the words of anonymous MOTC officials, it is incapable of running the THSRC as a state-run business at the moment?[29] For example, the executives of a government-run company could not possibly have annual salaries in the NT$10 million (US$330,000), as more than 20 incumbent THSRC executives, out of more than 3,000 employees, receive.[30] In other words, when talented individuals resign from the corporation due to a reduction in their salary, would this invite safety problems?

A related question must be posed: Was the government proactive? The answer is no. For example, in September 2009, chairperson of the Board of Directors of the Bank of Taiwan (BT), Susan S. Chang, said by October of the same year the debt-ridden THSRC can secure new funding as part of efforts to pay off earlier loans.[31] Yet, it was not until January 2010 that a NT$382 billion (US$12 billion) syndicated loan at an interest rate below 1.8% was signed to enable the THSRC to pay off existing loans, which were obtained at higher interest levels during the project's construction, thereby enabling the same corporation to save NT$2 billion per year.[32]

Fourth, several government or semi-official agencies and joint ventures were forced to contribute money to the THSRC, especially under the CHEN Shui-bian regime. For example, Aerospace Industrial Development Corporation (AIDC) had to invest by buying preferred shares, as opposed to common shares, amounting to NT$4.5 billion.[33] As another example, Taiwan Financial Holdings Group (TFHG), the parent of Bank of Taiwan, also bought preferred shares. Would that make the THSRC complacent, thinking that no matter what the government will have to make sure that the corporation is solvent?

---

[25] *BP*, March 15, 2010, p.B2.

[26] http://www.skyscrapercity.com/showthread.php?t=367080, accessed on May 7, 2010.

[27] Other figures include US$12.5 billion, US$16 billion, and NT$420 billion. The exchange rate is roughly US$1 = NT$33.

[28] TVBS, 2100 program (Taiwan, R.O.C.), dated September 21, 2009 at 9 pm.

[29] http://taiwantoday.tw/fp.asp?xitem=65921&CtNode=452, accessed on May 7, 2010.

[30] *SHDN*, September 25, 2009, p.11.

[31] *Ibid.*

[32] *BP*, January 11, 2010, p.B4 and http://www,mb.com.ph/articles/230499/taiwan-high-speed-train-company-refinance-debt, accessed on May 7, 2010.

[33] http://udn.com/NEWS/NATIONAL/NAT5/5115411.shtml. accessed on May 7, 2010.

Fifth, domestic politics was certainly involved. ING said: "I can't tell you how many people we offended from the south to the north. Out of concern for my security, one director told me, 'You have too many enemies. You will always be a target here.' From the time the project began, we have never given anything to any elected official," adding her own company since her father's days has never gotten involved with the government and the ING family had always steered clear of politics (WU and CHEN, 2009).[34]

It goes without saying that international politics was also involved. In October 1997, the Eurotrain consortium was declared the preferred bidder to supply trains and equipment and execute the actual construction. However, in December 1999, the THSRC instead chose the Japanese bidder, signing a memorandum of understanding (MOU). It goes without saying that Siemens and Alstom protested. However, their protest was also rejected by the High Court in the Taiwan area. Nevertheless, the THSRC in November 2004 agreed to pay US$65 million in compensation to the Eurotrain consortium, which in February 2001 filed a damage claim to the Singapore International Arbitration Centre (SIAC).[35] The reason is simple and straightforward, the Taiwan area needs help from Japan more than it needs assistance from European countries, so as to deter mainland China's military threat or attack or thwart the mainland's peaceful plan for the Chinese reunification.

Sixth, did the government have a strategy to try to help the four domestic airline companies and other transportation companies, such as conventional train and long-distance bus,[36] which obviously have to scale back their service, thereby inevitably becoming the main casualty? To be sure, at least one old airline company closed its doors in May 2008, after a chain of financial crises.

2.2. The Second Player's Fault: Original Shareholders

Again, a number of faults by the original shareholders can be easily cited. First, there was uncertainty all along in the minds of the original shareholders, who only took a chance to play the game. It is fair to say that, on the one hand, they were gambling and they feel that they have nothing to lose. On the other hand, they can always award the sub-contracts for core systems, trains, electrification, signalling, and other electric and mechanical systems to local companies that they have been associated with. There were also loopholes in the contract. Thus, in September 2009, ING reportedly asked for a compensation of NT$5 billion (US$1 = NT$32.5) for her loss from the government. If she gets the compensation, would she be richer than before, when she was in charge of the BOT?

Second, the second player had a bit of confidence but they are not fully sure whether they can operate the rail for 35 years. They can only tout for the best case scenario--being able to make at least a modest profit. In November 2006, the THSRC said it expected to be profitable by its second year and to break even 12 months after its first commercial operation, adding "[t]he plan is to manage returns from the investments after 16 years from construction."[37] So,

[34] Yin-chuen WU and Yi-Shan CHEN, "Nita ING Bows Out," *Commonwealth Magazine*, No.431 (September 24, 2009), http://english.cw.com.tw/article.do?action=show&id=11373, accessed on May 10, 2010.

[35] http://wapedia.mobi/en/Taiwan_High_Speed_Rail, accessed on May 7, 2010.

[36] http://life.chinatimes.com/2009Cti/Channel/Life/life-article/0,5047,11051801+112009111300042,00,focus.html, accessed on May 7, 2010.

[37] http://www.forbes.com/feeds/afx/2006/11/30/afx3215855.html, accessed on May 7, 2010.

their logic was simple and straightforward: Live day by day and make as much profit as possible, and, in the worst case scenario, they just have to choose not to serve in the board of directors, so long as they are clean. Besides, they can assure the government and the public that they will only commission the best experts, for example, Mott MacDonald and Moh & Associates, which can provide a comprehensive asset management strategy for the project's civil infrastructure, such as engineering for the inspection and maintenance, procedures and people competencies, as well as guidance on the inspection process itself.[38]

Third, they would usually only say good things about the THSR system, such as relief of traffic congestion, saving energy, and preserving the environment, as if the win-win scenario can materialize. Did the original shareholders of the THSRC mention to the public that the short Paris-Lyon and Tokyo-Osaka routes are the only ones in the world that have broken even?[39] It goes without saying that the original shareholders would not challenge the planners' (erratic) prediction of the projected passengers--280,000[40] each day, as opposed to a mere 87,000 in September 2009. In January 2010, we see an increase in the daily number of passengers, averaging 93,000, which represents an average seat use rate of about 46%.[41] What about the corporation, which in May 2008, aimed for a maximum of 145,000 trips per day by 2033.[42] However, it should be noted that ING herself admitted in September 2009 that the government, indeed, inflated the estimates to make the railway more attractive to investors (WU and CHEN, 2009).[43]

Fourth, estimates by the government's Council of Economic Planning and Development (CEPD) also painted a rosy picture, that is, the construction of the HSR network can create 480,000 jobs and may contribute 1% point to economic growth,[44] including property developments surrounding the bullet train stations and depots.

The operations of the THSR system had been re-scheduled a few times. A government newspaper mentioned October 2005 as the original launching date. However, a delay in the completion of the project's core electrical systems forced a further delay to October 2006.[45] On November 30, 2006, Lloyd's Register issues a safety certification. The corporation also cancelled a December 7, 2006 opening ceremony, after the government said further tests were necessary before the HSR system could be in commercial operation.[46] Finally, on January 5, 2007, the high-speed train was opened to paying passengers.

---

[38] http://www.railways.mottmac.com/projects/?mode=type&id=121502, accessed on May 7, 2010.

[39] http://www.newsgeography.com/content/001344-high-speed-rail-towar-least-worst-projections, accessed on May 7, 2010.

[40] Another source mentioned "carry up to 300,000 passengers." See http://findarticles.com/p/articles/mi_m0BQQ/is 11 46/ai n26709598/. accessed on May 7, 2010.

[41] http://focustaiwan.tw/ShowNews/WebNews_Detail.aspx?ID=201004260038&Type=aSOC, accessed on May 7, 2010. The Council for Economic Planning and Development (CEPD) passed a construction proposal to add four new stations to the system by 2015, so as to increase ridership by about 5%.

[42] http://www.reuters.com/asets/print?aid=USTP18201520080527, accessed on May 7, 2010.

[43] Yin-chuen WU, Yi-Shan CHEN, "Nita ING Bows Out," *Commonwealth Magazine*, No.431 (September 24, 2009), http://english.cw.com.tw/article.do?action=show&id=11373, accessed on May 10, 2010.

[44] http://www.forbes.com/feeds/afx/2006/11/30/afx3215855.html, accessed on May 7, 2010.

[45] http://washingtonpost.com/wp-dyn/content/article/2007/01/04/AR200710400255.html, accessed on May 7, 2010.

[46] *Ibid.*

2.3. The Third Player's Fault: Contractors

From the available source materials, the third player, the contractors, have been involved in the least. So long as the original shareholders of THSRC can initiate the move to find experienced, trusted, and internationally well-known consortiums, such as Japan's Mitsubishi Heavy Industries (MHI), Ltd. and Sumitomo Mitsui Banking Corporation (SMBC), bankers, both at home and abroad, can be easily persuaded, even though, on top of their head, they know that capital-intensive, credit environment of international infrastructure development is highly risky (Flyvbjerg, 2003 and Cox, 2006).[47] To be sure, some of the consortiums may even promise to provide soft loans with very low interest rates, only to charge higher service fees later on, so as to make up for the loss. This is a standard practice in almost every industry.

2.4. The Fourth Player's Fault: Consumers

The THSRC lost a lot of money, after less than two years' operations. In the context of the Taiwan area's foreign exchange reserve,[48] it may not mean much. What this means is that each tax-payer has to foot the bill. Before awarding the project to the THSRC, the Legislative *Yuan* withdrew the budget allocated to the HSR, as mentioned earlier. It seems to be a relief to the tax-payers at that point in time. However, it turned out that, after the mass media began to publicize the near-bankruptcy of the THSRC, the government had to absorb more loss, tangible and intangible. According to one report, the total cost of the HSR project grew, and critics pointed out that the cost meant about US$650 for every man, woman, and child in the Taiwan area.[49] What are some of the faults?

First, we learned from a news report that the Taipei-based Taiwan Institute of Economic Research (TIER) does have experts on BOT.[50] What did the experts on BOT have to say? Did their opinion made a strong impact on the government and so on and so forth?

Some research outputs can be easily accessed. In early 21st century, knowing that the double-track railway line runs through an extremely active seismic area, Ming-fu CHANG, *et. al.* wrote about the sealing work under difficult conditions in seismically affected ground, such as the Linkou tunnel.[51] Another research paper or scenario analysis introduced the financial model used by the BHSR for its BOT projects, presenting the parameters, such as debt/equity ratio, and variables, such as annual operating income and affiliated business income in the operating period, of the model, taking account of the investment proportions of the government and the concessionaire, the concession period, and other items featured in BOT projects, as well as discussing the model's basic assumptions, input data, cost

---

[47] http://www.gisdevelopment.net/proceedings/gita/1999/business/ba003pf.htm, accessed on May 8, 2010. See also Bent Flyvbjerg, *et. al.*, *Megaprojects and Risks: An Anatomy of Ambition* (Cambridge: Cambridge University Press, 2003) and Wendell Cox, *War on the Dream: How Anti-Sprawl Policy Threatens the Quality of Life* (Bloomington, IN.: iUniverse, Inc., 2006).

[48] As of April 2010, mainland China has the most foreign exchange reserve, to be following by Japan, Federation of Russia (FR), the Taiwan area, Republic of India (ROI), Republic of Korea (ROK), and Hongkong.

[49] http://wapedia.mobi/en/Taiwan_High_Speed_Rail, accessed on May 7, 2010. According to the June 9, 2009 issue of *ShangYeZhouKan* (Taipei), it is NT$17,000 per person in the Taiwan area, and the government could have used the money to build six 101 buildings in Taipei Municipal City.

[50] *BP*, September 28, 2009, p.B3.

[51] http://www.gquadrat.de/media/get_foto.php?id=33, accessed on May 7, 2010.

requirement, self-financing ability analysis, financial statements, and indices (CHANG and CHEN, 2001).[52] An ex post cost-benefit analysis of the HSR system including several policy suggestions was also conducted.[53] Studies have also been made in full detail with special discussion on major issues encountered during the design works for one of the special bridges. In addition, seismic design had been considered particularly critical for HSR structures, and it was based on an earthquake with a return period of 950 years.[54] For the record, the THSRC organized the HSR in Asia Symposium and the Recognition and Appreciation Ceremony in October 2007 in Taipei, sharing its experience with transport officials at home and abroad; system providers, suppliers, and operators; contractors; consultants; and investment bankers, as if private funding to the transport projects can be replicated elsewhere in the world, with success. The related problem is that many legislators, bankers, etc. are not experts on BOT, engineering, and other related matters. So, how can they pin point the real problems?

Second, riders or commuters are actually powerless, because of lack of information from the experts and agencies responsible for reporting to the public. Therefore, commuters can only complain, if something went wrong. The THSR system encountered some operational problems, such as lingering safety concerns and embarrassing, widespread technical ticket glitches, plus the fact that some ticket buyers could not swipe their credit cards. In March 2010, a Richter scale 6.4 earthquake jolted Taiwan, and one of the THSRC's lead cars was derailed. In April 2010, a driver, while operating the bullet train, was found to be overdosed with sleeping pills.[55] The THSRC people in charge can only apologize to the passengers and/or make refunds.

Third, needless to say, some consumers, who choose not to heed what the chairman of the Consumers' Foundation Chinese Taipei (CFCT) had said--cherish your life, don't be a guinea pig, until extensive safety data has been released[56] – are happy that, as a result of having the HSR system, the people of Taiwan Island can live in an "one-day peripheral circle" or "one-day community,"[57] meaning that a housewife can take the train in the morning from Kaohsiung to Taipei, so as to eat a delicious bowl of beef noodle or visit a close friend as well as come back before dinner time, without rush. If one were to take a slower train, it would usually mean four or five hours. And, if one drives a car, normally, one has to be on the wheel for six hours or more, if there was a car accident on the superhighway.

---

[52] See Luh-Maan CHANG and Po-Han CHEN, "BOT Financial Model: Taiwan High Speed Rail Case," *Journal of Construction Engineering and Management*, Vol.127, No.3 (May/June 2001), pp.214-222.

[53] Yung-hsiang CHENG, "High-speed Rail in Taiwan: New Experience and Issues of Future Development." See http://www.sciencedirect.com/science/article/B6VGG-4XM6N9T-1/2/f006e0c3311300f3ee5ea15a806baf, accessed on May 7, 2010.

[54] http://www.maa.com.tw/common/publications/2000/2000-067.pdf, accessed on May 7, 2010.

[55] http://news.chinatimes.com/focus/0,5243,50105318x112010051100133,00.html, accessed on May 11, 2010.

[56] http://www.nytimes.com/2007/01/04/world/asia/04taipei.html, accessed on May 7, 2010. Incomplete data can affect assessments of the locations of temblors' epicentres and would undermine the ability of the early warning system to perform its proper functions. See http://taiwantoday.tw/ct.asp?xItem=95614&ctNode=413, accessed on May 7, 2010. In May 2010, it was confirmed that a driver of the bullet train in April 2010 was overdosed with sleeping pills. See http://news.chinatimes.com/focus/0,5243,50105318x11201005 1100133,00.html, accessed on May 11, 2010.

[57] On June 14, 2010, direct flight between Taipei Municipality's Taipei Songshan Airport and Shanghai Hongqiao International Airport began. This cuts short the distance between the two cities.

3. CONCLUSION

Lessons should be learned from this case study, because another BOT project, the Kaohsiung Metro, which capitalized at NT$10 billion and which opened service in March 2008, is also in trouble since September 2009, already losing 60% of its paid-in capital or NT$6 billion, when CHUANG Chi-wang, speaker of the Kaohsiung City Council (KCC), said that the Kaohsiung Mayor must get ready to take over the ailing Kaohsiung Rapid Transit Corporation (KRTC) by the end of 2009.[58]

First, there is no guarantee that all BOT projects can be successful. ING in September 2009 began to, in public, blame the government, for being untrustworthy and consistent (WU and CHEN, 2009).[59] Yet, there are always some entrepreneurs coupled with government officials and politicians who want to take risks, if the government has made promises again.

In April 2009, the Barack H. Obama, II administration initially released an outline for a national 10 high-speed rail corridors across the United States. In January 2010, Obama at the State of Union speech announced the program, and, a day later, he said the federal government will spend $8 billion developing the nationwide high-speed train system, probably using Japan's latest N-700-I system, a variant of the 700 Series *Shinkansen* and an investment which is much needed to help spur long-term economic growth and which will be funded through the government's US$862 billion economic stimulus package.[60] In the same month, a HSR Seminar, Kawasaki's High Speed Train Technology and Contributions to the US Society, was held in Washington, D.C. In May 2010, The American Transportation Secretary took a test ride on Japan's super-fast magnetic train. However, would the United States repeat the THSRC's near-bankruptcy blunder? The following citation should be remembered: "The recent failure of Taiwan High-Speed Rail raises questions about the role of private investment in new trains systems. The California High-Speed Rail Authority projects that it will need about 33 billion in 2008 dollars to complete its initial San Francisco-Anaheim link, a reasonable estimate considering the cost of peer systems. In addition to the 9 billion in state funds devoted to the project by last November's referendum, the Authority is banking on $2-3 billion in local money and $12-16 billion in federal contributions," adding "[b]ecause this aid won't be enough to cover the full costs of the line."[61]

If not, would the American aviation industry be hurt, because, once in full operation, lesser people would take the airplanes or even drive. In this connection, America can cut use of oil by 125 million barrels a year, says Rob McCulloch, transportation advocate for Environment America, a citizen-based environmental advocacy group.[62]

Another lesson is that, in all phases, everything must be transparent. A sanctions regime must be set up, so as to monitor as much as possible the whole development, including various community-centered arrangements. This applies to the period after the transfer of

---

[58] Http://www.chinapost.com.tw/business/asia/b-taiwan/2009/09/25/226072/Kaohsiung-Metro.htm, accessed on May 7, 2010.

[59] Yin-chuen WU, Yi-Shan CHEN, "Nita ING Bows Out," *Commonwealth Magazine*, No.431 (September 24, 2009), http://english.cw.com.tw/article.do?action=show&id=11373, accessed on May 10, 2010.

[60] http://edition.cnn.com/2010/POLITICS/01/28/obama.trains/index.html, accessed on May 8, 2010. In May 2010, it was reported that California may buy high speed rail system from mainland China.

[61] http://www.thetransportpolitic.com/category/places/california-high-speed-rail/. accessed on May 7, 2010.

[62] http://www.csmonitor.com/USA/Politics/2010/0128/Obama-s-high-speed-rail-plan-Which-states-get-the-money, accessed on May 8, 2010.

operation from the government to the private owners, so that officials will not be erroneously regarded as corrupt and business people, villains.

Some findings can be noted. First, it is a human tendency to blame others first. Whether the HSR is in the hands of the government or privately run, some day, somehow, the system will malfunction. So, blame can be easily lodged. If blaming is the name of the game, should we blame harshly on each key player in this case study? It is not necessary, because business failure is very common. According to observation, nine out of ten businesses fail. Besides, the passengers and consumers should be blamed the least, because they are like a heap of sand, unable to stick together like clay.

Second, ING said she indirectly felt deceived by the Government, emphasizing "we were too naïve" (WU and CHEN, 2009).[63] In human affairs, we often see conspiracy theories (Haniff Hassan and Redzuan Salleh, 2010),[64] hoax,[65] etc. Many audiences have also watched the movie, *The Sting*. The authors believe that none of them can be applied 100% to the THSRC case. There are simply too many things beyond the ability of an individual or a small group to conspire, command, and ultimately control the whole operation.

Third, why did not the THSRC declare bankruptcy? Trying to preserve the government's face may have played an important role. The premier may have to step down, to take the final responsibility. Thus, the government could not allow the corporation to declare a worst-case scenario – default on loans, and there is consensus on the matter between MAO and ING. The former said, after becoming the minister in May 2008, he had talked to ING in person about five or six times.[66]

Fourth, not all government officials were corrupt, because ING mentioned that "[o]ur original shareholders invested in the project based on a package of incentives that lured them on board. Later, the government said it was unable to help, because such assistance would constitute graft."[67] Sometimes, the original shareholders were wrongly blamed, because it is difficult to engage in land speculation and because the government is by far the biggest landowner.[68]

Last but not least, there is one potential issue, which remains to be seen, that is, would mainland China, with a huge foreign exchange reserve, ranking number one in the world, take over the HSR system one day, as one ruling party legislator guessed, in which the financial obligations will be its responsibility?[69]

---

63 Yin-chuen WU, Yi-Shan CHEN, "Nita ING Bows Out," *Commonwealth Magazine*, No.431 (September 24, 2009), http://english.cw.com.tw/article.do?action=show&id=11373, accessed on May 10, 2010.

64 See, for example, Muhammad Haniff Hassan and Mohamed Redzuan Salleh, "911 Conspiracy Theories: The Absent Perspectives," *RSIS Commentaries*, No.46 (May 7, 2010), three pages.

65 Some argue that the United States did not land on the moon in the late 1960s.

66 *SHDN*, September 23, 2010, p.11.

67 Yin-chuen WU, Yi-Shan CHEN, "Nita ING Bows Out," *Commonwealth Magazine*, No.431 (September 24, 2009), http://english.cw.com.tw/article.do?action=show&id=11373, accessed on May 10, 2010.

68 *Ibid.*

69 http://news.chinatimes.com/2007Cti/2007Cti-News/2007Cti-News-Content/0,4521,50102535+112009090300068,00,focus.html, accessed on May 7, 2010. In the year 2010, mainland China will invest 700 billion *yuan* (US$102 billion) in high speed rail construction. By the end of the year, it should have over 11,000 kilometers of high speed track in operation, up from just over 6,500 kilometers. See *BP*, June 8, 2010, p.B16.

REFERENCES

Reference to a Journal Publication

CHANG, Luh-Maan and Po-Han CHEN (May/June 2001), "BOT Financial Model: Taiwan High Speed Rail Case," *Journal of Construction Engineering and Management*, Vol.127, No.3, pp.214-222.

Hassan, Muhammad Haniff and Mohamed Redzuan Salleh (May 7, 2010), "911 Conspiracy Theories: The Absent Perspectives," *RSIS Commentaries*, No.46, three pages.

Reference to a Book

Cox, Wendell, *War on the Dream: How Anti-Sprawl Policy Threatens the Quality of Life* (Bloomington, IN.: iUniverse, Inc., 2006).

Flyvbjerg, Bent, *et. al.*, *Megaprojects and Risks: An Anatomy of Ambition* (Cambridge: Cambridge University Press, 2003).

Wild, John J., *et. al*, *International Business*, 4th ed. (Upper Saddle River, N.J.: Pearson and Prentice Hall, 2008).

Reference to a Web Source

Chang, Ming-fu, *et. al.*, http://www.gquadrat.de/media/get_foto.php?id=33, accessed on May 7, 2010.

Cheng, Yung-hsiang, "High-speed Rail in Taiwan: New Experience and issues of Future Development," online.

Wu, Yin-chuen and Yi-Shan CHEN, "Nita ING Bows Out," *Commonwealth Magazine*, No.431 (September 24, 2009), online.

Zhao, GuoFu and ShouQing WANG, "Indicators of Social Impact Assessment for BOT/PPP Projects," http://management.kochi-tech.ac.jp/PDF/SOCIAL_MANAGEMENT_INFRA/SESSION_B4/smsri_29_Zhao.pdf, accessed on May 17, 2010.

In: International (Corporate) Governance
Editor: Peter Kien-Hong Yu
ISBN: 978-1-61122-645-4

Chapter 9

BUSINESS SUCCESS AND FAILURE: MALAYSIAN BUMIPUTRAS AND NON-BUMIPUTRAS

Peter Kien-Hong Yu, Jawed A. Mohammed and Jokull Johannesson

ABSTRACT

This paper explores some of the reasons and factors for Bumiputras and Non-Bumiputras' success and failure in doing business in Malaysia in general and the State of Sarawak in particular.

Depending on the section, it is both inductive and deductive. A model and theory will be applied to describe and explain the seemingly contradictory relationship between success and failure, Bumi and non-Bumi, etc., so as to help readers to conceptualize everything. As a sequel, a survey, subject to approval and funding, has been planned to test whether or not the qualitative analysis is rigorous and valid.

The major finding is that when it comes to business, the government can indirectly help Bumi in general and non-Bumi in particular to compete, for example, globally.

The attempt to rationalize seemingly contradictory relationships logically in terms of the *Yin* and *Yang* diagram is new. In addition, not many literature is related to Sarawak.

Keywords: business, Bumiputras, non-Bumiputras, Malaysia, success and failure

Malaysia is big, with diverse socio-cultural and racial/ethnic groups and regions. Usually, we talk in terms of the following regions: Sarawak (East Malaysia), Sabah (East Malaysia), and the southern, northern, and east coast regions of West or Peninsula Malaysia.

In this case study of mainly the State of Sarawak in general and Kuching, Sibu, and Miri in particular,[1] with occasional mentioning of examples taken from elsewhere, we will focus

[1] There are many secondary towns in the Sarawak state, such as Mukah, Serian, Marudi, Lawas, Betong, and Sri Aman. Other isolated, smaller towns are Kapit, Kanowit, Long Lama, Belaga, and Limbang. When the

on the Bumiputras,[2] namely, the Malays, who constitute about 60% of the total population, and indigenous people, such as Organg Asli and Orang Ulu,[3] and Lun Bawang as well as the non-Bumiputras, to wit, Chinese and Indians, although there are not many Indians living in Sarawak and Sabah.[4]

At political functions, usually only the Malays, Chinese, and/or Indians were mentioned. For example, on the parliamentary by-election polling day in April 2010, Deputy Prime Minister Tan Sri Muhyiddin Yassin, said all voters in the Hulu Selangor constituency were important as they were "kings" who would determine the ruling party, Barisan Nasional (BN),'s fate, adding "[w]e will not segregate the Malay, Chinese or Indian voters in our campaign."[5] What about business? It seems to be the same.

The mass media in the country is somewhat controlled by the Federal Government[6] for the sake of, to some political observers, maintaining peace and tranquillity. However, when it comes to reporting on business matters, the newspapers and related mass media in both English and non-English are candid, honest, etc. Occasionally, newspapers such as *Borneo Post* (BP) would conduct interviews and surveys to find out the truth.[7] Therefore, it is quite balanced to say that we can mainly first rely on them to conduct a content analysis on Bumi and Non-Bumi's success and failure, while doing their business, especially in Sarawak.

This paper is divided into five sections. In the first section, we will identify reasons and factors for Bumi and Non-Bumi's success in doing business. In the second section, reasons and factors for their failure will be pointed out. In the third section, we will discuss reasons and factors under wait-and-see. By that, we mean sometimes either success or failure cannot be treated as 100%. There could be ambiguous reasons and factors, which fall somewhere in between the extremes of success and failure, fertilizing or cross-cutting each other. In the fourth section, we will argue that it is a mistake to merely talk about the reasons and factors for success or failure in doing business. Therefore, we will apply the *Yin* and *Yang* diagram to describe and explain, for example, their relationship at the macro-level, so as to see whether or not they can cooperate and coordinate to bring about further success and to refrain from making or repeating mistakes, resulting in possible business failures. In the concluding section, we will highlight the major findings.

---

proposed Sarawak Corridor of Renewable Energy (SCORE) can be implemented, those isolated, smaller towns could move ahead.

[2] There are eight criteria that one must meet to be qualified or deemed as a Bumiputra: Firstly one must be a citizen; secondly, domiciles in Sarawak; knows the language of the community applying for; married to a Bumi, and their marriage must be more than five years; knows the local law and custom of the community; has own house (for those in a village) or "bilek" (for longhouse); has continuous relationship with the people of the community; and the wife or the mother must be a native of Sarawak. See *Borneo Post* (hereinafter BP)(Sarawak, Malaysia),April 16, 2010, p.D2.

[3] The Sultan of Perak said his state has the second highest number of Orang Asli, that is, 54,416 people or 38.5% of the total population. See *ibid.*, May 5, 2010, p.18. Sino-Kadazans have always been regarded as Bumi in Sabah State. However, Peninsular Malaysia does not recognize the ethnic group as Bumi. See *BP*, August 25, 2009, p.7. Non-Bumi Straight-A achievers in the Sijil Pelajaran Malaysia (SPM) cannot enrol at Unimas. The term, racial discrimination, was mentioned. Sarawak students were given only 10% of Petronas scholarships when the state contributed some RM20 million in revenue to the federal government through its petroleum and natural gas. See *ibid.*, March 17, 2010, p.13.

[4] Or Sikhs to be more specific. Conversation with VieMing TAN, dated April 26, 2010 and another colleague on August 19, 2010.

[5] *BP*, April 17, 2010, p.1. A ranking official of the Malaysian Chinese Association (MCA) said his party has 8,000 members in that electoral district, and there are 16,000 Chinese voters. See *GuoJiShiBao* (hereinafter GJSB)(Sarawak, Malaysia), April 19, 2010, p.B3. BN won the April 2010 by-election.

[6] *SheeHua Daily News*b(hereinafter SHDN)(Sarawak, Malaysia), May 4, 2010, p.4.

[7] *BP*, September 3, 2009, p.9 and January 6, 2010, p.12.

REASONS FOR SUCCESS

The notion, success, is certainly on many, if not most, business people's mind.[8] A Bidayuh website asked the following question: What are the most successful people have in common? The answer is as follows: great attitude, discipline, and determination plus "a knowledgeable and trusted advisor or even an entire group of supporters that pulls and pushes them toward accomplishments."[9] To others, confidence is the key.[10] What about trust, the recommendation of not diversifying business interests at the very beginning,[11] sincerity,[12] brisk activities, good branding, repackaging, luck,[13] etc.? A successful company or corporation generates profit and it must have the ability to maintain and/or sustain its good reputation, etc. It goes without saying that a successful business person's words and deeds certainly can carry heavier weight than others.

In this section, we will cite some examples, related to business success, which are applied to all; to Bumi; and to non-Bumi.

Applied to all

Sometimes, some reasons and factors can be applied to all business people. In other words, race, ethnicity, color, etc. do not matter at all. Usually, we are looking at everything from the macro-level point of view. We can cite some examples. First, the future seems rosy for Malaysia. This may well mean more prosperous economy for the country. For example, in the global competitiveness report 2009-2010, Malaysia is ranked 24th among 133 countries. Malaysia's productivity level was US$12,793; Thailand, US$4,596; mainland China, US$3,734; Philippines, US$3,192; Indonesia, US$2,471; and India, US$2,051.[14] If Malaysia can enhance its productivity, its (small-scale) traders can be in a better position to compete with foreign traders, although empirical research on Malaysian SMEs in the area of internationalization has been limited.[15]

In this connection, while in the United States for a state visit in April 2010, Prime Minister Datuk Seri Najib Tun Razak said the following words to the United States-Association of Southeast Asian Nations (ASEAN) Business Council (USABC): "... we will be pursuing an economic policy that will be more open, more merit-based and more supportive entrepreneurship and innovation...."[16]

---

[8] See, for example, *ibid.*, November 15, 2009, p.7 and p.B3.

[9] http://www.bidayuh.com/reference.htm, accessed on April 30, 2010. Minister of Infrastructure Development and Communication Dato Sri Michael Manyin Jawong called upon the Bidayuh community not to be complacent. See *BP*, July 11, 2010, p.8. The term, great attitude, was mentioned. See *BP*, Sept. 4th, 2010, p.D3.

[10] *BP*, April 12, 2010, p.B1.

[11] Conversation with VieMing TAN, dated April 26, 2010.

[12] Prime Minister Datuk Seri NAJIB Tun Razak mentioned sincerity and willingness to work hard were among "the first and foremost attributes I will be seeking from people who come into my office." See *BP*, May 15, 2010, p.16.

[13] Conversation with a hawker, Jong Kim CHO, dated May 4, 2010.

[14] *BP*, April 21, 2010, B1.

[15] Shankar Chelliah, Mohamed Sulaiman, and Yusliza Mohd Yusoff, "Internationalization and Performance: Small and Medium Enterprises (SMEs) in Malaysia," *International Journal of Business and Management*, Vol.5, No. 6 (June 2010), pp.27-37.

[16] *BP*, April 16, 2010, p.B11.

As to Sarawak, its Chief Minister, Pehin Sri Abdul Taib Mahmud reminded the people about the income of Sarawakians. In 1981, the average per capita income was RM4,600 annually. In 2010, it is RM27,000. By 2020, he expects the per capita income to be RM80,000; and, by 2030, it will probably increase to RM130,000 per capita income.[17]

Second, in late 2010, the ASEAN Trade Centre (ATC) will be established. Its objective is to support small and medium enterprises (SMEs) to penetrate the ASEAN market as well as new markets. The initiative will also help SMEs to reduce their production costs through contract manufacturing, assist them in buying raw materials in bulk, and possibly offer financing for the SMEs.[18] In August 2010, it was reported that, in the last five years, Sarawak has not less than 100,000 entrepreneurs.[19]

Third, business communities are invited to participate in various kinds of functions such as expositions and exhibitions and no one is excluded. For example, Malaysia External Trade Development Corporation (Matrade) in January 2010 held a free of charge seminar, which is entitled "Optimising Opportunities Under Malaysia's Free Trade Agreement." It is especially for all exporters, as they will enjoy lower tariff for their products.[20] Apart from that, Matrade Sarawak director, Omar Mohd Salleh, said other advantages included gaining a wider access of customers' base and enhancing the competitiveness of products made in Malaysia in other markets particularly mainland China, and he added that local entrepreneurs can voice their concerns and spell out issues at the platform.[21]

As a second example, local government and non-governmental organizations (NGOs) would hold regular dialogues to address all sorts of issues. They would step in to help local business people, if and when necessary. For example, in April 2010, the Sibu Municipal Council (SMC) said it will continue to impound goods offered for sale by illegal hawkers and foreigners.[22] In 2009 alone, SMC impounded 35 foreign illegal hawkers, surprisingly most of them come from mainland China. The Miri City Council (MCC) for the first time in late June 2010 began to clean up the city of errant traders or more than 200 out of the existing 1,300 licensed market hawkers.[23]

As another example, Small and Medium Enterprises Corporation Malaysia (SME Corp Malaysia) in January 2010 organized a free of charge talk, which is entitled "Seven Secrets of Success in Business."[24] The speaker was a local Bumi woman entrepreneur, who operated a boutique firm.

Applied to Bumi

In October 2009, it was reported that the number of Bumi entrepreneurs has doubled. "It went up by 100 per cent compared to four years ago."[25] This is certainly a piece of good

[17] *Ibid.*, May 1, 2010, p.3. However, it should be noted that Sarawak's unemployment rate of 4.8% is slightly higher than average national rate of 3.6%. See *ibid.*, May 11, 2010, p.8.
[18] *Ibid.*, April 21, 2010, p.B11.
[19] *Ibid.*, August 21, 2010, p.6.
[20] *Ibid.*, January 15, 2010, p.B3.
[21] *Ibid.*
[22] *Ibid.*, April 18, 2010, p.22.
[23] *Ibid.*, June 22, 2010, p.D3.
[24] *Ibid.*, January 15, 2010, p.B3.
[25] *Ibid.*, October 26, 2009, p.6.

news. In June 2010, the government said it aims to increase the number of Bumi exporters in the manufacturing sector to 1,000 by 2015 under the Master Plan for Bumi Development (MPBD), thereby to help Bumi companies to accumulate investment of RM25 billion in the sector.[26] Academics are also studying some of the reasons and factors.[27] First, foreign nationals will not be issued license to conduct trade in the Federal Territories, according to Federal Territories and Wellbeing Minister Datuk Raja Nong Chik Raja Zainal Abidin, adding "[i]f licences were given to foreigners, I am sure 100 per cent of the hawker areas would be controlled by them," while noting that the number of foreigners hired to work are doing heavy chores at hawker centers and operating their own stalls--whether illegal or on local hawker's license--was balanced.[28] Thus, this policy was taken to secure a sustainable source of income for local hawkers and petty traders. Yet, some traders still hired foreigners to sell their produce at pasar tani/farmers markets, and those errant traders' licenses were suspended for three months.[29]

Second, many people, including the Indonesians, apply for Sarawak's Bumi status. Once they get it, they can inherit native lands or get other privileges, such as scholarships and Amanah Saham Bumi (ASB) saving scheme.[30] Some local Chinese were under the false impression that they cannot apply for educational assistance from the Sarawak Foundation (SF), when they face financial problems.[31] It goes without saying that the money saved can be used for doing business.

Third, some Bumi do grab the business opportunity. For example, an enterprising Bumi entrepreneur, Azrol Hidzam Hussin, claimed to have discovered the technology to produce an environmental-friendly water-based fuel, Banapi, which can be used for industrial and domestic purposes.[32] As another example, several restaurants and food stalls in Hulu Selangor have extended their operating hours, so as to meet the needs of people who have camped over there for the by-election. Many of them would open until late in the night, in view of increased number of customers.[33]

Applied to Non-Bumi

It is not difficult to find out the reasons and factors. First, Chinese are well known for their willingness to work long hours, even for low pay. This has been the tradition. In Hongkong today, there is still no ceiling for how many hours can one work each week.[34]

---

[26] *Ibid.*, June 22, 2010, p.12.

[27] See, for example, Firdaus Abdullah, *et. al.*, "Developing a Framework of Success of Bumiputera Entrepreneurs" *Journal of Enterprising Communities*, Vol.3, No.1 (2009), pp.8-24.

[28] *BP*, February 24, 2010, p.18.

[29] *Ibid.*, March 25, 2010, p.10.

[30] *Ibid.*, April 16, 2010, p.D2 and conversation with my colleague on August 19, 2010.

[31] *BP*, April 16, 2010, p.7.

[32] *Ibid.*, June 22, 2010, p.1.

[33] *Ibid.*, April 18, 2010, p.7.

[34] *SHDN*, April 16, 2010, p.11. See also *ibid.*, October 26, 2009, p.13. Africans marvel and fret at hard workers from mainland China, who are pursuing wealth. "A Chinese worker gets about 300 dirhams (RM135) a month. A Moroccan wants around 2,000 dirhams. For 300 dirhams, you might as well commit suicide." See *BP*, September 6, 2009, p.B7.

Mahathir bin Mohamad, writing in Singapore in April 1950, mentioned the Chinese in Singapore as being "native diligence and business drive born out of the hard life in China."[35]

Second, having a good strategy of doing business is also important. A Chinese owner of a building invites different food stall owners to do business, while he only sells drinks of various kinds.[36] The rent is very cheap. For example, the noodle stall owner just has to pay RM100 per month to the building owner, as opposed to RM400 per month to another building owner at a popular eatery. Another stall owner in the same building just has to pay RM150 for two stalls selling different types of non-halal (meaning non-"lawful/permissible" in Arabic) food, which has not been prepared according to the prescriptions of the Quran and which could be mixed with pork, lard, alcohol, etc.[37] Asked about the reason, the lead co-author was told that the building owner just wants to make sure that, when the rent is cheap, the food stall owners can reduce their price of selling, for example, a box-lunch. In the long run, the same hawkers can do business at the same place, and there could be more customers, old and new. It follows that, when there are more customers, the building owner can make more money on selling more drinks.

As another example, Chillipepper's owner is a Chinese. However, he only employs Malays as his workers, because, by doing so, he is able to attract more Muslim customers with his halal food. In passing, it should be noted that Muslims account for one-fifth of the world population, with between 1.4 and 1.8 billion spread across 148 countries.[38] By mid-2011, the Halal Development Corporation (HDC) and Neguin Group of Companies of Iran will open 1 Malaysia Departmental Store, serving as a shopping haven where halal product and service can be sources and obtained from Malaysia.

Reasons for Failure

Applied to all

It is not difficult to cite reasons and factors from local newspapers, which are faced by all business communities. First, Malaysia has a population of 28 million and some 35% are rural folks. In some states, 70% of its people are staying in villages and to this date, many of them are still behind in terms of benefitting from the prosperity that Malaysia has enjoyed in the past five decades, such as getting water and power supply.[39] Without basic infrastructure, how can one do business? In passing, it should be noted that, as of December 31, 2009, the country is in debt,[40] implying the Federal Government cannot take care of every business person. As a

[35] http:/zakisamsudin.blogspot.com/209/06/why-mahathir-hates-lee-kuan-yew, accessed on April 10, 2010. The former prime minister also once labeled the Bumi "as lazy individuals." See http://www.themalaysianinsider.com/index.php/opinion/breaking-views/56856-how-can-bumiputeras-surge-ahead--george-lee, accessed on April 30, 2010. A Bintulu businessman, Dato Seri TIONG King Sing, said Chinese are good at making money but not at forging unity. See *BP*, July 5, 2010, p.6.

[36] Conversation with Collin CHONG/ZHANG JianQiao, dated April 17, 2010.

[37] Conversation with a Swinburne University of Technology, Sarawak Campus, food stall owner, YAP Chong Hock, who sells chicken rice, dated April 20, 2010. His wife is an Iban. Chinese eat all kinds of food. See the heading, for example: Import of US beef tongues, penises, and testicles halted. See http://taiwantoday.tw/ct.asp?xItem=99900&ctNode=452&mp=9, accessed on April 22, 2010.

[38] *BP*, July 17, 2010, p.B3.

[39] *Ibid.*, March 19, 2010, p.9.

[40] In May 2010, one official, Datuk Seri IDRIS Jala, who is a minister in the Prime Minister's Department, said the country may be bankrupt by 2019. See *SHDN*, May 28, 2010, p.1. For a rebuttal, see *BP*, June 1, 2010, p.1 and

percentage to Gross National Product (GNP), it is equivalent to 53.7%. Nationally, it amounted to RM 348.6 billion (or 96.2%). Externally, the outstanding amount is RM 13.9 billion (or 3.8%).[41]

Second, many Bumis, especially those in Sarawak, do not understand how government machinery works. Accordingly, they would just become "by-standers."[42] Many places are lagging behind others. For example, Bumi living in Kapit still has to travel three hours by boat in order to reach Sibu.[43]

Third, can SMEs in Malaysia compete with foreign giants? It is doubtful, unless companies merge[44] or SMEs would latch on to larger firms for business via supply chain.[45] Thus, the Ministry of International Trade and Industry (MITI) plans to integrate 3,000 Bumi companies into the domestic supply chain.[46] However, would some ambitious business people be willing not to be a boss? To be sure, SMEs comprises over 90% out of three million active businesses registered under Companies' Commission of Malaysia (CCM), and only 960 companies are listed on Bursa Malaysia, which offers the complete range of exchange-related services including trading, clearing, settlement, etc., with total market capitalization amounting to RM one trillion.[47] Needless to say, it is not much.

Thus, in July 2009, the Federation of Malaysian Consumer Associations (FOMCA) called on the government to be "cautious" when listing government linked companies (GLCs) on the stock exchange as it could be detrimental to the well-being of the people and country, because such listing might erode the controlling stake in the companies and subject them to foreign domination, while citing the example of a Hong Kong-based company, Wang Tak Company, Ltd., which had emerged as one of the biggest shareholders of Padiberas Nasional Berhad (Bernas), a GLC, which holds the monopoly for rice import.[48]

Fourth, according to Omar, shipping cost in East Malaysia is higher than in Peninsular Malaysia. So, the question before all the Sarawak business people is: How can logistics operators especially shipping companies leverage on Free Trade Agreements (FTA) to reduce their cost of doing business?[49]

Fifth, it seems that Sarawak cannot provide more economic opportunities for some Bumi. Thus, it was reported that some 40,000 Ibans left Sibu, which is dominated by local Chinese, to choose to work in Senai town, the State of Johor,[50] which is close to the Republic of Singapore (ROS). Another high-ranking official said there are some 700,000 Malaysians working overseas, and the government hopes to attract 25% of those talents to return home.[51]

June 3, 2010, p.10. Jeremy TAN said, so long as Malaysia can issue its currency, it would not collapse. Conversation with him, dated June 5, 2010. So long as the Government is willing to sell it public land to the common people, it can have revenue.

41 *XinZhouRiBao* (hereinafter XZRB)(Sarawak, Malaysia), April 23, 2010, p.14.

42 *BP*, June 18, 2010, p.D3.

43 *Ibid.*, June 18, 2010, p.D2.

44 *Ibid.*, November 23, 2009, p.6.

45 *Ibid.*, March 31, 2010, p.B12.

46 *Ibid.*, June 22, 2010, p.12.

47 *Ibid.*, April 25, 2010, p.B1.

48 http://www.theedgemalaysia.com/features/148211-tradewiands-to-take-over-bernas.html, accessed on April 23, 2010.

49 *BP*, January 15, 2010, p.B3.

50 *SHDN*, May 10, 2010, p.A4.

51 *Ibid.*, June 17, 2010, p.1. Najib mentioned some 700,000 Chinese from Malaysia are working abroad. See http://www.zaobao.com/yx/yx10085.oo601.shtml, dated August 15, 2010.

Sixth, many business people had to quit for fear of losing larger sum of money, even for a short period of time. Assistant Minister of Sarawak Bumi Entrepreneur Development Unit (UPUB), Mohd Naroden Majais, said high returns only come to those who understand the kind of industry they are in.[52] Entrepreneurs are advised not to abandon their other businesses halfway. "For example, if you are rearing catfish before, don't give up halfway. Understand the concept of running the business first, and focus on it in the long term as revenue does not come in a short period of time."[53]

Seventh, Malay, Chinese, and Indians eat chicken. However, chicken vendors are struggling for survival, especially on weekdays, at least in Sibu, unless running cost can be lowered, bearing in mind that each vendor has to spend at least RM12 a day on ice to keep the chicken fresh plus the fact that chicken suppliers are unwilling to lower the price of every chicken by RM1 and plastic bags are getting costlier.[54]

Eighth, local traders have been advised not to borrow money from loan sharks or Ah Longs, because they impose a very high interest rate making it impossible for the borrower to pay back the loan.[55]

Applied to Bumi

It is not difficult to find some weaknesses of Bumi. First, Najib pointed out that most of the Bumi prefer to go into sectors which are already saturated and often referred to as "sunset industries."[56] They sometimes fight among themselves, scrambling to get, for example, halal certification. The Islamic Development Department (Jakim) has set standards that had to be met to get the halal certificate and this applied to all applicants without discrimination.[57] The question of whether the certificate is fake or not had been brought up.[58] Needless to say, there were complaints that conditions set by the department were too strict and ridiculous.[59]

Second, in August 2009, Sarawak Economic Development Corporation (SarawakEDC) chairman Datuk Talib Zulpilip said business operators at its Medan Niaga Permaidani Kampang Tebingan Boyan-Gersik-Surabaya (BGS), in particular, must have the discipline to open their shops early and close late daily, so as to enjoy a good and loyal clientele, adding the SarawakEDC will issue a warning to those who fail to do so (extend operating hours) to follow regulations and, after that, the SarawakEDC "will give the business opportunities to others, who are more serious in the endeavour." To be sure, this is not the first time that a high-ranking official has made this remark.[60] For the record, SarawakEDC built and manages the RM4.3 million BGS, which includes 34 units for eateries, 20 units of business kiosks and toilets.[61] It is a Sarawak Government project aimed at increasing the residents' income.

---

[52] *BP*, April 20, 2010, p.3.
[53] *Ibid.*
[54] *Ibid.*, January 8, 2010, p.10.
[55] *Ibid.*, April 9, 2010, p.18.
[56] *Ibid.*, May 15, 2010, p.16.
[57] *Ibid.*, March 17, 2010, p.15.
[58] *Ibid* and June 22, 2010, p.B11.
[59] *Ibid.*
[60] *Ibid.*, August 13, 2009, p.1 and April 20, 2010, p.3.
[61] *Ibid.*, p.5.

Third, some GLCs hold the view that projects given to local or Bumi companies will involve higher costs, because they are not competitive, although United Malays National Organization (UMNO) economic bureau chairman, Datuk Awang Adek Hussein, said that such issues could be discussed and resolved.[62] The question posed by some observers is: How long can the business community wait?

Fourth, United Malays National Organization (UMNO) information chief, Datuk Ahmad Maslan, said Malays should change mindset.[63] Najib said he is confident that Bumi "can succeed at the highest level without quota or government help."[64] Bumi Chamber of Commerce Sarawak (DUBS) Kapit branch president, Bangsa Untang, told Bumi entrepreneurs in general and Dayak in particular not to wait for government's project or contract handouts, earning only a commission. (According to a report, they get 4 or 5% by practicing Ali Baba.[65]) He added that being hard working was not enough for them to succeed.[66] Bangsa urged them to learn how to earn, spend prudently, and go for management and human resources training to stay relevant.[67] In this connection, "[e]asy financial facilities like Agrobank, Tekun, Mara are all there to assist us. Equally important, after successfully obtaining the bank loan, we must honour and pay the instalments accordingly to build a good reputation so that others can trust us."[68]

Another news report cited what Assistant Land Development Minister Datuk Francis Harden said. He advised the people with wrong attitude not to set up associations or clubs just for the purpose of getting government grants.

Fifth, Deputy International Trade and Industry Minister, Datuk Mukhriz Tun Mahathir, pointed out one reason why Bumi entrepreneurs in the retail sector cannot succeed. It is because "[m]any shopping centres still employ favouritism and there are not known reasons for it," adding "Bumiputeras are not given the space they should be given although they can afford to pay rent like anyone else..... I would like to call on them to be more fair in this matter as I am convinced that given the chance, Bumiputera entrepreneurs will not have problem in the fields they are entering."[69]

Sixth, Kuching City North Commission (DBKU) "spends up to RM558,000 annually on electricity, garbage collection, cleaning and operations" at Satok Market, a tourist destination. Yet, the Commission can only collect RM173,000 per year from traders and hawkers, who should be blamed for the dirty conditions, while the DBKU has to subsidize the rest.[70] In a word, if the place is dirty, how can it attract (foreign) tourists?

Seventh, in Sarawak, some 20,000 illegal workers (as opposed to some 120,000 legal ones) are unaccounted for, and there are only 120 under-staffed enforcement officers, who can track down them.[71] Some leaders perceive that Malaysians can get higher income, if the numbers of cheap, unskilled foreign labours, who are willing to take any job for minimal pay,

---

[62] *Ibid.*, October 13, 2009, p.B2.
[63] *Ibid.*, June 20, 2010, p.23.
[64] *Ibid.*, June 21, 2010, p.5.
[65] *SHDN*, April 9, 2010, p.A2. Non-Bumi tried to obtain government-tendered projects by teaming up with Bumi. Ali refers to the former and Baba, the latter. The non-Bumi would pay the Bumi a certain sum in exchange. See http://en.wikipedia.org/wiki/Bumiputera_(Malaysia), accessed on April 26, 2010.
[66] *BP*, January 31, 2010, p.11.
[67] *Ibid.*
[68] *Ibid.*
[69] *Ibid.*, March 4, 2010, p.D4.
[70] *Ibid.*, March 10, 2010, p.8.
[71] *Ibid.*, April 15, 2010, p.3.

both legal and illegal, can be reduced. This is because the bottom 40 per cent of workers cannot demand higher wages, as there are substitute foreign workers. In a word, if a Bumi cannot earn enough income per month, how can he or she save money in the long run, in order to become an entrepreneur?

Eighth, Najib, since April 2009, is fully aware of the fact that many people are talking about the widening disparities and growing polarization among the different communities as the New Economic Policy (NEP), which can be dated back to the early 1970s, was seen to be benefiting a narrow group of Malays.[72] To some people, this calls for concern. In this connection, we see remarks made by the Liberal Democratic Party (LDP) Youth leader, Ir CHIN Shu Ying, regarding government's allocation of projects to multi-cultural companies: "Currently 99 percent of the projects are given to Malays, but the reality is that 90 per cent of Malay contractors subcontract the projects to Chinese contractors," adding "[i]f all decisions have to be based on race or quota, how can we achieve 1 Malaysia?"[73] In other words, if Bumi were receiving privileges since early 1970s, why do some politicians still say that Bumi are unable to achieve the 30% equity ownership? One Malay in February 2010 offered an explanation. Coordinating Director of Gagasan Baan Ekonomi Melayu (GABEM) Sahlan Saruddin identified the main reason why equity ownership by Bumi in companies is still around 19%, while they should have achieved 30%. It is none other than Bumi entrepreneurs' attitude, because they are always getting support from the government in terms of capital or moral support.[74] However, Taib reminded the Chinese living in Sarawak, saying they are more fortunate than those in other states.[75]

Ninth, business may be interfered by politics. For example, in April 2010, Miri Bumiputra Traders Association (PBMS) slammed Pakatan Rakyat (PR)/People's Pact or People's Alliance, which is an informal Malaysian coalition formed in April 2008 by opposition political parties, for having said that the Saberkas night market has no surau (prayer) rooms, which are provided to all Muslims to perform their "salat/salah (Muslim ritual prayer)" and toilet for traders and consumers or shoppers. PBMS said the surau and toilet are located in the same building at PBMS' office free of charge, and it advised PR to wise up and do not disturb the night market.[76]

Applied to Non-Bumi

What kind of disadvantages does the non-Bumi face? First, Malaysia is well known for serving halal standard of food. At schools, a food court cannot sell pork. In passing, it should be noted that, so long as there is a Malay student, a Chinese private school also cannot sell pork.[77] This mean is that a Chinese or Indian hawker and, for that matter, Chinese or

[72] *Ibid.*, April 18, 2010, p.23. Not all Bumi can be taken care of. See, for example, *ibid.*, March 20, 2010, p.D3. See also James Chin, "The Malaysian-Chinese Dilemma: The Never Ending Policy," *Chinese Southern Diaspora Studies*, Vol.3 (2009), pp.167-182.

[72] *BP*, August 25, 2009, p.7.

[73] *Ibid.*, August 25, 2009, p.7.

[74] *Ibid.*, February 28, 2010, p.17.

[75] *Ibid.*, June 16, 2010, p.4.

[76] *Ibid.*, April 24, 2010, p.13.

[77] Conversation with TAN Lee Suang, dated April 19, 2010.

indigenous pig farmers, who serve non-halal food, cannot earn more income, because a Malay simply would not approach the food stall or eating place.[78]

Second, many documents are written in Bahasa Malaysia. Some local Chinese and Indians cannot fully understand either Bahasa Malaysia nor English.

REASONS UNDER WAIT-AND-SEE

If we adopt a linear thinking, a 100% success is a 100% success is a 100% success. In other words, a 99% success is not a 100% success. The same speaks for failure. However, if our thinking is non-linear, on the one hand, perhaps success can lead to failure, if, for example, one expands his or her business too fast. On the other hand, failure may be a catalyst as a lesson for staging a comeback. Thus, we say, to be successful, one has to pass through many trials and tribulations. In short, there could be many reasons and factors beyond Bumi and non-Bumi's control, while doing business. We will cite some examples.

Applied to all

First, the NEP and NEM have the same intention, that is, to reduce the gap between the rich and the poor in Malaysia. This applies to all the races and ethnic groups in the country. In April 2010, while in Washington, Najib, who met U.S. President Barack H. Obama, II earlier, made a similar remark. He said questions had been asked if the United States would depend more on domestic consumption and less on export-driven growth or whether the untrammelled pursuit of trade had exposed the United States to unacceptable risks.[79] Najib added, saying "[i]t is my hope, of course, that the United States will resolve this question in a way that addresses its national interest without sacrificing that of the rest of the world," while urging the United States to share and help other nations grow and develop to generate a more prosperous world and a prosperous America.[80] For the record, Obama on April 27, 2010 laid a key plank of his strategy to mend ties with Muslim nations, hosting a summit with around 250 entrepreneurs from 50 countries to boost economic development in the Islamic world, with over a billion people. In June 2009, the American president in a landmark speech called for a "new beginning" to relations between the United States and the Muslim world.

Second, on January 1, 2010, the China-ASEAN Free Trade Area (FTA) was established. In the year 2009, trade volume between Malaysia and the People's Republic of China (PRC) reached almost US$52 billion, from which the former enjoyed US$12.7 billion trade surplus.[81] Would this trend continue? If so, more Malaysian traders can be benefited. If not, they will most likely suffer.

Third, we should get an overall picture. According to Muhyiddin, some 40% of Malaysians earned less than RM3,000 or even RM1,500 a month.[82] [In passing, it should be pointed out that, on August 12, 2008, Malaysian Economic Council (MEC) advisory group

---

[78] Conversation with YAP Chong Hock, dated January 18 and 20, 2010 as well as April 20, 2010.

[79] *BP*, April 16, 2010, p.B11.

[80] *Ibid.*

[81] *Ibid.*, April 27, 2010, p.B11.

[82] *Ibid.*, September 3, 2009, p.9 and April 16, 2010, p.6. See also *GJSB*, March 11, 2010, p.B4.

said 57% of Malaysians earned less than RM3,000 per month.[83] In this connection, a postman's starting salary is RM610. A person with income below RM700 per month is regarded as poor.[84]] In the same news report, we see that around 600,000 civil servants earn less than RM3,000 each month and that the country had more than a million private sector workers earning less than RM1,000 per month. For example, a housemaid in Malaysia or the Arab world can get only RM500, as contrasted to the ROS's RM2,400 or the Republic of China (ROC) on Taiwan's, RM1,700 per month or Hongkong's, RM1,680.[85] To be sure, there was no change in minimum wage in the Taiwan area from 2007 to July 31, 2010, and the previous basic monthly wage of NT$15,840/RM1,584 remained unchanged for 13 years. If the minimum wage is raised, this might result in more layoffs and, in turn, hurt the workforce.[86] The victims could be of any races, ethnic groups, etc. in the country.

Fourth, Bandar Kuching Member of Parliament, CHONG Chieng Jen, urged the Kuching South City Council (MBKS) to be more transparent in the implementation of public projects, such as telling people about the contractor, engineer, architect, and employer involved, plus whether there was a tendering process.[87] Indeed, this transparency proposal can benefit all potential bidders. In June 2010, Transparency International Malaysia (TI-M) was alarmed by the apparent lack of transparency, governance, and integrity in government contracts. In other words, there have been many awards without tender, open or otherwise.[88]

Fifth, experience and exposure are needed in order to generate brisk business activities. Several factors are involved for a manager's success: intellectual ability and skills, capability to conduct critical and systematic analyses of situations he or she confronts, and to come up with conventional as well as creative answers to problems, the manager's ability to access other people, and not the least, their personal qualities.[89] In short, who can possess them all? A follow-up question is: How long would it take to train each entrepreneur to possess them or should they experience it by themselves?

Sixth, officials themselves cannot speak in one voice. If so, the common people will be confused. For example, on the one hand, in September 2009, the Cultural and Training Manager, Sabah Entreprenuer Development Centre (SabahEDC), Jusil Potoh, said youths, especially jobless graduates, should not rely on the government/government linked companies or the private sector to find employment.[90] On the other hand, in April 2010, Minister in the Chief Minister's Department Datin Fatimah Abdullah urged job seekers, especially school graduates and leavers, to look beyond public sector.[91] In October 2009, she, as the then Assistant Minister, urged graduates to grab abundant or available opportunities in entrepreneurship.[92] Yet, she did not caution the job seekers as a principal of an institution of higher education had advised that certain risk is involved in entrepreneurship.[93]

---

[83] *SHDN*, September 16, 2009, p.A8.
[84] *BP*, May 5, 2010, p.18.
[85] *Ibid.*, December 29, 2009, p.4.
[86] http://taiwantoday.tw/fp.asp?xItem=58208&CtNode=452, accessed on April 26, 2010.
[87] *Ibid.*, August 27, 2009, p.16.
[88] *BP*, June 19, 2010, p.15.
[89] *Ibid.*, April 24, 2010, p.B3.
[90] *Ibid.*, September 13, 2009, p.10. In 2008, the Centre trained 1,251 Bumi entrepreneurs, 836 of them women on how to run and manage food catering, child nurseries, beauty saloons, tailoring, entrepreneurship, and contract businesses.
[91] *Ibid.*, April 9, 2010, p.10.
[92] *Ibid.*, October 13, 2009, p.12.
[93] *Ibid.*

Seventh, corruption may affect business. The Malaysian Anti-Corruption Commission (MACC) has repeatedly urged witnesses or informers to come forward and assist the commission during investigations involving bribery cases. A MACC director said in April 2010 that, in the last 10 years, 866 offenders were arrested for bribery, an average of 87 people each year.[94] In 2009, 500 people, including 23 politicians, were investigated for alleged corruption.[95] MACC Commissioner, Datuk Abu Kassim Mahamed, said: "Cases will be lost if witnesses fail to turn up or decide to make a u-turn at the last minute," adding "[w]e have the law. So if a witness is afraid, they can provide the information and they will be protected. Let us know what their problems are."[96] However, would the corrupt business people threaten the lives of witnesses and their family members? Such is the lingering fear of any witness.

Eighth, efforts have been made to produce more capable traders and business people from the Bumi community, which is concerned with the NEM.[97] In March 2010, it was reported that the government targets by 2012 to create 4,000 women entrepreneurs among the hardcore poor, who are those with a household income of less than RM440 each month.[98] Other schemes like Program Sejahtera Ekonomi Bandar (Proseb), which was created by the BN Government to provide meaningful economic assistance to the *rakyat* (people), irrespective of their ethnicity and background, would advise Bumi traders and business people to embrace a high degree of discipline, diligence, commitment, and hard work to succeed plus a host of other traits, such as "giving priority to cleanliness and hygiene of shops and premises; being ethical, reliable, trustworthy and punctual, and, most importantly, giving good service to customers."[99] It is said that they can be learned and embraced by all of us.[100] However, it may take a long period of time for some Bumi and non-Bumi to acquire them.

Ninth, conservativeness can be identified as another problem. "Commercialize your product," "don't focus on food products only," and "look for niche market" constantly ring bells.[101] Industrial Development Minister Datuk Patinggi Tan Sri George H. N. CHAN regards Sarawak's small and medium industries (SMIs) and enterprises (SMEs) as being "too conservative" in today's challenging market, adding it is time to wake them up, so that they would not do the same thing and continue the same effort.[102] Later, Taib pointed out that the traditional logging of primary forests was a dying industry, which should be replaced by planted forests, downstream wood-based activities, and commercial oil palm plantations.[103] As to Sabah, Chief Minister Datuk Seri Musa Aman pointed out that "Sabah has too long relied heavily on exporting commodity products such as palm oil, rubber, and cocoa." Instead, it should increase production of higher value-added products, arising from greater

---

[94] *Ibid.*, April 27, 2010, p.4. An investigation has begin on the *Port Klang Free Zone* (*PKFZ*) scandal in Port Klang, Malaysia, since the second half of 2008. See http://www.zaobao.com/yx1yx100308_001.shtml, accessed on March 8, 2010.

[95] *BP*, May 12, 2010, p.16.

[96] *Ibid.*, March 10, 2010, p.9.

[97] In April 2010, 22 members of Gabungan Usahawan Bumiputera Sarawak (GUBS) paid a courtesy call on officials in Putrajaya and Kuala Lumpur. In December 2009, the GUBS had a meeting, urging the government to help make the Bumi economic agenda a success. See *ibid.*, April 28, 2010, p.10.

[98] *Ibid.*, March 18, 2010, p.10.

[99] *Ibid.*, November 15, 2009, p.7. The Miri City Council (MCC) wants all food outlet operators to maintain a high standard of hygiene and cleanliness or face the music, if they fail to do so. See *ibid.*, May 1, 2010, p.5.

[100] *Ibid.*, March 18, 2010, p.10.

[101] *Ibid.*, April 30, 2010, p.11 and p.18 and May 1, 2010, p.9.

[102] *Ibid.*, August 20, 2009, p.11.

[103] *Ibid.*, April 25, 2010, p.3 and April 30, 2010, p.B1.

downstream activities.[104] In the World Banks' *2010 Malaysia Economic Monitor,* released in November 2010, we were told that Sabah has about 10% of the population but it has more than 40% of the poor people.

Tenth, having unskilled foreign workers, who accept low pay, may help a country's economy. For example, they may be willing to build roads or railway. Yet, we see what Minister Datuk S. Subramaniam said, that is, the Malaysian Government wanted to limit the recruitment of foreign workers to 1.5 million in three years, as proposed by the Cabinet Committee on Foreign Workers laboratory.[105] Malaysia has about 1.8 million foreign workers in manufacturing (39%), construction (19%), plantation (14%), housemaid (12%), services (10%), with the rest in agriculture.[106] Does that mean owners and operators of coffee shops and restaurants can employ more locals, if they receive tax incentives from the government? To be sure, for several decades, the Malaysian Government did not adopt the national minimum wage policy (as opposed to the let-the-market decide policy).[107] Yet, at present, there are more than 150,000 foreigners in the restaurant sector.[108] Part of this figure could include nearly 40,000 Indian citizens who went "missing" after their tourist visa issued by Malaysia had expired.[109] At the same time, many Malaysian sought jobs outside the country, and this is because of the low wages being offered at home.[110]

11th, hawkers at Suajana Food Center at Jalan Masjid, Kuching, claim that the management was not paying attention to their poor business plight, did not hold monthly meetings, and did not make effort to promote the once popular eatery, so as to attract more customers.[111] The rent has also gone up over the years. According to Ibrahim Junal, the management had raised the rent from RM200 in 1989 to RM680 today.[112]

12th, talking to Bumi in the small town of Lawas, Sarawak, Second Minister of Planning and Resource Management, Datuk Amar Awang Tengah Ali Hassan, said "[d]o not give the excuse of being fated to be poor…."[113] Does luck or fortune play a role in our lives? Why are some business people more successful than others only to fail later on?

Applied to Bumi

First, lack of competitiveness is among the reasons that Bumi in Sabah, especially the Kadazandusun and Murut (KDM), are economically more backward compared to the other races and ethnic groups. However, Parti Bersatu Rakyat Sabah (PBRS) president Tan Sri Joseph Kurup stressed that KDM should not point fingers for their backwardness and "[n]obody should be blamed in this matter as it occurred because the KDM community is not competitive," while urging the same not to choose to ask for assistance from the government

[104] *Ibid.*, November 15, 2009, p.B2.
[105] *Ibid.*, April 14, 2010, p.17.
[106] *Ibid.* Up to December 31, 2009, more than 1.91 million legal foreign workers were recorded in Malaysia, while "… the government estimates that there are 1.9 million illegals in this country, on the basis that for every legal foreign worker there is one illegal." See *ibid.*, May 4, 2010, p.19.
[107] *The Star* (Sarawak, Malaysia), August 13, 2009, p.N27.
[108] *BP*, March 20, 2010, p.17.
[109] *Ibid.*, January 15, 2010, p.17.
[110] *The Star*, August 13, 2009, p.N27.
[111] *BP*, April 18, 2010, p.22.
[112] *Ibid.*
[113] *Ibid.*, October 20, 2009, p.5.

for their livelihood.[114] Would the Sabah Bumi make an effort to reverse the trend, since the problem has been identified?

Second, an experienced leader in entrepreneurial initiatives, who can offer coaching and training programs, said it takes only a few thousand dollars to help an entrepreneur to begin a small business that could grow to a greater height, minus all the company overheads, because "[w]hat we need is not more funds to fill the financial holes dug-up by the corporate world, but a redirection of funds to a new generation of entrepreneurs who have new mindsets to tap the opportunities of the new economy."[115] However, can a small business entrepreneur have an initial capital or sufficient money for business start-ups? Can he or she succeed after three months, when the government tries to provide them with a net to catch fish as opposed to providing them with fish?[116] We need just to look at a figure related to Sabah's Bumi. "For instance, as of December 2008, the performance of Bumiputra in terms of company ownership only recorded 27.45 per cent compared to non-Bumiputra's 72.45 per cent."[117] It should also be noted that "[t]he number of bumiputra companies involved in the industrial sector , especially manufacturing, was at just 9.1 per cent compared to 90 per cent for non-bumiputras."[118] And, in respect of the ownership of real estate, Bumi in Sabah at present is only 44% as compared to the 54.9% by non-Bumi.

What about Sarawak? For example, according to Assistant Minister in the Chief Minister's (Entrepreneur Development) Department Mohd Naroden Majais, Bumi's participation in franchise businesses[119] is still very low at just 10%, and one of the factors deterring them from getting, for example, KFC, is the start-up capital, which requires at least RM200,000.[120]

Third, Ministry of Energy, Green Technology and Water Datuk Peter CHIN Fah Kui said, although the Chinese community is seen as the most successful in their respective fields by the other races, the Chinese community should work together with other races in the country as they need their support and cooperation.[121] What if the Chinese community still plays a passive role? Or is it possible that support has already been rendered, with no concrete results? To be sure, recent news reports said that many Chinese schools are still in need of financial assistance.[122]

Needless to say, not just the Chinese community has been called upon to help, the corporate sector in general has also been urged to help the less fortunate, so as to fulfil their corporate social responsibility.[123] Yet, we read the following July 2009 remarks by the secretary-general of the FOMCA, Muhammad Shaani Abdullah: "Investors the world over is interested in only profits and little else, and hence depending on them for social contribution to national development is not an option at all."[124]

---

[114] *Ibid.*, August 22, 2007, p.17.
[115] *Ibid.*, November 24, 2009, p.13.
[116] *Ibid.*, January 4, 2010, p.11.
[117] *Ibid.*, February 13, 2010, p.10 and p.B12.
[118] *Ibid.*, February 13, 2010, p.B12.
[119] Zahariah Mohd ZAIN, *et. al.*, "Why Malaysian Bumiputera Franchisees Purchase Franchise Business?" *International Bulletin of Business Administration*, No.6 (December 2009), pp.50-58.
[120] *BP*, November 3, 2009, p.13.
[121] *Ibid.*, August 24, 2009, p.8.
[122] *Ibid.*, April 5, 2010, p.13.
[123] *Ibid.*, February 11, 2010, p.8.
[124] http://www.bernama.com/bernama/v5/newsgeneral.php?id=429286, accessed on April 28, 2010.

Applied to Non-Bumi

First, in Malaysia's armed forces, non-Malays only make up 15.3 per cent or 17,521 of the whole strength. According to Defense Minister, Datuk Seri Ahmad Zahid Hamid, studies showed that the group made up of Chinese and Indians was less keen to join the forces, because of the high degree of discipline needed, the rigid nature of the job, and the need to prepare to sacrifice times and lives.[125] In June 2010, the Malaysian Maritime Enforcement Agency (MMEA) said only 10% of the 4,000 MMEA personnel were non-Malays. A question ought to be asked: Are the Chinese and Indians perceiving that doing business would be better off in the long run? One Chinese-Malaysian professional soldier said the Chinese community simply does not understand what is going on in the armed forces.

A *YIN* AND *YANG* DIAGRAM INTERPRETATION

In this section, we will apply the *Yin* and *Yang* diagram, , to study the relationship between success and failure and, for that matter, the relationship between Bumi and Non-Bumi, because sometimes we cannot treat some people as 100% a Bumi or non-Bumi. It is a fact that some Chinese's spouses are non-Chinese. Their spouses could also be Malays. The same speaks for the Indians. Thus, we see the term, *mamak* or Indian Muslim community. The finest example is the former Malaysian prime minister, Mahathir Mohammed, whose father was from India.

Applied to all, Bumi, and non-Bumi

If a business person can be successful, we would not need to use the diagram, because we can think of success in terms of a pure circle or dot with nothing negative inside. Since nobody can be successful all the time, the diagram is needed to describe and explain further development. So, whether a Bumi or non-Bumi, they must look at the diagram. We can say that the white portion of the diagram is success, whereas the black portion, failure. Inside the failure portion, we still see possible success or a ray of hope, couched in terms of a small, white dot. Most likely, after many failures, one will learn to avoid them. If so, failure can turn into success. If one begins to have success, he or she would navigate to the success portion. Needless to say, most likely, one cannot be successful all the time, and, therefore, we see the necessity of having the small, black dot in the success portion, which represents failure. Sometimes, we hear people say 50% successful and 50% not successful. In that case, the snake-shaped line in the diagram represents just the mixture.

The above-mentioned logic applies to Bumi and Non-Bumi or a mixture of Bumi and Non-Bumi, who are represented by the snake-shaped line. A follow-up question can be posed: Can Bumis and non-Bumis cooperate and coordinate? No, if we read the following sentence: The former should emulate the Chinese and Indian business communities.[126] If they can, they would be likened to that snake-shaped line in the diagram. Indeed, Naroden urged Bumi

---

[125] *BP*, March 19, 2010, p.22.
[126] *Ibid.*, November 15, 2009, p.7.

entrepreneurs to work with non-Bumi entrepreneurs to market and set their business on a bigger scale.[127]

Sometimes, Malays, Chinese, and Indians cannot cooperate nor coordinate. Indeed, Malays can be separated from, for example, the Chinese, because the former does not eat pork, lard, etc. One noodle stall owner said usually you do not see a Malay food stall in the same canteen with non-Malay food stalls. Another chicken rice stall owner said it is difficult to do business with Malays, because they will first look at whether their compatriots are serving food,[128] whereas the Chinese can eat almost every kind of food.

CONCLUSION

We can note some major findings, which can be applied to all, applied to Bumi, and applied to Non-Bumi.

Applied to all

First, as a ruling party, BN can legitimately use the national budget. It has been using the tangible and intangible resources to help the business people and non-business people.[129] When it tries to assist, it usually does so not along racial lines, even the dominant component party, UMNO, in October 2009, began to say that they can consider to assist non-Malays, if and when necessary.

Second, many government and non-governmental organizations (NGOs) are involved in helping Bumi and Non-Bumi. We will list them from the newspaper editions mentioned in this study:

Government agencies: Ministry of Entreprenuer and Cooperative Development (MECD); Ministry of International Trade and Industry (MITI); SMC; etc.

NGOs, semi-official agencies, private entities: ATC, Bumipretutra Entrepreneurs Development Unit (UPUB); CIMB Bank Berhad (formerly known as *Bumiputra*-Commerce Bank Berhad); DUBS; eXfuse Asia Pacific Sdn. Bhd; Entrepreneurship Institute of Malaysia (EIM);[130] Federation of Malaysian Manufacturers (FMM); FOMCA; Gabungan Usahawan Bumiputera Sarawak (GUB);[131] Halal Industry Development Corporation (HDC); Koperasi Usahawan Tani Batu Kawa Berhad (KUTBKB);[132] Kota Kinabalu Chinese Chamber of Commerce and Industry (KKCCCI); Kuala Lumpur Chamber of Commerce and Industry (KLCCI); Malaysia Co-operatives Commission (MCC), Sarawak branch; Malaysian Industrial Development Finance, Bhd (MIDF); Malaysian Islamic Training Institute (ILIM); Malaysian Trades Union Congress (MTUC); Matrade; Penang Bumiputera Assets Foundation (PBAF); Penang Malay Association (Pemenang); Sarawak Chamber of Commerce and Industry (SCCI); SabahEDC (SEDCO); Sarawak Dayak National Union (SDNU);

---

[127] *Ibid.*, February 14, 2010, p.10.

[128] Conversation YAP Chong Hock, dated January 18 and 20, 2010.

[129] See, for example, *ibid.*, April 17, 2010, p.1.

[130] This is headquartered in Kuala Lumpur with professional development centers in Peninsula Malaysia as well as Sarawak and Sabah.

[131] It represents Bumi entrepreneurs in the state.

[132] It is located at Batu Kawah, trying to improve the economy of the Bumi. See *BP*, April 5, 2010, p.D4.

SarawakEDC (SEDC); Sarawak Islamic Information Centre (SSCI); Sarawak-Sabah Foochow Association Malaysia (SSFA);[133] Sarawak Timber Industry Development Corporation (STIDC); Selangor Indian Chamber of Commerce and Industry (SICCI); Sibu Chinese Chamber of Commerce and Industry (SCCCI); SME Corp Malaysia; UPUB; financial facilities, such as Agrobank, Tekun, and MARA; etc.

Schemes and programs: 1Azam Programme Sarawak (1APS); Entrepreneur Development Fund (EDF);[134] Matrade Sarawak's seen programs mainly in Kuching, Sibu, and Miri; Micro Economy Stimulus Package (ESP-i);[135] MoneyTree Young Entrepreneur Startup Challenge;[136] Private Financing Initiative (PFI); Proseb; Minggu Saham Amanah Malaysia (MSAM) 2010; SEDC's Small Scale Bumiputera Entrepreneur Development Programme (Putera);[137] Skim Bantuan Galakan Perniagaan *Orang Kurang Socio-economic Assistance Programme;*[138] *Upaya/persons with disabilities* (SBGD-OKU);[139] Tekun Nasional (TN); etc.

Third, surveys or public opinion polls must be conducted as the next step,[140] so as to test whether has been written in this paper is closer to reality. The above-mentioned government agencies, NGOs, etc. could be approached, so as to find out their opinion. Questions like the following ought to be asked: 1. What comes first, if a business person wants to be successful: a) confidence; b) attitude; 3) trust; etc.; 2. is it necessary to categorize Malaysians into Bumi and non-Bumi, when it comes to business? 3. What do you think are the problems with the Non-Bumi and Bumi? A host of other 17 questions can be raised. To be sure, asking too many questions would get fewer respondents, who may not have the incentive to answer any one of them.

Fourth, Sarawak State Education director, Julaihi Bujung, lamented that, in Malaysia, workplace ethics and attitude, such as punctuality and obedience to all the orders given by the management are still lagging behind those of other countries, especially Japan.[141] That being the case, when can Malaysians' behavior be rectified or improved upon?

Fifth, the world has been changing. When many people were poor, they worked hard. As the society becomes more affluent, some people, especially the younger generation, began to have poorer work ethic, namely, spoiled and lazy.[142] Since it is a general trend, should Malaysia be concerned? The lead co-author is really surprised to see that many local Chinese shops in Kuching do not open on Sunday afternoons.[143]

---

133 There is also a Kuching Foochow Association (KFA).

134 This is created by the Society for the Blind, Malaysia (SBM), providing zero-interest loans.

135 The credit scheme is offered by Agrobank, which tries to help operators of small and medium enterprises in the agriculture and farming industry.

136 This is sponsored by the Maybank.

137 *BP*, May 27, 2010, p.D2.

138 *Ibid.*, May 26, 2010, p.5.

139 This was introduced in March 2007 under the Ninth Malaysia Plan (9MP), trying to help Orang Kurang Upaya to become independent. The RM22 million grant was provided by the government for free. The grant would not be distributed in the form of cash but would go to buy equipment or for upgrading work to the business premises. See *BP*, November 5, 2009, p.12.

140 See, for example, M L. Menefee, *et. al.*, "The Role of Human Resources in the Success of New Businesses," *Southern Business Review*, Vol.32, No.1 (Fall 2006), pp.23.-32; A. V. Bruno, *et. al.*, "Why Business Fail?" *Business Horizons*, Vol.30, No.2 (March/April 1987), pp.50-58; R. N. Lussier, "A Nonfinancial Business Success Versus Failure Prediction Model for Young Firms," *Journal of Small Business Management*, Vo.33, No.1 (January 1995), pp.8-20; and J. A. Parnell, *et. al.*, "Profiting from PastTriumphs and Failures," *SAM Advanced Management Journal*, Vol.70, No.2 (March 2005), pp.36-44.

141 *Ibid.*, November 17, 2009, p.13.

142 *Ibid.*, April 6, 2010, p.B8.

143 One academic explained that it is because many Chinese go to church on Sunday mornings.

Sixth, it is appropriate for us to apply the *Yin* and *Yang* diagram to study 1/*Satu* Malaysia, because the 6th Prime Minister of Malaysia for the first time in April 2009 put forward the slogan, which can be properly understood in terms of the *Yin* and *Yang* diagram.

Applied to Bumi

Bumi can get easier grants. Someone should help them to manage the money wisely, so as to really enable the Bumi entrepreneurs to be more successful.

Applied to Non-Bumi

Many of them still quite feel uncomfortable with the NEP and NEM. Ironically, they can still make profit, if not more profit. Does that imply that they should stay in their country and continue their business?

One academic made the following observation: "In Malaysia, Malays have political power which can be used to gain money from Chinese. In contrast, Malaysian Chinese have controlled most business activities in the nation. They use money to purchase political power from Malay politicians. Majority of Indian and some bumi ethnic groups [Bidayuh, Iban, (and) Kadazan] gain no political power and economical control in Malaysia. One way for them to gain these two benefits is to convert themselves as Muslims."[144] MCA president, Datuk Seri Dr. CHUA Soi Lek, called upon the Federal Government to relax the 30% Bumi equity requirement, so as to liberalize the economy. He was quoted as saying the MCA was not afraid to share similar views with the DAP when fighting for the Chinese community's interest.[145]

In sum, Malaysia is trying its best to fulfil the 2020 vision by becoming a developed country. After studying the Bumi and Non-Bumi business people, there is room for improvement on both sides.

References

Abdullah, Firdaus, *et. al.*, "Developing a Framework of Success of Bumiputera Entrepreneurs" *Journal of Enterprising Communities*, Vol.3, No.1 (2009), pp.8-24.

Bruno, A. V., *et. al.*, "Why Business Fail?" *Business Horizons*, Vol.30, No.2 (March/April 1987), pp.50-58.

Chin, James, "The Malaysian-Chinese Dilemma: The Never Ending Policy," *Chinese Southern Diaspora Studies*, Vol.3 (2009), pp.167-182.

Chellian, Shankar Chelliah, Mohamed Sulaiman, and Yusliza Mohd Yusoff, "Internationalization and Performance: Small and Medium Enterprises (SMEs) in Malaysia," International Journal of Business and Management, Vol.5, No. 6 (June 2010), pp.27-37.

[144] Email from him, dated May 3, 2010.

[145] *BP*, August 19, 2010, p.18.

Idris, Aida, "International Marketing Strategy for Bumiputera Entrepreneurs in the Tourism Industry," *Proceedings of the Asia Pacific Management Conference* (2001), pp.623-634, unpublished paper presented at the 7th Asia Pacific Management Conference, November 2-4, 2001, Kuala Lumpur, Malaysia.

Lussier, R. N., "A Nonfinancial Business Success Versus Failure Prediction Model for Young Firms," *Journal of Small Business Management*, Vol. 33, No.1 (January 1995), pp.8-20.

Menefee, J. A. Parnell, Ed Powers, Chris Ziemnowicz, "The Role of Human Resources in the Success of New Businesses," *Southern Business Review*, Vol.32, No.1 (Fall 2006), pp.23.-32.

MHD Juri, Khairul Anuar and Aida Idris "The Effect Of Values On Innovativeness: A Study of Malay and Chinese Entrepreneurs in Peninsular Malaysiathe National Management Conference 2008, December 13-14, 2008, Terengganu, Malaysia.

Mohn Zain, Zahariah Mohd, *et. al.*, "Why Malaysian Bumiputera Franchisees Purchase Franchise Business?" *International Bulletin of Business Administration*, No.6 (December 2009), pp.50-58.

Parnell, J. A. *et. al.*, "Profiting from Past Triumphs and Failures," *SAM Advanced Management Journal*, Vol.70, No.2 (March 2005), pp.36-44.

Sarawak Trades and Development, Sarawak Chamber of Commerce and Industry, celebrating 57th anniversary.

In: International (Corporate) Governance
Editor: Peter Kien-Hong Yu
ISBN: 978-1-61122-645-4

Chapter 10

GOVERNING 1 MALAYSIA AS ONE DOT?

Peter Kien-Hong Yu

ABSTRACT

In April 2009, the new Prime Minister of Malaysia, Datuk Seri Najib Razak, officially propounded a concept or formula, namely, 1/*Satu* Malaysia. Another way of saying the same thing is: People First, Performance Now. This chapter will examine this not so new concept from three perspectives, namely, those who support it, against it, or take a wait-and-see attitude, in terms of the one-dot theory, which is accompanied by the crab and frog motion model.

Later, a few thorny, lingering issues challenging the 1 Malaysia concept will be discussed.

Keywords: 1 Malaysia, one dot theory, politics, economic affairs, religion

The Federation of Malaysia (FOM) since its establishment is a multi-race and multi-ethnic country. The First People are the Orang Asil (oringal peoples) in Peninsula Malaysia, and the main Malaysian races are Malays, Chinese, and Indians. However, since April 2009, there is a picked-up movement calling for the formation of a single or new race in Malaysia.[1]

In April 2009, Datuk Seri Najib Razak, who is a Malay, became the 6th Prime Minister of Malaysia. In the same month, he officially propounded a concept or formula,[2] namely, 1/*Satu* Malaysia. Another way of saying the same thing is: People First, Performance Now.[3] This came about as a reaction to the following facts.

In May 1946, the United Malays National Organization (UMNO) was founded, having, as of today, about three million members, representing the interests of the Malays and

[1] *Burneo Post* (hereafter *BP*) (Sarawak, Malaysia), October 4, 2010, p.4.
[2] *New Sunday Times* (hereinafter NST)(Sarawak, Malaysia), October 18, 2009, p.23.
[3] In Mandarin Chinese, *YiMinWeiBen,JiXiaoWeiXian* or *XianZaiJiuBiaoXian.* Minister's Department Senator, Tan Sri KOH Tsu Koon said no local or foreign public relations firms are paid to promote the 1 Malaysia concept. However, KOH said the government did appoint Apco Worldwide Sdn. Bhd. to handle communication-related services for the federal government and to enhance Malaysia's image abroad. See *Borneo Post* (hereinafter BP)(Sarawak, Malaysia), October 23, 2009, p.23. Another newspaper reported that Kuala Lumpur had spent Ringgit 20 million to promote the concept. See *See Hua Daily News* (hereinafter SHDN)(Sarawak, Malaysia), October 19, 2009, p.3.

Bumiputras/Bumiputeras, the latter of whom can be translated as son of earth, referring to the indigenous people of the Malay Archipelago, such as the Orang Asil, Negrito, Senoi, and Proto Malays, 26 ethnic and sub-ethnic groups with Dayak as the main ethnic group in Sarawak State,[4] which has been hailed as the best example of the 1 Malaysia concept,[5] 32 ethnic and sub-ethnic groups with Kadazans as the main ethnic group in Tawau Division of Sabah State,[6] which was acknowledged by Najib as a role model for the 1 Malaysia concept[7] and which, in August 2010, was declared Sabah's first poverty-free district, etc.

The UMNO managed to form an Alliance [in July 1974 expanded as the Barisan Nasional (BN)/National Front] with 15 other component political parties or member constituents, as of August 2009,[8] to become or remain as the ruling party. In March 2008 at the general election, the BN, for the first time, was not able to maintain its two-thirds majority in the Parliament, in which the loose coalition of three opposition parties or Pakatan Rakyat/People Alliance since April 1, 2008, to wit, Parti Keadilan Rakyat (PKR)/People's Justice Party, Democratic Action Party (DAP), and Parti Islam Se-Malaysia/Pan-Malaysian Islamic Party (PAS), had gotten majority in five states, namely, Kelantan, Kedah, Penang, Perak, and Selangor or also known as Pakatan Rakyat state governments, or a total of 82 seats as compared to the BN's 140 in the *Dewan Rakyat* (literally "Hall of the People") or House of Representatives, which is the lower house of the Parliament of Malaysia.[9] Earlier in May 2006, the BN lost nine out of 71 seats to the opposition in the Sarawak election.[10] Selangor, Kedah, Kelantan, and Trenganu are supposed to be conservative states, peopled by Malays.

In January 2010, Najib said the UMNO and the BN should learn from the downfall of the Japanese ruling party, Liberal Democratic Party (LDP), which was replaced by an opposition party, Democratic Party of Japan (DPJ), in August 2009, ending a half-century of virtually uninterrupted one-party rule in the country. The then Japanese prime minister, HATOYAMA Yukio, who stepped down in June 2010 by a row over an unpopular Unites States Marine Corps airbase on Okinawa Island, told Najib the reasons: The LDP was no longer close to the people, could no longer feel the pulse of the people, and did not understand the wishes and aspirations of the people.[11]

---

[4] *Borneo Post* (hereinafter BP)(Sarawak, Malaysia), September 2, 2009, p.13.

[5] *BP*, November 2, 2009, p.8 and November 12, 2009, p.12.

[6] *Ibid.*, December 28, 2009, p.3. Another report mentioned more than 30 ethnic groups. See *Ibid.*, January 9, 2010, p.14.

[7] *BP*, December 23, 2009, p.20.

[8] *SHDN*, February 18, 2010, p.6. Besides the UMNO, which has 3.16 million members as of the latest count which was released in May 2010, there are the following component parties: Malaysian Chinese Association (MCA), Parti Gerakan Rakyat (Gerakan), Malaysian Indian Congress (MIC), People's Progressive Party (PPP), Parti Pesaka Bumiputera Bersatu/Parti Pesaka Bersatu Sarawak (PBB), Sarawak United Peoples' Party (SUPP), Parti Bersatu Sabah (PBS), Liberal Democratic Party (LDP), Parti Bersatu Rakyat Sabah (PBRS), United Pasokmomogun Kadazandusun Murut Organisation (UPKO), **Sarawak Progressive Democratic Party (SPDP),** Parti Rakyat Sarawak (PRS), Parti Cinta Malaysia (PCM), Parti Gerankan Rakyat Malaysia (PGRM), and Parti Semangat Rakyat Malaysia (PSRM).

[9] A by-election in October 2009 at Bagan Pinang somewhat reversed the trend, because a Barisan Nasional (BN) candidate won and the Parti Islam Se-Malaysia (PAS) candidate was lost. It is said that 70% Chinese voters would vote for the main Chinese opposition party, while 30% of them are for the SUPP. See *SHDN*, May 29, 2010, p.A9.

[10] The SUPP president in February 2010 said the DAP is "not a strong opponent…" any more. See *BP*, February 22, 2010, p.1.

[11] *Ibid.*, January 10, 2010, p.23.

Since April 2009, many academics and experts plus government officials have positively treated 1 Malaysia, depending on the context, as formula, spirit, *wawasan* (vision),[12] philosophy,[13] (pragmatic) *LiNian* in Mandarin Chinese/ideal (concept),[14] principle,[15] value,[16] approach,[17] aspirations,[18] policy,[19] national drive,[20] feature/*tese*,[21] event,[22] situation,[23] action, brand,[24] logo,[25] placard,[26] gesture,[27] 1 Malaysia checking and balancing/*ZhiHeng* extremism,[28] oneness, wholeness, and togetherness,[29] etc. Najib has gone to at length describing and explaining his concept. Some of the important passages are mentioned below.

1 Malaysia is applied to all Malaysians. The concept is synonymous with the unity aspirations of the late Tun Hussein bin Dato' Onn, the third prime minister of the country.[30] Najib made following remarks, as a third priority point, to his UMNO members: "… the party culture… must be inclusive not insular. More outreach programmes must be implemented. In this context, one matter must be remembered, this need not be limited to UMNO members but must be expanded to all Malays and non-Malays."[31] It should be reminded that the UMNO constitution already has principles of the 1 Malaysia concept, under Clause 3 (6), emphasizing the creation of a single Malaysian race.

One Malaysia has several pillar principles, "among them a departure from unity based on tolerance to that of acceptance, social justice and shared values, taking into consideration the nation's historical reality and guided by the supremacy of the Constitution and Rukun Negara [National Principles instituted by royal proclamation on the August 1970 Merdeka/ Independence Day]."[32]

Najib reminded us that "… the 1 Malaysia concept does not digress from the spirit of the Federal Constitution as the law of the country, either written or unwritten. In fact, we will continue to uphold core provisions such as Article 3, Article 4, Article 152, Article 153, as well as Part II and III of the Federal Constitution… . Ultimately, 1 Malaysia is a celebration of Malaysia's plurality and diversity from which the country draws its strength."[33] However, UMNO executive committee (exco) youth Datuk Muhd Khairun Aseh said 1 Malaysia will

---

[12] *Ibid.*, October 26, 2009, p.3.
[13] *Ibid.*, January 24, 2010, p.14.
[14] *SHDN*, January 23, 2010, p.2 and *GuoJiShiBao* (hereinafter GJSB)(Sarawak, Malaysia), July 27, 2009, p.A14.
[15] *SHDN.*, January 29, 2010, p.4.
[16] *Ibid.*, December 30, 2009, p.21.
[17] *Ibid.*, October 13, 2009, p.13.
[18] *BP*, February 23, 2010, p.17.
[19] *SHDN*, January 28, 2010, p.1.
[20] *Ibid.*, January 27, 2010, p.9.
[21] *GJSB*, February 22, 2010, p.A20.
[22] *SHDN*, October 13, 2009, p.13.
[23] *Ibid.*, September 2, 2009, p.13.
[24] *Ibid.*, January 18, 2010, p.15.
[25] About 800 pupils used 220,220 pieces of 20 sen coins created the 1 Malaysia logo in Kuala Lumpur. See *BP*, November 2, 2009, p.14.
[26] *SHDN*, January 27, 2010, p.A6.
[27] *Xinzhouribao* (hereinafter XZRB)(Malaysia), October 15, 2009, p.17.
[28] *SHDN*, August 23, 2010, p.6.
[29] *BP*, November 4, 2010, p.19.
[30] *BP*, July 26, 2010, p.14.
[31] *NST*, October 18, 2009, p.23.
[32] *Ibid.*, October 18, 2009, p.23.
[33] *Ibid,*, October 18, 2009, p.23.

not override the country's constitution, meaning, for example, West Malaysians cannot go to Sarawak without any restrictions.[34]

He also said the following: 1 Malaysia has a noble purpose. It is a call to action underpinned by age-old, fundamental values that have always existed with us, such as integrity and loyalty. These core human values are woven together into the fabric of our national identity... our Malaysian identity... ."[35]

In February 2010, Najib drew an analogy between 1 Malaysia and "*yee sang*,"[36] saying there may be different ingredients in *yee sang*, such as herbs, salmon, fish, vegetables, nuts, and so on and so forth, making the dish to look like one hell of a mess, but, when the ingredients were tossed, it looked colourful and tasted very nice, and adding his dinner table is a perfect "1 Malaysia table," having Malay, Melanau, Chinese, Iban, Fuzhou/Foochow, Hokkien, Kelabit, and Guangdongren/Cantonese.[37]

Positive Information, Data, and Analysis on One Malaysia

There are supporters of the 1 Malaysia concept. If Najib can translate rhetoric of 1 Malaysia into action, he can further whip up the sentiments of his supporters or spur the people to a higher level of optimism to maintain and sustain 1 Malaysia.

The UMNO does not want to see a repetition of the May 13, 1969 racial riots tragedy, the outcome of which was the formulation of the New Economic Policy (NEP), which was introduced in the Second Malaysia Plan (1971-1975), trying to reduce the socio-economic disparity between the Chinese minority and Malay majority in the federation. From an international regimes perspective, this is a wise move: What is good for Malaysia will be good to its neighbours, if not other countries and regions.

While emphasizing that 1 Malaysia "is not a new[38] concept or formula,"[39] Najib in October 2009 explained in the following words: "The [NEP], when it was first formulated, targeted increasing Malay and Bumiputra equity ownership from 2.4 per cent to 30 per cent, in 20 years. But, until the [NEP] ended, the objective could not be achieved. The equity ownership of the Malays and Bumiputras only reached 19.2 per cent. Therefore, this objective was continued under the National Development Policy, the Vision Development Policy and now, the National Mission using approaches that are not all very different."[40] In September, 2010, he gave the assurance that the March 2010 New Economic Model (NEM) is not about removing the NEP but move towards "progressive liberalization" of the economy[41]. On another occasion, Najib in his personal statement cited the Gawai celebrations in longhouses

[34] *BP*, May 9, 2010, p.3.

[35] *BP*, February 1,2 010, p.14.

[36] *Yee Sang* or Yusheng literally means 'raw fish' but since 'fish' is commonly conflated with its homophone 'abundance/*yu*', [it] is interpreted as a homophone for Yúshēng meaning an increase in abundance. Therefore, yusheng is considered a symbol of abundance, prosperity and vigor." See http://en.wikipedia.org/wiki/ Yusheng, accessed on March 1, 2010.

[37] *BP*, February 24, 2010, p.1.

[38] On another occasion, NAJIB said the concept was "still new." See *ibid.*, October 14, 2009, p.18.

[39] *Ibid.*, October 16, 2009, p.21.

[40] *Ibid.*, October 18, 2009, p.22 and p.23. The Malaysian Government's Government Transformation Program (GTP) roadmap, launched in January 2010, wants to catalyze Vision 2020 though 1 Malaysia, People First, Performance Now. In the year 2008, the percentage is 21.9%. According to CHONG Chieng Jen, the percentage is over 30%, if we talk about the government linked companies. See *SHDN*, June 12, 2010, p.A31.

[41] *BP*, September 1, 2010, p.1.

in Sarawak as an example: He could not help but think that the people of Sarawak had already adopted the values of 1 Malaysia "long before I explained its various elements."[42]

Najib assured others that Malays are an all-inclusive race, far from being a racist party,[43] unlike the Americans who openly practiced racism until the mid-1960s or the South African whites, who formulated and implemented the apartheid policy.[44]

Some political observers and politicians regard 1 Malaysia as a slogan, something in the air. However, we do see implementation of some ideas. Examples are many, to name but a few.

First, the Malaysian Federal Government allocated a total of Ringgit (RM) 10 million to establish a total of 50 people-oriented 1 Malaysia clinics, manned by non-greenhorn medical assistants and nurses[45] from Monday to Sunday and public holidays and usually set up in low and medium cost of housing estates. The first clinic was opened on December 28, 2009. The one in Batu Melintang District, opened on January 31, 2010, in Kelantan, which is the most socially conservative state, is the first clinic in the rural district.[46] Each patient just have to pay a nominal registration fee of RM one to get basic medical attention.[47] From December 28, 2009 to July 24, 2010, over 721,888 patients visited the clinics.[48] There will be more 1 Malaysia clinics.

Second, the National Service (PLKN) (as opposed to pusat indoktrinasi politik/political indoctrination center) [49] intake in the year 2010 reflects the racial composition in line with the 1 Malaysia concept: Bumiputras (60%); Chinese (28%); Indians (10%), and others 2%, unlike the previous six times, which were done at random. About 120,000 trainees were selected.[50] In February 2010, Kuala Lumpur announced a 30% increase in the intake of non-Malay students at the Royal Military College (RMC). This is good news, because there were only about 5% in Forms four and five.[51]

Third, as Minister in the Prime Minister's Department, Senator Tan Sri KOH Tsu Koon, after officiating the November 2009, first-ever World Chinese Economic Forum (WCEF), said, the diversity of religious and cultures actually can be a major asset to the nation. For example, the Chinese community in Malaysia has been encouraged to use their linguistic capability and cultural affiliations to help the country in gaining access to mainland China's huge market. Malay and Muslim businessman and professionals have been exploring economic collaborations and other potential ventures with Islamic countries, while Indian-

---

[42] *BP*, September 17, 2009, p.1 and February 20, 2010, p.11. In September 1963, Sarawak agreed to be independently ruled through Malaysia by retaining certain rights and conditions, such as it has the rights over immigration control as well as policy implementation on land and forestry issues, while the state civil service is free from any Federal Government's interference. See *ibid.*, February 20, 2010, p.11.

[43] Extremists in the UMNO exist, and they would remind others that Malaysia is the land of Malays and non-Malays are "émigrés/*WaiLaiRen*." See *SHDN*, February 23, 2010, p.8.

[44] *NST*, October 18, 2009, p.21.

[45] *BP*, January 16, 2010, p.11. The SUPP maintains a "People's Clinic," trying to solve the people's problems.

[46] *Ibid.*, February 12, 2010, p.21. In January 2010, six suspects broke into a 1 Malaysia clinic at Taman Lee Ling in Matang Jaya. See *ibid.*, January 29, 2010, p.10.

[47] There are, of course, problems. For example, 1 Malaysia clinic at the Sungai Plan housing area does not have enough experienced medical staff. See *ibid.,* January 26, 2010, p.11. At bigger public clinics and hospitals, one also just have to pay RM1.

[48] SHDN, July 29, 2010, p.2.

[49] *Ibid.*, January 16, 2010, p.5.

[50] *BP*, January 13, 2010, p.14.

[51] *Ibid.*, February 26, 2010, p.21.

Malaysians could work on relationships with the Republic of India (ROI) and the global Indian diaspora.

Fourth, visits by government agencies especially from Peninsular Malaysia to Sabah and Sarawak can indeed create further understanding and integration.[52] Seeing is believing. If East Malaysia can be the best example or role model, why cannot West Malaysia?

Fifth, the International Society for Krishna Consciousness (ISKCON) Malaysia, Kuching Branch hailed Sarawak for truly practicing the 1 Malaysia concept by recognizing minority religious groups, such as the ISKCON. This is because the state government had proven this by allocating a piece of land next to the temple at Jalan Ketitit, Batu Kawa Township, Kuching City, for the ISKCON's moral uplifting, youth development, festivals activities.[53] As another example, Che Hui Khor Moral Uplifting Society (CHKMUS)'s vision is similar to 1 Malaysia, as it promotes mutual understanding and tolerance, while encompassing five major religions, namely, Confucianism, Buddhism, Daoism, Christianity, and Islam.[54]

Sixth, in November 2009, a deputy minister in the Prime Minister's Department suggested that a 1 Smile 1 Malaysia campaign to be held, so as to forge closer relationship among the Malaysians.[55] In December 2009, the Ministry of Information Communication and Culture announced that activities to popularize the 1 Malaysia concept nationwide will involve government agencies and the private sector and will be held at the state level throughout next year. In February 2010, the Biro Tata Negara (BTN)/National Civics Bureau (NCB) said it will conduct 500 1 Malaysia seminars for the private sector and non-governmental organizations (NGOs) throughout the year. For example, in July 2010, some 50 community leaders and village chiefs from Matu District, Mukah Division, Sarawak attended the seminar.[56] 1 Malaysia can demonstrated by celebrating together major festivals like Hari Raya (Aidilfitri),[57] Deepavali,[58] Christmas, Gawai Dayak, Pesta Kaamatan, and Chinese Lunar New Year[59] when lion and dragon dance troupes in Sarawak truly epitomize the 1 Malaysia concept as they comprise multi-racial members, such as ngajat, performing dance routines.[60] So, we saw 1 Malaysia (in) Christmas being celebrated in December 2009[61] and we see the Chinese New Year 2010 1 Malaysia gathering.[62] The Education Ministry has considered the suggestion to create 1 Malaysia Clubs in schools, organized the 1 Malaysia camping activities, and put 1 Malaysia hostels into operation.[63] Tourism Assistant Minister believed that the concept is aimed at creating a single Malaysian race, whose thinking

[52] *Ibid.*, January 30, 2010, p.6.

[53] *Ibid.*, October 20, 2009, p.14.

[54] *Ibid.*, September 26, 2009, p.14.

[55] *Ibid.*, November 16, 2009, p.6.

[56] *Ibid.*, July 31, 2010, p.D2.

[57] *Ibid.*, September 22, 2009, p.12. The Malaysian Prime Minister, Datuk Seri NAJIB Tun Razak, said the Hijrah (flight from Mecca to Medina in 622 A.D.) spirit is in line with 1 Malaysia concept. See *ibid.*, December 18, 2009, p.23.

[58] *Ibid.*, October 16, 2009, p.26 and October 18, 2009, p.21. In keeping with the 1 Malaysia concept, the national Ponggal festival, the harvest thanksgiving celebrated by Tamils, has been opened to all races from January to February. See *ibid.*, January 13, 2010, p.17.

[59] *Ibid.*, February 22, 2010, p.11.

[60] *Ibid.*, January 26, 2010, p.5 and February 17, 2010, p.14 and p.17. NAJIB said the 1 Malaysia Lantern Festival to be yearly affair. See *ibid.*, September 28, 2009, p.3. See also *ibid.*, September 24, 2009, p.19.

[61] *Ibid.*, November 29, 2009, p.22 and December 5, 2009, p.9.

[62] *Ibid.*, February 22, 2010, p.11.

[63] *Ibid.*, November 26, 2009, p.23.

transcend factors, such as state, district, race, religion, and culture.[64] Over 2,000 facilitators and lecturers at the BTN were asked to intensify the elements of 1 Malaysia concept in its courses and seminars, so as to nurture patriotism.[65] And, the state-owned Petroliam Nasional Berhad (Petronas), an oil and gas corporation, would advertise "One Legacy. One Destiny. 1 Malaysia" in newspapers.[66]

Seventh, Sarawak Orphans Welfare Board (Peryatim) practices the 1 Malaysia concept by accepting eligible non-Muslim orphans to enrol at Peryatim centers, and the board will not force non-Muslim orphans to embrace Islam when they stay in its institutions.[67]

Eighth, Malaysian Chinese Association (MCA), a component party of BN, which only has influence and clout in Peninsula Malaysia and Sabah, after the Chinese Lunar New Year in February 2010, urged Najib in writing to drop the usage of the terms, Bumiputra and the non-Bumiputra.[68] To be sure, according to Mahathir bin Mohamad, who is the former prime minister, each political party controls 20% of Malay voters.[69] A non-Chinese, Marcella Gider, also said that the term, Bumiputra should not exist, because there are three contrasting and inconsistent definitions as stated in Article 161a of the Federal Constitution: If both parents are indigenous natives of Sarawak, the child is considered as Bumiputra; whereas in the Peninsular and Sabah, the definitions are different as night and day.[70] In West Malaysia, a child is a Bumiputra, if any one of the parents is a Bumiputra, while in Sabah a child is a Bumiputra, if the father is a Bumiputra.[71]

Ninth, the Sarawak United People's Party (SUPP), a state BN component, said it is proud of the fact that it is a multi-racial party, despite being labelled by some as an urban-based party for the Chinese.[72] This is because, since its formation, its slogan is *Sa'ati*, which translated from Iban means one heart, or *Sehati* in Malay.

Tenth, the Federal Government continues to subsidize Malaysia Airlines (MAS) to provide rural air services (RAS) to the remote and interior parts of Sarawak.[73] In August 2009, it was reported that the Ministry of Domestic Trade, Cooperative and Consumerism (MDTCC) in line with the Price Control Act (PCA) will target to standardize the prices of 100 essential items, such as sugar, rice, etc. in Sarawak before the year-end, under the "1 Sarawak, 1 Price" program.[74] In July 2010, a ranking official said a total of 20 villages comprising 192 localities are involved in the project, and the project will be expanded to 39 new areas.[75]

---

[64] *Ibid.*, August 18, 2009, p.12. In one important January 2010 document, *Government Transformation Program (GTP) Roadmap*, the following was mentioned: The people of Malaysia/Malaysians come first, while race, religion, birth place, and class (*SeHuiJieJi*) come second. See *SHDN*, July 12, 2010, p.8. However, an opposition party leader, LIM Kit Siang, said Malaysians should come first, while race, district (*DiQu*), religion, and ethnic group come second. See *ibid.*, July 10, 2010, p.A41.

[65] *BP*, December 15, 2009, p.17 and 16, 2009, p.8.

[66] *Ibid.*, August 31, 2009, p.3 and January 1, 2010.

[67] *Ibid.*, September 15, 2009, p.14.

[68] *SHDN*, February 12, 2010, p.1.

[69] *Ibid.*, June 15, 2010, p.2.

[70] *BP*, November 18, 2009, p.15. This has to do with a Sri Aman, Sarawak case related to Marina Undau, whose father is an Iban and mother, Chinese. In November 2009, the Federal Government has recognized Undau, a Bumiputra.

[71] *Ibid.*, November 5, 2009, p.6.

[72] *Ibid.*, September 2, 2009, p.13.

[73] *Ibid.*, August 6, 2009, p.4.

[74] *Ibid.*, August 6, 2009, p.4.

[75] *Ibid.*, July 19, 2010, p.2.

11th, some foreigners also appreciate the 1 Malaysia concept. In the words of Harold J. Raveche, who is the president of the U.S.-based Stevens Institute of Technology (SIT), said the concept fits nicely with innovation, which can help Malaysia to transit from a knowledge-based economy to innovation-based economy.[76] President of Bosnia and Herzegovina said "[t]he concept will be the foundation to our policies in" his country.[77] A calligrapher from mainland China presented his 1 Malaysia brush writing to Najib.[78]

In sum, it is not difficult to find evidence, which are in line with Najib's 1 Malaysia concept.

NEGATIVE INFORMATION, DATA, AND ANALYSIS ON ONE MALAYSIA

Some skeptics,[79] critics, detractors, etc. have treated One Malaysia as a (sugar-coated) slogan,[80] rhetoric,[81] empty words/promise,[82] not possible to be a "one size that fits all,"[83] meaningless without fair distribution,[84] vague,[85] cease to exist except in name/exist in name only,[86] stumbling block,[87] cannot stand up to any test,[88] like a piece of melting ice,[89] a façade,[90] obscurantism,[91] laughingstock/joke,[92] bring about hindrance or obstruction,[93] *HouJingFaLi*/lack stamina in long-distance race,[94] a symbol at ceremony,[95] an incomplete/*CanQue* 1 Malaysia,[96] 1 Muted Malaysia,[97] etc. In July 2010, Mahathir said the slogan needs to be explained in-depth or in detail.[98] It is not difficult to find evidence. In the following month, the chief minister of Sarawak, who has been in power for a few decades, said he still does not know what the Chinese community want.[99]

First, in the words of Deputy Transport Minister, Datuk Robert LAU Hoi Chew, some 300,000 Malaysians left the country in 2009, causing brain drain.[100] This includes young Malays.[101] In May 2010, at the Sixth World Islamic Economic Forum (WIFE), Muhddin

[76] *Ibid.*, December 10, 2009, p.9.
[77] *Ibid.*, November 12, 2009, p.6.
[78] *XZRB*, December 27, 2009, p.17.
[79] *BP*, January 24, 2010, p.14.
[80] *SHDN*, October 2, 2009, p.*zeng*1.
[81] *NST*, October 18, 2009, p.21.
[82] *BP*, January 24, 2010, p.3 and *SHDN*, January 30, 2010, p.8.
[83] *BP*, September 20, 2009, p.9.
[84] *Ibid.*, September 5, 2009, p.14.
[85] *Ibid.*
[86] *SHDN*, January 27, 2010, p.A2.
[87] *GJSB*, November 9, 2009, p.B2.
[88] *Ibid.*, December 13, 2009, p.3.
[89] *Ibid.*, December 20, 2009, p.B2.
[90] *Ibid.*
[91] *Ibid.*
[92] *Ibid.*, January 18, 2010, p.B5.
[93] *XZRB*, October 17, 2009, p.8.
[94] *SHDN*, February 23, 2010, p.8.
[95] *Ibid.*, July 25, 2010, p.5.
[96] *Ibid.*, August 23, 2010, p.A12.
[97] A small group of people called for freedom of speech in Kuala Lumpur. See *LianHeRiBao* (hereinafter LHRB)(Sarawak, Malaysia), August 23, 2010, p.A4 and *SHDN*, August 23, 2010, p.7.
[98] *BP*, August 3, 2010, p.17 and November 2, 2010, p.14.
[99] *SHDN*, August 25, 2010, p.A1.
[100] *BP*, January 18, 2010, p.7.
[101] *GJSB*, February 27, 2010, p.B1.

candidly mentioned that "[s]ome studies have indicated that in the last 50 years, a huge number of intellectuals had migrated from the Muslim world to industrialized countries," adding, to reverse the brain drain to brain gain so as to ensure young entrepreneurs to remain in the country, a right strategy should be mapped out.[102] Another report mentioned 304,358 Malaysians from March 2008 to August 2009.[103] In 2007, the number was 139,696.[104] One of the worries is that there is no future for their children, had they stayed on.[105] Usually, a Chinese or an Indian may have to learn three languages from childhood. After years of schooling, many of them cannot command each language, by being trilingual.

Second, in February 2010, a five-man bench of the Federal Court unanimously ruled as constitutional the appointment of Datuk Seri Zambry Abdul Kadir as Menteri Besar[106] of Perak, which is one of the 13 states of Malaysia and the second largest in Peninsular Malaysia, to the post by Sultan Azlan Muhibbuddin Shah to succeed another political figure from another political party. Some political observers feared that, one day, as a result of this decision, Malaysia could become an absolute monarchy, as opposed to constitutional monarchy.[107]

Third, there are 35 active political parties.[108] The BN has 16, plus the fact that there are 16 small parties and, of course, the People Alliance. Yet, we see many power struggles even within the BN. The UMNO is suffering from *lagak* (to boast or brag about), *laga* (to fight or clash), and *leka* (to cause to become careless).[109] People's Progressive Party (PPP) is based in Kuala Lumpur. It was warned by another BN component party, Sarawak Progressive Democratic Party (SPDP), that it should only set up clubs not registered 28 or even 42 branches in Sarawak, because the PPP, trying to spread its wings to Sarawak or even "steal" members of other political parties, had caused uneasiness among the State BN.[110] The opposition camp is also sometimes divided. For example, each party in the People Alliance has its own objectives and, therefore, they cannot really work together.[111] As another example, some cracks seem to appear in the People Alliance, so a meeting had to be held among the top leaders in February 2010 in setting up a disciplinary committee.[112]

Fourth, Minister in the Prime Minister's Department, Datuk Seri Mohamed Nazri Abdul Aziz, said he is touched by the racial harmony and religious tolerance as enjoyed by Sarawakians. He admitted that the political culture in West Malaysia is not healthy, because West Malaysians are narrow-minded as far as politics and religion are concerned, adding he

[102] *BP*, May 19, 2010, p.B12.
[103] *SHDN*, December 18, 2009, p.4.
[104] *GJSB*, December 27, 2009, p.A14.
[105] *SHDN*, February 9, 2010, p.1.
[106] In Malay, it means grand minister, who is the chief executive of the state government for one of Perlis, Johor, Kedah, Perak, Selangor, Negeri Sembilan, Pahang, Terengganu and Kelantan, i.e., all states with royal rulers. In other states without a monarch, the title, Ketua Menteri (Chief Minister), is used. "Menteri Besar" is often un-translated in local English mass media. See http://en.wikipedia.org/wiki/Menteri_Besar, accessed on February 12, 2010.
[107] *SHDN*, February 10, 2010, p.1.
[108] *Ibid.*, February 18, 2010, p.6. This edition mentioned 33. In August 2010, the SUPP said "quitting BN was never discussed in KL meeting." See *BP*, August 24, 2010, p.4.
[109] *SHDN*, October 16, 2009, p.1.
[110] *BP*, February 3, 2010, p.10, February 10, 2010, p.4, February 18, 2010, p.1 and February 19, 2010, p.6.
[111] Conversation with one of my colleagues, dated February 20, 2010. Indeed, one BN assemblyman said that, should the PAS become a ruling party, it would drop the secular part by making Malaysia a pure Muslim country. See *GJSB*, January 20, 2010, p.A15.
[112] SHDN, February 23, 2010, p.1 and 3. For the friction between two leaders in the DAP, see BP, January 20, 2010, p.9 and *XZRB*, February 7, 2010, p.6 and 8, 2010, p.6.

would prevent the 1 Malaysia concept, which originated from Sabah and Sarawak to be intruded by the negative political culture of Peninsular Malaysia.[113]

Fifth, Malaysian Indian Congress (MIC), a component party of BN, said there are some Indian NGOs, funded by certain Indian opposition figures, including elected representatives, instilling hatred among certain sections of the Indian community towards the government and the BN.[114]

Sixth, Selangor State Government in November 2009 barred its state civil servants, students in state-run institutions of higher learning, and employees of state government-linked companies from attending the BTN courses, because they were an indoctrination process, with possible intention of converting participants to the UMNO or the BN, and smacked of racism.[115]

Seventh, Miri Division chairman for Parti Keadilan Rakyat (PKR), Michael TEO Y.K., noted that one of the biggest flaws in the distribution of the country's wealth is the way projects were given out to individuals and companies, not open to public tender. Sarawak, endowed with land, timber, oil, and gas, "has contributed much money to the country but is only given about five per cent of the share in return.... A fair figure should have been 14 per cent and not just five."[116] In May 2010, TEO said: "The Chinese are not anti-government, it's just that they have a good memory of the injustices they had to endure," adding it is a misconception that al Chinese were rich.[117] In December 2009, it was reported that, due to corruption, each year RM 10 billion were wasted, amounting to 1 to 2% of Gross National Product (GDP).[118] A DAP assembly person, TING Tzi Fui, said "millions and millions of ringgit unaccounted for precisely, squandered."[119] CHONG Chieng Ren, Member of Parliament (MP) for Bandar Kuching, said if the opposition parties were to become the ruling party, they will conduct anti-corruption campaigns.[120] At lower level, we also see nepotism, cronyism, and favouritism, when it comes to distributing government aid to the people by the community leaders, especially *penghulus* (village headman) and village chiefs.[121] For the record, 34% of the Malaysian workers earn less than RM700 per month, as of August 2010.[122]

Eighth, 1 Malaysia clinics may take away business from private clinics. Besides, would it be possible for a 1 Malaysia clinic to be upgraded to polyclinic?[123] What about the fact that there is a 60% shortage of medical doctors at government hospitals and clinics nationwide and the problem can only be overcame five years later?[124]

---

[113] *BP.*, August 17, 2009, p.20 and May 3, 2010, p.10.

[114] *Ibid.*, December 17, 2009, p.21.

[115] *Ibid.,* November 27, 2009, p.23.

[116] *BP*, September 5, 2009, p.14. Senadin assemblyman, who is also Assistant Minister of Infrastructure Development and Communication, Datuk LEE Kim Shin, said there is no favouritism in awarding of projects to the people. See *ibid.*, January 7, 2010, p.8. About 30% of the projects were unable to be finished in the Ninth Malaysia Plan and they have to be shifted to the 10th. See *GJSB*, January 30, 2010, p.B8.

[117] *Ibid.*, May 15, 2010, p.5.

[118] *SHDN*, December 18, 2009, p.2.

[119] *Ibid.*, January 3, 2010, p.A4.

[120] *Ibid.*, January 3, 2010, p.A6.

[121] *BP*, December 28, 2009, p.9.

[122] *SHDN*, August 20, 2010, p.4.

[123] *BP*, January 11, 2010, p.4.

[124] *Ibid.*, February 19, 2010, p.20. See also *SHDN*, January 13, 2010, p.6. Another report mentioned that Sabah and Sarawak lack 80% of the medical doctors. See *XZRB*, February 7, 2010, p.23.

Ninth, we sometimes see open threats. For example, Lubok Antu District Member of Parliament, William Nyakillau Badak, said community leaders, including village and longhouse chiefs, found unsupportive of the BN or joining with the opposition against the BN in the coming election would have their appointments revoked.[125] In other words, they must be 1 Malaysia-compliant,[126] and both the leaders and the people cannot be "*alang alang* (half-hearted).[127]

Tenth, in December 2009, the Republic of Indonesia (RI) and Malaysia signed a brotherhood alliance called *Persaudaraan Serumpun Indonesia Malaysia* (PSIM). The question is: Would the former also adopt 1 Malaysia?

11th, leaders in the Bidayuh community in Sarawak were forthright in calling upon the Bidayuhs to get rid of their old mentality of being envious and pulling each other down. Dayak Bidayuh National Association (DBNA) chief advisor, Dato Sri Michael Manyin Jawong, referred to what is famously called the "crab mentality," whereby the envious would work hard to bring down those who are successful much like the crabs that would claw their way up receptacles by clinging and climbing onto one another, thereby bringing those on top down with their sheer weight, emphasizing that "... if we fight each other, we will become smaller."[128] However, in August 2010, at the Bidayuh Youth Symposium 2010, Minister of Infrastructure Development and Communication Dato Sri Michael Manyin spoke on "one frequency" and called for 1 Bidayuh.[129] The question is: Is the concept part of 1 Malaysia?

12th, Najib launched the *Subur* (rice subsidy program) in Selangor, which is Malaysia's most populous, richest state and which was declared as developed in August 2005. It was an effort under the Agriculture and Agro-based Industries Ministry (AIM) to alleviate the burden of the lower-income group via the use of coupons. In November 2009, Sabah announced that 1,043 people comprising the hardcore, poor, and under-privileged were eligible for the subsidy program. A chairman for Chinese Kapitan Association (CKA) in Tawau Division, Sabah, YAP Kin Vui, said the perception that the Chinese including those who lived in urban areas were rich was inaccurate, as many of them, staying in squatter settlements and low-cost housing estates, were under the poverty line.[130] YAP also called for the program to be transparent in line with the slogan of "People First, Performance Now," which is derived from the 1 Malaysia concept.

13th, transparency sometimes is an issue. If the Malaysian Government is not corrupt, it does not have to take nine initiatives as shown in its unprecedented, January 2010 Government Transformation Program (GTP) Roadmap to fight against corruption in three phases [Horizon I (2010-2012); Horizon II (2012-2015); and Horizon III (2015-2020)]. For example, the following was mentioned: regarding its 1.2 million strong civil service workforce: To reduce the opportunity for corrupt practices to take place at... enforcement agencies, job rotation will be instituted to help prevent enforcement officers from forming collaborative relationships with criminal organizations and also create a league table of performance for all local authorities.[131]

---

[125] *BP*, January 31, 2010, p.12.
[126] *Ibid.*, October 3, 2009, p.13.
[127] *Ibid.*, September 22, 2009, p.11.
[128] *Ibid.*, November 7, 2009, p.10.
[129] *SHDN*, August 8, 2010, p.Zeng1.
[130] *BP*, December 22, 2009, p.15.
[131] *Ibid.*, January 29, 2010, p.2.

Sometimes, even when there is transparency, unfairness can be seen. For example, in August 2009, the RM10 bullion 1 Malaysia Unit Trust or Amanah Saham 1 Malaysia (AS 1 Malaysia) was opened for subscription. The management urged the Malaysians to seize the opportunity to get high returns.[132] During the offer period, subscription of the units is subject to an allocation of 50% for Bumiputras, 30% for local Chinese, 15% for Indians, and the remaining 5% for other minorities. In addition, 50,000 public university (as opposed to both public and private university) students can each get 100 free units.[133] To be sure, many Chinese and Indian students can only attend private universities, due to the quota system, which began to change since April 2009.

14th, another news report mentioned that as compared to the year 1970 the number of Chinese and Indian civil servants dropped by 4% and 6%, respectively.[134] Is this because one can make more money by working in the private sector?[135]

15th, Malaysia's Information Communication and Culture Minister said the 1 Malaysia message must be spread in the rural areas or at the grassroots level, using various communication methods and debates as well as the use of visual aid and interesting story-telling technique, so as to enable the rural folks to know about and appreciate the concept.[136] What does this imply is that many, if not most, people living in rural areas cannot or could not really understand the abstract concept, even though Najib as early as September 2008 initiated his 1 Malaysia website[137] and in October 2009 the country ranks 11th in electronic-government implementation.[138]

16th, the Ministry of Home Affairs, with the cooperation of the Malaysian Communications and Multimedia Commission (MCMC) are monitoring blogs and websites that touch on the people's sensitivities, involving race, religion, and the institution of Malay rulers.[139] Bernama is Malaysia's national news agency. Although practicing parliamentary democracy, the press and the publishing industry are usually controlled for the sake of stability, peace, and harmony in the country, as the following statement in the GTP shows: "While censorship is anti-ethical to democracy, there is a need to introduce, instil and internalize a commitment to journalistic professionalism, a sense of responsibility and self-restraint, with sensitivity to the divergent views and feelings of the divergent communities in Malaysia."[140]

17th, the country is not 100% safe, even though Najib said 1 Malaysia can help to counter terrorism.[141] A few examples can be noted. First, in January 2010, Home Affairs Minister, Datuk Seri Hishammuddin Tun Hussein, said a local and nine foreigners were detained under the Internal Security Act (ISA) for alleged link with international terrorism. Some reports said

---

[132] *Ibid.*, August 6, 2009, p.B3.

[133] *Ibid.*, August 6, 2009, p.B3.

[134] *SHDN*, November 8, 2009, p.4. In the 1970s, the quota system on civil servants disappeared. See *SHDN*, September 12, 2010, p.5. However, we do read reports saying, in May 2010, some 400 Chinese applied to join the Malaysian Anti-Corruption Commission (MACC) and, in the same month, some 200 Chinese youths eager to join the Civil Defence Department. See *BP*, May 8, p.D2 and May 10, 2010, p.14. Assistant Minister of Infrastructure Development and Communications Datuk LEE Kim Shin called on Chinese to join the police force. See *ibid.*, May 8, 2010, p.D3.

[135] *BP*, September 4, 2010, p.15.

[136] *BP*, November 25, 2009, p.23 and January 9, 2010, p.18.

[137] www.1Malaysia.com.my. See also *BP*, September 16, 2009, p.20.

[138] *BP*, October 14, 2009, p.18.

[139] *Ibid.*, February 1, 2010, p.15.

[140] *Ibid.*, January 29, 2010, p.5. See also *ibid.*, December 8, 2009, p.9.

[141] *SHDN*, March 28, 2010, p.1.

that they are linked to a Nigerian bomber, who was going to blow up a U.S. commercial airplane on December 25, 2009.[142] Second, in February 2010, five armed robbers, who are not linked to Abu Sayyaf, abducted two local seaweed farm workers at a sea hut on a seaweed plantation in shallow waters around Pulau Sebangkat, about eight nautical miles from Semporna Peninsula, Tawau, Sabah. This incident, like the previous one in April 2000, had not been prevented, because, in January 2010, Deputy Prime Minister Tan Sri Muhyiddin Yassin, referring to a warden notice issued by the United States Embassy, which is a much lower level than a travel advisory, regarding Sabah's security, said the Malaysian Government has never issued any notice on any security threat in the area, because it knows the situation better.[143] It is also interesting to note that, in January 2010, members of the armed forces, since the launch of "Ops Pasir (an operation to curb crimes and encroachment of Malaysian waters) after the Malaysian dive resort island Sipadan hostage crisis in May 2000, have been urged to be vigilant and not to become oblivious to the situation around them due to relative calm in the waters off eastern Sabah.[144]

In sum, it is not difficult to find evidence, which are not in line with Najib's 1 Malaysia concept.[145]

SOMEWHERE IN BETWEEN THE TWO EXTREMES

On the one hand, positive information, data, and analysis on 1 Malaysia can be regarded as one extreme (or 1) in the author's crab and frog motion model, which will be introduced later on. On the other hand, negative information, data, and analysis on 1 Malaysia can be regarded as another extreme (or E). In other words, there are bound to be information, data, and analysis, which are in the grey area, meaning that, pending further development and observation, can we tell whether the information, data, and analysis can be either positive or negative. Some examples can be noted.

First, Najib is very aware of the imbalance between the Bumiputra and the non-Bumiputra. For example, foreign nationals will not be issued license to trade in the Federal Territories. Otherwise, "[i]f licenses were given to foreigners,… 100 per cent of the hawker areas would be controlled by them."[146] Thus, in October 2009, although he said the time has come for the UMNO, as the backbone of the ruling coalition, to be the main political party to take charge of the welfare and well-being of not only the Malays and Bumiputras but of all Malaysians, adding that this did not mean that the UMNO would open its doors to all races right now and that it would be left to the members to determine that sometime in the future when they are ready to do so.[147]

Second, former Dewan Negara Speaker, Tan Sri Abdul Hamid Pawanteh, said "I see 1 Malaysia as an implicit reminder and admission that after 50 years of independence, we have

---

[142] *BP*, January 29, 2010, p.20.

[143] *Ibid.*, January 17, 2010, p.17 and February 26, 2010, p.2.

[144] *Ibid.*, January 26, 2010, p.14.

[145] The opposition leader and Permatang Pauh MP Datuk Seri ANWAR Ibrahim said the 1 Malaysia concept was copied from the "One Israel" concept and was allegedly related to Apco Worldwide. NAJIB said 1 Malaysia is his original concept. See GJSB, April 5, 2010, p.A11. On September 16, 2008, ANWAR was alleged to plan to take over the federal government.

[146] *BP*, February 24, 2010, p.18.

[147] *Ibid.*, October 14, 2009, p.19.

strayed a little, and 1 Malaysia enjoins us to go back to our original path in the interest of the nation."[148] The question is: How long would it take to really come back to the original path?

Third, Deputy Works Minister Datuk YONG Khoon Seng said when children were still in kindergartens or earlier they should be introduced to 1 Malaysia.[149] If so, in a world of globalization, isn't they should be first taught what are international regimes, which are beneficial to all the countries, political and economic entities, and individuals like you and me?

Fourth, former deputy prime minister, Tun Musa Hitam, said the Malay psychology and mentality are still coupled with the "cannot do" excuse, pointing out that Malay thinkers and proponents kept saying things like "*Habislah Melayu* (Finish lah the Malays) and "*Apalah nak jadi pada Melayu*? (What will happen to the Malay? When faced with national issues).[150] The solution was "*ketuanan Melayu* (Malay supremacy)." Musa said modern history had proven that the master race concept has failed, especially when faced with competition from those with a high level of knowledge and expertise in various fields, such as science and technology, while challenging the young Malays then by saying that the Malays ought to feel ashamed if they were forever given a special position in whatever field just because they were Malays.[151] Musa was confident that the Malays can compete with anyone, adding "*Alhamdulillah* (the time has already come)."[152]

Fifth, in October 2009, NajibB[153] tabled his maiden Tenth Malaysia Plan (2011-2015) budget with the theme, 1 Malaysia, Together We Prosper, emphasizing three-pronged strategy: 1. Driving the nation towards a high-income economy; ensuring holistic and sustainable development; and focusing on well-being of the people. We still need to see whether Kuala Lumpur can achieve its goals, because we receive different messages. On the one hand, the GTP said the government and the people need to put in a tremendous effort for Malaysia to record eight per cent growth annually in order to achieve a developed nation status by the year 2020.[154] Yet, we were told that "[b]y the World Bank's definition, the minimum standard set for achieving developed nation status is achieving a per capita income of US$14, 800... . Hence, the country's economy has to expand at an average of at least 5.4% per cent from 2011 till 2020," so as to reach a per capita income of US$15,340 by 2020.[155] To be more specific, Sarawak aims at increasing its per capita income from US$7,000 to the region of US$15,000 by the year 2002.[156] And, to be sure, Najib, in August 2009, said Malaysia must grow 8% annually over 10 years to meet the developed nation status by 2020.[157] In July 2010, he mentioned 6% to achieve the 2020 vision, which is a brainchild of Mahathir.[158]

---

148 *Ibid.*, August 26, 2009, p.6.
149 *Ibid.*, August 17, 2009, p.4.
150 *Ibid.*, October 16, 2009, p.1.
151 *Ibid.*
152 *Ibid.*
153 In September 2009, it was reported that Harvard Business School (HBS) will undertake a case study, highlighting Datuk Seri NAJIB Tun Razak's bold initiatives to tackle Malaysia's financial crisis or neo-economics/Najibnomics. See *ibid.*, September 26, 2009, p.B12. For a previous case study on Malaysia, see Rawi Abdelai and Laura Alfaro, *Malaysia—Capital and Control* (April 2002).
154 *BP*, January 29, 2010, p.4.
155 *Ibid.*, January 29, 2010, p.B1. Malaysia's Gross National Income (GNI) is US$7,000 in 2008, ranking 85th in the world. The World Banks uses GNI, not Gross Domestic Product (GDP).
156 *Ibid.*, January 26, 2010, p.5.
157 *Ibid.*, August 29, 2009, p.B10.
158 *Ibid.*, July 20, 2010, p.15.

Sixth, Najib urged the UMNO members to reject negative elements like money politics.[159] However, would a number of power-thirst party members really follow his instructions? This remains to be seen.

Seventh, Deputy Minister in the Prime Minister's Department, Datuk Ahmad Maslan, said the BTN course modules are not racist.[160] Why did some participants worried about it?

Eighth, Deputy Minister of Housing and Local Government, Datuk Seri Panglima Lajim Ukin, singled out political stability in Sarawak as the major factor for the state to become more developed than his home state of Sabah over the last 20 years or so, adding "[i]n fact, development in Sabah started to slow down when we (in Sabah) adopted a system to rotate the chief ministership among heads of our political parties in Sabah several years back. That destabilized our political unity and infrastructural development."[161] Can this logic be applied to West Malaysia?

In sum, some evidence are not very clear as to whether they are in line with Najib's 1 Malaysia concept.

How to Conceptualize One Malaysia?

Najib said his party's philosophy is for *wasatan* (moderation) or what some political scientists call a centrist political party, adding "UMNO cannot be an ultra-left or ultra-right party. Since its establishment, the UMNO ideology has not leaned towards a liberal or a conservative ideology."[162] This implies that he is Confucian, not an extremist.

In January 2010, Secretary-general of the DAP and Penang State Chief Minister, LIM Guan Eng, at the party's 15th national conference, put forward the slogan of "Middle Malaysia."[163] The BN said it does not feel threatened by the DAP's middle path strategy. UMNO Supreme Council member and Information Communication and Culture Minister, Datuk Seri RAIS Yatim, said: "As far as I know, the DAP has not done anything yet except being like '*pungguk rindukan bulan* (the owl pining for the moon) and the moon will not drop unless if Allah wills it."[164] SUPP branch publicity secretary Daniel NGIENG asked why is the DAP so scared of the 1 Malaysia concept preached by NAJIB? "Is it because they have three versions [or directions] of 1 Malaysia—1 Malaysia for DAP Malaysian Malaysia, 1 Malaysia for Keadilan's Anwar Ibrahim and 1 Malaysia for PAS Islamic state…?"[165]

There are also other seemingly contradictory facts. For example, the PKR also regards itself as a centrist party.[166] Yet, it opposes the BN.

How do we rationalize the seemingly contradictory party agendas? It is necessary to apply the one-dot theory and the crab and frog motion model, which are interrelated. Since

---

[159] *Ibid.*, October 16, 2009, p.6.
[160] *Ibid.*, December 15, 2009, p.17.
[161] *Ibid.*, January 17, 2010, p.11.
[162] *NST*, October 18, 2009, p.21. See also *SHDN*, September 16, 2009, p.6.
[163] One important Democratic Action Party (DAP) leader in Sarawak said he does not understand what the term means. Conversation with him, dated February 14, 2010. A Kaohsiung Municipal City, Taiwan-based Chinese-Malaysian academic, Tee Kim Tong, put forward the term, *YiGeMaLaiXiYaGuoZhu*/1 Malaysia Nation-state. See *SHDN*, August 9, 2010, p.8.
[164] *BP*, January 20, 2010, p.16.
[165] *Ibid.*, May 12, 2010, p.4 and May 14, p.4.
[166] http://en.wikipedia.org/wiki/Parti_Keadilan_Rakyat, accessed on February 11,2 010.

both the theory and the model are derived from the *Yin* and *Yang*, the following diagram will be applied to rationalize everything:  (see the Preface).

Najib's 1 Malaysia concept does not equal to the diagram. It should be depicted in terms of one white, pure dot, like a circle, symbolizing stability, peace, and harmony. However, in real life or reality, can we have that? It is not possible most of the time, unless all the Non-1 Malaysia concept, which are the opposite of the 1 Malaysia concept, have been gone.

Can we say the 1 Malaysia concept is equivalent to either the white portion or the black portion of the diagram? The answer is neither, unless we treat the 1 Malaysia concept as either the white portion which includes the black dot or the black portion which includes the white dot. If the 1 Malaysia concept is equivalent to the white portion which includes the black dot, then the black portion which includes the white dot stands for Non-1 Malaysia concept. So, we are actually talking about the 1 Malaysia concept versus Non-1 Malaysia concept, when we look at the *Yin* and *Yang* diagram. What is Non-1 Malaysia concept, it could refer to God, Allah, Taiwan, mainland China, Middle Malaysia, etc.

Another way of calling the 1 Malaysia concept is new. In other words, the white portion of the *Yin* and *Yang* diagram is new. Indeed, the 1 Malaysia concept was only officially pronounced in April 2009. From LIM's perspective, the white portion which includes the black dot can also be called the Middle Malaysia. If so, we still see struggle between the 1 Malaysia concept and Middle Malaysia at a higher level.

Let us only regard the 1 Malaysia concept as the white portion which includes the black dot or new. Actually, the black dot is old, as Najib said his 1 Malaysia dot is not really new. The Sabah and Sarawak experience at the macro-level already embraced what he had in mind. In short, the 1 Malaysia concept is a hybrid of old and new. We can say that old includes Tunku Abdui Rahman Putra Al-Haj ibni Almarhum Sultan Abdul Hamid Shah's Malay Malaysia or LEE Kuan Yew's Malaysian Malaysia, when he put forward it in May 1965 at the Parliament in Kuala Lumpur. Tunku Abdul Rahman was the Father of Independence and the first prime minister of Malaysia, while LEE later became the prime minister of the Republic of Singapore (ROS) in August 1967.[167]

Where do we place Middle Malaysia, since it is very similar to the 1 Malaysia concept? We can treat it as the snake-like line in the *Yin* and *Yang* diagram. Here, one must apply the crab and frog motion model, so that we can see where is the 1 Malaysia concept and Middle Malaysia.

The model's structure is as follows:

1 2 3 4 5 A B C D E

time/space sequence (1)
time/space sequence (2)
....
time/space sequence (n)

1 2 3 4 5 is a spectrum or what I called the safe zone, while A B C D E is another spectrum or what I refer to as the danger zone. Each spectrum can be expanded or contracted.

[167] Singapore has defended its race policies after a United Nations (UN) envoy, Githu MUIGAI, called for reforms including lifting restrictions on the public discussion of sensitive issues like ethnicity, language, and religion. The Foreign Ministry said it could not risk allowing such open discussions, emphasizing that the Government, not the UN, would bear the consequences of ethnic strife. See *BP*, April 30, 2010, p.A1.

For example, 1 2 3 4 5 can be expanded to become 1 2 3 4 5 6 7 8 or 1 to 1,000; or contracted to be only 5 A. Scale is involved. 1 means 100%; 3, 50%; and 5, 1%, while E means 100%; C, 50%; and A, 1%. As can be seen, there is a scale, that is, from E to A, there is a downward trend of movement, whereas from 5 to 1, there is an upward trend. Anyway, 1 weighs the most and 5 the least. Also, E weighs the most and A, the least. Whenever confronted with a dilemma, one would go to the middle road or 5 of the safe zone or A of the danger zone in 1 2 3 4 5 A B C D E. There could also be a middle road between 5 and A. Due to its flexibility in application, such is the beauty of dialectics.

Applying the dialectical model, the 1 Malaysia concept would be positioned at 1, while Middle Malaysia is at 5. In other words, to NAJIB, his concept carries more weight than Middle Malaysia. It has to be, because the BN is the ruling party in his country. When one day LIM's party and others become the ruling party, Middle Malaysia would be put at 1, while the 1 Malaysia concept is at 5, from LIM's perspective.

It must be noted that further studies may have to be conducted to place Malay Malaysia and Malaysian Malaysia.

Issues Challenging the One Malaysia Concept

There are a few issues after April 2009, which pose a doubt over what Najib had hoped for--stability, peace, and harmony in his country under 1 Malaysia. They can be discussed.

First, in February 2009, (the very irresponsible, to some)[168] Archbishop Tan Sri Murphy Nicholas Xavier Pakiam filed for a judicial review on the usage of the word, Allah, in the church's publications, naming the Home Affairs Ministry and the government as the respondents, claiming that the word, Allah, was not exclusive to the religion of Islam.[169] In December 2007, the Malaysian Government banned the *Herald* to use the word, Allah, in Semenanjung (Peninsular Malaysia or Malays before independence).[170] For the record, Islam is the country's official religion, and Malaysia regards itself as both a secular and theocratic state and it also bans the use of three other words related to Islam.[171] Two years later in the same month, Malaysia's Court Justice, Datuk LAU Bee Lan, decided that non-Malay Catholics and Christians have the constitutional right to use the word, Allah, so long as the periodical, *Herald*, was confined to educating the Christians. Before that the Christians have been using the word, God, in English or Allah in Malay and Kinoingan in Kadazandusun in Sabah's urban areas.

The court decision has wide spread implications on the unity of Malaysians, especially the mosque, *surau*/small Muslim chapel or place of worship, church, temple, synagogues, and other houses of worship.

Worried that the decision had offended some Muslims, the Prime Minister's Department, together with the cooperation of the Home Affairs Ministry, appealed on January 4, 2010 against the High Court's decision for a stay of execution of the court order, justifying the ban on grounds of national security and to avoid misunderstanding and confusion among

---

[168] *BP*, January 16, 2010, p.10.

[169] *Ibid.*, January 3, 2010, p.27.

[170] Malaysia has also banned books mentioned words like Baitullaha (an Arabic phrase meaning House of God), Solat (prayer), and Kaabah (a cube-shaped building in Mecca, Saudi Arabia) were not allowed to be imported to the country. See *SHRB*, March 6, 2010, p.1.

[171] *BP*, January 16, 2010, p.10 and *GJSB*, January 20, 2010, p.A5.

Muslims.[172] While LAU agreed to record the stay by consent, the case can be moved to the Appeal Court and the Federal Court.

Others offered their own reasoning: "This is because 'God' in other religions is translated as '*Tuhan*'[173] in Bahasa Malaysia or Arabic, not 'Allah.' 'Allah' specifically refers to God in Islam. If they understand that, they would use the word '*Tuhan*' instead." *Tuhan yang Maha Kuasa*/in Mandarin Chinese, *QuanNengDeShangDi* could also be used.[174] Indeed, Christians believes in the concept of Holy Trinity, whereas the Muslims do not, because Allah is the only God--*tawheed* in Bahasa Malaysia or *DanYiDeShen*[175] in Mandarin Chinese--and Allah does not have a son.[176] To Muslims, Jesus Christ is only a human being.[177]

The Prime Minister's Department in charge of law, Datuk Seri Mohamed Nazri Abdul Aziz made the following remarks, when he was interviewed by a group of local Chinese news reporters, while wearing a traditional Chinese *Tang* costume:[178] In the federal constitution of Malaysia, there is an article which says that no other religions except Islam can be propagated among the Muslims or the Malay community. However, other religions can be propagated in Sabah; Sarawak; Wilayah Persekutuan (WP)/Federal Territory, which is a collection of Kuala Lumpur, Putrajaya, and Labuan; Malacca, with the first two territories or enclaves in the Selangor State; and Penang, which do not have such law but which can use the Printing Act at the discretion of the Minister of Home Affairs to ban the use of any word, if he foresees that it may cause some problems and later on affect the national security of Malaysia. So, in the Selangor State, it is the right of Sultan or any Muslim to insist the authorities to take any action against any group wanting to use the word, Allah, as reference to their God. To set the record straight, the *Herald* in November 2008 also received a letter from the Home Affairs Ministry saying it cannot use the word, Allah.[179] And, in September 2009, about 15,000 copies of the Bible, which were shipped from Indonesia to Kuching, Sarawak, Malaysia, were confiscated.[180]

Some others disagree, saying the UMNO wants to retain Malay voters' support. Therefore, only the Muslims can use the word, Allah. A prominent opposition party, DAP, leader, LIM Kit Siang, said the word, Allah, appears at seven states' anthems: *Allah peliharakan*; *Allah lanjutkan usia Tuanku; Segala Kebesaran Allah cucurkan;* and *Allah selamat Sultan Makhota*. If a non-Muslim were to sing it, would he or she be allowed? If so, would that not being regarded as offending the Muslims?[181] In passing, it should be noted that there are close to 60,000 Muslims in Malaysia, who are ethnic Chinese, according to a 2000 census.[182]

There could be another reason. Some Muslims, with the word, agenda, in mind, are worried that when mentioning the word, Allah, some Catholics and Christians may convert some Muslims into Catholics or Christians.[183] 10% has been mentioned.[184] That has been a

---

[172] *Ibid.*, January 5, 2010, p.12.
[173] In Mandarin Chinese, it is translated as *ShangCang*.
[174] *SHDN*, January 12, 2010, p.3.
[175] *Ibid.*, January 4, 2010, p.8.
[176] *BP*, January 15, 2010, p.2 and January 16, 2010, p.10.
[177] Conversation with my relatives, dated February 28, 2010.
[178] *BP*, January 16, 2010, p.10 and *SHDN*, January 19, 2010, p.A6.
[179] *SHDN*, January 20, 2010, p.*zeng*4.
[180] *Ibid.*, January 6, 2010, p.A6.
[181] *Ibid.*, January 23, 2010, p.5.
[182] *Ibid.*, October 25, 2009, p.6. In summer 2010, another round of census was held.
[183] *BP*, January 4, 2010, p.13.

fact in Indonesia.[185] Other Muslims perceive that one day the word, Allah, may appear on a cross.[186] However, former prime minister, Tun Abdullah Ahmad Badawi, who chairs the Institute of Islamic Understanding of Malaysia (IKIM), said his organization has *ulama* (Islamic religious scholars) or Islamic experts who can provide the explanations on the issue through articles or forums.[187] In the same month, a closed-door Muzakarah Pakar forum, organized by the Movement to Protest the Usage of Kalimah Allah, was held at the Federal Territory Mosque, Kuala Lumpur, while Sarawak's Malaysian Royal Police 69 Squad, led by Abdul Rahman Hashim, said that "Allah Taala," as stated in the al-Quran/Koran, which was written in Arabic, never allowed Muslims to trespass any house of worship even during war.[188] However, on January 12, 2010, a Sikh Temple at Sentul in Kuala Lumpur also became a victim, because some 20 stones were hurled from outside the temple compound.[189] The office of a lawyer, who is an Indian and who defended the *Herald*, was broken into by thieves on January 13, 2010.

To be sure, some Muslims, such as those belonging to the PKR and PAS,[190] can accept God as Allah, because the word, Allah, is widely used among indigenous Christian tribes in Sabah and Sarawak, most of whom speak Bahasa Malaysia.[191] The Sabah Council of Churches (SCC) stated the following:[192] From a historical perspective, the Christian community speaking Bahasa Malaysia has been using the word, Allah, since the completed translation of the Bible in 1733 and 1879, respectively. According to another report, as early as the 15th century, both Christians and Muslims began to use the word, Allah.[193]

Assistant Minister's Department (Islamic Affairs) Datuk Daud Abdul Rahman said there was never any religious tension in Sarawak.[194] What he said can be proven by the following facts: a church and a mosque side-by-side at one place as well as a Muslim burial ground next to a Chinese cemetery at another place.[195] (In passing, one writer wrote the following words: "This is a place where a Muslim food stall can occupy a place in a coffee shop where pork leg rice is also being sold.[196] This is a place where one can find Tai Chi, that pre-eminent Chinese art, being taught by a Malay instructor. This is a place where during Hari Raya, there are as many non-Muslims as there are Muslims in all the open houses."[197] To be sure, many non-Chinese attend Chinese primary schools.[198] To be objective, a window-smashing incident took place at the Anglican Good Shepherd Church in Lutong, a suburb of Miri City, on

---

[184] *SHDN*, January 12, 2010, p.3.
[185] *GJSB*, January 14, 2010, p.B3.
[186] *Ibid.*
[187] *BP*, January 5, 2010, p.15.
[188] *Ibid.*, January 13, 2010, p.3.
[189] *Ibid.*, January 14, 2010, p.3. A Muslim house of worship was also the victim. See *SHDN*, August 14, 2010, p.2.
[190] *SHDN*, January 6, 2010, p.3 and January 13, 2010, p.A5. The DAP holds the same view. See *ibid.*
[191] *BP*, January 5, 2010, p.12.
[192] *Ibid.*, January 13, 2010, p.3.
[193] *GJSB*, January 18, 2010, p.A8.
[194] *BP*, January 6, 2010, p.4. However, In May 2010, Minister of Housing and Urban Development Datuk Amar Abang JOHARI Tun Openg issued an ultimatum to the opposition to stop using the "Allah" issue in the forthcoming Sibu by-election just to canvass for more votes. See *ibid.*, May 13, 2010, p.5. See also *ibid.*, May 12, 2010, p.1.
[195] *Ibid.*, January 10, 2010, p.5.
[196] *GJSB*, February 22, 2010, p.A20.
[197] *BP*, January 24, 2010, p.14.
[198] *GJSB*, February 22, 2010, p.A20.

January 10, 2010 spoiled the record[199] or as the Minister of Energy, Green Technology and Water, Datuk Seri Peter CHIN Fah Kui had wrongly predicted a day earlier, saying Sarawakians are sensible.[200] CHIN could be based on the fact that the Anglican Good Shepherd Church existed side by side a mosque with only one fence diving them for some half-a-century already, without any incident.[201] Thus, some people inferred that it was either the hooligans or naughty kids who smashed the windows of the church.[202]

In January 2010, 13 houses of worship were set ablaze after the controversial Allah ruling.[203] PKR Vice President, Mohamed Azmin Bin Ali, alleged that UMNO Youth members were involved in the arson attack on Metro Taberacle Church, which was destroyed and which was later given by the Malaysian Government a grant of RM500,000 to relocate from Desa Melawati, Klang Valley, suburban Kuala Lumpur to another place.[204] The police began investigations and it soon arrested offenders, including the son of a policeman.[205] Fortunately, 130 Muslim NGOs and the People's Volunteer Corp (RELA) offered to help the authorities to monitor security at houses of worship in the Klang Valley.[206] On January 17, 2010, Muslim NGOs and Christian NGOs in Kuantan, Pahang State, met to seek consensus in addressing the issue of attacks on houses of worship.[207] However, on January 28, 2010, two pig heads plus RM 30/35[208] were thrown at a mosque. In August 2010, a court judge sentenced two arsonists to a jail sentence.[209]

Some people including Christians have urged the *Herald* weekly magazine, to drop the claim for the sake of peace, harmony, and security.[210] In August 2010, Muhyiddin said all the political parties including BN should not discuss openly the issue of the use of the word, Allah, which is still being heard by the courts.[211]

The following is an open letter from the editor of the *Herald*, which was published in the January 19, 2010 edition of *Malaysian Insider* (MI):[212]

Recently, someone whom I consider a very close and trusted friend, and who is a Muslim, wrote an email to me with a very simple question: "What was *The Herald* asking for exactly?"

As someone who knew what the issue was from the start, having once been a freelance contributor to *The Herald*, I gathered my thoughts and spoke to a few relevant people and started writing down the facts of the whole issue.

Instead of the creative and open writing style that is normally employed in any article, I decided to keep it strictly to the point with the facts itself, following the style of a former prime minister whose blog name is one letter short of the anagram for the word

[199] *BP*, January 11, 2010, p.5. On January 11, 2010, Sidang Injil Borneo/ Borneo Evangelical Church also suffered from arson. See *SHDN*, January 12, 2010, p.1.
[200] *BP*, January 10, 2010, p.4.
[201] *SHDN*, January 14, 2010, p.A2.
[202] *BP*, January 14, 2010, p.3.
[203] *SHDN*, August 14, 2010, p.2.
[204] *BP*, January 9, 2010, p.1 and January 29, 2010, p.17.
[205] *Ibid* and January 21, 2010, p.1.
[206] *Ibid.*, January 11, 2010, p.1.
[207] *Ibid.*, January 18, 2010, p.5.
[208] *SHDN*, February 2, 2010, p.4.
[209] *Ibid.*, August 14, 2010, p.2.
[210] *BP*, January 12, 2010, p.4.
[211] *Ibid.*, August 5, 2010, p.7.
[212] Email from the editor, dated February 3, 2010. For the original version, see *http://cyrildason.com/2010/01/19/facts-on-the-herald-and-allah/, accessed on February 3, 2010.*

"CHEATED", which is rather ironic since many of us still feel that way over events of the past 28 years.

Anyway, this was my letter to that Muslim friend.

Dear brother Malaysian,

I wish all Muslims (and even some non-Muslims) were like you, stopping to ask what the issue was instead of playing straight into the tactics of people (and some media) who have personal and political agendas. Here are the facts of the issue, which I am sure will answer your question easily.

1. *The Herald* has been around for more than 15 years. The first edition of Herald appeared on September 8, 1994. It was a 12-page compact (tabloid) size fortnightly.
2. *The Herald* was first published in English only.
3. A year later, other languages, Malay, Tamil and Chinese were added as sections with one page for each section or language. This was to allow Catholics who were more familiar with those languages to have their community news and spiritual guidance explained for their better understanding.
4. The thousands of East Malaysian students in government universities in Peninsula Malaysia, who are active in the Catholic Students Society in their respective universities, so more pages were added in Bahasa Malaysia... .
5. Over the past 15 students were educated completely under the Bahasa Malaysia medium and with little exposure to English.
6. In addition to the students, thousands of East Malaysians have been flocking to the Klang Valley for better prospects and simply to "cari makan", just like other Malaysians from all over the peninsula. Ag ain, the majority would be [Bahasa Malaysia-educated and more comfortable worshiping in Bahasa Malaysia than in English.
7. Bahasa Malaysia was, after all, their common denominator, i.e. the national language, propagated by the government themselves over all other languages since the late 1970s.
8. Both East and West Malaysians themselves wrote the original content and translated some of the English pages in *The Herald* to Bahasa Malaysia. One can easily surmise this from the writers' by-lines as well as from the "Letters to the Editor" in the Bahasa Malaysia edition since its beginnings, around 12 years ago.
9. If these East Malaysians used "Allah" in their praise and worship all their lives — as did their parents, grandparents and the generations before them — it would only be natural that they would write their articles and reflections, as well as do translations, using the only word they know for the "Lord our God", the God of Abraham and Moses. The one Almighty God.
10. When former Home [Affairs] Minister Tan Seri Datuk SYED HAMID bin Syed Jaafar Albar imposed a blanket ban on the use of the word "Allah" in *The Herald*, as well as on imported Christian Bibles and other literature in both print and multimedia formats from Indonesia, the church appealed.
11. After appeals and all other avenues failed, the Catholic Church had no choice but to go to court because it is a basic deprivation of human rights in not allowing East

Malaysian Christians the right to worship God in a manner they have used to worship Him all their lives and for generations past.

12. *The Herald* just wants the right for fellow Catholics who speak Bahasa Malaysia to practise their faith, and share their community information, while learning about their own faith, in the only language they share.
13. *The Herald* is only sold within church grounds, and has also complied with government requests to have "TERHAD (restricted)" and "FOR NON-MUSLIMS ONLY" on the cover, even if it was never to be sold or distributed outside church grounds in the first place.
14. The greatest lie being repeated over and over again, by ministers, morally-corrupt politicians, some Muslim scholars, some government-controlled media as well as misinformed members of the public is that the church started using the term "Allah" in *The Herald* since only a few years ago.
15. The other great lie is that the term is also intended for use in the English edition."

In sum, religious matters cannot really be resolved by law. If it is a hybrid solution, it could be done. Needless to say, 1 Malaysia concept should be able to embrace it. If not, something is wrong with Najib's 1 Malaysia, and many people are waiting for an answer, satisfying to them all. It can be done, if it is dialectically arranged.

Second, Datuk Nsir Safar, the prime minister's special officer, who had known Najib for more than 30 years, in February 2010 at a 1 Malaysia seminar, which was attended by about 1,000 people, at the Malacca State said the Indians were pendatang (immigrants)(in Mandarin Chinese QiShi/QiTao/begging for food) and the Chinese women came to Malaysia to indulge in the "flesh trade (in Mandarin Chinese MaiSheng/sell oneself." [213] As a result of the racist remarks, five MCA and MIC leaders simply walked out.[214] 1 Malaysia Youth Graduates Club deputy chairman said Nasir conducted 60 ceramah (talks) in 2009 and 22 talks so far in that year, and the speeches were never misconstrued nor misunderstood.[215] In any case, Nasir within 12 hours tendered his resignation,[216] and then he was probed for sedition under the Sedition Act 1948. Najib later said Nasir's statement did not affect the 1 Malaysia vision.[217]

Needless to say, Nasir was not the first one to make such derogative remarks. Some BTN lecturers would utter words offensive to the Chinese and Indian participants.[218] Some opposition party leaders still accuse the UMNO as being racist.[219]

To be sure, the number of Chinese and Indians residing in Malaysia could decrease, every ten years.[220] By the year 2020, Bumiputras' percentage could be 63.9%, showing an increase. For the Chinese, it is 20.6%, a drop of about two percent. Najib said there are about 700,000 Chinese-Malaysians working overseas.[221] And, for the Indians, 6.4%, a drop of about 0.4%. A

---

[213] *New Straits Times* (hereinafter New ST)(Malaysia), February 4, 2010, p.N2 and p.4 and *SHDN*, February 3, 2010, p.1 and p.2.

[214] *NST*, February 4, 2010, p.N2 and p.4. MCA said the party should not be made the scapegoat for the dip in Chinese support for BN in the April 2010 Hulu Selangor by-election, in which BN won. See *BP*, May 4, 2010, p.17.

[215] *Ibid.* p.N8 and p.4.

[216] *SHDN*, February 3, 2010, p.1.

[217] *BP*, February 5, 2010, p.18.

[218] *SHDN*, November 29, 2009, p.2 and *GJSB*, December 13, 2009, p.B3.

[219] *SHDN*, January 19, 2010, p.4.

[220] *Ibid.*, January 27, 2010, p.3 and *GJSB*, January 22, 2010, p.A1.

[221] http://www.zaobao.com/yx/yx100815_006-1.shtml, dated August 15, 2010, accessed on August 15, 2010.

PKR Pulau Coast District State Legislator, HUANG River/HUANG Jinhe, said close to five million Malaysian eligible citizens over 21-year of age have not registered for elections.[222] This calls for concern, because many, if not most, of them are Chinese and Indians, who are apolitical or disappointed with politics.

Third, how would the driving forces of globalization affect 1 Malaysia? Should each Malaysian still identify with their homeland or learn to adjust their psychology, mindset, etc, and accept the One Global Village concept? In August 2001, Youth and Sports Minister Datuk Ahmad Shabey Cheek said 1 Malaysia concept could inspire what he called a "1 World Nation."[223]

Fourth, propaganda by some foreign media, saying that the 1 Malaysia concept has been rejected by the people, raised concerns by some leaders in Malaysia.[224]

CONCLUSION

From the party politics perspective, 1 Malaysia can, indeed, attract or get some votes at elections. Many Chinese and Indians would still be willing to give the BN a last chance. However, we should not forget that even major Sarawak-based BN component party chairman and deputy chief minister of Sarawak, *Datuk Patinggi Tan Sri George* CHAN Hong Nan, said if there are no change nor reform within the SUPP there will be no hope for the party.[225]

However, from the academic perspective, if 1 Malaysia continues to be accepted by BN and others after NAJIB's term has expired, Najib would remain in history, because it reflects "a single Malaysian race whose thinking transcended the demographic factors"[226] and because *so far none of the following have been accepted as official: 1)* Tunku Abdul Rahman Putra Al-Haj ibni Almarhum Sultan Abdul Hamid Shah's Malay Malaysia;[227] 2) LEE Kuan Yew's Malaysian Malaysia[228]; and 3) LIM's Middle Malaysia.

---

[222] *SHDN*, January 20, 2010, p.A4.

[223] *BP*, August 17, 2010, p.17.

[224] *Ibid.*, January 13, 2009, p.12.

[225] *GJSB*, February 18, 2010, p.A20.

[226] *BP*, August 18, 2009, p.12.

[227] In March 2010, Deputy Prime Minister Tan Sri MUHYDDIN Yassin said he was a Malay first. See *BP*, April 2, 2010, p.16.

[228] Because Malaysia is far different from that of Singapore, former Prime Minister BADAWI said Malaysia does not need LEE Kuan Yew's advice. See *BP*, September 19, 2010, p. 22.

In: International (Corporate) Governance
Editor: Peter Kien-Hong Yu
ISBN: 978-1-61122-645-4

Chapter 11

SUGAR SHORTAGE: ANALYZING SARAWAK, MALAYSIA'S GOVERNANCE

Peter Kien-hong Yu, Asleena Helmi, and Vie Ming Tan

ABSTRACT

In this paper, the co-authors try to find out as many reasons possible for sugar shortage in various parts of Malaysia in general and the State of Sarawak in particular. A combination of reasons accounted for the shortage, such as hoarding by wholesalers and retailers; panic buying by families who go to supermarkets in droves; distribution network/chain or logistics and transportation problem; as well as smuggling by violators who dare to challenge government rules and regulations of one kind or another. Delay of bulk shipment is also possible due to weather conditions, which will usually affect the smooth transportation of sugar from one place to another.

This paper also tries to give some evidence to show that governments at the federal, state, division, and district levels are trying to resolve the shortage problem, including urging consumers to take less sugar, since too much sugar is harmful to one's health. Over-consumption of sugar is linked to over 60 types of diseases or sugar is the mother of various ailments.

In May 2010, the Subsidy Rationalisation Lab proposed to abolish subsidies on sugar and other commodities in stages. Would that decrease sugar consumption? Would that affect business before and during a festive season? Would low income earners and the poor suffer more?

Keywords: Sugar shortage, Sarawak, Malaysia, governance, business

In a globalizing world where the private sector has become more vocal and financially more powerful, using the term, governance,[1] is very appropriate, because of its two major

[1] On May 28, 2010, the American president in his 52-page *National Security Strategy*'s Preface and on page 21 mentioned the term, governance, the U.S. capacity to speak to other people's hopes, as well as American troops and diplomats, private sector, nongovernmental organizations (NGOs), and citizens, who all have a role to play. While mentioning mainland China, India, and Russia, this is a new strategy, which has abandoned George W. Bush's

dimensions: state-sponsored and non-state-sponsored. For example, under the 10th Malaysia Plan (10 MP), more projects would be implemented through the Private-Public Partnership (PPP).[2] Indeed, there is an increasingly public-private partnership at work. One needs the other, and one must not do without the other, due to the lack of ample tangible and intangible resources on each side. From the governance perspective, our analysis should be closer to reality.

The issue that we are going to discuss is the shortage of sugar, which is a hardy crop. Currently, the consumption of sugar in the Federation of Malaysia (FOM) is about 130 million metric tons, while the production capacity to produce *gula pasir* (refined sugar, mainly used for making cakes) is up to two million metric tons per year.[3]

The International Trade and Industry Minister Datuk Seri Mustapa Mohamed[4] said the bulk of the country's sugar, 41%, was imported from the Federal Republic of Brazil (FROB) with 509,630 metric tons, followed by 447,480 metric tons from the Commonwealth of Australia (COA), 36%, and 174,000 metric tons from the Kingdom of Thailand (KOT), 14%, adding his country also received raw sugar from the Republic of Nicaragua (RON) amounting to 99,400 metric tons or 8% and the Republic of Guatemala (ROG). In addition, local sugar production contributes to only 1% of sugar supply with 17,000 metric tons.[5]

According to a statement issued by Malaysia's Domestic Trade, Cooperative and Consumerism Ministry (MTDCC), Malaysians in general and Malays and Ibans in particular,[6] consumed 21 tablespoons or around 120 grams of [either coarse white/brown[7] or refined sugar each day, which was 10 tablespoons or 50 grams more than the recommended amount.[8] Moreover, the problem of sugar shortage among the 13 states including Sarawak, Sabah, Kedah, Kelantan, and Perils, plus the duty-free Federal Territory of Labuan, has been recurrent almost every time before a major festival, such as Hari Raya (Aidilfitri),[9] Chinese Lunar New Year,[10] Deepavali, Christmas,[11] and Pesta Kaamatan. For example, a month before the June 2010 Gawai Dayak celebration,[12] demand for sugar in the Kapit, Sarawak area increased by 15%, because each family needs at least five to 10 kilograms of sugar and

---

unilateralism of September 2002. The term, international regimes, was mentioned on page 13. On page 23, "a global nonproliferation regime" was mentioned. The term, international norms, was mentioned on page 11, page 17, page 40, and page 50. The term, international nonproliferation norms, was mentioned on page 24. On pages 12-13, he said international cooperation since World War II has been an architecture of institutions, organizations, regimes, and standards that establish certain rights and responsibilities of all sovereign nations. On page 19, he mentioned public-private partnerships. A section was devoted to (alternative) mechanisms of cooperation.

[2] *Borneo Post* (hereinafter BP)(Sarawak, Malaysia), June 4, 2010, p.8 and June 11, 2010, p.B2.

[3] *Ibid.*, August 9, 2010, p.12.

[4] Mohamed is the last name.

[5] *BP*, June 11, 2010, p.22.

[6] *Ibid.*, March 29, 2010, p.4.

[7] Brown sugar may have a lot of impurities. See *BP*, January 10, 2010, p.1.

[8] *Ibid.*, November 25, 2009, p.6. Another report mentioned 26 tablespoons. See *ShiHua Daily News* (hereinafter SHDN)(Sarawak, Malaysia), May 24, 2010, p.A13.

[9] 18 essential items were under the PCS during the celebration. See *BP*, September 14, 2009, p.12 and September 15, 2009, p.15. Another report mentioned 17. See *ibid.*, September 12, 2009, p.13.

[10] 11 items were under the PCS during the celebration. See *ibid.*, February 11, 2010, p.10. Pork in February 2010 was for the first time under control. It is said that the Chinese are not using a lot of sugar during this festival. See *BP*, June 25, 2010, p.6.

[11] 13 items were under the Price Control Scheme (PCS) in 138 areas and districts. In addition, "[t]he 3,588 controlled prices include chicken, imported turkey, local beef, etc." See *BP*, December 17, 2009, p.12.

[12] 12 items were under the PCS during the celebration. See *SHDN*, May 24, 2010, p.A13.

other ingredients to make home brewed rice wine.[13] Families go to supermarkets, mini-markets, retail outlets, sundry shops, etc. in droves to buy the commodity, unlike the normal days. In the year 2009, Sarawakians consumed 89,237 metric tons or 89,237,000 kilograms of sugar, one of the highest in the county.[14]

WHO ARE INVOLVED OR BEING AFFECTED?

The Government is, needless to say, involved, because it has policies related to sugar and other controlled items, a few years after launching the Malaysian New Economic Policy (NEP)(1971-1990). It is aware that, to alleviate the burden of each household, it should heavily subsidize the price of sugar.

In May 2010, Minister in the Prime Minister's Department and also the Chief Executive Officer of the Performance Management and Delivery Unit (Pemandu), Datuk Seri Idris Jala,[15] said Malaysians need to be aware that their country is giving the highest subsidies--4.6% of Gross Domestic Product (GDP), which is even higher than the Republic of Indonesia (ROI)'s 2.7% and the Republic of Philippines (ROP)'s 0.2%.[16]

In the year 2009, the Malaysian Federal Government forked out a total of RM74 billion (RM33 = 1US$) to subsidize sugar, wheat flour, cooking oil, liquefied natural gas for cooking, gasoline and diesel, electricity, etc.,[17] and this is equivalent to RM12,900 per household.[18] If we were to only discuss sugar, the amount is RM1.008 billion, which can bring harm to our health. However, it is said that subsidy is needed until people have higher or sufficient income.[19]

The main government agency in charge of controlled items is the MTDCC, which has an annual budget of RM960 million to subsidize, for example, transportation of controlled items, including sugar. Surprisingly, Sarawak received RM690 million for the year 2010.[20]

Knowing that, for example, about 30% of the cooking oil subsidy has been abused,[21] Prime Minister Datuk Seri Najib Tun Razak[22] is concerned. So, the sugar issue was elevated to the national level. In January 2010, he asked the following question: Lacking logic, should the Federal Government continue subsidizing the sugar price?[23] He is aware of the statistics from the International Diabetes Institute (IDI), showing that Malaysia has the fourth highest

---

[13] *SHDN*, May 24, 2010, p.A13 and *BP*, May 5, 2010, p.D2. Sometimes, due to sugar shortage, icing sugar/gula pasir would be used. See *BP*, May 23, 2010, p.11.

[14] *SHDN*, May 24, 2010, p.A13 and *BP*, March 29, 2010, p.4. Sabah State needs about 68,000 metric tons of sugar each year. In the year 2009, it only received 62,000 metric tons. See *BP*, April 22, 2010, p.14.

[15] Jala is the last name.

[16] *BP*, May 28, 2010, p.13, June 30, 2010, p.11, and August 5, 2010, p.10.

[17] *SHDN*, January 27, 2010, p.1. In the area of social, it is RM42.8 billion; fuel, RM23.5 billion; infrastructure, RM4.6 billion, and food, RM3.1 billion. There is a discrepancy in the total subsidy figures issued by the Ministry of Finance (MOF) and Permandu. It is due to the differences in the definition and classification of expenditure and their sources. The MOF's figures of RM 18.4 billion referred only to direct subsidies involving the Treasury, while that of Permandu, all indirect subsidies and from all public sources. In other words, the MOF was looking strictly from their angle and their own budgeting concern, while Permandu, the overall picture. See *BP*, June 10, 2010, p.9.

[18] *BP*, May 28, 2010, p.13.

[19] *Ibid.*, June 13, 2010, p.7.

[20] *SHDN*, January 27, 2010, p.1 and June 30, 2010, p.11.

[21] *BP*, May 28, 2010, p.13.

[22] Razak is the last name.

[23] *BP*, January 4, 2010, p.1.

number of diabetes in Asia.[24] In August 2010, Najib "announced that the RM750 million we save out of this subsidy rationalization will be used for scholarships, 1 Malaysia clinics and other long-term and urgent needs."[25]

There are four sugar refineries/mills/manufacturer in the Peninsula or West Malaysia, namely, Malayan Sugar Manufacturing Company (MSM) in Pulau Penang, which has garnered 50% of the domestic sugar market;[26] Gula Padang Terap Sdn Bhd (GPT) in Padang Terap, Kedah; Central Sugars Refinery Sdn Bhd (CSR) in Shah Alam, Selangor;[27] and Kilang Gula Felda Perlis Sdn Bhd, in Chuping, Perlis. There were no new refineries since November 28, 1990.[28] Each one of them possesses an approved permit (AP) to buy sugar in bulk from abroad. These companies would sign long-term contracts with foreign suppliers.[29] "If sugar import is not controlled by the government, it is feared that the importers will not bring in the sugar when the price is high in the international market."[30] Therefore, a Ministry of International Trade and Industry (MITI) official, Datuk Jacob Sagan,[31] said the existing import system for essential goods should not be seen as a monopoly to benefit only certain parties. Such a system can enable the Federal Government to control the supply and prices of the commodities, besides encouraging local refining of raw sugar for added values.[32]

Wholesalers are part of the whole picture. At the moment, there are 25 sugar wholesalers in Sarawak: five in Kuching, one in Sarikei, nine in Sibu, four in Bintulu, and six in Miri.[33] The Malaysian Federal Territory of Labuan has four wholesalers, each one of which can monthly import 100 metric tons of sugar.[34] In June 2010, The MTDCC Minister, Datuk Seri Ismail Sabri Yaakob[35] said the Ministry allowed the Small and Medium-Scale Industries Association (SMIA) to form a sugar wholesaling company, so as to distribute sugar to its members.[36] Once receiving the sugar, they would distribute to the retailers, supermarkets, outlets (such as 7-Eleven), etc. Large food and beverage companies, which can be regarded as second tier wholesalers so long as they have a valid permit from the Ministry of Domestic Trade, Cooperatives and Consumerism (KPDNKK), may not suffer from costlier sugar, because they tend to buy sugar in bulk. However, operators of drink business may have to absorb the costs despite the price hike, in order to keep their loyal customers. Bakeries[37] and coffee shops would also try to directly source the much desired commodity from wholesalers, so as to reduce their operation cost.[38]

Other people, such as operators in the food manufacturing industry, restaurants, and other eateries, would be affected, if insufficient and erratic sugar supply in the local wet market

---

[24] *Ibid*, August 22, 2009, p.20. However, a medical doctor said that the public has a misconception, that is, taking more sugar can cause diabetes, adding excessive intake of sugar could lead to obesity. See *ibid.*, June 21, 2010, p.12.

[25] *Ibid.*, August 5, 2010, p.10.

[26] *Ibid.*, August 27, 2009, p.13.

[27] A supermarket in Kuching gets sugar from this refinery.

[28] *SHDN*, October 21, 2009, p.5.

[29] *BP*, December 8, 2009, p.1.

[30] *Ibid.*

[31] Sagan is the last name.

[32] *BP*, December 8, 2009, p.1.

[33] *Ibid.*, June 21, 2010, p.4.

[34] *Ibid.*, September 8, 2009, p.6.

[35] Yaakob is the last name.

[36] *BP*, June 30, 2010, p.11.

[37] Sugar is a natural preservative for cakes, and to use less of the item might make the cake spoil faster. See *ibid.*, June 25, 2010, p.6.

[38] *Ibid.*, December 31, 2009, p.8.

would occur. Nationwide, there are, as of September 2009, traders with 15,057 licenses, issued by the MTDCC on controlled items, including sugar.

Last but not least, consumers,[39] who are the end-users, may have to pay more money for the same pack of sugar, if the Federal Government stopped subsidizing sugar price. One unconfirmed report said, during sugar crisis, certain retail shops would secretly sell the commodity to favoured customers at an exorbitant price of RM2.5 per kilogram.[40] Some smaller producers and retailers would feel the pinch from higher raw material costs.[41]

WHAT WENT WRONG?

Ismail Sabri acknowledged that the price of all goods would not remain the same as now. This is because it is beyond the Federal Government's control of the world market price and because it cannot cope with prolonged inclement weather or climate conditions, such as drought, bulk shipment problems related to rough seas and water level in a river, which could be too shallow,[42] and heavy rain, which could push crop prices up.[43]

Ismail Sabri also specifically blamed three types of people for the (artificial) sugar shortage: wholesalers and traders;[44] sugar smugglers who diverted sugar to neighbouring countries where the profit is bigger; and consumers who engage in panic purchase.[45] What the minister said can be backed up by evidence. For example, an owner of a cafe shop said some sundry shop owners were hoarding sugar and selling them at high prices or overcharges them.[46] As another example, a pack of one kilogram of sugar can be sold at RM2.9 across the Malaysian-Thai border or RM3.1 across the Malaysian-Indonesian border.[47] RM4 per pack was also mentioned in a news report.[48] To be sure, Sarawak's interior areas have a long and porous border, coupled with thick forest and deep terrains.[49]

However, what the minister said can also be challenged. For example, one politician said the people in Lawas District should not be blamed for buying sugar in bulk, adding "[t]here is no sugar supply or transportation problem as the government has good networking to send over the sugar supply."[50] Another politician of the Parti Keadilan Rakyat (PKR) said the MTDCC should stop playing the "blame game."[51] Indeed, how come in June 2010 did we learn that Kuala Lumpur began to consider a proposal to appoint special wholesale sugar suppliers (or even petroleum stations/kiosks) to small and medium sized retailers as a mechanism to overcome sugar shortage, so as to avoid small and medium sized retailers from

---

[39] Malaysia Cooperatives College or Maktab Kerjasama Malaysia (MKM) said cooperatives are consumers as well. So, they can determine prices of goods. See *BP*, November 13, 2009, p.12.

[40] *Ibid.*, June 17, 2010, p.9. During the Gawai Dayak, a one kilogram of sugar could be resold at RM2.5. See *ibid.*, June 25, 2010, p.6.

[41] *Ibid.*, January 10, 2010, p.1.

[42] To go to Limbang River, Lawas District from Bintulu sub-district, a ship is needed. See *BP*, December 10, 2009, p.8.

[43] *BP*, January 9, 2010, p.16, April 1, 2010, p.15, and May 21, 2010, p.D2.

[44] Another report mentioned retailers. See *ibid.*, June 4, 2010, p.5.

[45] *BP*, August 14, 2009, p.11 and June 4, 2010, p5.

[46] *Ibid.*, January 7, 2010, p.6 and January 19, 2010, p5.

[47] *Ibid.*, May 1, 2010, p.4 and May 21, 2010, p.18.

[48] *SHDN*, June 15, 2010, p.A2.

[49] *BP*, August 21, 2009, p.10.

[50] *Ibid.*, December 12, 2009, p.13.

[51] *Ibid.*, September 12, 2009, p.16.

depending on hypermarkets and supermarkets for their supply when faced with the shortage?[52]

Ismail Sabri also failed to mention that MSM Company's domestic sales accounted for 90% of its turnover, while its exports to the Republic of Singapore (ROS), New Zealand, and Hongkong Special Administration Region (SAR) accounted for the remainder.[53] The KPDNKK from September 2009 to late 2009 revoked the licenses of seven sugar wholesalers.[54] Yet, the same Ministry's Head of Enforcement, Mohammad Rahim Ibrahim,[55] said sugar shortage at the distribution points was due to logistic, leakage, or supply disruption[56] rather than a real shortage, adding "[w]e have sent our officers to all the relevant areas including suppliers, retailers, wholesalers and sea ports [and the border]."[57] It should be noted that the same KPDNKK official failed to mention another three problems, that is, the authorities concerned sometimes only pay lip service of monitoring,[58] there are no deliveries on weekends,[59] and some lorry drivers would go home to celebrate festive occasions.[60] Besides, sometimes manufactures did not know that they were selling sugar to industries whose products were meant for export.[61] And, sometimes, manufacturers have to refuse to supply sugar to some retailers, because the latter had failed to pay money on time.[62]

At other times, some retailers/traders were reported to be unwilling to sell the sugar for RM1.60 after getting it for RM1.57 per kilogram from the supplier/distributor. To the former, the profit margin of three, five, or ten sen was too little, while the supplier/distributor nets 13 sen per kilogram.[63] In June 2010, it has been agreed that five sen per kilogram is a reasonable profit for the retailers/traders. In August 2010, the MDTCC Deputy Minister, Datuk TAN Lian Hoe said the wholesaler (*pifashang*) can earn eight sen from six sen, while the retailer can earn eight sen from five sen.

Some consumers chose to believe in some shopkeepers, as if they are the ones to announce the sugar price hike, for example, on June 1, 2010,[64] resulting panic buying. In this connection, border enforcement officers may have to show a bit of compassion, allowing some foreigners to carry any of the nine controlled items, including sugar.[65] In passing, it should be noted that shopkeepers in Daro town would stock up sugar to sell to foreign oil palm plantations workers from Indonesia at a higher price.[66] It should also be noted that a person can bring in RM600 worth of goods at any one time by sea.[67]

---

[52] *Ibid.*, June 9, 2010, p.1 and p.3.
[53] *Ibid.*, August 27, 2009, p.13.
[54] *Ibid.*, January 17, 2010, p.4 and January 20, 2010, p.17.
[55] Ibrahim is the last name.
[56] *BP*, September 8, 2009, p.6 and June 25, 2010, p.6..
[57] *Ibid.*, August 14, 2009, p.11.
[58] *Ibid.*, September 1, 2009, p.8.
[59] *Ibid.*, January 31, 2010, p.12.
[60] *Ibid.*, June 5, 2010, p.5.
[61] *Ibid.*, August 25, 2009, p.5.
[62] *SHDN*, June 1, 2010, p.2.
[63] *BP*, November 28, 2010, p.13 and June 9, 2010, p.8 and *SHDN*, June 9, 2010, p.1. If the sugar price is RM1.8, traders would sell it at RM2 or RM2.2, so as to cover the transportation cost. See *BP*, June 9, 2010, p.13.
[64] *SHDN*, June 1, 2010, p.2 and *BP*, June 1, 2010, p.1.
[65] *BP*, August 25, 2009, p.5.
[66] *Ibid.*, June 23, 2010, p.D4.
[67] *Ibid.*, June 12, 2010, p.8.

There is still another reason. TAN, who has a fuller picture,[68] said the long distance involved in the delivery of sugar between one state and another had contributed partly to a delay in the supply reaching distributors in the northern part of a state, if sugar is sent from the south, and from the south to the east, and the distance was one of the factors which contributed to the unnecessary delay of the supply reaching the distributors concerned.[69] The finest example has to do with the shortage in Kedah. It turns out that 70% of sugar supplies were channelled to Kelantan, which is not a neighbouring state of Kedah.[70]

Rural area/district and sub-urban village folks have to pay RM1.9 or RM2 or even RM2.2 and RM2.5 per kilogram for the same commodity.[71] Yet, a MTDCC Sibu head said the Ministry does subsidize cooking gas for the Kapit consumers.[72] In other words, what happened to the subsidy of sugar?

Another issue has to do with unscrupulous traders.[73] A MTDCC official said, for example, sundry shops, petty hawkers, or small time traders are afraid to make reports to the Ministry for fear that they might not be able to buy sugar from their suppliers.[74] This is because some of the latter would demand the former to buy other commodities from them. If the sundry shops failed to comply with, they may not be able to get the amount of sugar they wanted from the suppliers. For example, the amount could be reduced from 2,000 kilograms to 300 or 400 kilograms.[75] In this connection, some shops, contravening the MTDCC guidelines, would insist customers to buy other goods, if they wanted their two kilograms of sugar.[76] In June 2010, a local daily reported that those who need to buy a large amount of sugar for wedding can do so at Terengganu KPDNKK office, with the condition that they show their invite/invitation cards. This is, to some people, an absurd proposal.[77]

Last but not least, in May 2010, Infrastructure Development and Communication Minister, Dato Sri Michael Manyin Jawong,[78] vowed to ensure that there will be roads to almost every village and bazaar in Sarawak's rural areas by the year 2020. What does this imply? It simply means that there were delays in transporting sugar at present. As a reminder, it has been estimated that the road to Kapit from Kanowit would cost RM700 million. A kilometre could cost RM8 million to build and even RM13 million, if we include a bridge.[79]

WHAT HAS BEEN DONE?

There are about 180 million diabetes (mellitus) worldwide.[80] The Federal Government has been trying to urge the public to take less sugar, reminding them that 14.5% of the 26 million Malaysians are down with and about 54% of adults in the nation faced weight

[68] *GuoJiShiBao* (hereinafter GJSB)(Sarawak, Malaysia), June 6, 2010, p.A6 and *SHDN*, June 7, 2010, p.2.
[69] *BP*, August 23, 2009, p.9.
[70] *Ibid.*, August 27, 2009, p.13.
[71] *SHDN*, January 11, 2010, p.A2 and *BP*, May 5, 2010, p.D2.
[72] *BP*, September 17, 2009, p.7.
[73] *Ibid.*, January 19, 2010, p.5.
[74] *Ibid.*, January 19, 2010, p.5.
[75] *GJSB*, June 6, 2010, p.A6 and *SHDN*, June 7, 2010, p.2.
[76] *BP*, May 1, 2010, p.1.
[77] *Ibid.*, June 5, 2010, p.5.
[78] Jawong is the last name.
[79] *BP*, May 23, 2010, p.9.
[80] *GJSB*, May 27, 2010, p.Zeng2.

problems or obesity, as compared to only 24.1% in the past 10 years, adding over-consumption of sugar is linked to over 60 types of diseases or sugar is the mother of various ailments, such as allergies, asthma, blindness, cancer, cavities, hypertension, kidney problems, heart ailments, obesity, and osteoporosis.[81] A medical doctor said sweetness is just a matter of taste and human body can survive, if he or she does not take any sugar, adding our body has its own system to produce sugar after carbohydrates, like unpolished rice, potatoes, tapioca, fruits, and flour, when they are broken down.[82]

The Federal Government's MITI in December 2009 said it does not intend to do away with giving APs for the import of sugar and other essential consumer items, as it will only expose the prices to speculation and fluctuations in the international market, emphasizing that the Government has a mechanism to intervene if there were elements of consumer exploitation.[83] In June 2010, Mustapa said that issuing more AP to import sugar would not lower the price of the commodity, if the government did not increase the current allocation of RM1+ billion.[84] So, for example, at the Bintulu sub-district, inspection officers would check the prices of wholesale and retail items twice a week, on Tuesdays and Thursdays.[85] The newest MTDCC guideline, which was postponed to July 1, 2010[86] from the original set date, June 15, 2010, is that each retailer, who wants to sell sugar, wheat flour, cooking oil plus cooking gas, petroleum, and diesel, must have a Sundry Sales License (Lesen Jualan Runcit), costing nothing (as opposed to the original RM 10) each and to be renewed every five years (as opposed to the original two years),[87] and each retailer, including petroleum station for the first time for the sake of the convenience of the drivers, can be allocated 200 kilograms of sugar on its premise, provided their application was backed with invoices of purchase for two previous months or past transactions history.[88] To be sure, about 19 years ago, the license was abolished, for fear that some consumers might be victims.[89]

Ismail Sabri, in August 2009, warned (inactive) wholesalers,[90] who hoard sugar without getting consent from either him or the secretary-general, thereby causing sugar shortage in the market, would face stern action including an immediate revocation of their licenses, adding the Federal Government would monitor the movement of container lorries, which transport sugar from the factories to the designated destinations.[91] The minister also said the Federal

---

[81] *BP*, August 22, 2009, p.20, November 25, 2009, p.6, and December 5, 2009, p.4.

[82] *SHDN*, January 11, 2010, p.A2.

[83] *BP*, December 8, 2009, p.1.

[84] *Ibid.*, June 11, 2010, p.22.

[85] *Ibid.*, February 11, 2010, p.10.

[86] Some retailers belonging to the Federation of Sundry Goods Merchants (FSGM) were tough. They aired their grievances against the licensing, and they want to boycott the guidelines. Some complain that the government only target the small sundry shops. See *SHDN*, June 13, 2010, p.1 and June 14, 2010, p.A4 and *BP*, June 13, 2010, p.23.

[87] *BP*, June 21, 2010, p.4.

[88] *Ibid.*, June 5, 2010, p.D1, June 9, 2010, p.3, and June 15, 2010, p.2 as well as *SHDN*, June 4, 2010, p.7 and June 8, 2010, p.3. Each retailer may have to buy 9-11 licenses, amounting to RM1,107 per year. See http://www.chinareviewnews.com, dated June 8, 2010 at 11:51:42. In late June 2010, an official said that due to ample supply, each sundry shop can order up to 500 kilograms of sugar at any one time. See *ibid.*, June 25, 2010, p.6.

[89] *BP*, June 8, 2010, p.3. It was done by the Malaysian Chinese Association (MAC). See *SHDN*, June 8, 2010, p.3. In June 2010, a newspaper reported that MAC may well be called upon to talk to the Federal Government. See *SHDN*, June 14, 2010, p.2.

[90] In Miri, there are five wholesalers, and three of them of major ones. See *BP*, June 10, 2010, p.8. However, there are four major *PiFaShang* (wholesalers) in Miri. See *SHDN*, June 13, 2010, p.A6. Felda Trading Sdn. Bhd. Owns 226 retail shops and the D'Mart supermarkets and 13 outlets in Sabah and Sarawak. See *BP*, June 10, 2010, p.4.

[91] *BP,* August 14, 2010, p.11.

Government was also offering a reward of RM10,000 to anyone who could provide information on the hoarding of sugar, which could lead to the case being solved. As a stringent measure, the MTDCC's Sibu head, BALRAJ Singh, in September 2009, said six enforcement officers were deployed to escort the sugar from the Rajang Port Authority (RPA) to the three wholesalers, so as to prevent errant traders from manipulating the sugar supply in the wet market or channelling the same to other places.[92] In January 2010, fresh stock or consignment of sugar was transported to the four wholesalers' warehouses again under strict watch.[93] As a step further, the KPDNKK since December 2009 would assign two enforcement officers at every wholesaler to ensure that sugar will reach the retailers, so as to prevent the former stocking up sugar supply.[94] In May 2010, it reminded consumers that retailers are not allowed to insist that their customers must buy additional items, and that any retailer caught indulging in such a practice could be charged under the Control of Supply Act (1951), in which the maximum penalty is RM100,000.[95] In June 2010, the KPDNKK said, if sugar supply is sufficient, one can buy more than two kilograms at a time.[96] However, small-time retailers, who cannot obtain sugar directly from suppliers, can call up KPDNKK Sarawak Hotline at 082-466052, which opens daily from 8 am to 7pm. Consumers can also channel to the KPDNKK via e-aduan@kpdnkk.gov.my.[97]

One MDTCC official assured owners of businesses that, if they cannot get sufficient sugar supply, they could contact the Ministry, and the latter would direct suppliers to meet the demand. Failure to do so, the suppliers would be regarded as committing an offence.[98] Meanwhile, coffee shop operators are requested to display prices of drinks and charge customers according to the price list, failing which they would be liable to a maximum of RM7,500 fine, under the Price Control Act 1946.[99]

The MDTCC in August 2009 is also looking into the possibility of restructuring the sugar distribution network/chain in the states to present any delay in supplying the commodity to the distributors. TAN said her ministry was considering confining sugar distribution to a particular state, without the need to distribute the commodity to other states. "For instance, in future, distributors in Selangor would only have to supply sugar within Selangor, without having to send it to other states."[100] In spring 2010, the old distribution system was supposed to be replaced by the new system, which began outside of a festive season.[101] However, it should be noted that, in early May 2010, the Sarawak Dayak Iban Association (Sadia) Kapit branch, which was worried about the depleted sugar stock, urged the Federal Government to appoint a direct sugar supplier to cater for their Gawai Dayak celebration on June 1st and 2nd.[102] As a reminder, in December 2009, Kapit, which is the heartland of the Dayak community, with more than 80% of the total population residing in over 350 traditional longhouses,[103] was out of sugar for over a week.[104]

---

[92] *Ibid.*, September 8, 2009, p.6.
[93] *Ibid.*, January 12, 2010, p.7.
[94] *Ibid.*, January 17, 2010, p.4.
[95] *Ibid.*, May 4, 2010, p.14.
[96] *Ibid.*, June 18, 2010, p.D3.
[97] *Ibid.*, August 29, 2009, p.13.
[98] *Ibid.*, January 19, 2010, p.5.
[99] *Ibid.*, January 17, 2010, p.4.
[100] *Ibid.*, August 23, 2009, p.9.
[101] *Ibid.*, October 8, 2009, p.12 and January 17, 2010, p.4.
[102] *Ibid.*, May 5, 2010, p.D2.
[103] *Ibid.*, June 3, 2010, p.D2.

The Federal Government also encourages the public for providing information to the police about, for example, smuggling subsidized sugar to other countries. The public can just inform the MTDCC the location of the suppliers.[105] The MTDCC does not allow the export of sugar by land/highlands,[106] air, or at sea, and it has been cooperating with other Malaysian enforcement agencies to thwart the smuggling of goods. Throughout 2009, the Sabah region Marine Operations Force (MOF) inspected 44,562 boats in the country's waters, a rise of 55% from 2008.[107] In January 2010, the Malaysia Maritime Enforcement Agency (MMEA) patrol vessel, KDR Maritim, in the Sandakan waters off Berhala Island, Sabah State, seized a Philippines-bound vessel with about RM200,000 worth of sugar or 3,500 bags of sugar, at a time when Malaysia is facing sugar shortage.[108] The Malaysian [Anti-Smuggling Unit (UPP)], employing undisclosed new strategies, and Thai customs departments have been joining force at the border to curb sugar smuggling into the Kingdom of Thailand (KOT).[109] In May 2000, both countries signed a border agreement. In August 2010, an improved accord was signed during the 50th Thai-Malaysian General Border Committee (GBC) meeting. There are also laws ready to punish the convicted smugglers. Section 135 (1)(e) of the Customs Act carries a fine of not more than 10 times and not less than 20 times the value of the seized items, or jail of up to three years.

The Selangor State's MTDCC officials and police, in August 2009, acting on a tip-off, seized 11,400 kilograms or 228 bags of sugar worth RM16,500 from two houses in Taman Teratai, Bukit Beruntung.[110] The owner was charged with stocking up sugar at the illegal premises without a license, under Section 21 of the Control of Supplies Act 1961, who could be fined RM250,000 or jailed not more than three years or both.

It was not until September 2009 that the MTDCC requested all the supermarkets, retail outlets, and sundry shops located within 10 kilometers of the international border between Malaysia and the State of *Brunei* Darussalam (SBD)/Nation of Brunei to apply for a RM10 special license to sell controlled items, such as sugar, so as to deter traders taking the festive season as an opportunity to jack up prices of goods in general and controlled items in particular. Penalty of RM15,000 and RM25,000 in fines for sole proprietors and companies, respectively, will be imposed on violators. Among the areas gazetted within the 10 kilometers mark are the Emart Commercial Centre (ECC), Bandar Baru Permyjaya, Senadin (BBPS), and Kuala Baram (KB). In February 2010, the Federal Government, in a directive under the Price Control Act 1946, asked the KPDNKK to make sure that operators of hypermarkets, supermarkets, superstores, and chain stores to apply for RM10 trading license in order to sell sugar, etc.[111] Any violation to the Act will mean a maximum compound of RM7,500 or a maximum penalty of RM15,000.

---

[104] *Ibid.*, December 15, 2009, p.6.
[105] *Ibid.*, January 19, 2010, p.5.
[106] *Ibid* and September 8, 2009, p.6.
[107] *Ibid.*, January 7, 2010, p.8.
[108] *Ibid.*, January 20, 2010, p.12.
[109] *Ibid.*, August 14, 2009, p.11 and January 7, 2010, p.17.
[110] *Ibid.*, August 20, 2009, p.21.
[111] *Ibid.*, February 6, 2010, p.4.

OTHER RELATED ISSUES

Sugar is a heavily controlled item in Malaysia. Traders are directed to display pink price tags. It is done on the interest of the people. The following are several issues related to sugar.

It is suggested that the Malaysian Government should promote plantation of sugar locally by offering low interest agriculture loan to support the farmers' initial set-up costs. Besides that, the progress of agriculture activities is also able to generate more job opportunities to local people, too. If the sugar plantations can be run in big scale with advance technology, the country may able to export sugar in future which can improve the balance of payment in the international trade.

There is confusion regarding the issue of how many licenses are needed to sell controlled items. It was not until late June 2010 that a KPDNKK official said only one license, not 11, is needed. Probably the 10 other licenses are required by other ministries and local authorities, like business license and fire safety license from the fire department.[112]

On January 1, 2010, the MTDCC announced the price increase of 20 sen per kilogram of sugar, that is, from RM1.55 to RM1.75. In July of the same year, the price increased again by 25 sen. Would this decrease the sugar intake of many people, thereby gradually changing the dietary habit of those people for their own good health? More importantly, would this trigger a domino effect, indiscriminately soaring the prices of other controlled goods or commodities, such as condensed milk, cooking gas, wheat flour, etc.? According to analysts at OSK Research Sdn Bhd, which is one of the largest investment research firms in Malaysia with sister regional teams in Singapore, Indonesia, and Hongkong, sugar price hike posed a minimal impact.[113] In a later study,[114] it was shown that, based on a 325 milliliters can of Pepsi and assuming sugar subsidies were cut as proposed in 20 sen increments and this would completely passed through to consumers, the price per can of Pepsi would rise by 0.7% of every 20 sen raise in sugar prices. Furthermore, if sugar prices were hikes by a fill RM1 per kilogram, the price of a can of the same sparkling beverage could rise from RM1.8 to RM1.87. To the analysts, consumers would be generally able to absorb this 3.6% raise. One Sibu branch head of the MTDCC explained why cooking gas price is cheaper in Kapit than Sibu, for example.[115] The reason is none other than that, under the Pilot Project Scheme (PPS), the price-controlled item under discussion has been subsidized by the Federal Government to cushion rural folks from higher transportation cost, freight, and labor charges. Without the subsidy, a consumer will have to pay RM35 per cylinder, instead of RM24.5. The price could even be higher, if we include delivery and handling charges, as some retailers would take them into account.

Another related issue is when to announce the price hike? A government official revealed that, from past experiences, when there was speculation that the price would be increased, people would start panic buying and some traders would irresponsibly stock up and hoard their supplies. Thus, the government's strategy is to offer no warning on price hike, so as to avoid hoarding.[116]

---

[112] *Ibid.*, June 25, 2010, p.1.
[113] *Ibid.*, January 6, 2010, p.B12.
[114] *Ibid.*, June 24, 2010, p.B11.
[115] *Ibid.*, September 17, 2010, p.7.
[116] *Ibid.*, August 5, 2010, p.10.

In September 2009, the Tawau marine police during Operations Octopus detained two passenger ferries that were on the way to Nunukan, an Indonesia town. 227 kilograms of sugar worth RM350 and other controlled-items were seized from the ferries. Yet, because nobody admitted to owning the items, no suspect was detained.[117] In another operation in December 2009, a smuggler offered a RM5,000 bribe to the policemen, so as not to take stern action against him. Although these policemen ignored the offer and went ahead to arrest the smuggler,[118] what about the integrity of other policemen? This is because, in June 2010, the Congress of Unions of Employees in the Public and Civil Services (Cuepacs), which is an umbrella union for Malaysia's civil servants, is only hoping to see a zero graft or corruption by 2012,[119] but not earlier.

In August 2009, the General Operations Force (GOF) in Sarawak, the leading agency with over 2,000 personnel deployed at 25 posts,[120] plus selected members of the People's Vigilante Corps (Rela) from the announcement of the 10MP at a total cost of about RM31 million, began to carry out operation, surveillance, and inspection, so as to curb smuggling activities along the border and on express buses,[121] said the smuggling of controlled items like sugar over the border with the Indonesian province of Kalimantan is not serious, because these items were being brought out of the state for villages, which were located much nearer to Sarawak and not the major towns in Kalimantan, adding "[w]e have our [six main customs, immigration, and quarantine (CIQ)] for export but the problem here is some try to get more out."[122] In other words, the GOF is more concerned about the smuggling of other items like alcohol and cigarettes through illegal routes/*jalan tikus*.[123] Yet, in January 2010, *Borneo Post* reported that smuggling of sugar across border is rampant.[124]

A related issue is: Has, for example, the GOF being able to pin point and, more importantly, patrol places where smuggling can be easier conducted, such as Tebedu, which is a border town in southwestern Sarawak along the Malaysia-Indonesian border in the island of Kalimantan?[125]

Restaurants and coffee shop owners in Kuching, the capital of Sarawak, following the Federal Government's announcement of a hike in price of sugar, said they will not burden consumers. However, how much longer can they hold on at their old price? If a business cannot generate profit, the owner might as well quit it.

The Sibu Division's Consumers Association (SCA) has been calling for a boycott of sugar as a sign of protest over the January 1, 2010 sugar price hike. Earlier in August 2009, it urged consumers to exert collective bargaining power to pressure either suppliers or retailers to bring down prices of goods.[126] In this connection, Labuan Indian Chamber of Commerce and Industry was also against the government decision to have license to sell sugar, etc.[127] Are consumers like a heap of sand or a heap of clay, even though a KPDNKK official urged

---

[117] *Ibid.*, September 4, 2009, p.15.
[118] *Ibid.*, December 25, 2009, p.21.
[119] *Ibid.*, June 4, 2010, p.18.
[120] *Ibid.*, January 7, 2010, p.1.
[121] *Ibid.*, August 21, 2009, p.10.
[122] *Ibid.* In Sabah, only 50 kilograms are allowed. See *SHDN*, February 17, 2010, p.A9.
[123] *BP*, August 21, 2009, p.10.
[124] *Ibid.*, January 7, 2010, p.6.
[125] *Ibid.*, January 19, 2010, p.5.
[126] *Ibid.*, August 29, 2009, p.1 and p.6.
[127] *Ibid.*, June 10, 2010, p.8.

consumers to complain if their rights were violated?[128] Who really have the time to demonstrate in front of government buildings, supermarkets, etc.? More importantly, how come the SCA has not been cooperating with the Malaysian Consumer Protection Association (PPPM), which prides itself as being able to make sure that the consumers' rights are always protected?[129] What about forming a coalition or alliance with the Federation of Sundry Goods Merchants Association (FSGMA), which has 20,000 retailers[130] in the country? Besides, how come the SCA has not pointed out that Sarawak is not complying with the national policy on consumerism movement by appointing government officers or civil servants in the state consumerism drive council, instead of leaders or representatives from non-governmental organizations (NGOs)?[131]

It is said that Sarawakians consumed 66.1 metric tons or 66,100 kilograms of sugar each day.[132] Should we include a discussion of the foreign tourists as well as legal and illegal foreign workers in the state? For example, in January 2010, Najib disclosed that 39,000 Indian nationals who entered the country could not be traced.[133] At the end of May 2010, Malaysia is the haven for 88,100 refugees and asylum-seekers, and 90% of them are from the Union of Myanmar (UOM).[134] In May 2010, we were told that Sarawak had 3,280,656 visitor arrivals in the year 2009. Out of the total number recorded, 2,117,447 were foreigners,[135] while 1,163,209 were domestic visitors from the Peninsula and Sabah.[136] Do they consume a lot of sugar?

It should also be noted that sugar prices, heading for the biggest quarterly drop since the 1985/1986 season, will extend a slump as Brazil and the Republic of India (RI), the world's largest producers, harvest bumper crops next season.[137] To be sure, Brazilian yields are beating forecasts as a waning El Nino brings dry weather, boosting prospects for a record harvest.[138] In short, would Malaysians have to pay less money for buying sugar? And, what will happen to the subsidized sugar price?

CONCLUSION

As of May 2010, Malaysia has a big national debt of RM103 billion,[139] and the Federal Government intends to reduce it in five years. It also has a record high deficit of RM47 billion

---

[128] *Ibid.*, June 25, 2010, p.6.
[129] *Ibid.*, February 6, 2010, p.6.
[130] *SHDN*, June 11, 2010, p.A11 and *BP*, June 9, 2010, p8. According to *BP*, there are a total of about 70,000 or 80,000 retailers nationwide. See *BP*, June 9, 2010, p.3 and June 10, 2010, p.1. Angkatan Koperasi Kebangsaan Malaysia Berhad (Angkasa) has over 7,000 cooperatives across the country. See *BP*, June 9, 2010, p.8. In mid-June 2010, it revoked its decision of boycott the sale of sugar, after the government had accepted its reasoning. See *ibid.*, June 17, 2010, p.4.
[131] *BP*, February 6, 2010, p.6.
[132] *Ibid.*, February 6, 2010, p.4.
[133] *Ibid.*, January 14, 2010, p.18.
[134] *Ibid.*, July 13, 2010, p.15 and *SHDN*, July 13, 2010, p.6.
[135] Malaysia has the "Malaysia as My Second Home (MM2H)" program.
[136] *BP*, May 27, 2010, p.6. There are 288 foreigners who chose to make Malaysia their second home. Among them, 118 are British and 84, from the Republic of China (ROC) on Taiwan. See *SHDN*, May 27, 2010, p.A4.
[137] *BP*, April 2, 2010, p.B9 and http://www.fao.org/docrep/003/s8850e/S8850E09.htm, accessed on June 2, 2010.
[138] *BP.*, April 2, 2010, p.B9.
[139] The question of would Malaysia become a second, bankrupt Greece by 2019 was posed by Datuk Seri Idris Jala, who is a minister in the Prime Minister's Department. See *SHDN*, May 28, 2010, p.1. For a rebuttal, see *BP*, June 1, 2010, p.1, June 3, 2010, p.10, and June 9, 2010, p.5. Jeremy TAN said, so long as Malaysia can issue its currency, it

in 2009.[140] It is certainly contemplating to stop sugar subsidy, withdrawing it in stages.[141] If phased out, the Federal Government can save a whopping figure of RM1.008 billion per year. Perhaps the shortage problem can also be alleviated, due to more expensive sugar. Infrastructure Development Assistant Minister, Datuk Daud Abdul Rahman,[142] said, with that amount of money, at least 200 kilometers of roads can be built in Sarawak.[143] Political will is certainly needed to execute the exit strategy for the subsidies, if the Federal Government wants to save the national budget and reduce deficit. Perhaps, it might be thinking of doing it after the next general election. The last one was held in March 2008, and the ruling party was for the first time unable to maintain a two-third majority in the Parliament.

Drawing from the various data and feedback as discussed above, it is, needless to say, after having successfully tackled the sugar shortage, it is not the end of the whole battle, because there are also (glutinous) rice shortage,[144] cement or crust gravel shortage,[145] and diesel shortage[146] to name but a few. As a final remark, the shortage issue relating to any commodities of the country would include both the socio-economic and operational factors, which require a more comprehensive agenda, apart from curbing the level of subsidy.

would not collapse. Conversation with him, dated June 5, 2010. So long as the Government is willing to sell it public land to the common people, it can have revenue.

[140] *BP*, May 28, 2010, p.1.

[141] *Ibid.*, April 8, 2010, p.10 and May 28, 2010, p.4.

[142] Rahman is the last name.

[143] *BP*, March 29, 2010, p.4.

[144] *SHDN*, January 30, 2010, p.A11. Some imported products look shrivelled.

[145] *BP*, December 12, 2009, p.4, December 22, 2009, p.10, January 31, 2010, p.12, and August 7, 2010, p.17.

[146] *Ibid.*, June 14, 2010, p.4.

In: International (Corporate) Governance
Editor: Peter Kien-Hong Yu

ISBN: 978-1-61122-645-4

Chapter 12

THE STUDY OF POLITICS AND NON-POLITICS SHOULD BEGIN WITH ONE DOT

Peter Kien-Hong Yu and W. Emily Chow

ABSTRACT

There are many models and theories in the West, such as game theory, systems theory, and rational (choice) theory. Each one of them and the lead co-author's dialectical framework of thought and action can be respectively regarded as a dot. Argubly, we should begin with one dot, when we study politics and non-politics. Otherwise, we will encounter many contradictions and unable to dissolve them.

In this paper, comparison and contrast have been made with regarding to all the above-mentione models and theories. The two co-authors have attempted to demonstrate that, by using the lead author's dialectical model, more phenomena since the beginning of human beings can be logically, systematically, and coherently described and explained, if not inferred or predicted.

Keywords: one-dot theory, dialectics, game theory, systems theory, rational (choice) theory

It should be stated at the outset that a model is either a simplification or compression of certain things or phenomena. In each model, there should be at least two concepts interrelated to each other. At a higher level, a theory is either a simplification or compression of the model itself or what some social scientists prefer to call the theoretical framework.[1] Just as a model can be simplified or compressed into a dot, the same thing speaks for a theory.

In this research paper, we will first introduce the lead co-authors' framework of thought and action. In the next section, we will spell out the reasons why it is better for us to begin with one dot when we study dialectical and non-dialectical politics. By politics, we mean both domestic and international. The word international could subsume interplanetary, because mainalnd China plans to land on the Moon in the foreseeble future. In the third section, we

[1] Some social scientists refer to paradigm as a philosophical framework.

will conduct an exercise in parsing the one dot and some sentences, so that readers can understand more fully about what we are trying to drive at. In the fourth section, we will compare and contrast the lead co-author's model with other (supposedly) non-dialectical models and theories but having inner dialectics, which were first developed in the West.

THE INTEGRATED, MODIFIED MODEL

In September 1994, the lead co-author constructed his first working, dialectical framework of thought and action. Over the years, it was very convenient for him to apply this model to describe, explain, and interpret some 60 different topics.[2] In July 2004, the lead co-hor found a copy of William (Bill) H. Gates, III's November 1996 revised and updated book on computer science's binary system, *The Road Ahead*. The wattage of eight light bulbs was depicted on pages 27 and 28: 128, 64, 32, 16, 8, 4, 2, and 1. Later in the same month, he asked LI Chuang, a professor of computer science at Qinghua University (Beijing), whether we can say that the binary system is another way of saying *Yin* and *Yang*, and, in less than a few seconds, he said "Yes!" In October 2004, the lead-co-author came across the following phrase: (the) snake in the tunnel (mechanism). Simply put, in April 1972, the European Community Council (ECC) passed a resolution on an exchange rate limit or fluctuation margin of +2.25% and -2.25%. In other words, some Europeans like many Germans do subconsciously accept dialectics, because the two percentages refer to two extremes, respectively. Since our study almost has do to with Chinese (Communist) politics, we will change the word from snake to dragon, the latter of which can bring about luck.[3] In order to make our original model easier to grasp and to be appreciated by more experts and layman, the lead co-author will (slightly) modify his model for the third time by integrating the latter two contributions in modified forms.

---

[2] See my books, *Bicoastal China: A Dialectical, Paradigmatic Analysis* (New York: Nova Science Publishers, 1999), *The Crab and Frog Motion Paradigm Shift: Decoding and Deciphering Taipei and Beijing's Dialectical Politics* (Lanham, MD.: University Press of America, 2002), and *Hu Jintao and the Ascendancy of China* (Singapore: Marshall Cavendish International Academic Publishing, 2005).Thomas A. Metzger pointed out that there are basic contradictions between contemporary China's complex market-place and Western liberalism. See his book (2004), *A Cloud Across the Pacific: Essays on the Clash between Chinese and Western Political Theories Today* (Hongkong: The Chinese University Press). China is sitting atop 10,000 years of history. In November 2005, it was reported that Chinese archaeologists for the first time discovered 4,500-year-old fortune-telling instruments. The *Yin* and *Yang* can be dated back to 3,100 years. September 28, 2005 marked the 2555th birthday of Confucius, who is well known for his middle-way teaching. In January 2006, the 80th generation of Confucius was born in Taipei. However, in April 2007, we were told taht there are 83 generations. See *China Times* (Taipei), April 2, 2007, p.A13. March 14, 2006 (or February 15, 2006 in the Chinese Lunar calendar) markes the 2577 birthday of Laozi.

[3] The Chinese people are regarded as *longdechuanren* (descendants of the dragon) or *longzhong* (dragon seeds). The first image of a Chinese dragon can be dated back to more than 6,400 years ago, and it was excavated in 1987/1988 in Puyang City of Henan Province. Zhejiang Province people liken tornadoes to dragon's breath or dancing or waving. *Shuilongjuan* (literally water dragons)'s watersprouts were spotted in waters off the Donsha (Pratas) Island Group in the South China Sea (SCS) in May and June 1998. In December 2004, the State Administration for Radio, Film and Television (SRFT) in Beijing banned a controversial Noke commercial, because the advertisement insults Chinese national dignity and inerest as well as national culture. The Nike television commercial shows LeBron James in a video-game-style settting defeating the *kung fu* master, two women in traditional Chinese attire, and a pair of dragons, which is considered a sacred symbol in traditional Chinese culture. In *Snakes in Suites: When Psychopaths Go to Work*, Robert Hare and Paul Babiak said the psychopaths "use arrogance and superficial charm to scale the top of the ladder, knocking off whoever gets in their way" and "they see the world as one large watering hole. Their resources are sex, power and money." In short, snake has a negative connotation.

Figure 1 shows the lead co-author's theoretical framework. He will describe and explain the following model in more detail:

1 2 3 4 5 A B C D E

time/space sequence (1)
time/space sequence (2)
....
time/space sequence (n)

Figure 1.

On surface, 4, and 5 constitute a spectrum or what we called the safe zone each Number or Letter represents a static concept. 1, 2, 3,, and A, B, C, D, and E, the danger zone spectrum. Each Number is a synonym or a variation of the next Number. Similarly, each Letter is a synonym or variation of the next Letter. A dialectician would refrain from entering into the Letter zone, unless absolutely necessary or compelled to by objective circumstances.

In the face of constant change, a dynamic, operational concept [or what the Chinese Communists called *fangzhen* (or guided principle)] is needed to reconcile the two extremes, to wit, 1 and E (or two spectrums), or to eventually bring about the disappearance of the right extreme by elimination, cooptation, absorption, etc. (See Figure 2.) Another way of saying this concept is action. Such a concept/action must work in favor of the left extreme (that is, 1).

Dialecticians must take action to reduce (or reconcile) contradictions in a time-frame that proceeds from time/space sequence (1) up to the time/space sequence (n-1),[4] which just precedes time/space sequence (n). Time/space sequence (n) is the last, decisive action or the end move of the game that brings the game to an ascendant or higher stage, to wit, a synthesis.

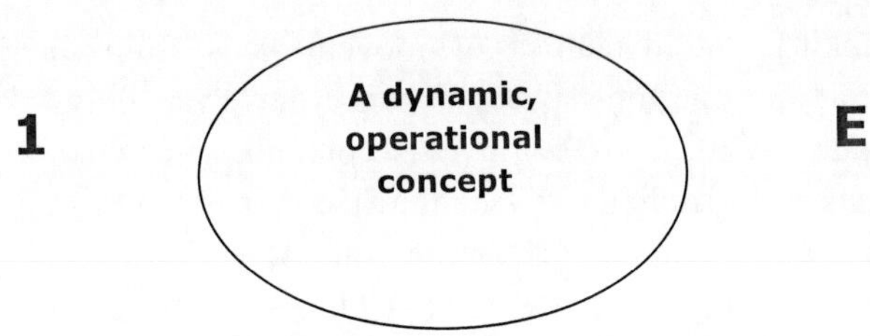

Figure 2.

To feel secure and comfortable and to talk in the same political language, dialecticians navigate within a series of dialectical models and, as a step further, navigate through the shifting *luxian* (path/line/middle way/road/track), which is either shown by a Number or a

[4] My student, Sawagodo Wilfrid Relwende, on October 31, 2006 suggested me to treat n or time/space sequence (n) as 1, the time/space sequence before the last time/space sequence or time/space sequence (n) as n-1 and so on and so forth, and the time/space sequence after the time/space sequence (n) in my model as n+1. My reply to him on November 1, 2006 is as follows: I have never thought of n, n+1, and n-1, collectively. However, if n means synthesis, there can be no n+1. N+1 could also be misunderstood by some people, because, at n+1, the synthesis will have to be divided into two-halves. One half is thesis and the other half, anti-thesis (or non-thesis). In other words, there will be problems applying what you have suggested. In any case, I will note what you said in my model's footnote.

Letter. They can react to some phenomena or take initiatives, using a particular framework which may not be known to the outsiders. In other words, a dialectician has to apply a series of dialectical frameworks in order to emerge as the winner at time/space sequence (n). Like a frog, one would leap from one framework to another framework at any time/space sequence, thereby being able to refrain from taking a tunnel vision, that is, by sticking to only one dialectical model. If one framework cannot describe and explain a phenomenon, another framework certainly can. This means that, of all the frameworks, there should be a paradigmatic framework which is primary. One can rely on the primary framework for the purpose of making moves or apply the other frameworks at other specific time/space sequences. Hence, all frameworks should not been seen as mutually exclusive.[5] Another way of looking at this is to imagine a second window within a first window with yet another, sub-dialectical window (or sub-game) within the second window.

Playing sub-games is always possible. [For example, Socialism (with Distinct Chinese Characteristics) versus Capitalism is a sub-game of Communism versus Capitalism.] Since a dialectician will pick any two dots in a framework, the sub-model can be 1 versus 3, 1 versus A, 3 versus 4, A versus B, C versus E, 1 and 5 versus Non-1-and-5, 5 and A versus Non-5-and-A, etc. However, preferably, it is the following: 1 versus A, 1 versus B, 1 versus C, 1 versus D, 2 versus A, 2 versus B, 2 versus C, 2 versus D, 2 versus E, 3 versus A, 3 versus B, 3 versus C, 3 versus D, 3 versus E, 4 versus A, 4 versus B, 4 versus C, 4 versus D, 4 versus E, 5 versus A, 5 versus B, 5 versus C, 5 versus D, and 5 versus E. And, right after making a move, what has been said or done is a thing of the past, and, in the course of making moves in a game or sub-game, the negation of negation, the affirmation of negation, the affirmation of affirmation, and the negation of affirmation may also appear (respectively) before time/space sequence (n).

"Time," which is part of the time/space sequence component, could refer to seconds, days, or years. "Space" could refer to any place involving the Chinese, which could also be on the Moon, for example.

Normativelly speaking, the dynamics of movement is from the right to the left. Empirically speaking, at any one time/space sequence, however, only one static concept is thought about or in play. While there is obvious contradiction when we see the Number spectrum versus the Letter spectrum, there is none when making a move, just as when we key in one Number, Letter, symbol, etc. in our computer at a time. These concepts are allowed to change between time/space sequences and do not have to exhibit any continuity between sequences, and, therefore, apparent contradictions between different time/space sequences are not recognized as contradictions by the dialecticians, because the rules and regulations of the game do not bind the dialecticians in one time/space sequence to the same concepts that may bind the dialecticians in the previous or next time/space sequence (*YinShiZhiYi*/因時制宜 or *CiYiShiBiYiShi*/此一時彼一時). This means that no contradiction is possible from time/space sequence (1) to (n), when a word has been said or an action has been taken. Chinese people believe in change. Hence, it is usually acceptable when one makes changes according to (time/situation) change. In this connection, any move is considered logical but not necessarily

[5] An anology will be the Chinese I-Ching (Classic of Changes), its 64 Hexagrams are not mutually exclusive. When consulting one Hexagram, one must also consider the two neighboring Hexagrams and an opposite Hexagram to understand its meaning. For example, if you consult Hexagram 3, Hexagram 4 will be the situation if you overdo 3 (or future) and Hexagram 2 will be the situation if you do less than 3 (or past). You also must consider Hexagram C for contingencies of the situation.

always rational, because one can (be forced to) be in the danger zone for a period of time, due to certain circumstances (or *QngShi* in Mandarin Chinese) or as in Confucius saying, *ShiShiWuZheWeJunJi*/識時務者為俊傑). An event may take days to finish but it could be described and explained second by second or decade by decade within the framework.

Dialectics is both normative [when we see the Numbers and the Letters, given the decrease in wattage from E to A and the increase in wattage from 5 to 1, the dynamics of which can be likened to a crab, moving side-ways from the right extreme to the left extreme, resulting the ultimate elimination, cooptation, absorption, etc. of the right extreme concept by the left extreme concept at time/space sequence (n)] and empirical (when a word has been uttered or a deed taken). Dialectics is also both inductive and deductive. The former is associated with Numbers and Letters, while the latter, each time/space sequence.

There is no doubt that dialectics is scientific.[6] For this reason, sometimes we hear Chinese Communists prefer using the word scientific to refer to dialectics. If this dialectical model cannot describe, explain, and infer certain phenomena, another framework certainly can, hence the necessity of leaping or jumping like a frog. Indeed, from a Marxist point of view, the Chinese Communists have not abandoned Marxism for one second! We may have to set up another model to link the two strikingly similar or different dialectical models. However, a dialectician may err when wrongly applied a certain dialectical model. The finest example is what DENG Xiaoping once said about the Chinese reunification. In January 1980, he said both mainland China and Taiwan can be reunited in the decade of 1980s. By the time this writing is published, it is already the second decade of 21st century, and the possibility of arranging or having it to the satisfaction of both the mainland and Taiwan is not in sight.

A la maniere de Gates, showing the lead co-author's crab and frog motion model in terms of light bulb wattage can help us to have a fuller and quicker understanding of the dynamics. (See Figure 3.) We can designate both 1 and E as having 100 watts respectively; both 3 and C, 50 watts each; and both 5 and A, 1 watt respectively. This kind of arrangement for Numbers and Letters suggests that there are three basic stages (or nodal points) of development: nascent, ascendant, and mature for the Numbers and mature, descendant, and moribund for the Letters. In other words, 5 is nascent; 3, ascendant, and 1, mature. On the other hand, E is mature: C, descendant; and A, moribund. Last but not least, a series of other dialectical, theoretical models must be applied, in order to describe, explain, and infer (or predict) more phenomena.

At this juncture, a caveat should be added, that is, whenever we use the word, versus, it means that the concept or whatever on the left extreme, say, Yes, or 1 will eventually defeat, coopt, absorb, etc. the concept or whatever on the right extreme, say, No, at time/space sequence (n). However, in the process, the following arrangement may be necessary, such as flexibly positioning Yes at 1 and No at 5. In other words, a contradictory or even adversary relationship between Yes and No has been transformed into a non-contradictory, non-adversary relationship, meaning that whoever chose Yes or whoever opted No should learn to tolerate the existence of each other, because they are in the safe zone spectrum.

In sum, a dialectician plays two roles when playing games, that of a crab by moving side-ways and a frog by leaping from one model to another model at he or she sees fit.

---

[6] According to Michael Barnett's observation, Kenneth "Waltz aspired to make Realism more rigorous, scientific, and amenable to hypothesis testing." See his chapter, "Social Constructivism," in John Baylis and Steve Smith, editors, *The Globalization of World Politics*, 3rd ed. (N.Y.: Oxford University Press, 2005), pp.254-270.

Both 1 and E (just as others, such as 5 and A) are being positioned in parallel, and they each represent an extreme. 1 is positive or it can be equivalent to a plus sign, while E is negative or shown by a minus sign. (Of course, there are more than one tunnel in a dialectical model, depending on which two dots one chooses at any time/space sequences. Thus, 1 versus A can be the second tunnel, 5 and C can be another tunnel, A and E can be the fourth tunnel, etc.) (See Figure 4.) Given the time/space sequence element, we can watch the movement, just like what we see in the fluctuation of a foreign exchange currency or stock prices over time. The fluctuation certainly looks like a dancing or waving dragon (or snake).

In sum, one cannot just use the word, for instance, versus in writing. This word is definitely associated with dialectics. In other words, throughout the writing, one should apply the dialectical approach and method, not just here and there. Otherwise, one will inevitably face methodological problems, unless one is conducting a dialectical and non-dialectical comparative study of the same topic, using the same literature.

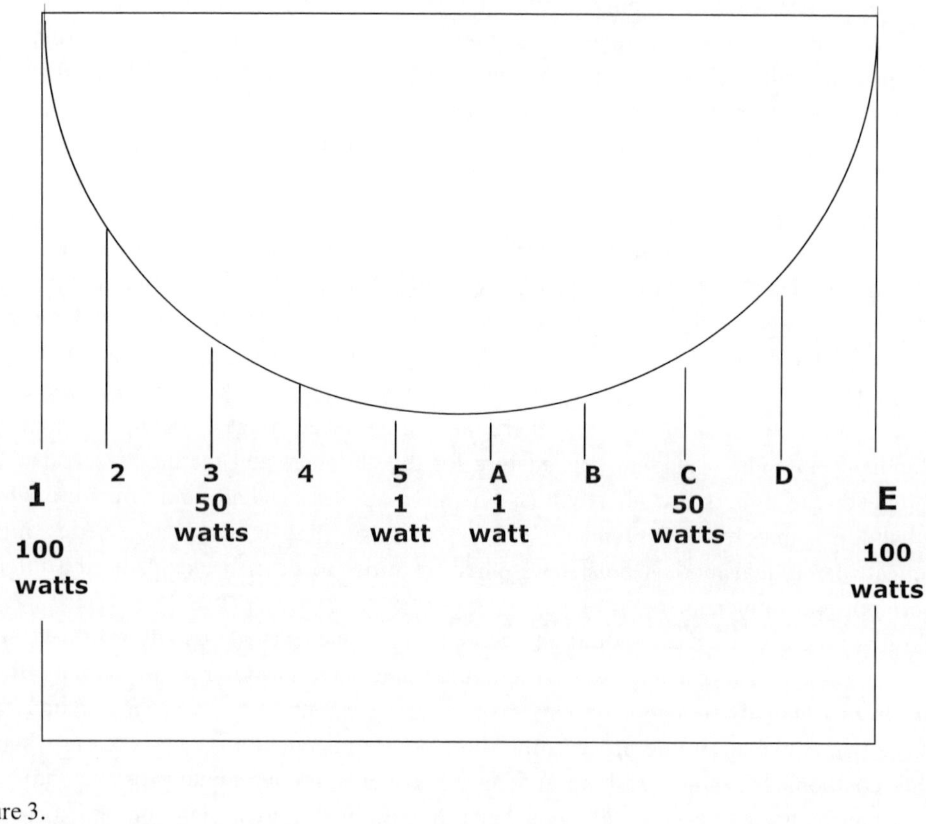

Figure 3.

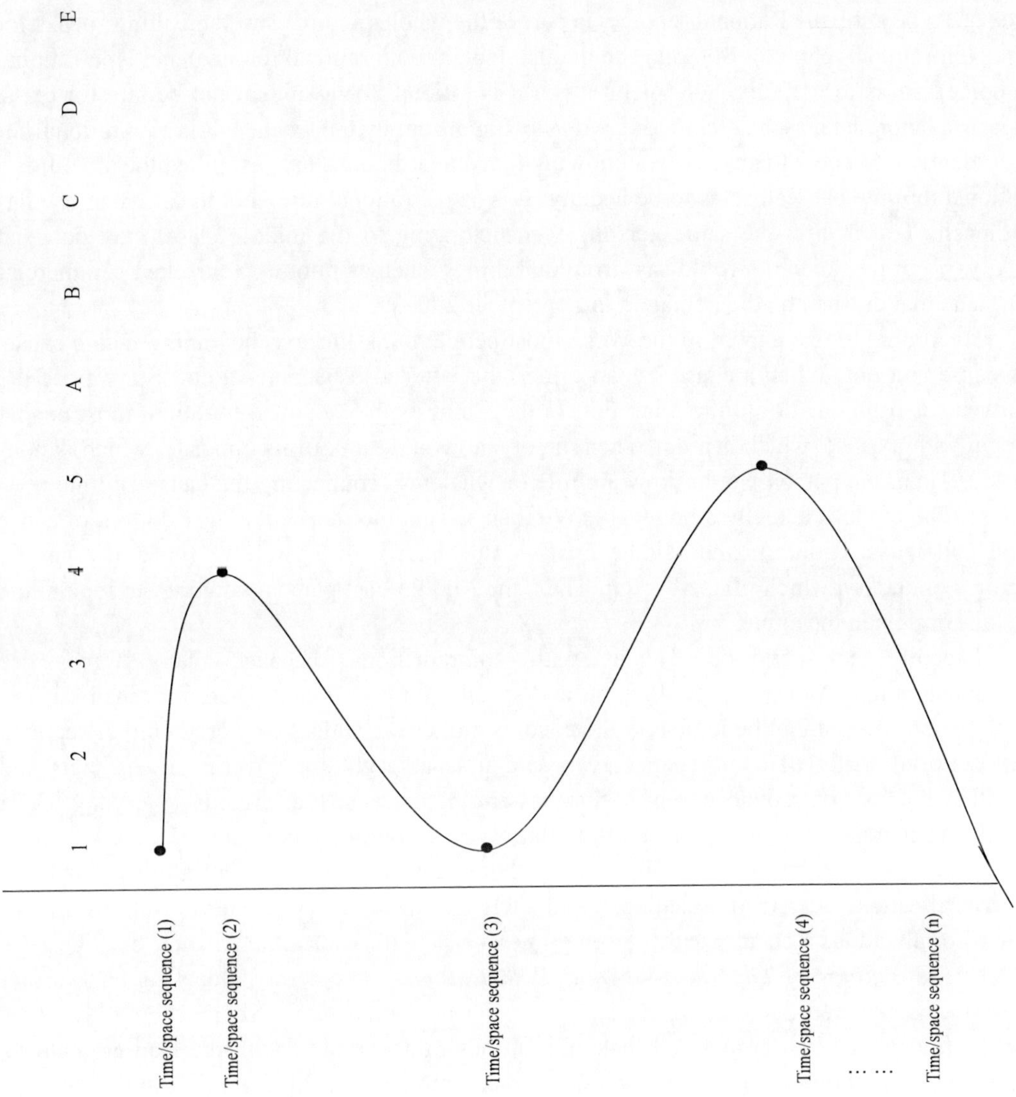

Figure 4.

Reasons for Studying Politics from One Dot

There are several reasons. First, a dot is a whole. Yet, it could also be part of a bigger whole or be equivalent to two-halves. We need to see a whole from the very beginning. For example, is God, Buddha, or Allah the original dot?[7] In Buddhist language, which also has a heavy influnce in Chinese values, this is named *YiHeXiang*/一合相 As another example, some social scientists prefer applying the non-dialectical rational (choice) theory.[8] Dialectically, we

[7] See my manuscript, *God is, by Inferrence, One-dot:* Paradigm Shift (Boca Raton, Florida: Universal Publishers, 2010).

[8] Rational choice is "an approach that emphasizes how actors attempt to maximize their interests, how they attempt to select the most efficient means to achieve those interests, and endeavours to explain collective outcomes by

could construct the following model: Rational (choice) versus Non-rational (choice) or vice versa. To be sure, the Rational (choice) is part of the whole picture. The same thing speaks for the Non-rational (choice). But, one should also look at both rational (choice) and Non-rational (choice), so as to get the whole picture. So, it is rational for a student not be late for class, because he or she may be recorded down as being absent by the teacher. It is also rational for a student not to come to class, when knowing that an earthquake has just jolted the area. It is a rational thing to eat well so as to be healthy. It is also a rational thing not to eat when one has stomach. Yet, in life, the same person, even belonging to the middle class, may do what many, if not most people would say, irrational things, such as piloting a hijacked commercial airplane that crushed on the Pentagon in September 2001.

According to one expert, in the West, most people think linearly, beginning with a cause. A cause is a dot. When a cause has an effect, the latter also becomes a dot. So, we see the movement from one dot to the other dot. In the Chinese philosophical tradition, most people begin with a cause, which is a dot. Then, he or she would think of its opposite, which is non-cause. Then, the person would draw a circle or whatever, connecting the cause and the non-cause. The circle is actually a boundary. We then see another dot or a bigger dot out of cause and non-cause. People in the Middle East would begin with a circle or find out a certain thing's boundary, which in itself is dot. Then, the Middle East person would try to look at the details or dots in the circle.

Second, the world is fraught with contradictions, because many forces are complementing, co-existing, conflicting, and so on with each other. Therefore, many, if not most, politicians cannot be logical in their words and deeds, unless they are being dialectical. An editorial writer of a newspaper even said it is all right for government officials and politicians to be contradictory in what they say and do, because they are busy everyday.[9] As a political scientist, it is our foremost task to dissolve the contradictions. In the lead co-author‘s study of globalization, he realized that there are at least 20 definitions, such as universalization, deterritorialization, and territorialization (yes, territorialization) or reterritorialization. Yet, all of them sometimes clash with each other, hence the title of a book--*The Politics of Globalization and Polarisation*.[10] The term „glocalization" further describes a situation that two contradictory concepts/situations can co-exist even at the same time. However, if you arrange all those definitions in accordance with the lead co-author‘s crab and frog motion model, there would be no contradictions at all from time/space sequene (1) to the last time/space sequence, the reason being, at each time/space sequence which could be 0.00001 second away from the next time/space sequence, one only thinks about one concept at a time.

Third, we want to be closer to reality, when we conduct research and writing. To begin with, the universe can be regarded as a dot. It could also be part of a larger dot, God. Earth can also be regarded as a dot. But, it is part of the universe, the Milky Way galaxy, or the solar system. Everything on Earth including nature from the beginning to the demise of human beings can also be regarded as one dot, if we were looking at the Earth from the

virtue of the attempt by actors to maximize their preferences under a set of actors to maximize their preferences under a set of constraints. Deriving largely from economic theorizing, the rational choice approach to politics and international politics has been immensely influential and applied to a range of issues." Cited in Baylis and Smith (note 5), p.267.

[9] *Shi Hua Daily News* (hereinafter SHDN)(Sarawak, Malaysia), July 14, 2007, p.10.

[10] Maurice Mullard, *The Politics of Globalization and Polarisation* (Cheltenham, U.K.: Edward Elgar, 2004).

International Space Station (ISS), Moon, or Mars. There are other concrete examples. A human being can be regarded as one dot but it comes from two dots, namely, a male sperm and a female egg. As a second example, knowledge can be divided into natural science and social science. As a third example, the study of natural science or social science can be break down into dialectical or non-dialecitcal approaches and methods.

Last but not least, a one-dot theory is much easier to remember. It is the easiest way to simplify or compress complex reality. The dot may mean one thing or it may mean, collectively, a zillion or googol (which means the largest number or *TianWenShuZi* in Chinese translation) of phenomena since Adam and Eve. The same thing speaks for game theory, systems theory,[11] and rational (choice) theory. Looking in the back of a classroom, each theory is a dot on the whiteboard or blackboard or in the PowerPoint slide(s).

Parsing the One Dot

We are not the first one to talk about the one dot. YI Junbo, a professor of political science, said a theory has to be begin from a dot, i.e., the definition of a concept itself.[12] What we are going to say below differs a great deal from what YI said.

We should begin from a dot, which could be a whole, depending on the context. A dot is a model or theory, because it is part of the whole truth, reality, etc. Similarly, the whole is a theory, if it is part of something which is bigger or larger.

A one-dot theory should be able to be broken down into an at-least-two-dot model, with each dot representing a concept which has to be interrelated to the other concept or concepts. In other words, any concept in a model must do without the other concepts in the same model.

Let us position the Earth in the lead co-author‘s model in the safe zone spectrum. If we regard Earth as a dot, 1 is a dot, 2 is a dot, 3 is a dot, 4 is a dot, and 5 is a dot. The difference between them lies in the degrees, with 1 carrying the most weight or being most important, while 5 the least weight or less important.[13] We can, for example, say that before there is Moon, the original, young Earth was positioned at 1. A non-dot on the right extreme or E would be designated as Non-Earth. Examples of Non-Earth are many, for example, an individual, a comet, or universe.

Because many phenomena had been existed before and after the birth of Adam and Eve, we can domonstrate that the lead co-author‘s model can describe and explain all the phenomena minus 1. Using the following model can demonstrate what we have just said: Future as 1, Present as 3, and Past as 5. There would be no redundancy in having the

---

[11] David Easton, *The Political System* (Chicago: University of Chicago Press, 1981).

[12] Email from David Dirkwen WEI, dated November 12, 2005. YI taught WEI at the National Cheng-chi University in Taiwan, Republic of China (ROC). But, when WEI emailed me for the first time in July 2005 mentioning YI's one-dot statement, my 2005 book was already published in January of the same year. In the preface, I urged research centers to develop a One-Dot-School of Thought and Action. See p.xi.

[13] "[T]he problem with dialectic is not in its mathematical formulation, which is just a simple duality based on binary analysis. Its problem comes from empirical test, for which you need statistical techniques, i.e., how to quantify different degrees of responses and how to put a weight on each response." Email from John Wong, dated November 11, 2005. My former student, CHIANG Chun-chi, said, when time is ripe, it is possible to figure out the mathematical form (*SuXueXingShi*) of dialectics. His email to me, dated November 10, 2005. The second co-author made the following remarks: "[I]f we can 'quantify' the model, it will no longer be the 'one' dot theory <holistic thinking>? The gist of One Dot is to desert the current arithmatic/ categorical thinking logic," dated August 25, 2010.

normative Future, Present, and Past as well as the empirical time factor in the time/space sequence component in the lead co-author‘s model. At time/space sequence (1), Earth can be placed under Past or 5. At time/space sequence (2) or even (100), we can put Adam and Eve under 3. This is because it is a fact that Earth existed before Adam and Eve. In this connection, why minus one phenomenon? This is because, when human beings do become extinct, no one can employ the lead co-author‘s model or other versions of dialectics to continue to describe and explain new phenomena.

The lead co-author‘s model has its descriptive and explanatory power. To play on the safe side, his framework of thought and action can also infer (as opposed to predict) future, given that (n) is the last time/space sequence. We can make the following descriptive statement: This apple is red. We can also say: This "apple" is red. On the one hand, we are describing an apple that we know, see, or eat. Such an apple is equivalent to 1 in the lead co-author‘s model. On the other hand, an ordinary apple may have been mixed with another type of fruit, resulting what we called "apple." This kind of apple with quotation marks could be placed at 5, which in the middle of the Apple (or 1) versus Non-apple (or E) model. Needless to say, we need a second framework, namely, red (or 1) versus Non-red (or E). In a word, at time/space sequence (1), we should choose the This (or 1) versus Non-this (or E) model. We would, then, look at This or 1. At time/space sequence (2), we choose the apple (or 1) versus Non-apple (or E) framework, and, similarly, we look at apple or 1. At time/space sequence (3), we choose the is (or 1) versus Non-is (or E) model, and we, again, look at is or 1. Finally, we look at red or 1 in the red (or 1) versus Non-red (or E) framework, thereby completing the descriptive exercise. If the reader has understood what we had done, he or she would realize that there is still a train of thought, accomplishing the same task as what a non-dialectician would rely on, to wit, the cause and effect method, although we need a series of dialectical models to demonstate it. This could be cumebrsome to some people.

The lead co-author‘s model can also be used to explain certain phenomena. We can make the following statement: The reason why many consumers buy this kind of apple is because it is sweet (or, for that matter, sour). Dialectically, it is necessary to construct at least 15 models, because there are 15 words in the sentence. The first framework is The (or 1) versus Non-The (or E). The second framework is reason (or 1) versus Non-reason (or E). The third model is why (or 1) versus Non-why (or E). The structure for other words from the fourth one on up to the last word is the same. And the last one would be sweet (or 1) versus Non-sweet (or E). So, at time/space sequence (1), we will look at The (or 1). At time/space sequence (2), we will look at reason (or 1). The same logic applies to the rest of the words in the sentence. Nonetheless, it is not necessary for us to use, for example, the first model or, for that matter, the is (or 1) versus Non-is (or E) model, because they should be understood as non-dominant in the sentence. For this reason, if a sentence is long, we need only to pick out the dominant framework(s) of thought and action, so as to reduce confusion on those who have not yet fully understood the lead co-author's model. And, if we put all these frameworks about the apple together, it becomes another one dot.

The lead co-author's model can still interpret linear or cause-effect statements or sentences like logic is logic is logic; a rose is a rose is a rose; and 1 is 1 is 1. To a person whose thinking is non-dialectical, to begin with, the first logic in the sentence is the cause. If it is the cause, the second logic becomes the effect. Similarly, when the second logic in the same sentence becomes the cause, the third logic in the same sentence becomes the effect, which,in turn, becomes cause again if we want to mention the fourth logic. However, if we regard logic as one dot, we can parse it as inductive logic, deductive logic, or a hybrid logic of induction and deduction, each one of which is part of the original logic. Generally speaking, the inductive logic means from the general to the particular, and deductive logic is just the reverse. However, arranged dialectically in the lead co-author‘s model, the inductive logic could be 1; the hybird logic, 3; and deductive logic, 5. There are other possibilities: deductive logic as 1 and inductive logic, 5; deductive logic as 1 and inductive logic, E; inductive logic as 1 and deductive logic, E, etc. In short, non-dialectically, one would only mention logic from time/space sequence (1) to (n), whereas, dialectically, one can break down logic into inductive logic and deductive logic or say you can have your logic and I can have mine.

What about the sentence: A rose is a rose is a rose? Again, non-dialectically, one cannot see the difference between the first word rose from the seocnd word rose or from the second word rose to the third word rose. Dialectically, one can think of a wide range of colors: red, white, pink, yellow, organge, etc.[14] So, dialectically arranged, the red rose could be positioned at 1; white, 2; and so on and so forth accordingly. In other words, at time/space sequence (5), one may buy a red rose and at time/space sequence 1,000, white rose.

Because rose is perishable, we can talk about wheat, another perishable farm product. In October 2005, it was reported that wheat entered into mainland China’s Central Plains about 4,000 years ago.[15] This was a new discovery.[16] The wheat noodle which was preserved in a special, sealed vase remained intact after all those years, except that it went mouldy or became mildewed. How do we apply the lead co-author‘s model to describe and explain this phenomenon? The applicable, normative model is Past and Future (or Past versus Non-Past). That is to say, Past is 1; Present is 3; and Future is 5. The reason that we did not apply the Past versus Present, the Present versus Future, Future versus Non-Future, or another arranged, normative model is because the discovery was made in October 2005. We will stick to 1 (or Past) from time/space sequene (1), that is, the moment when the noodle was put into the vase, up to the last time/space sequence or (n), which could be 10, 100, or even 4,000 years from the moment that the discovery was made. There is nothing wrong by sticking to 1, because, in the lead co-author‘s crab and frog motion model, there are three stages, namely, nascent, ascendant, and mature to each Number or Letter, which appears to be static on surface or appearance. Empirically, at time/space sequence (1), the wheat can be positioned at the nascent stage of 1, because the noodle has not been broken into pieces. At the next time/space sequence, it is the same. However, due to changes within the vase, the wheat gradually became carbonized. In other words, a chemical reaction has been taken place in the unbroken noodle. So, when the wheat was discovered recently, we can put the same but mouldy wheat at 1 but of the mature stage.

It is important for us to point out one more thing. That is to say, from time/space sequence (1) to the time/space sequence just before the discovery, they are empirically,

---

[14] Each different color has a different meaning. It conveys a silent, yet extremely important message from the sender to receiver. Thornless rose signifies “love at first sight.“

[15] *United Daily News* (hereinafter UDN)(Taipei), October 10, 2005, p.A9 and conversation with my student, Eric Y. H. Wu, dated November 9, 2005.

[16] We the humen beings often belately study something that had already existed. In other words, we give a name to that something later. In November 2006, a finding by the researches at the University of Hong Kong indicated that many Hoingkongers who had colon cancer can be traced back to the same Guangdong Province ancestor 550 or more than 2,500 years ago. See http://www.mpinews.com/htm/inews/20061105/gb71447k.htm, dated November 5, 2006.

collectively being regarded as past. At the moment of discovery, it is present. And, after the discovery, it becomes future, because we do not know what will happen to the wheat noodle. Hence, the present will become the past „at" the future. In a word, there is no redundancy when we use both the normative Numbers and Letters and the empirical time/space sequence components.

As to 1 is 1 is 1, the logic is the same. The first 1 could be 0.5 + 0.5; the second 1 could be expressed in terms of 100 - 99; and the third 1 could be understood as 1 x 1. If 100 - 99 carries the greatest weight, it will be placed at 1. If not, it could be positioned at 2, 3, 4, or 5. We have often heard of the One China Principle of the Communist Party of China (CPC) several months before the signing of a mutual defense treaty between the United States and the Republic of China (ROC) in December 1954. This Principle could be regarded as 1, 2, 3, 4, and 5. As of September 1, 2010, there are 192 Member States in the United Nations (UN). Swiss Confederation (SC) is not a member and it does not have diplomatic relations with either the People's Republic of China (PRC) or the ROC. As of September 1, 2010, 171 countries have diplomatic relations with the PRC and 23 of them have such relations with the ROC. Since there are no overlaps, 171 plus 23 equal to One China. So, 171 could be postitioned at 1 and 23, at 5, and they still mean One China.

The application of or a series of the lead co-author's models could be linear, because dialectics can interpret something that has been linearly expressed in the first place. Let us examine the following sentence again: The reason why many consumers buy this kind of apple is because it is sweet. As mentioned ealier, at least 15 models are needed for the purpose of demonstrating the linear progression. At time/space sequence (1), we look at the 1 in the first dialectical model, to wit, The (or 1) versus Non-The (or E). At time/space sequence (2), we jump to the second model, which is reason (or 1) versus Non-reason (or E). Here, we look at 1 again but the time/space sequence number is (2), not (1). At time/space sequence (3), we leap to the third model. This model is why (or 1) versus Non-why (or E). At this juncture, we look at (1) again but the time/space sequence number is (3), not (2). The same logic applies for other words that follow. So, for the last word, we would be looking at (1) again but the time/space sequence number is (15), not (1), (2), (3), (4), (5), (6), (7), (8), (9), (10), (11), (12), (13), or (14). In short, if we can describe and explain 15 words using at least 15 models, we can equally describe and explain one zillion phenomena minus one, because the logic throughout is the same.

Thus, the lead co-authors' model can describe and explain what has been happening to Robert B. Oxnam, who is a well-known person or an expert on Asia. In his October 2005 book, *A Fractured Mind: My Life with Multiple Personality Disorder*, he said that, in his life, he has 11 personalities or alters, including old man, young man, males, and females. He did not know about them until he went to have therapy. Today, three still remain. At least one dominant model can be discussed, that is, Oxnam versus non-Oxnam. Since he has 11 different personalities, we can arrange them in accordance of their importance, the real one being himself at 1, while the other 10 personalities in the danger zone spectrum. At each time/space sequence, he would travel in between the two extremes. When he is in the danger, it means pain and suffering for him. When he said he still has three personalities, the game continues, until time/space sequence (n) arrives. It is at (n), we probably can see the real Oxnam defeating the Non-Oxnam.

COMPARING AND CONTRASTING THE THEORY WITH OTHER NON-DIALECTICAL THEORIES

There are many models and theories in the West, such as game theory, systems theory, and rational (choice) theory. Among them, game theory has been quite popularly accepted by social scientists in the West and East. In October 1994, John F. Nash and two others received the Nobel Memorial Prize in economic sciences for their non-cooperative games. 11 years later, Thomas C. Schelling and Robert J. Aumann received the same prize for their work on game theory which can help explain and resolve trade and business conflcits, and even play a role in avoding war. It does not matter which model or theory, each one of them can be regarded as a dot to begin with. In dialectics, after looking at one dot, we will have two half-dots, when competition or conflict appears. It is simple and straightforward. But, it is better to show them in terms of Numbers and Letters. Nonethless, this is not so in game theory, whereby we see the matrix, two persons, etc. at the same time, unless we think of the two persons first. It is also not the case in systems theory, because we see the Inputs (demand and support), the Outputs (allocative such as policy making and policy application as well as symbolic), the Feedback, and especially the Blackbox (or the political system). As to the rational (choice) theory, one may have to think of many choices and then arrive at one choice, which can maximize one's interest at a particular point in time. However, where is the model? Posing this question is necessary and important, because, when one applies a model, he or she does not have to have a theory but, when one applies a theory, he or she must show the model in the form of a diagram or at least verbally.

In the lead co-author's model, whenever making a move, one only thinks of one concept, be it couched in terms of a Number or a Letter. This is the same as key in something in a (personal) computer. The game theory does not function that way. The same thing speaks for the other two theories. The Blackbox in the systems theory makes us to wonder what is really going on, that is, is there an invisible hand or inscrutable force at work?

From one dot, we proceed to think of another, anti-thetical dot. Another way of saying one dot is one zillion phenomena minus one. Can the game theory accomodate so many phenomena logically, without even a contradiction in one out of zillion second? As to the systems theory, we can throw in the one zillion minus one phenomena into the Blackbox, by becoming, like the international/global governance theory, the virtually everything theory[17] or the globalization theory, the almost everything theory. However, while the Outputs are clear, we do not really know what is going on in the box and the reason why they do not come out of the box. As to the rational (choice) theory, may be it is rational to leave aside the irrelevant phenomena. However, what happens when an irrational choice at time/space sequence (5) became rational at time/space sequence (10)), to recall the term, (*YinShZzhiYi*/因時制宜)? For example, most countries ban cloning. However, when the number of Earthlings decreased from 7 billion, reportedly, as of 2011, to 2 persons as a result of waves of natural disasters or nuclear wars, should we begin to clone human beings right away?

International governance has been criticized as "virtually everything." The globalization has also been accused as being "almost everything." Since the one-dot theory has the same

---

[17] Martin Hewson and Timothy J. Sinclair, "The Emergence of Global Governance Theory" in *id.*, eds, *Approaches to Global Governance Theory* (New York: State University of New York Press, 1999), p.17.

feature, can we say it is also "virutally or almost everything"? If it is so, the game theory and other theories have the same problem, because we can regard them as one dot as well.

A student of the lead co-author said he came across a statement in a textbook saying a model or theory cannot describe or explain itself.[18] In other words, to him, the lead co-author can only claim that his dialectical model can only describe and explain one zillion phenomena minus two but not 1. The lead co-author told him that he can use any word, number, letter, symbol, and so on and so forth in his One Zillion Phenomena versus Non-One Zillion Phenomena framework to describe and explain his theoretical framework. In other words, he can say that his model can describe and explain one zillion phenomena minus one. However, non-dialectically, the student is correct. Such is the paradox between dialectics and non-dialectics.

Many, if not most, academics and expert have regarded any versions of dialectics as being ideological. On the one hand, it is partially correct, if we try to decode and decipher, for example, Chinese (Communist) politics.[19] The same thing can be said of game theory. In his summer 1964 article in *Daedalus* on page 860, Daniel Bell wrote that "... any monistic theory--that in explaining everything, it really explains nothing." (In fact, nothing is a part of everything.) And, as Robert W. Cox has noted and as many academics and experts have subsequently acknowledged, "[t]heory is always for someone and for some purpose. All theories have a perspective. Perspectives derive from a position in space and time, specifically social and political time and space."[20] It follows that game theory also has a pre-determined feature. For example, one assigns 0 or -1 for a particular cell in the matrix. By doing this, one would be evitably rationally locked into those four choices. On the other hand, it is partially incorrect to say that dialectics is ideoligical, because ideology can be put into practice. When ideology has been practiced, it is no longer ideological. There are many models that we can choose from when we have determined what are the two extremes. For example, A as the left extreme and B, the right extreme. However, B could also be 1 and A, E. Again, A could be positioned at 1 and B, at 5, and vice versa. There could be many other dialectical arrangements. In this connection, when we talk about nature and human beings, we cannot be ideological to begin with.

CONCLUDING REMARKS

Many well-known political scientists apply a version of dialectics, such as James N. Rosenau,[21] who is not a Marxist, and Bertell Ollman, who is a Marxist. Rosenau discussed both integrating and fragmenting influences, both globalizing and localizing tendencies, as well as both cohesive and conflicutal dynamics. He also mentioned the continuum stretching between the transnational and the subnational, the macro and the micro, the informal and the institutionalized, the state-centric and the multi-centric, as well as the cooperative and the

[18] Conversation with him, dated November 23, 2005.

[19] See, for example, Peter Kien-hong YU and Shawn S. F. KAO, "The Study of China Should Begin with One Dot," *The One-dot Center Occasional Working Papers Series in International Governance, Regimes, and Globalization*, Vol. 1 (April 2008), No.1, 46 pages.

[20] Hewson and Sinclair, p.17.

[21] Martin Hewson and Timothy J. Sinclair, "The Emergence of Global Governance Theory" in *ibid.*, eds., *Appraoches to Global Governance Theory* (New York: State University of New York Press, 1999), p.7.

conflictual.[22] However, he and others have not shown their dialectical arrangements in terms of a diagram for us to see. Moreover, we cannot simply look at, for example, integration and fragmentation as an either or thing. In other words, integration, just as fragmentation, should be more sophisticated.

Many political scientists are not aware that game theory or others have their dialectical roots. -1 and +1, for example, in one of the four cells in the game theory matrix is opposite of each other. The Inputs and Outputs components in the systems theory can also be regarded as being structured dialectically. If a rational (choice) theorist think of the opposite of the adjective rational which is irrational, he or she has also been dialectical. And, in his discussion of political culture and the presistence of inequality, Richard W. Wilson, applied a four cell, two dimensional space model to describe and explain rights and globalization in general and ideal property rights regimes in particular, with the upper right quadrant reflecting the realization of an ideal.[23] Many political scientists before him had used the same model to study other topics. But, he said he had never really thought of the figure as being dialectical, because he does not want to cast his analysis into a predetermined mold that might be inappropriate.[24] Nonetheless, flexibility in jumping from this dialectical model to that dialectical theoretical framework suggests that dialectics does not have to be totally predetermined.

In the paper, it has been stated that the lead co-author's dialectical model can describe and explain one zillion phenomena minus one. Can he also say his one-dot theory, which is derived from the model, can perform the same function? The answer is yes, because, if there is something larger than the universe, such as God, because either one of them can destroy human existence.

Finally, according to James C. Hsiung, who is well versed in both Chinese and English, "[t]wo factors equally determine the salience and popularity of a particular approach/theory: (a) its perceived explanatory power, and (b) how powerful its 'proselytizers' (promoters) are. Both game theory and dialectics (of both the *Yin-Yang* and Hegelian-Marxian variations) have rich explanatory power. The rest depends on people's perception and the power of their respective champions. By comparison, game theory enjoys better perception, hence wider acceptance; and it is more readily comprehensible than dialectics. More important, game theory's champions are more powerful as its patron saints. Furthermore, dialectics has suffered from its readily perceived (assumed) linkage with Marxism. You notice I used 'Marxian,' not 'Marxist' in referring to the dialectics associated with Karl Marx. But, most people don't know the difference. Game theory has no such extraneous ideological problem. In fact, Marxian dialectics was derived from Hegelian dialectics, which in turn had been inspired by the Chinese *Yin-Yang* dialectics. But, interestingly enough, Marxian dialectics bears more resemblance to the *Yin-Yang* dialectics than does the Hegelian version."[25] Four comments can be made. First, not all dialectical models are ideological, as noted earlier. To give another example, Yes versus No can be formed as a non-ideological dialectical model. Second, game theory, for example, has its dialectical roots or inner dialectics, which began

---

[22] James N. Rosenau (1995), "Governance to the Twenty-First Century," *Global Governance*, Vol.1, No.1 (January-March), pp.13-43.

[23] Richard W. Wilson, "Political Culture and the Persistence of Inequality," *East Asia* (U.S.A.) (2005), Vol.22, No.1 (Spring), pp.3-17.

[24] His email to me, dated November 1, 2005. No, he is 50% correct, because concepts can be arranged flexibly.

[25] Email from him, dated November 6, 2005.

with two persons.[26] Third, when we study the Chinese (Communist) politics, it is better for us to first apply a version of dialectics. Otherwise, one may distort Chinese (Communist) politics. That is why, James R. Lilley, who is an avid China-watcher, for example, admitted in his October 19, 2005 public lecture at the Fairbank Center, Harvard University, that the U.S. Government up to this day still does not fully understand Chinese Communist thinking. In addition, he said that Taipei leaders have not explained to the Americans the deals between them and Beijing leaders.[27] Last but least, can game theory, for example, last for more than 3,100 years or becoming one of the timeless laws as in natural science? It is doubtful that the Chinese people will abandon the *Yin* and *Yang* after applying them more than 3,100 years ago, unless all the Chinese and the non-Chinese subscribers have been perished. Indeed, in November 2005, Beijing unveiled five doll mascots for the August 8, 2008 Olympic Games, which should be understood in terms of the Five Elements and which are the dynamic, operational concepts (see Figure 2) for reconciling the *Yin* and *Yang*.[28] And, as an extension of the "One China, Respective Interpretation," Beijing made a remark regarding the location of the Taiwan Pavilion in the Expo2010 Shanghai China site: "The location of the Taiwan Pavilion is a dot in Zone A, which hosts the China Pavilion and national pavilions for Asian countries except Southeast Asian ones. The China Pavilion is also a dot in Zone A." Simply put, the China Pavilion in the context of Zone A is a partial dot, just as China is made of many partial dots. Taiwan, (or, for that matter, the Chinese mainland) is one of them, which implies Taipei can have a seat in the UN only under China (Taiwan).

---

[26] As for an n-person game, mathematical formulas are needed.

[27] http://www.worldjournal.com/wj-us-news.php?nt_seq_id=1253092, dated October 20, 2005.

[28] They also represent the sea, forests, fire, earth, and air. See *UDN*, November 11, 2005, p.A8 and *China Post* (hereinafter CP)(Taipei), November 12, 2005, p.1.

ABOUT THE CONTRIBUTORS

Chunli Zhang (Ph.D. in social science, National SUN Yat-sen University, Taiwan, R.O.C.) is an assistant professor at Ta-jen University, which is located at Pindong County. He is an honourable member of the Phi Tau Phi Scholastic Honor Society. His teaching and research interests include methodology, philosophy of science, international relations, and national strategic studies.

W. Emily Chow (M.Phil & Ph.D., University of Cambridge; Ed.M., Harvard University; M.A., University of Chicago) is an assistant professor at the Graduate School of International Affairs, Ming Chuan University. Her research interests include cross-cultural communication; cultural globalization, international regimes, and democratization.

Asleena Helmi has been in the academic field for more than a decade in various institutions of higher learning in Malaysia. Prior to joining Swinburne University of Technology, she taught a variety of subjects which include entrepreneurship, management information systems and knowledge management at Multimedia University, Cyberjaya. She gained her Bachelors in Public Administration & Management from the Sheffield Hallam University, U.K. Apart from teaching, she participates in consultancies and presented research papers at the Harvard Asia Project for Asian and International Relations in 2008 and has published in numerous local and international journals & book chapters. She earned a distinction masters award majoring in Electronic Commerce from the School of Business at Curtin University of Technology, Western Australia and currently in completion of her Ph.D. study. Her areas of research interests are in the fields of knowledge management, e-commerce, and international business.

Kiat Sing Heng is a lecturer with the School of Business and Design, Swinburne University of Technology, Sarawak Campus. She has had wide teaching experience. Her research interests are integration of information and communication technology (ICT) in teaching and learning, environmental sustainability and public administration.

Jokull Johannesson is a senior lecturer in strategic management at Northampton Business School, University of Northampton. His teaching and research interests are in the fields of strategic management, international strategy, and corporate governance. Dr. Johannesson held lectureship positions at universities in the USA, UK, and Taiwan. Prior to his academic career, he combined his entrepreneurial activities in industry with consultancy in business strategy and organizational development to private-, public-, and international organizations including the Rockefeller Foundation and International Monetary Fund. Dr. Johannesson has published more than fifty papers in various international peer reviewed journals, books, and conference proceedings in the USA, UK, and Asia. He is a regular reviewer for textbook publishers, journals, and international conferences. He is a member of the Academy of Management, Academy of International Business, and the British Academy of Management. Jokull Johannesson can be reached at: jokull.johannesson @northampton.ac.uk

Shawn S. F. Kao (Ph.D., University of Virginia) is Associate Professor of International Politics, Department of Political Science, Tung-hai University, Taiwan, Republic of China (R.O.C.). He has been working in various capacities, such as Dean of International College, Director of Graduate School of International Affairs (GSIA) at Ming Chuan University (MCU); Senior Staff Officer, Taipei Office on Education Forum, Asia-Pacific Economic Cooperation (APEC); Deputy Secretary General, People-to-people International (PTPI-ROC). His teaching and research interests include China in Southeast Asia, East Asian Regional Security, and International Relations. His publications include: "*US Strategic Policy Toward Occupied Japan*" (1985); "*A Potential Threat to the Peace of the Southeast Asian Region*: *A Study of the Problems in the South China Sea*" (1999); "*State Sovereignty in the Internet Era*: *Puzzles and Prospects*" (2000); "*Whether CHINA, China, china: Threatening or Non-threatening?*" (2007); and "*China Rise and the Myth of ASEAN/East Asian Regional Integration*" (2009).

Bibiana Chiu Yiong Lim holds a Master Degree in Cognitive Science and Human Resource Management by dissertation from the Universiti Malaysia Sarawak (UNIMAS) in Malaysia in the year 2007. Her Bachelor Degree in Business was from Swinburne University of Technology, which she obtained in the year 2004. Currently, she is a PhD candidate in UNIMAS under the research area of education technology in business statistics and management.

Bibiana started her career as a tutor in Swinburne University of Technology (SUT) (Sarawak Campus), teaching Marketing, Business Statistics, and Electronic Commerce subjects in undergraduate program. She is lecturer in SUT (Sarawak Campus). Presently, she is a program coordinator for undergraduate Business/Commerce programs.

Her teaching philosophy is that the keys to effective teaching and learning include interactivity and student-centred. Her research areas are more to education technology as well as management and marketing areas. Basically, she is also interested in Electronic Business applications or Electronic Commerce strategies, E-Marketing and new possible ways of conducting business. E.g: Mobile-commerce, podcasting.

Chui Ching Ling obtained her Doctor of Business Administration (DBA) from the University of Newcastle, Australia. As a professional member of the Malaysian Institute of Accountants and CPA Australia, she has more than five years of audit and lecturing experience. Prior to joining Swinburne University of Technology (Sarawak Campus), she worked as a Programme Coordinator with SEGi College Sarawak and was responsible for developing and managing the Faculty of Business, Information and Technology & Accountancy. Currently, she is engaged by the University as a full-time accounting cum taxation lecturer.

Jawed A. Mohammed is a lecturer of International Business at the Faculty of Business at Swinburne University in Melbourne and is the convenor of units in the International Business discipline. He has over ten years of academic (teaching and research) and nearly ten years of industry experience in the field of international business. This enables him to integrate theory with practice providing high standard of excellence in teaching, research and administration. He is of Indian origin educated in India, UK and New Zealand.

Dr. Mohammed has held variety of responsible positions ranging from management to international operations. His entrepreneurial venture in foreign trade adds to his expertise in international business. He has travelled widely and gained valuable cross-cultural experiences as well as established network of international contacts with senior management of business corporations, government officials and scholars in different parts of the world. He has also been engaged in an advisory role with the United Nations (UNIDO) and an non-governmental organization (NGO) in Turkey.

Dr. Mohammed has been a regular speaker in corporate, parliamentarians, and defence personnel seminars, business meetings of Rotary and Lions Clubs, several social and church groups in New Zealand and Australia on contemporary Islam and various international affairs and relations issues. He has also provided consultation to several businesses.

Dr. Mohammed is committed to research with a clear understanding and comprehensive knowledge in the area of international business and Islamic studies. He is currently embarked on a research project studying business practices in Islamic countries and its implications on global strategies.

George K. S. Ngui, senior lecturer, teaches marketing and organizational behavior courses at Swinburne University of Technology, Sarawak Campus. He received his M.Sc. from the University of Leicester and his Ph.D. from Universiti Malaysia Sarawak. He has written numerous articles for journals and conferences, and has undertaken consulting projects for clients such as the Malaysian Furniture Promotion Council and the Ministry of Industrial Development. His current research focuses on industry competitiveness and strategic capabilities of small businesses.

Lisa Hua Ngui Lee obtained her Master of Arts in Management from University of Science Malaysia, Penang in 2001. Currently she is a lecturer at School of Business and Design at Swinburne University of Technology (Sarawak Campus), Sarawak, Malaysia.

Vie Ming Tan posses a Master degree in Business Administration from the University of Heriot-Watt, United Kingdom. His first degree is Bachelor of Commerce majoring in Finance from the University of Otago, New Zealand.

He has recently joined Swinburne University of Technology, Sarawak campus, Malaysia, as Lecturer in the School of Business and Design. He teaches Business Mathematics, Quantitative Analysis and Services Marketing for undergraduate programmes.

Prior to joining Swinburne University in February 2006, he taught Business Mathematics, Statistics, Finance, Research Methodology and Operations Management at both the diploma and degree levels for 7 years while working as a lecturer at Chermai Jaya College, Kuching. Apart from lecturing, he also served as a Programme Head of Business Administration Programmes with Chermai Jaya College, Kuching.

His research and teaching interests include service quality and time series analysis in services industry as well as innovative teaching techniques to enhance students' interest in quantitative subjects.

Mung-Ling Voon is a lecturer at the School of Business and Design, Swinburne University of Technology, Sarawak Campus. She graduated with Honours in Economics and International Business from Universiti Malaysia Sarawak (UNIMAS) and holds a Master of Science from University of Leicester, UK in 2003. She has taught the courses of Economics, Human Resource Management and Management. Besides teaching, she has published several articles in journals and conference proceedings.

Peter Kien-Hong Yu (Ph.D., New York University, October 1983) is Professor at Swinburne University of Technology (Australia) since June 2009 and Director of the One-dot Center for the Study of International Governance, Regimes, and Globalization at Ming Chuan University (MCU), Taiwan, Republic of China (ROC), since April 2007. From October 1983 to July 2009, he worked in various capacities, such as the Dean of Research and Development at an institution of higher education, Director of the Graduate School of International Affairs at MCU, professor at the National Sun Yat-sen University, senior research fellow at the National University of Singapore, etc. He is the author, co-author, editor, and co-editor of 15 books in both English and Chinese and some 90 journal articles and book chapters published in the West. He is the recipient of many fellowships, awards, and grants. His latest books are *The Second Long March* (2009), which is published by The Continuum (U.S.), and *International Governance, Regimes, and Globalization: Case Studies from Beijing and Taipei* (2010), which is published by Lexington Books (U.S.). His forthcoming books are: *International Governance and Regimes: A Chinese Perspective* and *The Politics and Business Dimensions of Governance and Regimes: A One-dot Theory Interpretation.*

INDEX

C

D

J

K

L

M

N

O

P

Q

R

Y

Z